Possessed

THE RISE AND FALL OF PRINCE

ALEX HAHN

BILLBOARD BOOKS
an imprint of Watson-Guptill Publications/New York

Senior Acquisitions Editor: Bob Nirkind
Editor: Michelle Bredeson
Designer: Michelle Gengaro-Kokmen
Jacket design by Spencer Drate and Judith Salavetz
Production Manager: Ellen Greene

First published in 2003 by Billboards Books, an imprint of Watson-Guptill Publications, a division of
VNU Business Media, Inc., 770 Broadway, New York, NY 10003
www.watsonguptill.com

Library of Congress Cataloging-in-Publication Data
Hahn, Alex.
  Possessed : the rise and fall of Prince / by Alex Hahn.
    p.   cm.
  Includes discography (p.   ) and index.
  ISBN 0-8230-7748-9
  1. Prince. 2. Rock musicians—United States—Biography. I. Title.
ML420.P974 H35 2003
781.66'092—dc21
                                        2002152603

Manufactured in U.S.A.

1 2 3 4 5 6 7 8 9 / 10 09 08 07 06 05 04 03

ontents

Source Notes and Acknowledgments   iv
Note on Sales Charts   vii
Prelude   1

Part One   Rise: 1958–1988

1. Home   4
2. One-man Band   20
3. Rude   31
4. Pawns   44
5. Majesty   58
6. Hangover   73
7. Counter-Revolution   84
8. Factory   97
9. Alone   109
10. Black   120

Part Two   Fall: 1988–2002

11. Fantastic   148
12. Hit   163
13. Games   180
14. Warfare   189
15. Escape   200
16. Gone   210
17. Larry   220
18. Comeback   228
19. Xenophobia   240

Discography   248
Index   274

Source Notes and Acknowledgments

Sources of information for this project included dozens of interviews with Prince's friends and associates. Interviews were conducted during 2001 and 2002 by the author and the following research assistants: Jacqueline Johansen (who interviewed Anna Garcia), Lisa Sabitini (who interviewed Pepé Willie), and Alan Freed (who interviewed Marylou Badeaux). In addition, Per Nilsen, the author of *DanceMusicSexRomance: Prince—the First Decade* (Firefly, 1999) and the editor-in-chief of *Uptown*, the unauthorized and independent Prince fanzine, gave the author access to numerous interviews undertaken (with the assistance of Alan Freed and others) from 1996 to 2001. In all cases, the questions were prepared by the author (in the case of interviews conducted by the author or his assistants) or by Nilsen (in the case of interviews conducted by Nilsen and his assistants).

The following individuals were interviewed, in many cases several times:

Marylou Badeaux (Hahn and Nilsen)
Tommy Barbarella (Nilsen)
Don Batts (Nilsen)
Roy Bennett (Nilsen)
Michael Bland (Nilsen)
Matt Blistan (Nilsen)
Howard Bloom (Hahn)
Mark Brown (Hahn)
Bob Cavallo (Hahn)
Terry Christian (Nilsen)
David Coleman (Nilsen)
Margie Cox (Nilsen)
Dez Dickerson (Hahn)
Matt Fink (Hahn and Nilsen)

Brett Fischer (Nilsen)
Steve Fontano (Nilsen)
Rosie Gaines (Hahn)
Anna Garcia (Hahn)
Jeff Gold (Hahn)
Craig Hubler (Nilsen)
Owen Husney (Nilsen)
Femi Jiya (Nilsen)
Coke Johnson (Nilsen)
Jellybean Johnson (Nilsen)
Michael Koppelman (Hahn and Nilsen)
Karen Krattinger (Hahn and Nilsen)
Alan Leeds (Hahn and Nilsen)
Eric Leeds (Hahn and Nilsen)
Paul Martenson (Nilsen)
Peggy McCreary (Nilsen)
Bob Merlis (Hahn)
Monte Moir (Nilsen)
Chris Moon (Nilsen)
Bruce Orwall (Hahn)
Robbie Paster (Hahn)
Bobby Z. Rivkin (Nilsen)
David Z. Rivkin (Nilsen)
Susan Rogers (Nilsen)
Charles Smith (Nilsen)
Arnold Stiefel (Hahn)
Sandra St. Victor (Hahn)
Pepé Willie (Hahn and Nilsen)

Various sources spoke only on the condition of confidentiality and are not identified by name in the text.

The following individuals either refused to be interviewed or failed to respond to multiple requests for interviews: Lisa Coleman, Morris Day, Carmen Electra, Sheila Escovedo, Madonna, Albert Magnoli, Denise Mathews (Vanity), Benny Medina, Susannah Melvoin, Wendy Melvoin, Mo Ostin, Levi Seacer, Jr., Lenny Waronker, and Miko Weaver. The following individuals could not be located or contacted: André Cymone and Tony Mosley.

The vast public record on Prince (which includes numerous print, television, and radio interviews with him) was also an important source of information. When directly quoted, such sources are referenced in the text. Reviews of Prince's music in the media are also referenced in the text.

Also helpful were three previous books about Prince: John Bream's *Prince: Inside the Purple Reign* (MacMillan, 1984), Dave Hill's *Prince: A Pop Life* (Harmony Books, 1989), and Liz Jones' *Purple Reign: The Artist Formerly Known as Prince* (Birch Lane Press, 1998). When directly quoted, these books are referenced in the text.

Of the many sources who helped with this book, Alan Leeds deserves special mention. From 1983 to 1992, Alan was one of Prince's most important associates. Even after leaving Prince's employ, Alan maintained close contact with current and former members of Prince's inner circle. Alan is also something of a living history of R&B and funk music, having worked over the years not only with Prince, but with James Brown, George Clinton, D'Angelo, Maxwell, and many others. Alan proved to be a patient, knowledgeable, and insightful source for this project.

In addition to the people who graciously agreed to be interviewed, many others were very helpful in the preparation of this book. Per Nilsen's insights on Prince's character were revealing, as was his intricate knowledge of Prince's music. Lisa Sabitini, a key researcher during the latter stages of the project, was extremely helpful. The following individuals also volunteered time as research assistants during various stages: Michael Walker (who was critical in locating former Warner Bros. vice president Jeff Gold), Jacqueline Johansen (who conducted the important interview with Anna Garcia), Joan Hopper (an extremely effective locator of sources), and Jennifer O'Neill.

For photos, special thanks again to Per Nilsen and also to Greg Helgeson.

My editor at Billboard Books/Watson-Guptill Publications, Bob Nirkind, was a constantly accessible source of constructive feedback, encouragement, ideas, and advice. Bob's enthusiasm, support, and counsel, along with his genuine passion for music, were integral to the project. Michelle Bredeson, *Possessed*'s project editor at Watson-Guptill, provided additional eagle-eyed editing and saw the project through the homestretch.

Rob McQuilkin, my agent at the Kneerim & Williams Agency, believed in this project from the beginning and was extremely important to its completion, especially during the critical early stages. He was also a consistently thoughtful and effective advocate for my interests.

Steven Fox, a talented author of many books, provided mentorship, encouragement, and an essential referral to the Kneerim & Williams Agency.

My parents, Robert Hahn and Nicole Rafter, were especially important during the early stages of developing the project. Both are outstanding writers and editors who provided excellent advice. My sister, Sarah Hahn, also made important early contributions, bringing her unique energies and discernment to the project at a pivotal time. And both of my grandmothers, Elizabeth Fischer and Berniece Hahn, were important sources of inspiration and support during this project.

Lauren Serreti, whom I met just weeks before embarking on this project, remained my closest friend throughout its development and contributed in ways that I am still beginning to appreciate.

Note on Sales Charts

The Billboard R&B Singles Chart was known as the Soul Singles Chart until 1982 and the Black Singles Chart from 1982 until 1990. These charts are referred to by their various names in the text, depending on the year of the release in question. The same is true with respect to the Billboard R&B Albums Chart: It was called the Soul Albums Chart until 1982 and the Black Albums Chart from 1982 to 1990. In the text, these album charts are referred to as the R&B Chart, the Soul Chart, and the Black Chart.

The Pop Singles Chart and Pop Albums Chart have retained the same names since their inception. These charts are referred to, respectively, as the Pop Singles Chart and the Pop Chart in the text.

The Recording Industry Association of America (RIAA) began certifying gold singles and albums in 1958, requiring sales of one million units for a gold single and $1 million in sales for a gold album. In 1975, the RIAA revised its qualifications for a gold album to require that an album sell a minimum of 500,000 units, in addition to reaching $1 million in sales. In 1976, platinum singles and platinum albums were introduced, requiring sales of two million units for a platinum single, and $2 million and at least one million units for a platinum album. The RIAA began certifying albums with sales of at least two million units as multi-platinum in 1984. In 1989, the requirement for a gold single was lowered to 500,000 units.

PRELUDE

april 21, 1996: chanhassen, minnesota

The problems in Prince's life had piled up to a point where not even his legendary talent, energy, and passion could resolve them. Control—the thing that possessed him most—was slipping away on any number of fronts.

Prince's finances were in a state of chaos. Just two days earlier, he had been forced to lay off most of the staff at Paisley Park Studios, his recording complex in Chanhassen, Minnesota. The red ink was entirely self-created; Prince continuously made expensive music and video projects that were never released. A host of local and national vendors—studio proprietors, clothing designers, video directors, and others—now found it nearly impossible to get paid. Prince no longer even had a band; in March, he had abruptly told the members of his backing ensemble, the New Power Generation, that they were being taken off the payroll.

Long a notorious bachelor, Prince was about to become a father. His young wife, Mayte Garcia, whom he married on Valentine's Day just a few months earlier, was pregnant and expecting to give birth in November. Having publicly embraced monogamy and family, Prince now faced the stress of having to conform to a lifestyle radically different from the one he had lived his entire adult existence.

Prince's most important business relationship, his eighteen-year involvement with Warner Bros. Records, was about to end. In recent years, Prince's fanatical desire to gain exclusive control over both his music and his career prompted a bitter, high-profile battle against the label. He likened the company's executives to slave owners and scrawled the word "slave" on his face for public appearances. Now, as he waited in Chanhassen, Prince's legal representatives were in Los Angeles engaged in tense discussions with Warners officials about how best to terminate an association that had become unproductive and embarrassing for both sides. The contract that guaranteed Prince millions of dollars each time he delivered a new record was about to become null and void.

In recent months, Prince had experienced uncomfortable chest palpitations and occasional sharp pains, and had started to worry that he might be having heart problems. Having read that aspirin was good for the heart, he began taking at least four a day. Otherwise, Prince's exhausting lifestyle remained the same. He continued to work relentlessly, recording music at all hours and playing concerts that ended at five or six in the morning.

On the morning of April 21, the palpitations grew worse, and Prince drank wine to numb the pain. He consumed a full bottle and, owing to his small body and fast metabolism, became intoxicated quickly. He also popped several aspirin. Whether he ate anything is unknown, but in addition to being an incredibly light eater, Prince had just recently embarked on a radical vegan diet that cut all animal products from his diet. The combination of alcohol, aspirin, stress, and lack of sleep wreaked havoc on his slight five-foot-three-inch, 125-pound frame. He was buffeted by waves of nausea and then began vomiting.

Prince was taken to the emergency room at Fairview Southdale Hospital in the nearby suburb of Edina, where the doctors peppered him with questions: Had he been depressed? Had he taken drugs? Any history of heart problems? Despite his sickly state, Prince remained cogent enough to answer in the negative, but to the doctors, his responses sounded cagey, elusive, and incomplete.

After nearly two decades as a clean-living workaholic, Prince was perhaps the least likely star of his generation to self-destruct. If he was often bizarre in his actions—and few could deny this of a man who had changed his name to an unpronounceable symbol—he was nonetheless as disciplined as anyone in the history of pop music.

Yet here he was, inebriated and vomiting in a hospital emergency room. Somehow, Prince had lost control.

PART ONE
Rise: 1958-1988

chapter one

ℋome

When he was five years old, Prince Rogers Nelson's mother, Mattie Shaw, took him to a Minneapolis theater where his father, John L. Nelson, was playing piano in a musical revue. As he and his mother arrived at their seats and waited for the show to begin, Prince watched the hundreds of people filing into the theater and wondered what was supposed to happen next. Abruptly, the house-lights went down, shrouding him and the audience in darkness. Then, from the back of the theater came a bright spotlight, riveting everyone's attention to the stage. The curtain rustled, and from behind it stepped a smiling John Nelson, who sat down at a piano to hearty applause.

As Nelson began playing, his face became the picture of concentration while his hands darted about the keyboard. The audience remained rapt. To Prince, it seemed that his father owned special abilities that could entrance hundreds of people.

Behind Nelson, the curtain moved again. A group of stunning, scantily clad females—the chorus girls—joined him onstage. Prince watched as they danced around his father, who returned their seductive smiles.

After the show, Prince replayed the scene in his mind over and over. He envisioned his father at the front of the theater, illuminated by the lights that pierced the darkness. But as he fantasized, the script gradually shifted. Now it was Prince himself at the piano, basking in the crowd's adoring attention. Now he was surrounded by gorgeous women who danced to the rhythms he created.

Young Prince had discovered an obsession with the power of music. In the days and weeks that followed, he gravitated towards anything that resembled an instrument. His father kept a piano in the living room, and Prince started fiddling with it every day while Nelson was away at work. He was a natural; before long, he could string notes together into a coherent melody. On visits to department stores, Prince sped off to the musical instruments. He played with radios, organs, and pianos—anything that made noise. Because he was small and thus difficult to spot, his mother sometimes had to follow the trail of sounds to find him.

Always a quiet child who preferred playing alone, Prince seemed to have found the perfect outlet. Nothing else absorbed him like this new interest. A pattern of withdrawal from the world and retreat into music was quickly established in his life.

In Minnesota, Prince's birth state and lifelong home, automobile license plates are graced with the phrase "Land of 10,000 Lakes." The words evoke a semi-mythical Midwestern heartland—a wholesome and healthy, if bland, place, with suggestions of Protestantism, plain vanilla flavors, and a white-bread (and for that matter, white) ethos. The region was discovered in 1640 by a Calvinist priest, Father Louis Hennepin, who in his travels stumbled upon the picturesque Saint Anthony Falls cascading into the Mississippi River. The state's urban center, Minneapolis—founded in the 1840s by early industrialists who built sawmills and flour mills along the river and at the base of the energy-generating falls—even today retains a surprisingly scenic and unspoiled aspect. The state's name, which means "sky-tinted water" in the language of the Dakota Indians who once lived there, reflects its beauty.

It is not surprising that such territory would produce a sincere folksinger like Bob Dylan, a quintessentially American novelist like F. Scott Fitzgerald, or a populist politician like Hubert H. Humphrey. One would not expect, however, that it would serve as the home and lifelong base of a tormented, messianic, meteoric African-American pop musician—a driven, protean talent who would rocket to a fame that at its peak rivaled that of Michael Jackson and Madonna. Yet even after becoming an international superstar, Prince rarely strayed far from this cold Midwestern state. He would live all over the Minneapolis area—in a tiny downtown apartment that was his first home as an adult; in a pretty rented house overlooking Lake Minnetonka, where he recorded the hyper-explicit album *Dirty Mind*; and in a purple-painted home on the verdant Kiowa Trail. Later, using the largesse generated by the blockbuster 1984 film and album *Purple Rain*, Prince purchased a large home with a pool and tennis court in the exclusive Minneapolis suburb of Edina and also erected, just a few miles away in Chanhassen, a sprawling studio complex called Paisley Park. Initially open to other recording artists, Paisley soon became his private, hermetic universe, off-limits to everyone but himself, his employees, and a few chosen friends and collaborators.

While Prince would perform all over the world, most of his life was spent in small, quiet suburbs close to where he grew up. This environment became a metaphor for his insularity and distrust of outsiders. "I will always live in Minneapolis," Prince told Oprah Winfrey in 1996. "It's so cold, it keeps the bad people out."

John Nelson, the son of sharecroppers and the grandson of slaves, moved to this city in 1956 from Louisiana after divorcing his first wife, Vivienne. Drawn by the state's strong industrial economy and its reputation for tolerance toward minority groups, he settled with his two daughters, Lorna and Sharon, and his son, John Jr., in working-class, predominantly African-American North Minneapolis. Everyone called it the Northside. Nelson was short—about five feet four inches—but handsome and immaculately groomed. He landed a job as a plastic molder at Honeywell Electronics, where he worked until retiring thirty years later. He was a model employee—restrained in conversation, fastidious in his personal habits, and tremendously disciplined.

Nelson's true passion was music. A skilled pianist, he fit in perfectly on the Northside, which was peppered with jazz clubs and blues bars. Nelson's hardy constitution allowed him to toil every day at Honeywell and then play his piano in these local spots until the early morning. His group, the Prince Rogers Trio (after his chosen stage name) became a fixture on the circuit.

Nelson was a reticent man with a quirky sense of humor. While he exuded a quiet confidence, people often found him strange; one of Prince's associates in the 1990s compared Nelson to Chauncey Gardiner, the enigmatic hero of the film and novel *Being There*. Sometimes, though, Nelson encountered the rare person who understood perfectly his style of communication. One such individual was the great trumpeter and bandleader Miles Davis, whom he met in 1987 as a result of his son's fame. "They were both a bit eccentric and crazy—they hit it off very well," recalled Susan Rogers, one of Prince's longtime recording engineers. When they met at a recording studio where Prince had invited Miles, Nelson looked intently at him and said, apropos of nothing, "I liked those pants, the striped pants you were wearing at the Grammy Awards."

Miles pondered this, and then responded, "I don't own no striped pants."

"Yes you do, I saw you in them," Nelson insisted.

Fixating on the subject as if it were a matter of great urgency, the two jazzmen went back and forth on whether the pants existed. Prince, lurking in the background, watched the bizarre colloquy and suppressed an urge to laugh.

Finally, Miles recalled the outfit in question. "Yes, I remember now. I do have striped pants," he said. "They're made out of eel. Eel, like in Vietnam!"

Nelson smiled; he seemed to know exactly what Miles meant.

While hardly in a league with Miles (or his own son, for that matter) as a musician, Nelson was a talented jazz pianist. The Prince Rogers Trio not only played standards but some of Nelson's original compositions, which were abstract, nonlinear pieces that sometimes evoked Thelonious Monk or Duke Ellington. Like the man himself, Nelson's music could be a challenge to understand. "They were meandering ballads, very unstructured, with a lot of pauses and odd phrasings," said Rogers, who once engineered a session for Nelson.

In 1956, while playing a Northside dance, Nelson met Mattie Shaw, herself a jazz singer. She was also a transplant from Louisiana, having moved to Minneapolis with her twin sister, Edna Mae, in the 1950s. Her voice reminded listeners of Billie Holiday. She was in her early twenties and had previously been married; she had one son, Alfred. Nelson, who was sixteen years her senior, asked her to join his group, and she agreed; they soon became romantically involved as well, marrying in 1957. The entire family moved into 915 Logan Avenue, a modest Northside home.

Prince, their first child together, was born at Mount Sinai Hospital in downtown Minneapolis on June 7, 1958. His unusual name was taken from his father's stage name, and also reflected the high hopes that any couple has for a new baby. "I named my son Prince because I wanted him to do everything I wanted to do," Nelson told the television show *A Current Affair* in 1991.

A second child, Tyka, was born in 1960. The family was now complete—two parents and six children (from three different marriages) surviving on Nelson's modest income. Somehow, they escaped the depths of poverty. Charles Smith, Prince's second cousin, recalls the Nelson home as immaculate and even posh, at least compared to his own. When Nelson installed a television into the living room wall, which to Smith seemed the height of opulence, he had no luck getting his own father to follow suit. Smith also recalls Nelson impressing the whole neighborhood with his natty attire. "His shoes always matched his clothes, and he was clean and neat," Smith said. "We'd always beg him and say, 'Open up your closet, let us see your clothes.'" To his son, Nelson was a role model in all respects—Prince admired his musical creativity, his flamboyance, and his discipline.

Shaw, who usually called her husband Prince, gave her son the nickname "Skipper." It stuck; for years, he insisted that family and friends use it, and he bristled if anyone called him Prince. By age seven, he could play his father's piano with reasonable proficiency, and it was clear that music would be a significant part of his life. Yet he had other, more typical interests for a young boy—sports and exercise, especially Ping-Pong and basketball. Smith recalls that Prince was good at both sports and also exuberantly competitive. He loved to win, and always would. In the mid-1980s, during a visit with his arch rival Michael Jackson, Prince challenged him to a game of Ping-Pong. To intimidate the self-proclaimed King of Pop, Prince furiously smashed the ball across the table right at him.

Although spirituality would become central to Prince's life—he would always place God atop the list of thank-yous on his albums—this was not necessarily due to any indoctrination he received during childhood. The Nelsons were practicing Seventh Day Adventists, and Prince attended Bible-study classes. Later, in interviews, Prince complained that the most he got out of going to church as a child was listening to the choir. Still, while he developed no great affinity for organized religion, he certainly did absorb the basic lessons of Christianity, teachings that resonated deeply with him. The notion of an omnipotent God who would reward goodness and punish evil has rarely strayed far from Prince's mind during his life.

Prince attended Minneapolis public schools, starting with John Haye Elementary School on the Northside. The most difficult part of school for him was that he was significantly smaller than most of his classmates. In songs and in press interviews, he has made repeated references to the bullying he endured. In his 1996 conversation with Oprah Winfrey, Prince said that childhood traumas, including this teasing, prompted the emergence of a second, separate personality within him. "Recent analysis has proved that there's probably two people inside of me," he said without irony. "There's a Gemini. And we haven't determined what sex that other person is yet."

Fortunately, though, the schoolyard taunts did not prompt him to withdraw further into himself. Instead, by the time he was nine or ten, a comical side emerged in Prince, and he began to make more friends. Especially around people he knew well, he could shift quickly from a shy introvert into a boisterous and amusing child. "He was just like all of us—funny, telling jokes," recalled Smith.

Nor was Prince an odd figure among his peers. He dressed sharply but conservatively (a habit enforced by his father) and engaged in none of the cryptic mumbling that characterized many of his press interviews after he became famous. Yet, Prince wanted to do far more than just fit in; he was gradually developing a desire to surprise, titillate, and shock. This strand of his character was influenced by a peculiar and shadowy figure in his personal history—half-brother Alfred Nelson, the first son of Mattie Shaw. Several years older than Prince, Alfred was also musically talented—he sang along to his large collection of James Brown records with fervor—and he was also colorful and unconventional, wearing his hair in a crazed Little Richard–style do and flashing bills that came from goodness knows where. "We thought he was some kind of pimp or something," recalled Smith. Impervious to any sort of discipline, Alfred would sneak out of the house through his bedroom window late at night and return the same way, sometimes surprising Prince and Smith, who often came in to try on his wild outfits and listen to James Brown.

While little is known about the extent of Albert's musical gifts or ambitions, it is striking that so many of his quirks—strange sartorial habits and hairstyles, a fascination with James Brown, and an odd relationship with food, among others—emerged in Prince as well. But Albert was ultimately less successful than Prince in controlling and channeling his idiosyncratic impulses. According to Smith, he became disturbed and ended up in a Minneapolis mental institution.

Even as things got easier for Prince at school and with his peers, his home life deteriorated. John Nelson and Mattie Shaw had strikingly different temperaments and often got along poorly. "She was the one that was wild, he wasn't," remembered Smith. "I think that [Nelson] was really serious about Prince's mom, and that Prince's mom wasn't nailed down enough." Loud fights that left Shaw in tears were not uncommon. Adding to the tensions, Shaw put her musical ambitions on hold to care for her children, while Nelson continued to play clubs at night. The volatile atmosphere was frightening and disturbing for Prince, who would draw a grim portrait of his family life in the quasi-autobiographical film *Purple Rain* (1984). In 1996, he told Oprah Winfrey that a scene showing his mother crying after being struck by his father was the most true-to-life part of the movie. The arguments continued, and Prince's parents separated (and shortly afterwards divorced) when he was just ten.

When Nelson moved out, he left behind his piano, which Prince continued to play avidly. Shaw soon married another Minneapolan, Hayward Baker, who became Prince's stepfather. On the verge of adolescence, Prince resented the intrusion of a new male figure into his life, and clashed frequently with Baker. Years later, Prince described him as emotionally distant and materialistic. "I disliked him immediately," he told the magazine *Musician* in 1981. "He would bring us a lot of presents all the time, rather than sit down and talk with us and give us companionship."

When Prince reached age twelve, he asked his father to take him back in. Nelson agreed, but the reunion did not last. According to Smith, Nelson caught Prince in bed with a female friend and threw his son out of the house as punishment. As Prince recounted in a 1985 interview with *Rolling Stone,* he begged his father to let him stay and also solicited his sister Tyka's intervention, asking her to contact their father on his behalf. After reaching Nelson by phone, Prince learned that the answer was still no. "I sat crying at that phone booth for two hours," he said. "That's the last time I cried."

They would never again live together, but continued to oscillate between intense affection and angered estrangement until Nelson's death in 2001. Prince's repeated overtures to Nelson during his adult life—giving him songwriting credit for music he had nothing to do with, praising him in the media, and introducing him to luminaries like Miles Davis—demonstrated a desire to bond with his father and heal old wounds.

What exactly were those wounds? If having his father leave the family home and then later throw him out on the street were not destructive enough, Prince also received punishments from Nelson that left emotional scars. In *Purple Rain*, Prince plays a struggling young musician who endures physical abuse at the hands of his moody, unstable dad. Asked by Oprah Winfrey in 1996 if his father was ever "an abusive man," Prince replied, "He had his moments." In the song "Papa" (from the 1993 album *Come*), Prince whispers, "Don't abuse children, or else they'll turn out like me."

Yet Prince has wavered on this point, reflecting deeply conflicted feelings about his father. In 1999, he told Larry King that his experience with his father was "not rough" and made no mention of any physical abuse. "I mean, he was a very strict disciplinarian, but all fathers were," Prince said. "I learned the difference between right and wrong, so I don't—I don't consider it so rough."

Nelson, for his part, consistently denied abusing any of his children. Charles Smith, while unable to state categorically that Prince never suffered corporal punishment, certainly detected no signs of systematic abuse. "I never saw Prince or Tyka getting treated really badly," he said.

Nonetheless, after being evicted by his father—which arguably was itself a form of child abuse—Prince's life became more difficult than ever before. He stayed briefly with his aunt, Olivia Nelson (John Nelson's sister), but she was unable or unwilling to fulfill a permanent parenting role. For months, he bounced around the homes of relatives and friends. "I didn't like being shuffled around," he conceded in the 1980 *Los Angeles Times* interview. And for the first time in his life, he experienced genuine economic privation; among his forms of entertainment was standing outside a neighborhood McDonald's, sniffing the greasy air and wishing he could afford a burger.

Finally, Prince found a stable situation at the home of Bernadette Anderson, mother of Prince's close friend André. Mrs. Anderson, who, like the Nelsons, was a member of the local Seventh Day Adventist Church, was the sort of woman—certainly not an uncommon figure in poorer African-American neighborhoods—who treated the problems of the community as her own. Despite having six of her own children, she treated Prince as a son and raised him throughout the rest of his adolescence. "She was Mom to everybody," Smith said. "As soon as her car pulled up with groceries, she shared everything with everybody."

With a much-needed feeling of rootedness now present in his life, Prince settled into his studies at Bryant Junior High School. He made the junior varsity basketball team and developed a fast friendship with a teammate named Duane, who soon became Duane Nelson (and Prince's stepbrother) when John Nelson remarried. From the start, there was an element of competition in the relationship, particularly because the taller, more handsome Duane attracted more girls. (In the song "Lady Cab Driver" from *1999*, Prince would allude to his frustration over this state of affairs.)

In high school, Prince quickly concluded that his strengths lay elsewhere than sports. He became increasingly immersed in music at Central High, taking a variety of classes in the subject, and his talents did not go unnoticed. Instructor Jim Hamilton locked the band room at lunch time so that Prince could practice the piano and other instruments undisturbed. In addition, Prince took a special class offered by Hamilton called the Business of Music, where students learned the legal and financial basics of the industry. His instructor also gave Prince one-on-one instruction on piano and guitar. Mark Brown, a Central student who received similar mentorship from Hamilton (and who later became Prince's bass player), recalls the teacher as both encouraging and rigorous. "He wanted me to learn how to read music, and that's where we had our disagreements," Brown said. "But he was a great teacher, and he pushed you."

Prince's friend and surrogate brother, André Anderson (who later went by the name André Cymone), was also musically inclined, and the two began to jam together regularly in his mother's basement. It was around this time that John Nelson—perhaps as a peace offering in their difficult relationship—bought Prince a guitar. Anderson learned the bass, and Smith brought over a drum set to add to the din. "I told Prince there was no way he could play the guitar, because he was a piano player," Smith recalled. "He totally proved me wrong, because he picked up the guitar like it was nothing." The vocal duties in this ad hoc group, though, were at first handled exclusively by Smith.

Upstairs, Prince shared a bedroom with Anderson. Despite being good friends, they were poor roommates; Anderson's side of the room was cluttered and disorganized, while Prince's was as meticulously ordered as a Marine barrack. Although he no longer lived with his father, Nelson's disciplined approach to life remained a significant influence on Prince, who sought greater order and privacy by moving into the basement. Bernadette Anderson opposed this, worrying about perceptions that her foster son was being treated poorly, but Prince insisted.

Downstairs, he had much easier access to his instruments; already, Prince had started blending the distinction between home and musical workplace. Moreover, the basement became something of a private universe—a small slice of the world where he was in total control. A dark space with little natural light, it was nonetheless where he felt most comfortable, and it provided a prototype for the cloistered recording studios where he would spend the majority of his waking hours over the next thirty-plus years.

It was now 1974, and cities across the United States were convulsed by struggles over a host of sociopolitical concerns, foremost among them Vietnam and race relations. The latter issue became especially inflamed during the 1970s by the court-ordered practice of bussing, which resulted in African-American children being sent to schools in white neighborhoods and vice versa. Whites were indeed bussed to the predominantly black Central High, resulting in a student body that was almost equally balanced along racial lines by the middle of the decade. In 1996, at a Central High School reunion, former employees of the institution recalled little of the anguish that bussing brought to so many American cities. "In my opinion, the '71–'81 Central was the most peacefully integrated school in the history of the state," former Central music teacher Bea Hasselmann told the *Minneapolis Star Tribune* at the event.

Others dispute this rosy account. Mark Brown, a student in the late seventies after Prince graduated, recalls "a lot of tension, a lot of fights" over racial issues. "It was basically segregated; blacks hung out with blacks, and whites hung out with whites."

But if racial animosity was indeed part of the day-to-day experience at Central High School, Prince seems to have come away with little bitterness toward whites.

Just a few years later, when he began putting together his first professional band, Prince would consciously create a racially diverse ensemble. Nor did he during his teen years develop a strong sense of identification as a black American; indeed, although he grew up with mostly black friends and had black parents, he would, for the first decade of his musical career, consciously deny having any particular racial identity. (In early interviews he inaccurately portrayed his parents as a mixed-race couple.) Only in the mid-1990s, when he sought to escape a record contract that he likened to enslavement, would Prince actively self-identify as an oppressed black American. And even then, he treated broader issues of economic and social inequality as subsidiary to his own personal travails.

Nor did the anti-authoritarian ethos of the social movements of the '60s and '70s have much impact on Prince—or perhaps it is fairer to say that the impact was delayed. Although by his early twenties he would become a self-styled cultural rebel, in high school Prince was anything but a troublemaker or agitator. Smith recalls that Prince took a professional attitude toward school, always getting work done early or on time. This assessment is confirmed by his recording engineer Rogers, who in the mid-1980s came across one of Prince's report cards; she recalls it saying that he received two Bs and an A and was "a quiet, studious, obedient, respectful student who had respect for authority and his teachers."

But Prince's true interests did not lie in the classroom. Every day after school, he, Anderson, and Smith retreated to the basement and jammed for hours. In addition to creating their own songs—which were essentially formless instrumentals—they played a variety of covers, learning songs they heard on the radio by Santana, Grand Funk Railroad, and others.

The Anderson basement—Prince's bedroom and rehearsal space—also represented his first attempt to create an alternative community based around music and, perhaps, sex. Years later in interviews, Prince would recall it as a hedonistic wonderland where he and Anderson engaged in carnal acts with a variety of girlfriends. Although Smith says these accounts were exaggerated in order to generate publicity—something Prince himself affirmed after family members became embarrassed by the media revelations—others believe that the initial stories were actually close to the mark. "My impression is that there were a lot of girls in that basement," said Howard Bloom, Prince's press agent during the 1980s. "He had grown up in the 1960s, and the message was make love, not war. In the basement, he was going for liberation and entitlement to any sort of sexuality, pleasure, and enjoyment."

Still, it seems unlikely that Bernadette Anderson, who did her best to provide a disciplined environment for her children, would have allowed untrammeled excess. Pepé Willie, a friend and musical associate, remembers seeing Ms. Anderson spank Prince (who was sixteen at the time) one day when she discovered that he had skipped school to cavort with a girl in the basement. "She whooped him right there in front of me," Willie related. "He wasn't angry—he didn't try to strike back at her or anything—he just accepted the fact that he got a whooping."

In any case, the primary focus in the Anderson basement was music—not just making music, but learning about other artists. Prince and his friends listened to the radio frequently, and were treated to the same sugary Top 40 artists as the rest of the country—Tony Orlando & Dawn, Paul McCartney & Wings, America, and John Denver. Gradually, though, they were exposed to black rhythm and blues, a style that crept into the mainstream as No. 1 hits were scored by Stevie Wonder ("Superstition" and "You Are The Sunshine Of My Life" in 1973), Sly & the Family Stone ("Family Affair" in 1971), and the Temptations ("Just My Imagination" in 1971).

But learning more about this rich musical heritage was challenging in Minneapolis. Only one station, KUXL, played a steady menu of R&B, and it went off the air after sundown. Compared to other urban centers, the city was a barren place for black music, and the vibrant local jazz and blues scene of the fifties and early sixties had all but disappeared. Jellybean Johnson, who moved to Minneapolis as a teen and became friends with Prince at Lincoln Junior High (a school that Prince attended briefly before moving to Bryant), felt a sense of culture shock. "I had just moved from Chicago, where you heard nothing but black music twenty-four hours a day," recalled Johnson (who would later become a member of the Time, a Prince side project).

Still, for young black musicians who grew up in Minneapolis, being exposed to different sounds had its benefits. While R&B artists like James Brown and Sly Stone excited Prince most, he also came to appreciate pop groups like Fleetwood Mac and rock bands like Santana. A few years later, when he started composing his own songs, all of these influences would show up in some measure.

Prince, Anderson, and Smith dubbed their band Grand Central. They added neighbor Terry Jackson as a percussionist, in part because he had a basement that was less dank than Anderson's and that provided an alternative location on the days Bernadette Anderson couldn't endure the clamor any longer. Both Prince and Anderson had started singing as well; the three main members divided vocal responsibilities and ran the band in an essentially democratic fashion. Curiously, although Prince would use his falsetto almost exclusively on his first three albums, in Grand Central he relied primarily on his lower register. "If we played Sly Stone, Prince sang just like Sly," remembered Smith.

Stone (né Sylvester Stewart) emerged as Prince's most important musical influence and would remain so for many years. More than any other single artist, Sly provided the prototype for Prince's efforts in the 1980s to blend R&B with rock and pop. He formed his band, the Family Stone, in San Francisco's Haight-Ashbury of the 1960s, a milieu clouded with marijuana smoke and excessive idealism; Sly, as much or more so than anyone else, embodied the contradictions of that scene and that time. He was incredibly talented, yet also extremely self-destructive and chronically unmotivated; his lyrics urged people to strive for success, but he did practically everything possible to throw away the advantages that his musical skills gave him. Still, for a brief time in the late sixties and early seventies, Stone's creativity burned as brightly as that of any R&B artist before or since. The combination of rhythm, melody, and sheer energy in songs like "Thank You (Falettinme Be Mice Elf Agin)," "Sing A Simple Song," and "Dance To The Music" has rarely been matched in any branch of pop or rock music. And on mellower songs like "Family Affair" and "Time," Sly showed off the some of the greatest vocal gifts of his generation.

Sly & the Family Stone's music spoke directly to what Prince wanted to accomplish: to combine the best elements of funk, rock, and pop into a new and original idiom. But despite admiring Stone's musical prowess, Prince was disdainful of his drug abuse and lack of discipline; he preferred the model of James Brown, known as "the hardest working man in show business." As Prince exclaimed to Smith one day, "I'm not going to be like Sly, I'm going to practice my behind off like James Brown's band, and I'm going to have everything so tight that you're not going to be able to say anything about it." At a time when drugs were becoming widespread in America's high schools, Prince's lifestyle was notably straight; he didn't even drink an occasional beer. While many of his peers were partying their way to self-discovery, he was obsessed with music and interested in little else, save perhaps the girls who visited the basement.

If Stone was Prince's major musical influence, followed by James Brown in second place and Stevie Wonder in third, a very different figure would have the most impact on his lyrics: the folksinger Joni Mitchell. Both Prince and Mitchell, in separate media interviews, have recalled that when Prince was about ten years old, he attended one of her performances and sat in the front row. She noticed him perhaps because young African-Americans were not a fixture at her concerts—particularly in predominantly white cities like Minneapolis—but also because his strange, intense eyes remained locked on her throughout the show. Mitchell's lyrics, which are filled with allegory and visual descriptions (including frequent allusions to colors), would inform Prince's approach to such a great extent that he would even borrow complete phrases from her work. And while the sway of both her words and also her quirky, cross-disciplinary musical approach would not become readily apparent until years later, it is clear that Prince was impacted by Mitchell's work even before he became a teenager.

Grand Central practiced incessantly and began playing gigs at dance halls around the city. A smattering of original numbers appeared in the band's repertoire, although none were particularly memorable. But each member was musically talented, and Grand Central soon became a fixture in Minneapolis' tightly knit R&B scene. Other notable groups included Flyte Tyme, which featured future star producers Terry Lewis and Jimmy Jam (who would also be members of the Time), and yet another future R&B luminary, Alexander O'Neal. The groups engaged in friendly but intense competition. An ensemble called the Family, for example—led by Sonny Thompson, who would become a member of Prince's band in the 1990s—tried to appear intimidating by wearing long black jackets onstage like gang colors. "We weren't trying to kill each other; we just wanted to kill each other onstage," remembered Jellybean Johnson.

As the stakes became higher for Grand Central, Prince and Anderson made a rather unsentimental decision. Displeased that Charles Smith's commitment to the Central High football team was cutting into rehearsal time, they summarily replaced him with Morris Day, another friend from the neighborhood. Smith arrived in the basement one day to find that his drums had been moved aside to make way for another kit. Despite Smith's disappointment, he remained close to Prince for many years.

The arrival of Day brought a greater professionalism to the band, largely because his mother, LaVonne Daugherty, stepped forward to become the group's de facto manager. The name of the group was changed to Champagne after Smith claimed that the phrase "Grand Central" was his creation. (Prince, Anderson, and Day also wanted to avoid comparison with Graham Central Station, a solo project led by Larry Graham, bassist for Sly & the Family Stone.)

Daugherty, who had ambition but no music industry experience, was assisted by Pepé Willie, a New Yorker who moved to Minneapolis in 1974 after marrying Shauntel Manderville, Prince's cousin. Willie, a songwriter who had worked with the R&B group Little Anthony and the Imperials, answered numerous business questions posed by both Daugherty and Prince. More out of a sense of family obligation than anything else, Willie began attending the group's rehearsals, where Prince was fast emerging as Champagne's leader. "He would stop in the middle of a song and say 'Wait a minute,' and then go over to the keyboardist and show what he wanted," Willie recalled.

When Willie went into the studio to record with his own group, 94 East, in late 1975, he recruited Prince as a session guitarist. During rehearsals, Willie learned something about Prince's work ethic; when the group took a break to have a beer, Prince refused to join them and would keep practicing. "We would come back and he'd be laughing at us because our eyes were red," Willie recalled. "We thought he was kind of square." The sessions themselves, which took place at a Minneapolis studio called the Cookhouse, gave Prince his first look at a recording studio. (Later, in an attempt to capitalize on Prince's fame, Willie released various of these demos under the name 94 East on his own record label in 1986, 1995, and 2002.) Prince assisted in the writing for the project and seemed giddy about the prospect of hearing his music on tape. When Prince began work on a song, he refused to stop until it was complete, no matter how late the hour. "Some people would just say, 'Nah, I'm going to take a nap,' but he wouldn't," said Willie. "Once he got on a roll, he had to finish it."

And once a song was finally done, Prince experienced a wave of exhilaration. Willie recalls being woken up by a four a.m. phone call when Prince completed lyrics for "Just Another Sucker," a 94 East song. "He had just accomplished something—he was very proud and happy, and he had to let someone know," Willie remembered.

The experience whetted Prince's appetite to record more of his own material, and Champagne cut a demo in early 1976 at ASI Studio, a small, primitive sixteen-track facility on the Northside. "That studio was just a horrible piece of junk," recalled David Z. Rivkin, the engineer on the sessions, who would work with Prince many times in the future. With Daugherty paying for studio time, the group cut six original songs, including the Prince composition "Machine" (he later described it as being about a "woman's parts") and the Anderson number "39th Street Party." None of the recordings from the sessions are known to still exist.

Shortly thereafter, Prince gave his first interview to his school newspaper, the *Central High Pioneer*. Showing a certain swagger, he complained that it was difficult for a group to thrive in Minneapolis, far from the spotlight of places like Los Angeles and New York. He claimed that if his band lived in one of those cities, "we would have gotten over by now."

Both Prince and Anderson kept writing songs, and the group entered another studio, a less expensive eight-track facility called Moonsound, in spring 1976. The studio proprietor, a tall, lanky Englishman named Chris Moon, had moved to Minneapolis as a teenager when his father landed a job in the city, and he opened his studio after graduating high school. Moon eventually took a full-time job engineering music jingles for a local advertising agency but continued to book time at the studio on evenings and weekends, providing a low-cost opportunity for local groups like Champagne.

Something of a frustrated songwriter, Moon wrote reams of lyrics in his spare time. He had difficulty creating the accompanying music, though, and had long hoped to stumble upon an instrumentalist who could provide assistance. During the Champagne sessions he took immediate notice of Prince. The young man seemed quiet and shy, and his skills at first glance did not stand out from the rest of the group, but his passion and discipline soon distinguished him. Prince almost always arrived early for recording sessions to rehearse by himself, not only on guitar, but on piano and bass as well.

One afternoon when they were alone in the studio, Moon pulled Prince aside.

"Listen," he said. "I'm looking for someone to put together some music for some words that I've written."

Prince said nothing; thus far during the sessions, in fact, he had spoken little at all.

"I'm also looking to find an artist, provide him with some free studio time, get a package together, and get the music out there," Moon continued. Prince saw what Moon was proposing—in exchange for music, he was being given a chance to succeed as a solo artist, rather than as just one member of a collaborative ensemble.

He pondered the offer for a few moments, and then he grunted; it was hardly a definitive answer, but Moon chose to interpret it as a yes.

"Let's shake on it," Moon said, and Prince agreed. He was then given a key to the Moonsound studio.

When Anderson and Day found out what had happened, they were chagrined to learn that Prince had been singled out for special attention. Their pride injured, they issued Prince an ultimatum: He had to choose between Moon and Champagne. A deeply conflicted Prince phoned Moon; he wasn't sure if he wanted to leave his friends. The studio owner was anything but pushy and told him to make whatever decision he wanted. Two hours later, Prince called back: He would go with Moon.

Since Moon had to work at the advertising agency during the day, Prince was usually alone in the studio in the afternoons. Working with lyrics Moon had left for him, Prince would sit down at a piano to create melodies for the words. Moon showed his new partner how to work the studio equipment, and soon Prince started to construct full-fledged songs, playing one instrument after another. When the weekends arrived, freeing Prince from his academic responsibilities, he worked virtually around the clock at the studio. Like his father, he needed very little sleep to refresh himself. As the sessions continued in coming weeks, he became more sociable with Moon. Still, his work habits were relentless; when Moon smoked a joint or cracked open a beer, Prince shot him disapproving looks and insisted that they get back to recording.

Prince graduated from Central High in the spring of 1976, giving him even more time to spend at Moonsound. Music became his singular focus, and his skills increased exponentially. While piano remained his strongest instrument, he became an effective guitarist and bassist as well. And with just a little effort, he also became a competent drummer. Prince was a quick study on studio equipment, and could soon run the mixing board with the skill of a veteran. "He looked like this octopus, because there were hands all over the place," Moon said. As a vocalist, he was initially tentative, and his falsetto was so soft that it barely registered on the studio's VU meters. He seemed to gain more confidence, though, when Moon created ambiance by having him lie on the floor with his head on a pillow and all the lights turned off.

Moon and Prince, so different in appearance and temperament, developed a creative symbiosis. One morning, after a long night of partying with a group of women, Moon stumbled into the agency and began writing lyrics in a semi-coherent state. The first phrase was "soft and wet," which was followed by other metaphoric explorations of sex. When he brought the lyrics to the studio that afternoon and explained the double entendre, Prince sat down on the piano and wrote his catchiest musical theme yet. The song's carnal subject matter clearly resonated with Prince, and this new direction provided a unifying theme for their work at Moonsound.

He was resistant, though, to Moon's next suggestion—that he drop his last name. "I don't see putting you out as Prince Nelson; I know it's your name, but we don't need 'Nelson,'" Moon said. Eventually, after some grousing, Prince agreed.

As work continued at Moonsound, the focus steadily began to shift from Moon's ideas to Prince's. He started writing his own lyrics, and, in short order, he and Moon had assembled fourteen songs, including "Soft And Wet." All of the instruments were played by Prince himself. Although most of the songs ramble on far too long, Prince's raw talent is apparent on these early recordings. Among the standouts on the demo is "Leaving For New York," on which Prince, sounding not unlike a higher-voiced Stevie Wonder, coos, growls, and scats over a flowing piano pattern.

Those encountering Prince during this period came away believing that he might be a budding musical genius. One afternoon Moon invited drummer Bobby Z. Rivkin, David Z. Rivkin's brother, to the studio. (The brothers' shared middle initial was a nickname coined by their grandmother.) When he arrived and saw Prince playing piano for the first time, Rivkin was stunned. "It sounded like he had four hands; he was filling out more chordal information on the piano than I've ever heard," Rivkin remembered. In the weeks to come, Rivkin kept hanging around Moonsound. He had already decided that this young musician was worth devoting his entire career to.

The time had arrived, Prince believed, to begin shopping his music to labels in the hope of getting a contract. He had essentially outgrown the need for Moon as a collaborator, and asked him instead to begin serving as a manager. The Englishman declined, however. "The piece I don't do," he responded, "is booking your hotel, making sure you're wearing the right kind of clothes. I'm not interested in that."

Showing remarkable confidence, Prince decided to approach record companies on his own. Armed with a four-song demo tape he flew to New York, where he stayed with his half-sister Sharon Nelson. Predictably, labels were unwilling to meet with an unknown teenager. Frustrated, Prince called Moon and urged him to contact record labels. Moon relented and did as asked, although no one returned his calls either.

Moon then seized on a bolder approach. He contacted Atlantic Records and claimed to a secretary that he represented Stevie Wonder; moments later, an executive called back. Summoning all of the confidence he could muster, Moon admitted that he did not handle Wonder but claimed he had something better to offer. "I'm representing Prince," Moon said. "If you like Stevie Wonder, you're gonna love my artist. He's only eighteen, he plays all the instruments, and he's not blind."

Moon's audacity landed Prince an audience with Atlantic, but the label came away unimpressed with the tape. The Moonsound demo was simply not slick or professional enough for presentation to major labels. Disappointed but undaunted, Prince hunkered down in his sister's apartment and pondered his next step.

An important new patron quickly emerged. Moon one afternoon played the fourteen-song demo tape for Owen Husney, an ambitious Minneapolan in his late twenties who in past incarnations had been a member of a band called High Spirits (which also included David Rivkin), a radio announcer, and a tour promoter. Currently, Husney and a partner ran a lucrative business called the Ad Company that performed marketing for clients in the music industry and other fields.

Moon turned on the tape and Husney began tapping his feet and nodding his head. "Who's the band?" Husney asked.

"It's not a band," Moon responded. "It's one guy playing, singing, and doing everything." Husney, despite years in music, had never heard of such a thing.

"You gotta be kidding!" he shouted. "This is ridiculous, where is he? Let's get him on the phone, now!"

Husney contacted Prince in New York and made his pitch. Although he had never actively managed a group, he exuded confidence and savvy. "I presented myself as his 'protector of creativity,'" Husney recalled. "He was young and a lot of people were going to come at him, and he was very vulnerable at that time."

Prince remained very quiet through the phone call, but agreed to return to Minneapolis to meet Husney. A few days later, when Moon brought him over to Husney's house, they connected immediately, "I have a sense of humor that borders on the sick, and he got it right away," Husney said. "He loved to laugh."

Husney and Prince inked a management agreement. Husney then undertook a mission to transform his new client—a talented but unpolished teenager—into a professional musician. Even though his business was generating $8 million a year, Husney showed no hesitation in turning the Ad Company's operations over to his partner so that he could devote himself full-time to Prince. Along with his attorney Gary Levinson, Husney then began approaching wealthy acquaintances to raise funds. After collecting about $50,000 he formed a corporation called American Artists. Some of the money was used to rent Prince an apartment and place him on a fifty-dollar-a-week allowance. Having made it through adolescence despite the disintegration of his birth family, Prince now left behind the Anderson basement forever.

Husney offered creative input and encouraged Prince to pare down the meandering songs on the Moonsound demo into more compact pieces; he also recommended more pop songs in the vein of "Soft And Wet." Prince proved receptive to the feedback and quickly churned out a simple, almost nursery rhyme–like number called "I Like What You're Doing" (which remains unreleased). Husney purchased new musical instruments and converted a room in his office suite into a rehearsal studio where Prince could jam with other musicians. Bobby Rivkin became an employee of American Artists and frequently drove Prince from place to place; after mentioning repeatedly that he played the drums, Rivkin was invited down to jam. Prince liked his simple, steady style. Among the bassists who joined them was Robbie Paster, who later would spend years as Prince's personal valet, but more frequently André Anderson filled this slot. The dissolution of Champagne had cooled their relationship only briefly, and they retained a powerful musical chemistry.

Once Prince had polished his material, Husney booked recording time at Sound 80, a higher-tech facility than Moonsound. Chris Moon, having played a pivotal role in Prince's career, withdrew from the scene, although Prince continued to use smatterings of his lyrics on some songs. David Rivkin was brought back in to engineer the sessions, and the results were just what Husney wanted: a smooth demo that showcased Prince's skills as both a singer and multi-instrumentalist. After assembling a glossy promotional kit, Husney decided the time was right to approach record companies.

The task facing this one-man band and one-man management team was significant, however. There was still no reason to think that record companies would swoon over a small, shy Midwestern teenager whose music, while impressive from the standpoint of pure musicianship, showed limited songwriting ability. Moreover, Husney, for all of his energy and skill as a promoter, had never managed a client or negotiated a record contract with a major label.

But Prince and Husney had the advantage of being in complete agreement on their strategy. They would emphasize Prince's ability to record an entire album by himself; in the 1970s, long before the wide availability of sophisticated home studio equipment made do-it-yourself albums commonplace, this was an astonishing feat. And they would use Prince's natural shyness to build a sense of mystery and allure around him.

They also decided that creative control was essential. If possible, they wanted Prince to self-produce his first album, and they wanted a multi-record deal that would give his talents time to develop. The first demand, in particular, was audacious; why would a label cede so much power to a fledgling artist? The answer, Husney believed, was that record executives would bow to the clarity and forcefulness of Prince's vision. Husney's confidence had a powerful reinforcing effect on Prince; rapidly, this young musician came to believe that he deserved everything the manager would demand from the record companies.

But while the bond between Prince and his new manager was powerful, Prince saw Husney, like Chris Moon, first and foremost as an instrument of his success. Husney would eventually discover, as Moon did after his studio was no longer needed, that Prince's seemingly sincere affection toward a person could be turned off at will.

Like Chris Moon, Husney wasn't above using creative duplicity to entice labels. He called a contact at Warner Bros.—Russ Thyret, a high-level executive who had previously offered him a job at the company—and told him about Prince. Husney said that CBS Records was flying Prince out to Los Angeles for a meeting and wondered whether Warner Bros. might be interested in taking a meeting as well. Thyret said yes. Husney then called CBS and A&M Records, each time emphasizing the theme of Prince as a musical prodigy and representing that other interest existed. The labels, not wanting to lose a chance at an artist that their rivals were courting, all agreed to meetings. "I lied my way in everywhere to get him in," Husney recalled. "Jealousy is what makes this business go around."

Husney, Prince, and attorney Levinson got on a plane for Los Angeles and visited the swank offices of five labels: Warner Bros., CBS, A&M, RSO, and ABC/Dunhill. The manager and attorney made the initial pitch, after which Prince came in and said just a few words. The approach worked; after hearing the demo tape, the executives were curious to see the teenager who had pulled this off, and they were mesmerized by his oddly quiet manner. CBS then booked time at Village Recorders Studios and asked Prince to undertake an audition of sorts. He rerecorded "Just As Long As We're Together," one of the songs on his demo, as the executives looked on.

When the team returned to Minneapolis, Husney's phone started ringing. Although RSO and ABC passed, the other three labels were all interested and went about assembling offers. Husney then began making the demands he and Prince had settled on. A&M would offer only a two-record contract, which appeared to rule them out. Warners and CBS were offering lucrative three-record deals, but both voiced concerns about Prince's desire to produce himself. CBS proffered what it thought was a wonderful idea: Verdine White, bassist of the popular R&B group Earth, Wind & Fire, would produce the first album. "That destroyed the possibility of Prince going with CBS," Husney recalled.

This left Warners. It would go only so far as to allow Prince to coproduce the first album, but there were many other things about the label that attracted Prince and Husney. Throughout the 1970s, under the stewardship of chairman Mo Ostin and president Lenny Waronker, Warners had earned a reputation as a company that signed interesting artists and carefully nurtured their creativity. And Russ Thyret's approach during his meetings with Prince and Husney had left them impressed. "Basically, while everybody was wining, and dining, and giving us lunches, and promising us homes in Beverly Hills, Russ took us back to his house, sat on the floor, and talked music with us," Husney said. "There was a real genuine bonding there."

But before making his final decision, Prince voiced an important concern directly to Warner Bros. officials: He didn't want to be pigeonholed as an R&B artist. "I'm an artist and I do a wide range of music," Prince insisted. "I'm not an R&B artist, I'm not a rock 'n' roller." At a time when most labels, including Warners, had separate "black music" departments, Prince dreaded the idea of limiting his appeal in any respect.

The executives said all the right things, and Prince signed a three-album contract with Warner Bros. on June 25, 1977, just weeks after turning nineteen. An association began that would become one of the most fruitful and lucrative—but also one of the most frustrating and embarrassing—in the company's venerable history. For the moment, Ostin and Waronker felt nothing but confidence—they had an artist who might be a once-in-a-generation talent. Had they paused, however, the executives might have wondered about the darker side of Prince's passion and ambition, and they might have wondered how such a fiercely independent figure would react to the constraints that inevitably arise from working within a major U.S. corporation. For an artist like Prince, how much control would be enough?

At a celebratory luncheon with company executives, he seemed shy and awkward. After the fete, though, he recorded a song that represented his own way of communicating with his new patrons. Called "We Can Work It Out," the unreleased song's lyrics can only be interpreted as an expression of hope that the Prince-Warners partnership would be a happy one. It ended, though, with the sound of an explosion.

CHAPTER TWO

One-man Band

O nly weeks after Prince inked his contract with Warner Bros., questions began to arise over who would really control the relationship. Although the company had agreed to at least let him coproduce his first album, left unresolved was the choice of the other coproducer and, more fundamentally, how much of a role Prince would play in shaping the album's sound. In Prince's mind, it was simple: He had to run the show. His sense of destiny and entitlement had been amplified by the competition among three record companies for his services, and he now felt ready to make yet more demands. "He was definitely out to make a statement: 'I can do it all, and you can kiss my ass,'" noted Steve Fontano, assistant engineer on the album.

Still, the issue was one on which Warner Bros. was reluctant to yield completely to this young artist. Despite their belief in his talents, company chieftains Mo Ostin and Lenny Waronker weren't sure they could entrust him with this complicated and expensive task, which required both technical knowledge and an intangible known in the industry as "record sense"—that is, the ability to create a radio-ready sound. Throughout the 1970s and well into the 1980s, the role of the producer remained paramount, and skilled professionals were almost always brought in to shape the work of new artists. Men (almost exclusively men) like Nile Rogers (mastermind of the group Chic), James Anthony Carmichael (frequent producer of the Commodores), and Giorgio Moroder (producer of Donna Summer and others) ran the mixing board with iron hands. Charging a nineteen-year-old with such authority was unprecedented in Warners' history.

But the executives faced a dilemma: They realized that any heavy-handedness on their part could undermine Warners' status as an artist-friendly label, which was what had attracted Prince there in the first place. Ostin and Waronker, believing deeply in the label's mission of nurturing creativity, preferred to assert a measure of control over Prince without alienating him or his manager. The two executives' careers had been linked since 1966, when Ostin, a thirty-nine-year-old vice president at Reprise Records, hired Waronker, twenty-six, as part of his artist development team. When Ostin became chairman of Warners in the early 1970s, Waronker joined him as an executive. Both men developed a sterling reputation within the industry—they were seen as unpretentious, honest, and skilled at selecting artists for the label. Both were also low-key in personal style and avoided publicity, and they were used to dealing with brilliant, mercurial, and demanding artists.

Treading delicately, Ostin called Owen Husney in summer 1977 to discuss the coproducer issue. The chairman's initial suggestion was one of the biggest names in R&B music: Maurice White, the leader (and drummer) of Earth, Wind & Fire, a supergroup that had released a stream of successful albums during the 1970s. The group's danceable songs showed considerable songwriting craft, and its slick sound helped define 1970s urban radio. Singles like "Serpentine Fire" and "Shining Star" scored big on the charts and were also widely influential among R&B producers. Ostin saw White as someone who could both provide cachet and serve as the perfect mentor for a young artist. Husney knew, though, that Prince would be mortified by the idea—he had, of course, already rejected CBS Records' bid to have Maurice's brother Verdine produce his first album. Determined to succeed on his own, Prince had no interest in riding anyone's coattails. Moreover, he viewed Earth, Wind & Fire as falling within the category of disco, an R&B subgenre that emphasized simplistic melodies, novel electronic effects, and lightweight dance grooves. Convinced that this fad would soon run its course, Prince dreaded being lumped in with such groups.

Husney, while expressing his doubts to Ostin, agreed to take the proposal to Prince. Predictably, he rejected it out of hand, and then wrote a detailed memo to Husney that marshaled arguments against the idea. Earth, Wind & Fire's sound was dated and generic, he contended, and White's input would detract from, rather than enhance his own highly original vision. When Ostin and Husney spoke again, the chairman backed down regarding Maurice White, but argued that Prince was too green to be sole producer. In response, Husney floated the same idea that had worked so well with CBS: Prince would undertake an in-studio audition to prove his readiness. This time, though, he would not be informed what was happening; Husney would simply say that Warners wanted to give him a weekend of free studio time. During the session, the executives could stop by under the pretense of working at the studio.

Ostin agreed, and Prince was flown to Amigo Studios in Los Angeles. Waronker and other officials discretely drifted in and out as Prince recorded another version of "Just As Long As We're Together." As Husney recalled, "He thought these people were janitors." The executives, after watching Prince play every instrument as he constructed the song in the better part of a day, decided it would be folly to force a producer upon him; an artist this talented and headstrong would simply have to learn on the job. "Okay, we're going to have to burn a record on the guy," Waronker grumbled to Husney after the session.

But Warners added an important caveat: An "executive producer," someone with plenty of technical experience, would have to be present to oversee the recording process. Prince and Husney concurred, realizing that they were unlikely to wrest further concessions. Selected for the role was Tommy Vicari, a veteran recording engineer who had worked with Carlos Santana, Billy Preston, and others.

Since Prince wanted to record in Minneapolis, work began at Sound 80, where he had made his first professional demo. Vicari had favored an even more sophisticated facility, and when technical problems interrupted the sessions, he proposed relocating to a sleek L.A. studio. Husney disagreed, arguing that any nineteen-year-old—even one as disciplined as Prince—could be distracted by the city's party atmosphere. They compromised on the Record Plant in Sausalito, a pleasant northern California city near San Francisco. A beautiful house overlooking the San Francisco Bay was rented in nearby Corte Madera, where Prince, Vicari, Husney, and Husney's wife, Britt, all moved in.

A significant amount of pressure rested on Prince, about to become Warner Bros.' youngest producer ever, and he entered the studio with a great sense of mission. As usual, he recorded each song himself, creating a foundation of bass and drums and then adding other instruments. "He seemed to be one of these guys who could hear the entire song in his head, before he even played it," recalled assistant engineer Fontano.

While the recording of his demos at Sound 80 had been marked by moments of lightness and good humor, Prince was now deadly serious. Proceeding deliberately and making sure every note was right, he burnished the songs into a state of perfection. The music he created was mostly straightforward R&B, with an emphasis on ballads. He relied heavily on an Oberheim model synthesizer, often giving the tracks a heavily electronic feel. To distinguish himself from other contemporary R&B groups, who often used trumpets and saxophones, he employed the synth for parts that would otherwise have been handled by horns. At first, Prince barely spoke to Vicari or Fontano. He paid close attention, though, to how they ran studio equipment. Although sensing that his ultimate goal was to render them redundant, they marveled at his concentration and ability to acquire new skills. "Prince's greatest ability is that he is a sponge, and he can absorb anything from anybody," observed Husney.

Another engineer, David Rivkin, was flown in from Minneapolis to record Prince's vocals. Pleased to see a familiar face, Prince became more relaxed and friendly, spending time with Rivkin outside the studio as well. When they ate dinner one evening at an upscale Sausalito restaurant, Prince brought out a squirt gun that they took turns surreptitiously shooting at the ceiling. "People three tables away were looking up, wondering if something was leaking," Rivkin remembered. "We tried not to laugh."

But in the studio, getting the vocals into the shape Prince wanted was difficult and time-consuming, as he insisted on recording the parts again and again. Gradually, Rivkin became concerned that Prince's perfectionism was robbing the music of any sense of spontaneity. On "For You," an a cappella vocal piece, Prince overdubbed his voice forty-six times. "The pressure caused him to keep doing things over and over and over," Rivkin recalled. And layers of overdubs were added to show off his skills as a musician; the catchy "Soft And Wet" was cluttered with synthesizer embellishments that sapped attention from the primary melody.

As a result of the methodical pace, the album went significantly over budget. Although Warner Bros. did not complain, Waronker flew in one afternoon for a progress check. From the moment he arrived, it was clear that Prince viewed his very presence as corporate meddling. When Waronker suggested adding more bass to the song "So Blue," Prince erupted and insisted that the executive leave the studio. Waronker returned to Los Angeles, realizing even more clearly that the label had on its hands an artist who would never be satisfied with anything short of total command over his career.

Prince also had no interest in the input of the executive producer, Tommy Vicari, who had hoped to play a significant role in shaping the album. Recalled Fontano, "He kind of looked at Tommy like, 'Oh, the babysitter's here, Dad's home.'" After several weeks of quizzing Vicari about how to run the equipment, Prince started ignoring him. When Vicari offered substantive suggestions, the responses were curt and dismissive. And one evening, Prince's resentment of Vicari's presence was underscored through a bizarre practical joke. When everyone else was out, leaving Prince alone in the Corte Madera house, he stuffed an outfit of Husney's clothes full of leaves, placed this makeshift dummy on Vicari's bed, and stuck a knife in its back, Rivkin recounted. "Vicari came back at four in the morning and thought Owen had been killed," he said. "He was really screaming."

Obviously, Prince recognized no further need for an executive producer. "He had absorbed everything he needed out of Tommy Vicari's brain," Husney noted. "Prince already wanted him out by that time, and Tommy was heartbroken, because he had just been treated like shit."

Another frequent presence in the studio was André Anderson, who also wanted to contribute. But while Prince appreciated his friend's company, the bassist's creative assistance was not welcome. "He got left out, because Prince wanted to make the whole album himself," remembered Husney. Still, because some of the material had emerged from earlier jam sessions involving Anderson, certain associates felt that the bassist's role was important. "André's vibe is all over that album," Charles Smith contended. But whatever he had contributed earlier in the process, Anderson was forced to remain a passive observer in Sausalito. While Prince recorded, the bassist chattered impatiently about how he would soon be making his own album, Rivkin remembered. "He kept saying, 'I'm going do my thing, I can't wait to do my thing.'"

After months of long, tedious sessions that left everyone exhausted, Prince and his team left for Hollywood in January 1978 to add the final touches at Sound Labs Studios. His meticulously constructed debut was nearly complete. But while the material was undeniably polished and professional-sounding, Prince's songwriting skills had not yet caught up to his vision of a grand synthesis of funk, rock, and soul. Songs like the maudlin ballad "Crazy You" and the overwrought hard rock number "I'm Yours" showed stylistic range but lacked interesting musical ideas or effective hooks. As Rivkin and others had feared, the vocal harmonies had become perhaps too exact, sounding almost artificial in places.

Entitled *For You*, the album was pronounced complete after Prince and Vicari left Sound Labs. Cover art was quickly prepared and Warner Bros. slotted the album for release in early spring. Prince returned to Minneapolis, where he decompressed and spent time with Smith, Anderson, and others. "I was a physical wreck when I finished that record," he later told *Musician*. But when he previewed *For You* for his friends, his pride was unmistakable; Prince believed that he had delivered a perfect product. Recalled Husney, "I think that by that point he had been told so much that he was fantastic that he believed he was going to be successful right away."

april 1978: release of For You

Just as Prince had insisted, the album was billed as a one-man production. Chris Moon is credited as cowriter of "Soft And Wet," and Tommy Vicari gets his executive producer title, but the credits otherwise state that the album was "produced, composed, arranged, and performed by Prince." The cover photo, shot in dark and muted tones that suggest romance and mystery, shows Prince wearing a serious gaze and a sizeable afro. All told, the packaging of the album—like most of the music within—seemed aimed directly at an R&B audience. Despite the presence of the rocker "I'm Yours," the overall sound of *For You* was not especially different from that of leading R&B artists.

Predictably, media attention focused on the theme of a wunderkind who had created a major label release entirely on his own. This owed much to the efforts of Husney, whose press kits portrayed Prince as a multi-talented whiz kid. Still, the publicity campaign could not mask the lack of compelling material on the album, which was not widely reviewed. The commercial performance of *For You* also fell far short of what Prince had hoped for; it sold just 150,000 copies in the United States, reaching a respectable No. 21 on *Billboard*'s Soul Chart but only No. 163 on the Pop Chart. (The sales would increase in coming years to nearly a million worldwide after Prince enjoyed other successes.) Not surprisingly, he remained for the most part beneath the public's radar screen as pop music was dominated throughout 1978 by the soundtracks of two blockbuster films, *Saturday Night Fever* (featuring multiple No. 1 hits by the Bee Gees) and *Grease* (which generated cloying chart toppers by Frankie Valli and the singing duo of John Travolta and Olivia Newton-John).

But despite Prince's disappointment, the album did make a mark in select urban markets. Owen Husney continued to pour his energies into promotion, organizing an autograph-signing tour that drew significant crowds in some cities. The release of "Soft And Wet" as a single in June also helped; the song reached No. 12 on the Soul Singles Chart. During a promotional appearance in Charlotte, 3,000 boisterous young fans showed up, creating a scene that at once thrilled and perturbed Prince. "All of a sudden you get thousands of screaming kids saying that they love him—he didn't understand that," observed Pepé Willie. "He told me, 'How can they love me? They don't even know me.' He told me he felt like a piece of meat being carried around."

In the end, *For You* did about as well as could be expected. The album remains an interesting historical document, as it is one of the first major label releases in pop history to be composed and performed almost completely by one man. While other musicians, such as Paul McCartney and Stevie Wonder, previously accomplished the feat, neither had done so at such a young age. And with his skillful playing on a variety of instruments and his intricate vocal harmonies, Prince shows himself a remarkable musician. In terms of clever songwriting, though, *For You* offers little. "In Love" and "Soft And Wet" feature decent hooks, but much of the album is flat. The songs fail to build momentum, instead moving arbitrarily from verse to chorus. Far from a stunning debut, *For You* is one of the lesser works in Prince's catalog.

But despite the album's flaws and modest commercial performance, Warners remained strongly invested in Prince's career. While the music industry during the 1980s, 1990s, and beyond would become merciless in its quest to find artists who could deliver overnight hits, in 1978 a different ethos prevailed, particularly at Warner Bros. Talent was given reasonable time to reveal itself, and musicians were not consigned to oblivion for having failed to deliver instant blockbusters. While troubled that he had not yet become a major star, Prince knew he would get another chance.

*   *   *

After moving into a new home at 5215 France Avenue in the Minneapolis suburb of Edina in summer 1978, Prince began recording new material on a four-track, reel-to-reel machine. At about the same time, Charles Smith and Pepé Willie told him about a sixteen-year-old singer named Sue Ann Carwell whose astonishingly powerful voice had been winning talent shows around Minneapolis. Prince went to see her perform, and afterward approached Carwell about recording together. She agreed and soon became a frequent visitor to France Avenue, where Prince wrote songs for her and had her lay down vocals on the four-track. Although their relationship never became romantic, Carwell often spent entire nights with him working on material.

From the start, Prince conceived of Carwell as a solo artist whom he would guide from behind the scenes. As he wrote for her, he consciously sought to adopt a female perspective, both in terms of the lyrics and the sound. The coy and bouncy "Wouldn't You Love To Love Me," for example, was written from the viewpoint of a woman being pursued by a male suitor. Prince became excited about the potential of a Carwell side project and planned to take a demo of the material to Warner Bros. He began concocting an image for her and proposed that she adopt the stage name Susie Stone. She balked at the whole enterprise, however, not wanting to have her career co-opted. "I didn't really believe in Prince, and I definitely didn't want to have a fictitious name," said Carwell, who later became a successful session singer for artists ranging from Rod Stewart to Christina Aguilera. Her collaboration with Prince petered out as he became more and more focused on promoting *For You*. The songs he recorded with her, however, point toward the stronger pop material he would write in later years. Remnants of the sessions exist; "Wouldn't You Love To Love Me," was later recorded by another protégée, Taja Sevelle, and unreleased versions of that song and another Carwell number, "Make It Through The Storm," exist with Prince's original vocals on them.

Carwell was the first in a long line of women that Prince would try to mold into musical disciples. While much more talented than most of his future female protégées, she was the prototype for artists like Vanity, Apollonia, Carmen Electra, Elisa Fiorillo, and others—women around whom Prince built side projects as a means of expressing another side of his creative personality. Carwell learned, as many others would, that the price of working with Prince was high—he would always insist on complete domination of any endeavor involving his music.

Prince's next task was forming a band that could tour behind *For You*. He wanted to create an ensemble that, like his longtime influence Sly & the Family Stone, embraced different races and genders. The first and most obvious selection was Anderson (who now adopted the stage name André Cymone) on bass. Although his aspirations went well beyond being a sideman, he and Prince shared musical and personal chemistry. Next chosen was drummer Bobby Z. Rivkin, who by now had been playing with Prince on and off for about a year. Using a rehearsal studio at Del's Tire Mart in Minneapolis, this three-man nucleus began auditioning candidates for keyboards and guitar who responded to advertisements placed in local publications by Husney. Gayle Chapman, a quiet young woman and a devout adherent of a Christian sect called The Way, filled the first keyboard slot. Dez Dickerson, a rock-oriented guitarist with a punkish sense of fashion, was tabbed as the guitarist. Auditions for the second keyboard slot took longer, with Prince finally settling on Matt Fink, an acquaintance of Rivkin's. Sue Ann Carwell briefly joined on backing vocals and congas but withdrew when she and Prince ceased recording together.

The band members were attracted not just by Prince's obvious talents, but by his focus and drive. Dickerson, recalling a conversation with Prince after he auditioned on guitar, came away impressed by the nineteen-year-old's maturity. "He asked me deep, long-term-oriented questions," Dickerson said. "I could tell he was a thinker — he wasn't just saying, 'Gee whiz, we're all going to be rock stars.'"

After much of their equipment was stolen during a break-in at Del's Tire Mart, the band relocated to Willie's basement, where they rehearsed nearly every day. Live, Prince's songs took on a much rawer and more rock-oriented flavor. Dickerson, a fan of Led Zeppelin and other hard rock groups, raised the energy with his power chords and intense solos. Cymone, intent on establishing himself as Prince's instrumental equal, showed off his chops through busy bass parts. Fink also emerged as a flamboyant musician, laying down wild solos influenced by jazz-fusion artists like Jan Hammer and Keith Emerson. Showing the same perfectionism that he had demonstrated during the recording of *For You,* Prince pushed the band relentlessly to master the songs. But they also jammed for hours on raw ideas (one of Prince's favorite pastimes), and from these sessions emerged riffs that Prince took home and shaped into songs.

While usually cordial with his band members, Prince was, at first, more reserved than friendly, preferring to play music rather than socialize. "If he didn't know you well, he came across as very shy, and sometimes people would read it as being anti-social," Dickerson observed. Still, his new colleagues influenced his development in various ways. Chapman's religiosity was intriguing, especially given her frequent remarks that God had endowed Prince with unique gifts. "She did tell him he was blessed, and he did eat it up," recalled Rivkin. Dickerson, meanwhile, provided Prince a window to alternative musical movements such as punk and heavy metal. And the guitarist's colorful attire gave Prince ideas about his live image.

Prince was especially receptive to anything that would distinguish him from other R&B artists. In many respects, his first album fit squarely in the tradition of singers like Al Green and Smokey Robinson, who wrote primarily love songs and rarely challenged their audiences with new musical directions. Already, though, Prince was considering how to break out of this mold. "He was very clear that he wanted the band to be an amalgam of rock and R&B," Dickerson remembered. Modeling his band after Sly & the Family Stone, a group very much part of the counterculture of the sixties, showed his desire to incorporate a social and political edge. When Husney told him how the Beatles had shocked a generation by wearing haircuts that touched their ears, Prince became intrigued by the idea of capturing public attention through imagery.

His overall relationship with his manager, however, began to deteriorate after the release of *For You.* Believing that the album was not being effectively promoted, Prince started griping to Husney and Russ Thyret, the official at Warners with whom he had the most contact. A frustrated Thyret, who had energetically pushed the album to radio stations, complained to Husney that Prince had unreasonable expectations and didn't understand the music business. It was hard for the manager to disagree.

Prince also barraged Husney with all manner of unusual demands, including that he repair broken toilets and sinks. There was a strong passive-aggressive undertone in the badgering, as Prince seemed to be conveying his frustration about the performance of *For You*. Husney, justifiably incensed that his hard work on much more important issues was going unrecognized, began to feel like a glorified gofer. The manager had viewed himself as a partner and strategist, but it was becoming apparent that Prince would always insist on making most of the key decisions himself.

Finally, things came unglued over Husney's refusal to perform yet another menial task. While he was awaiting a phone call from the William Morris Agency about a potential concert tour, Prince called and insisted that he immediately bring a space heater to the rehearsal studio. The manager explained the importance of the William Morris call and asked if Pepé Willie or someone else could handle the chore. Prince became indignant.

"You know what, fuck you," Husney told him. "Just go get your own goddamn space heater. I'm not going to do that."

Later, even after tempers had cooled, Husney felt matters had reached an impasse and told Prince that they should part ways. Prince seemed surprised and told Husney he wanted to continue the relationship, but he made no concessions as far as what the manager's role should be. He wrote Husney a three-page letter outlining his duties; it was filled with just the sort of demands Husney felt were beyond the pale. Prince envisioned a life for himself where all his basic needs would be handled by others. "He can keep ten, twenty people busy working eight to ten hours a day with creative and sophisticated demands," noted Bobby Rivkin. But Husney had no interest in fulfilling this fantasy and stood by his decision to quit.

The rupture left Prince in managerial limbo. Willie stepped in to help on a temporary basis but lacked the time or experience to serve as a full-time manager. Prince himself began writing the band members' $150 paychecks, and Willie did what he could in other areas. With Prince's album not doing especially well, and expenses mounting, it was obvious that help was needed, and quickly.

january 5, 1979: the capri theatre, minneapolis

Among the more important tasks Willie handled as interim manager was to organize Prince's debut concerts. Two shows were booked at the Capri Theatre, and various Warner Bros. executives were invited to check out their new act on the second night. The first show drew a modest crowd of about 300 people. This audience, which included many friends, family members, and other local supporters, responded enthusiastically. Prince, however, showed himself a tentative performer. He kept his back to the audience at times and appeared uncomfortable with onstage banter.

The second show, two nights later, was even more difficult. The temperature in Minneapolis was below zero—typical for a midwinter night—and the group of Warners officials who flew in from Los Angeles did little to warm the atmosphere in the theater. Prince and the band, already feeling less than confident after the previous evening's show, felt tremendous pressure as the executives stood stiffly in the balcony while their limos idled outside. "The show was very tense, very awkward," recalled Rivkin. "He was nervous, and the band hadn't jelled." Making matters worse, Dez Dickerson used the occasion to experiment with a wireless guitar; predictably, it malfunctioned, creating embarrassing gaps in the set.

Charles Smith, who drove home with Prince after the show, found him nearly in tears. "He thought the show was shit," Smith recalled. "I kept trying to talk to him, and he wouldn't even talk." Husney, who remained in contact with Warner Bros., found company officials extremely disappointed as well. "They told me that the show was a complete disaster," he said. Soon after, the executives bluntly told Prince that he was not ready for a major tour. While not surprising in light of the weak performance, it was a painful message to hear. "He was crestfallen," Dickerson remembered.

Warners was also concerned about the economics of Prince's career. *For You* had cost over $170,000 to make, nearly exhausting the $180,000 budgeted for his first three albums. With a five-piece band on the payroll and a constant list of demands, he was proving a costly investment. "There was quite a bit of debt to the label, and his back was against the wall," observed Rivkin.

Warner Bros., realizing that a solid management team was needed to right the ship, contacted the Los Angeles firm of Cavallo & Ruffalo, which had handled Little Feat and other acts. Prince, anxious for help, agreed to give them a try. Firm president Bob Cavallo dispatched employee Perry Jones, who began handling Prince's day-to-day needs. He and Steve Fargnoli, who soon became Prince's key contact at the firm, were more willing than Husney to perform caretaking chores. Fargnoli brought in reinforcements, deputizing his assistant Jamie Shoop and others to help.

The arrival of Cavallo & Ruffalo stabilized Prince's business situation and gave him a renewed sense of personal security. His mood, which had been fraying under the pressure of promoting his first album and pulling together a band, was enhanced by the frequent presence of Kim Upsher, a young woman he had met in high school. She became Prince's primary girlfriend, spending many evenings with him and bringing over decorations and plants to brighten the house. But Prince had little interest in confining himself to one relationship, and his status as even a minor star offered plenty of new opportunities for female companionship.

Realizing that his songwriting needed to improve, he focused on creating strong, simple melodies on his new material. Numbers like "I Wanna Be Your Lover" and "Why You Wanna Treat Me So Bad?" were hooky and danceable, with lyrics that were easy to remember. In some ways less ambitious than the harmony-laden material on *For You*, these new efforts were nonetheless stronger in almost every respect.

In late April 1979, Prince flew to Los Angeles to start working on his second album at Alpha Studio, a facility in the home of engineer Gary Brandt, a friend of Bob Cavallo's. Warners agreed to dispense with an executive producer; label officials had no concerns about Prince's professionalism or technical abilities, and they realized he was impervious to feedback from people he perceived as supervisors.

Prince took a radically different approach to production than he had on *For You*; rather than laboring over every detail and larding the songs with overdubs, he worked quickly and efficiently, keeping the arrangements lean and completing the basic tracks in just a month. Ultimately, he had come to agree with David Rivkin and others that *For You* suffered from overproduction, and his new music sounded freer and fresher.

After principle tracking was complete, scheduling issues at Brandt's studio prompted a move to Hollywood Sound Recorders, where staff engineer Bob Mockler was assigned to work with Prince. Over a period of just a few weeks, overdubs were added and the album mixed. The sound, while refreshingly uncluttered, was very much in the vein of standard R&B; Prince's goal was not to experiment, but to score a hit. "Our competition on that album was Michael Jackson and Kool & the Gang, and I think we looked them right in the eye," Mockler noted.

Prince and Warners agreed on "I Wanna Be Your Lover" as the first single from his forthcoming record, and its release in August 1979 provided just the boost he needed. It rose quickly up the Soul Singles Chart and was still climbing when the album, entitled *Prince*, was released in October. "Lover" finally hit No. 1 on the Soul Chart in December and would eventually achieve gold record status, signifying one million units sold. In addition, it reached No. 11 on the Pop Singles Chart. The album itself also sold well, reaching No. 3 on the Soul Chart and No. 22 on the Pop Chart, going platinum (one million albums sold) by early 1980. It received much more media attention than *For You*, as many critics found it a pleasing contrast to the glossy R&B of the seventies. "Everything is kept to a minimum, a rarity these days in disco music," commented John Wall in *Melody Maker*. Stephen Holden wrote in *Rolling Stone* that "Prince teems with hooks that echo everyone from the Temptations to Jimi Hendrix to Todd Rundgren."

The album displays great improvement over *For You*. "I Wanna Be Your Lover" and "I Feel For You" are engaging and breezy pop songs with strong melodies. The workout "Sexy Dancer" and the lengthy coda of "I Wanna Be Your Lover" point toward the jammy funk that would become key to Prince's eighties sound. And the love ballad "It's Gonna Be Lonely," with its cascading harmonies, is more moving than anything on the first album. Another ballad, "When We're Dancing Close and Slow," while much less successful in musical terms, is interesting in that its title is taken from a line in the Joni Mitchell song "Coyote" (from *Hejira*, 1976).

Over time, *Prince* would have a modest impact on R&B music. The pop ditty "I Feel For You" was covered by Chaka Khan and became a No. 2 hit on the Pop Singles Chart in 1984. And the influence of ballads like "Still Waiting" and "It's Gonna Be Lonely" would later show up in the work of 1980s groups like Boyz II Men and New Edition.

But most importantly from Prince's short-term perspective, the album replenished his capital with Warner Bros., which now viewed him as a rising R&B star. And based on another live showcase for label officials, this time in Los Angeles, Ostin and Waronker concluded that he and the band were now ready to tour. A short U.S. swing began in November 1979 with the same lineup: Chapman and Fink on keyboards, Dickerson on guitar, Cymone on bass, and Rivkin on drums. Ticket sales were mixed— an engagement at the Roxy in Los Angeles sold out, while an appearance in Dallas drew only about 20 people—but Prince's confidence as a live performer increased dramatically. Moving from guitar to keyboards and showing off skillful dance moves, he evoked stars ranging from James Brown to Jimi Hendrix.

While the band's hotel accommodations were usually humble, life on the road proved to be great fun. Prince had by this time warmed up to his colleagues, and became something of a prankster. "During those early days, we were just laughing all of the time," Dickerson recalled. But Prince's gags, like the stunt with Owen Husney's clothing that had so frightened Tommy Vicari, often had a morbid, biting edge. In one recurring joke at airports, the band would grab the first wheelchair they saw and install Prince in it. He donned a pair of dark sunglasses and sat in the chair with a blank look, appearing nearly comatose. The band members then retreated into the background, making it seem that an invalid had been abandoned on the concourse. Prince then slumped forward in his chair and even drooled, which immediately attracted a shocked crowd. At that point the band members re-emerged, trying to suppress their laughter as they pretended to come to his assistance.

Unfortunately, the tour was cut short after a December 2 show in New Orleans when Prince suffered a real malady, coming down with a slight case of pneumonia. But he recovered quickly, and by early January his new management team had booked high-profile television appearances on *Midnight Special* and *American Bandstand,* which Prince used to portray himself as an elusive and mysterious character. The night before *American Bandstand* he told his band members not to say a single word to the interviewer. When Clark quizzed Prince on his background, all he would do was hold up four fingers in response to a question about how long he had been a musician. "He knew he wasn't going to suck up to Dick Clark and act like other idiots that go on that show," said one band member, recalling the meeting where Prince told them how to treat the host. "He wanted to come off cool and aloof."

If it had not been apparent before, it now became clear to the band members that the reticence Prince often displayed—be it towards Warners executives, fans and admirers, or Dick Clark—was not an inherent part of his emotional makeup, but rather a device he used to keep others off balance. He dominated people not through bluster or rhetoric, but through silence and distance. Each band member would eventually find this tactic used against them as well.

The tour resumed and eventually hooked up with the popular funkster Rick James, with Prince serving as the opening act. Featuring an established veteran and an up-and-coming artist, these shows were a bonanza for fans and were billed by promoters as "The Battle of Funk," which helped generate rivalry between the two bands. Often, Prince's concise, energetic sets were more appealing than James' ponderous two-hour performances. "We were young and hungry, and we started kicking his butt," remembered Rivkin.

Prince again felt supremely confident—not just about his ability to blow James off the stage, but about his career prospects in general. Warner Bros. was also pleased, believing that the second album had placed him on track to become a major R&B artist. They saw in him a tremendously disciplined figure and also a budding songwriter; perhaps the label had, after all, discovered another Stevie Wonder.

But Prince's plans for the future were surprisingly different from the expectations of his record company, managers, and even his band members. With the seventies about to end, Prince believed that music was about to change, and he now felt ready to lead the way.

CHAPTER THREE

Rude

E ven as he struggled to succeed as an R&B artist, Prince remained determined to avoid being pigeonholed. Only a month after completing his second album, he embarked on a side project that constituted his most concerted effort yet to incorporate rock 'n' roll into his sound. Settling into the Mountain Ears Studio in Boulder, Colorado, Prince and his band engaged in several weeks of unusually collaborative sessions that included songwriting contributions from André Cymone and Dez Dickerson. This music, which featured heavy drumbeats and layers of distorted guitar, was a striking departure from the vulnerable ballads and pop ditties of *For You* and *Prince*. As with the aborted Sue Ann Carwell project, his intent was to release an album of material while concealing his own involvement; this side group, which he dubbed the Rebels, became a way to anonymously explore a different facet of his artistic personality.

The foray into rock was not particularly successful, however, as the material, including the songs written by Prince, had a generic sound and few interesting melodies. Aware of these deficiencies, Prince shelved the project after returning to Minneapolis, although he would later resurrect some of the material; "You," for example, was revamped as "U" and given to Paula Abdul, who featured it on her 1991 album *Spellbound*.

The release of *Prince* in October 1979, while boosting his commercial standing, did little or nothing to expand his appeal among rock fans. The question remained: Could a young, black artist from the Midwest transcend the ghettoized genre that the record industry seemed intent on placing him in?

Despite his youth (he was only twenty-one when his second album was released), Prince had a sophisticated understanding of the quandary he faced. Throughout the 1970s, music executives both perceived and fostered a highly segregated industry. It was an article of faith that white consumers would gravitate towards so-called album-oriented rock—whether rougher-edged groups like Kiss, Led Zeppelin, and

Aerosmith, or mellower ensembles like Fleetwood Mac, the Eagles, and Steely Dan—while blacks would favor funk stars like Chic, Parliament/Funkadelic, and Earth, Wind & Fire. Only very rarely—Jimi Hendrix was a nearly singular example—were African-American artists viewed by record companies as viable rock acts. These industry divisions extended to the staffing structure of record labels themselves; Warner Bros.' urban music department, for example, had only one white member when Prince was signed to the label.

"In the 1970s, it was incredibly unhip for any white person to work with any black artist," observed Howard Bloom, whose agency began handling Prince's media relations in the early 1980s. "There was a wall, and it was segregation to the Nth degree."

While Warner Bros. chiefs Mo Ostin and Lenny Waronker had great faith in his talents as an R&B musician, few there or at any other major label foresaw the rapidly approaching day when white rock fans would embrace Prince, Michael Jackson, and other black artists. From the start, the record industry had conceived of Prince as a young Stevie Wonder or Smokey Robinson, not a rare, Hendrix-like figure who could traverse boundaries. "Prince was seen as a black artist," noted Bloom, who would encounter significant resistance from Warner Bros. when he tried to change this perception.

As the new decade began, Prince viewed the need to escape the confines of his current market niche as increasingly urgent. Believing that seventies trends like disco were about to fade, he feared being identified with soon-to-be-dated artists who were at best destined for the oldies circuit. He also realized that his own single, "I Wanna Be Your Lover," despite becoming a No. 1 hit on the Soul Singles Chart, hadn't built a loyal fan following; it was simply a catchy love song that appealed to large numbers of young (and especially young female) consumers. His current career path might lead to more hits, but was unlikely to establish him as an influential artist.

During the *Prince* tour, he struggled to differentiate himself from the R&B crooners to whom he was so often compared. In addition to featuring a raw sound, these early live shows showcased Prince's skills on that quintessential rock instrument, the guitar. Through his furious solos, he declared himself part of a tradition of guitar gods like Jimi Hendrix, Eric Clapton, Jimmy Page, Jeff Beck, and others.

But rock songwriting was another matter; on his first two albums, efforts to move beyond R&B had not been especially successful. Rock numbers like "I'm Yours" from *For You* and "Why You Wanna Treat Me So Bad?" from *Prince* evoked generic seventies groups such as Boston and Foreigner, rather than distinctive bands like the Rolling Stones or Pink Floyd. And the disappointing results of the Rebels sessions again showed his limitations in this area.

In addition, at the very time Prince was struggling to find his voice as a rock artist, this genre was itself entering a period of great change. While the blues-rock paradigm of groups like the Stones and Led Zeppelin remained dominant, a new segment of fans that came of age in the mid- and late 1970s—many of them young, male, and alienated—sought alternatives. These listeners became the core audience for punk, which started in England with groups like the Clash and the Sex Pistols, and quickly migrated to America. Soon, punk matured and diversified into a loose movement known as post-punk or New Wave, which included Talking Heads, the Police, Devo, Gang of Four, Television, the Cars, and others.

Prince gradually exposed himself to these new trends. "He had stacks and stacks of records in his house that he got free from Warner Bros.," recalled keyboardist Matt Fink. "He was listening to just about everything." He also frequented nightclubs, environments that he believed gave an accurate reflection of the new and hip. Through visits to trendy spots in Minneapolis, New York, and Los Angeles, Prince saw that the edginess and minimalism of New Wave were creeping toward the mainstream.

This atmosphere of upheaval in rock and pop provided a backdrop as work began on his third album. Settling into his new residence—a rented home in the picturesque Lake Minnetonka section of Minneapolis, wired with a sixteen-track studio for his use—Prince began laying down rough-draft versions of songs that he planned to later rerecord in a professional studio. This new environment was full of technical imperfections—the home studio was a jury-rigged affair, and the drum booth frequently became waterlogged as a result of seepage from an abandoned cesspool near the house—but Prince thrived there. He felt much more comfortable in Minneapolis, without Warner Bros. officials looking over his shoulder. Most of the time, the only other person present in the studio was an affable engineer named Don Batts.

As he wrote new material, it became apparent that Prince's goal was nothing short of redefining himself. Composing primarily on guitar rather than keyboards, he created songs that were much rawer than anything on his first two albums. New Wave textures started to permeate his sound. For the first time, Prince was creating a genuine synthesis of styles, rather than simply imitating the dynamics and bombast of rock. His facility with structure and pop melody also improved; instead of just laying down grooves, he was fashioning songs.

Among the many strong new numbers he taped was "When You Were Mine," a taut pop song with an infectious melody, which had been composed in a hotel room on tour. Prince has described the song as influenced by John Lennon, and the Beatles flavor is apparent. As with Lennon's best love songs (such as "Norwegian Wood" and "You've Got To Hide Your Love Away"), it features lyrics tinged with anger and sarcasm, as Prince laments how he lost a girlfriend by letting her sleep with other men.

Another new number, the New Wave–influenced "Dirty Mind," emerged from a keyboard riff composed by Matt Fink at rehearsal. Prince added a bridge section during a lengthy session at the Lake Minnetonka home, and by midnight they had completed the instrumentation. Prince told Fink he was free to go, and the keyboardist left for bed. The next day at rehearsal, Prince brought in a cassette of "Dirty Mind," complete with vocals and other overdubs; he had labored on it all night. Prince announced to the band that it would be the title track of the next album.

The lyrics of "Dirty Mind," which recount a sexual encounter in a car, indicated a trend in Prince's work toward graphic imagery. While sex and seduction had been at the forefront of his music since "Soft And Wet," Prince's treatment of these themes now became explicit and at times sensationalistic. The hard-rocking "Sister," for example, explored the taboo of incest, while the funky workout "Head" told of a bride-to-be who fellates another man on the way to her wedding. These lyrics, reflecting his fascination with deviant sexuality, helped imbue the music with a newfound urgency.

Prince's creativity was also fostered by the comfort he felt with his band members. Although they were again minimally involved in the recording process, he saw them nearly every day at rehearsals. He, Matt Fink, and André Cymone also spent free time exercising together—lifting weights at Minneapolis gyms, swimming at a YMCA, and roller skating around Lake Minnetonka. They sometimes visited a roller rink in Saint Louis Park, Fink remembered, "to try to meet girls."

In such social settings, Prince was far from the shy individual that he often seemed in the company of record executives and press interviewers. He enjoyed clowning around and adopting various personas he had invented; one of his favorites was a bawdy, Richard Pryor–like character that reminded Fink of a stereotypical street-corner pimp. "When Prince was growing up in North Minneapolis, there was a lot of pimping, drug dealing, and underwordly stuff going on, and that's where this character emerged from," the keyboardist observed. "He had a fantasy of being someone outside the law." But it was indeed a mere fantasy, and Prince never associated with the lowbrow types he caricatured; instead, he consciously chose as his associates people, such as Fink, Rivkin, and guitarist Dez Dickerson, who were ethical, low-key, and even a bit square.

Prince's most complicated relationship in the band was with Cymone, his former teenage roommate. Believing himself to be just as talented as Prince, the bassist carried around the resentment of having to play a subordinate role to a close friend. When Fink was singled out to contribute in the studio (on "Dirty Mind" and a wild keyboard solo he added to "Head"), Cymone became even more jealous. "They shared the same bedroom, and then Prince starts becoming this big, huge star," noted Owen Husney. "That's got to affect you one way or the other."

Prince, while realizing that he had the upper hand in the competition, also seemed genuinely fearful that Cymone might develop into a successful solo artist. Intent on beating down any competitors, Prince actively hindered Cymone's progress through various manipulations, according to Charles Smith. When Cymone expressed interest in setting up his own studio to work on songs, Prince insisted that this was unnecessary and that the bassist could use his equipment whenever he wished. This seemingly generous gesture allowed Prince to keep physical custody of Cymone's music. On one occasion, Smith says, Cymone came looking for demos only to be told by Prince that he had "accidentally" erased a tape.

While Prince's band members were mostly in sync with the rock-oriented direction of the new material, there was less agreement about the lyrics. Dickerson, unhappy with the brazen sexual content, was concerned about playing the new songs live. Keyboardist Gayle Chapman was pushed over the edge when, during the *Prince* tour, she was required to make out with her band leader each night during "Head" (which was played on the tour prior to being recorded in summer 1980). Shortly after the tour, Chapman quit.

Realizing that Prince wanted to carry forth the theme of gender diversity, his managers identified as a candidate nineteen-year-old Lisa Coleman, a classically trained pianist from the San Fernando Valley area of Los Angeles. When Coleman met Prince at his Minneapolis rehearsal space for an audition, both seemed uncomfortable and said little to each other. But once Prince led her over to a piano, they began playing without hesitation. "They conversed through their music," said Howard Bloom. "For three hours they talked to each other that way, and learned that they were kin."

Prince and Coleman rapidly became close, their friendship briefly taking on a sexual dimension that prompted him to write an unreleased song ("Lisa") that describes

1

a "nasty" girl with whom he goes to the movies. Coleman's greatest impact, however, would come through her expressive playing, which added an entirely new dimension to his live sound. "There was something about Lisa's sound as a keyboard player, particularly on acoustic piano, that Prince was very fond of and found hard to duplicate himself," observed Alan Leeds, who became Prince's tour manager in the early 1980s. Over time, Coleman would become one of the very few musicians to play a meaningful role in his songwriting.

After completing the rough drafts for *Dirty Mind,* Prince experienced a revelation: He had just finished his third album. This was exactly the sound he wanted—raw, spontaneous, and subversive—and rerecording the songs in a state-of-the-art studio would merely dilute their impact. Selecting the eight songs he felt were strongest, he brought them to Warner Bros. and declared the album ready for release.

Opposition immediately developed at Warners, where officials were concerned both about the intense lyrics and the spare production values. "He turned the record company into disarray," recalled vice president Marylou Badeaux. "The promotions people would call me and say, 'I can't take this to radio! Is he crazy?'" Adding to the furor, Prince showed up for meetings wearing attire like bikini briefs and fishnet stockings. Badeaux recalls one Warners staffer accosting him in the hallway and saying, "Does your mama know what you're doing?" Prince shot him a withering look that said, "You just don't get it, do you?" and stalked by.

Convincing the record company to support *Dirty Mind* fell to Prince's management team, which had become increasingly important in his career and life. Steve Fargnoli, Prince's day-to-day handler (who was named the third partner in Cavallo, Ruffalo & Fargnoli in recognition of his expanding role), was a mercurial and passionate man who quickly emerged as a true confidant, someone Prince turned to for advice even on stage design and concert set lists. Fargnoli was hedonistic and enjoyed the perks of fame—especially the many attractive women surrounding concert tours—but he also brought a laser-like focus to promoting Prince's career. "Steve was one of a tiny handful of people that Prince really trusted," said Badeaux. "He was very creative and had a sixth sense of what would work and what didn't work."

Bob Cavallo was in many ways the polar opposite, an avuncular family man with a crisp, calm manner. He often handled the purely business side of things, aided by his considerable expertise in financial matters. And while Fargnoli was most visible among Prince's managers, developing a unique personal relationship with Prince, it was Cavallo—a shrewd, tough executive later to head Disney's Buena Vista Music Group—who made many key strategic decisions. "The secret to Fargnoli was also Bob Cavallo," noted set designer Roy Bennett. "Bob is a brilliant man; a very stable, very smart business guy. He knew how to get things done; Bob is the one who kept things level." Publicist Bloom concurs: "Fargnoli was so dedicated it was ridiculous; every day of his life was Prince," he noted. "But Cavallo was the mastermind. He was the general and Fargnoli was the troops."

Neither Cavallo nor Fargnoli had any doubts about Prince's radical new direction. The arguments they presented to Warners for releasing *Dirty Mind* in demo form were forceful and sincere. Gradually, high-ranking officials like Mo Ostin, Lenny Waronker, and Russ Thyret lined up behind the project, and they in turn endeavored to turn around the company's rank-and-file, many of whom remained unconvinced. "Russ was a huge piece of the puzzle, and always saw Prince as an act for all formats," noted a Warner Bros. source. "There were times where he had to flat-out order his troops to work the music, to make them give it the push they might not have otherwise."

Pop music was already changing, as New Wave groups like the Knack (with the seminal "My Sharona") and Blondie (the equally important "Heart Of Glass") topped the charts at the very end of the seventies. Nonetheless, with *Dirty Mind*, Warner Bros. was asked to take a significant leap—could the company support an album by a black R&B artist that was rawer and more explicit than perhaps anything ever released by a major label?

The answer, albeit a somewhat hesitant one, was yes.

october 1980: release of dirty mind

The cover of Prince's new album displayed a punk sensibility that was in stark contrast to his first two releases. A grim black-and-white photo showed him standing in front of exposed bedsprings. He wore black bikini underwear, a trench coat, and a handkerchief around his neck. The "Rude Boy" pin on his coat had its origins in a punk-related style, England's "two-tone" ska movement. (*Rude Boy* was also the title of a 1980 film featuring the Clash, the most influential of the early punk bands.)

As some at Warner Bros. had feared, the album failed to carry forward the commercial momentum of *Prince*. Many radio programmers were deterred by the lyrics and by stickers Warners placed on promo copies urging stations to "please audition before airing." Sales were modest, and the album would not even achieve gold record status (indicating 500,000 units sold) until four years after its release. The first two singles, "Uptown" and "Dirty Mind," enjoyed some success on the Soul Singles Chart but failed to dent the Pop Singles Chart, and the album itself reached only No. 45 on the Pop Chart. The rock audience hadn't materialized, and—not surprisingly—some of the fans who had purchased his second album defected. "If he was a guy who was going to cater to an R&B base, *Dirty Mind* wouldn't have been the way it was," observed Leeds. "*Dirty Mind* to me was a guy standing up and saying 'Listen, I play black music, it's part of me, but an equal part of me is rock 'n' roll, and nobody's gonna tell me I can't play rock 'n' roll too.'"

Despite the weak sales, plans went forward for Prince's first full tour as a headline act. The chirpy R&B singer Teena Marie was recruited as the opening act to help stimulate ticket sales, and Roy Bennett, an experienced designer, was hired to create Prince's stage show. "For an artist on their first tour it was quite a big production for the time," noted Bennett, whose set placed drummer Rivkin and the two keyboardists, Fink and Coleman, on risers behind Prince. Unfortunately, pre-sales of tickets for the concerts, which were booked into mid-sized auditoriums with capacities of several thousand people, were sluggish.

As Prince and the band rehearsed for the tour, his managers huddled to find a solution to the riddle of his career. Despite the tepid sales of *Dirty Mind*, Cavallo and

Fargnoli remained foursquare behind their client. The support of the rock press was deemed a key goal; what was needed, the managers believed, was to convince the media, and through them the public, that Prince was not just a multi-talented curiosity, but a revolutionary figure, both musically and culturally.

Cavallo hit on the idea of hiring as a media relations representative the intriguing figure of Howard Bloom. An energetic, chatty man with a somewhat nerdy appearance, Bloom was unique among rock press agents—a scholar and intellectual who considered his work with musicians as a kind of field research for his pet subject of mass behavior. Trends in popular music, Bloom believed, provided a highly accurate reflection of the public's mood and even an indicator of future behavior.

Bloom's modus operandi with every new client was to sit down for a psychotherapy-like discussion to uncover what he called an artist's "passion points"—the inner feelings that are the wellspring of creativity. "What I would tell my artists is that there's a 'you' who walks around everyday saying 'Hi, hello, how are you?'—a rather bland personality," he recounted. "Then there's another 'you' that comes out when you sit down at a blank piece of paper to write a lyric or a melody. That's the part we're looking for."

Several days before the *Dirty Mind* tour began, Bloom met with Prince after a rehearsal in Buffalo, New York. Word had reached him from various sources that his new client was a withdrawn, arrogant figure who would never open up emotionally—all of which proved wrong. During a session that lasted from two a.m. until nine a.m., Prince rambled about his tumultuous childhood, his formative visit at age five to see his father in concert, the teenage shenanigans in the Anderson basement, and more. Prince's passion points, not surprisingly, turned out to be a lust for fame, a conflicted relationship with both parents, and a voracious sexual appetite.

When the tour reached Manhattan's trendy club Ritz on December 9, 1980 (the day after John Lennon was murdered), the room was only about half-full, but the luminaries in the crowd, including Andy Warhol, funk producer Nile Rogers, and singer Nona Hendryx, showed Prince's broadening potential. "The whole vibe of that room was amazing," recalled Bennett. "That was the point where we thought, this is happening!" But as the tour reached markets like Charleston, Chattanooga, and Baton Rouge, the crowds thinned out, and a decision was made to cut the southern swing short. Nationwide sales of the album also remained slow.

Even Prince was beginning to have his doubts. Back in Minneapolis, he invited Dickerson to dinner at an Indian restaurant and shared the concerns that Warner Bros. was voicing about his new direction. "He was using me as a sounding board to get a sense of whether there was validity to what these people were saying or not," Dickerson recalled. In part to be reassuring, but also because he genuinely believed in the direction of *Dirty Mind*, the guitarist urged Prince not to worry. "I really thought we were onto something that hadn't been done before," he recalled.

Howard Bloom, another true believer, pushed various media outlets to write about Prince. Finally, the floodgates opened with a February 1981 article in *Rolling Stone* entitled "Will the Little Girls Understand?" that was accompanied by a glowing review of *Dirty Mind*. "At its best, *Dirty Mind* is absolutely filthy," wrote Ken Tucker. "Prince's sly wit—intentionally coarse—amounts to nothing less than an early, prescient call to arms against the elitist puritanism of the Reagan era." With that review, the *Dirty Mind* publicity campaign fell into place, as other influential publications picked up on Prince. *New Musical Express*, for example, wrote that "[i]n the same assertive way as Sly Stone and George Clinton before him, Prince is keen to clear the decks and establish a new wave within the clichéd environs of black dance music."

In important urban centers like New York and Detroit, ticket and album sales spiked upward. A diverse mix of fans—blacks, whites, gays, and a not-insignificant number of transvestites—showed up at Prince concerts, indicating that the populist, pan-sexual message of *Dirty Mind* was taking hold. The record was not a smash (and in fact didn't nearly equal the performance of *Prince*), but Prince had connected with an important new audience of critics and tastemakers.

The attention was deserved; Prince's goal of redefining his sound was achieved convincingly with *Dirty Mind*. Clocking in at under thirty minutes, the album is a brisk, invigorating ride that squeezes in plenty of highlights, including the fierce and hypnotic "Head," the blues-and-gospel-tinged "Partyup," and the pop classic "When You Were Mine." While the album's raw, guitar-driven music is a major departure from Prince's first two albums, the lyrics are an equally important step. Even as he explores the darker regions of his sexuality, Prince moves in the direction of becoming a political artist; the anti-war anthem "Partyup" evokes the protest music of the sixties, and "Uptown" describes a countercultural utopia where people of different races unite under a banner of sexual freedom.

But in the end, *Dirty Mind* is notable not because it represented the complete realization of Prince's style, but because it kick-started a run of creativity that would establish Prince, for a time, as the single most influential artist in pop. In terms of the development of music during the 1980s, 1990s, and beyond, *Dirty Mind* was prophetic, helping mark the transition from the glossy, bombastic sounds of the 1970s to a tighter, more compact aesthetic. Two decades later, artists like Macy Gray and D'Angelo would still be emulating the basic sound Prince outlined on this album. Only in his early twenties, Prince had helped redefine pop music.

Although the credits of *Dirty Mind* state that the album was written entirely by Prince (with the exception of the title track, which is attributed to him and Matt Fink), the compositional origins of two of the album's eight songs have been questioned. For "Partyup," it has been widely reported that the music (although not the lyrics) was written by longtime friend Morris Day, who played drums in Prince's first band. During the summer of 1980, Day played a groove he had recorded to Prince, who promptly wrote lyrics and re-tooled the song into "Partyup." Prince then approached Day with an offer: Either he would pay $10,000 for the song, or, alternatively, build a side project around Day. Day selected the latter option, which also gave Prince the opportunity, after the demise of the Rebels project, to find another outlet for the music flowing from him at a torrid pace.

"Uptown," the second contested song on *Dirty Mind*, is said to have been based around music by André Cymone. "The bass line of that song is based on something André came up with in a jam that we did at rehearsal," Dickerson told Prince biographer Dave Hill. (Charles Smith also confirmed this.) Additionally, Pepé Willie, who recorded music with Prince and Cymone in 1979, recalls that the music for "Do Me, Baby," which would appear on Prince's 1982 album *Controversy,* was also introduced by Cymone during those sessions. When *Controversy* was released, an upset Cymone contacted Willie for assistance. "I told André he should have copyrighted it, and that there was nothing I could do," said Willie.

Although many such claims have been made during Prince's career, some associates consider them inaccurate. Drummer Rivkin, while acknowledging that band members offered up riffs at rehearsals, noted that Prince fashioned this raw clay into finished pieces. "There's a big misconception between a riff, a lick, and a songwriter," he argued. "The songwriter is the guy who conceptualizes the words and the music. Ninety-nine percent of the time, when Prince says he wrote the song, he wrote the song." Owen Husney concurs that Cymone's claims in particular are difficult to prove, given the way the disputed songs developed. "When people are jamming, ideas float around," he said. "When Prince and André would jam, and something cool came out of it, Prince was the outlet to make it happen on record and on radio. André wasn't."

Still, there is plenty of evidence to demonstrate that, at the very least, Prince is not overly generous in recognizing songwriting and production contributions. For example, engineer David Z. Rivkin, who played a significant production role on Prince's debut album, goes uncredited on the back cover, receiving only a vague thank-you on the inner sleeve. And in 1986, when both Rivkin and Mark Brown contributed significantly to the hit "Kiss," Rivkin received merely an "arrangement" credit, and Brown no credit at all. In 1990, when Rivkin and bassist/guitarist Levi Seacer, Jr., collaborated with Prince on the song "Well Done," they received no credit whatsoever when it was released on the album *Heaven Help Us All* by the gospel group the Steeles. "That was his ego taking over again, I guess," said Rivkin. "Levi and I were not very happy about that. Prince is very proud, and it's pretty hard for him give up any kind of [credit], that's for sure."

For Rivkin, who was content with his behind-the-scenes role in Prince's career, such slights could be written off as the cost of doing business. But for Cymone, they were much more painful. After the *Dirty Mind* tour, a combination of grievances—a belief that his contributions were going unrecognized, his lack of input in the studio, and his hopes for his own career—prompted him to quit the band. "André was just not good at playing second fiddle, and would only take direction for so long," Bobby Rivkin observed. "He always saw himself as big as Prince someday."

Another part of the problem was that Cymone believed that he deserved better treatment in light of what his mother had done for Prince. "André felt slighted," Dickerson observed. "He believed that if not for him and his family, Prince wouldn't be where he was."

may 1981: european tour

As *Dirty Mind* garnered critical accolades, Prince made his first overseas visit for a brief promotional and concert tour. Utterly unconcerned with historical sightseeing, he instead spent his free time investigating the state of European pop culture. While in London, he and Steve Fargnoli attended a birthday party at a nightclub for Steve

Strange, a leading musician and impresario of the so-called New Romantic movement, a branch of New Wave known for outrageous clothing styles. Prince and the band then traveled to Amsterdam, where they made their European debut before a small crowd. The audience was sparse for a show in Paris as well, with mainly record industry insiders attending.

Prince continued to visit nightclubs, becoming inspired by the eclectic mixture of styles and sounds that fans overseas were embracing. "I think he knew better than the record companies what the mood of the street was," recalled Mark Brown, who replaced André Cymone on bass after the *Dirty Mind* tour. "He went over to Europe and studied what was going down, and he wanted to bring it to the United States."

The question was whether America was ready. Although critics felt that *Dirty Mind* had established Prince as an artist capable of attracting both R&B and rock fans, the sales figures suggested that he had instead become neither fish nor foul in the pop marketplace. After three albums, he had scored just one modestly successful hit single ("I Wanna Be Your Lover"), and his career lacked commercial momentum.

While pleased with the critical reaction to *Dirty Mind*, Prince was hardly unaware of this problem. When Brown auditioned for the band in early 1981 and asked about the follow-up to *Dirty Mind*, Prince seemed pensive, just as he had been during his recent conversation with Dickerson at the Indian restaurant. "He looked at me and he said, 'The next album has to make it,'" Brown remembered. "Musically, he definitely knew what he was doing, but I don't think he had a clue if it was going to work. I think he was feeling that if it didn't sell, he'd be dropped by Warner Bros."

Still, Prince showed no signs of retreating from his new course. After purchasing a home (which he promptly had painted purple) in the verdant Lake Riley region of Minneapolis, he again had Don Batts install a sixteen-track studio in the basement. The equipment was more advanced than that used on *Dirty Mind*, allowing for a more polished sound. The larger space allowed Prince's piano—which hadn't been used at all on *Dirty Mind*—to be wired from the living room down to the studio.

A pastiche of new influences emerged in Prince's songwriting as he prepared his fourth album, to be titled *Controversy*. Cold, electronic textures—a staple of New Wave bands like Kraftwerk and Devo—made their way into music that, more than ever, evoked a multiplicity of genres. "Controversy" combined a scratchy, James Brown–style guitar riff with a rock-like synth line and a multi-voice harmony that included Prince's lower register, part of his singing repertoire rarely displayed on his previous three albums. The funk outing "Sexuality" used the same approach, again showcasing his ability to coax a wide variety of sounds from his vocal chords.

Among Prince's management team and at Warner Bros., there was an almost unanimous consensus that this new material could establish Prince as an underground phenomenon with crossover potential. "I thought it was a brilliant album," said Marylou Badeaux, who felt the simmering anger of Prince's sound and lyrics dovetailed perfectly with the growing commercial prominence of New Wave.

While much of the new album was completed in his Edina home, Prince also worked at two Los Angeles studios, Hollywood Sound and Sunset Sound. At the latter facility he cut a song, "Private Joy," that proved a turning point in his approach to rhythm tracks. Rather than live drums, Prince used the Linn LM-1, the first drum machine on the market to incorporate sounds sampled from real drums. Whereas earlier models had had a plastic, disposable feel, the Linn sounded much more like a true instrument.

Prince loved the Linn and realized that it would allow him to work with even less assistance from other musicians and technicians. Creating full-band recordings in hotel rooms suddenly became possible. "When I heard 'Private Joy' for the first time, that was the moment I knew things were going to change," remarked Bobby Rivkin. "Recording drums is an expensive and slow process; it takes a long time to get a good sound. The Linn gave him an instant good sound."

The lyrics to "Private Joy" were directed at Susan Moonsie, a longtime friend whom he began dating after the *Dirty Mind* tour. Prince had met her in high school and even spent some nights on her family's couch before the Anderson family took him in. When she emerged as his principal romantic interest in late 1980, his associates found her to be an intelligent, grounded, unmanipulative person—perhaps the perfect complement to a mercurial, egocentric artist. "She was more of a girlfriend than any girlfriend he had ever had," observed Rivkin. Added Alan Leeds, who also got to know her well in coming years: "Like many a young lady, she was attracted to the fun of the rock 'n' roll lifestyle, but she could never be confused for a groupie. She saw Prince as a hugely creative, but lonely, young fellow who needed tons of support, tender loving care, and encouragement. This was all at a crucial time in his development."

Moonsie struggled, however, with a basic problem in the relationship: Prince's resistance to monogamy. As his notoriety grew, so did opportunities for casual sex. Moreover, the *Dirty Mind* tour introduced him to another young woman who became a significant love interest: Jill Jones, a backup vocalist for Teena Marie. Prince began dating Jones and promised to record an album of music for her to sing. With all of this going on, Moonsie was caught between her affection for Prince and her unwillingness to facilitate his unfaithfulness. "Unlike the majority of his subsequent girlfriends, Moonsie's boundaries were not negotiable," observed Leeds. "She wouldn't jump up and down or holler and scream, but Prince knew she would never tolerate any behavior that even bordered on disrespect." When Prince became flagrant about his affairs, Moonsie would temporarily withdraw, leaving him wounded and angry. But while Prince expected Moonsie to tolerate his dalliances, he was possessive of her, as the lyrics of "Private Joy" indicated. "He didn't want her as his exclusive girlfriend, but he wanted her around," said one source. "Other guys knew not to mess with her."

october 1981: release of controversy

Visually, *Controversy* carried forth the post-punk vibe of *Dirty Mind:* The cover shows Prince in a lavender trench coat, again with the Rude Boy pin attached. Floating behind him and on the back cover are faux tabloid newspaper headlines, such as "Lingerie—New Fashion Trend" and "Annie Christian Sentenced to Die!," that mock society's fascination with sensationalism. More and more, it seemed, Prince was adding social commentary to his message.

Musically, it was his most kaleidoscopic venture yet, featuring everything from rockabilly ("Jack U Off") to a seductive R&B ballad ("Do Me, Baby") to a spoken-word experiment ("Annie Christian"). But the diversity was at times dizzying, and critics found *Controversy* an enigmatic and inconsistent work. Stephen Holden in *Rolling Stone*, while calling Prince a potential heir to Sly Stone, criticized the album's "frequent fuzzy-mindedness and eccentricity." Others saw it as a sign of better things to come. The magazine *Sweet Potato*, put off by the mishmash of styles, observed that "the sequencing of *Controversy* is atrocious...[but] the next LP should be a fully formed delineation of Prince's vision."

Controversy is indeed something of a jumble. While the title track and "Sexuality" are as strong as anything he had written to date, songs like "Annie Christian" and "Ronnie, Talk To Russia" (a generic rock number exhorting Reagan to make peace with the Soviets) show his propensity for whimsy and excess. Still, the album is never less than interesting and displays an artist struggling to challenge himself and his audience. The energy is often palpable, with songs like "Jack U Off," "Sexuality," and "Private Joy" capturing some of the anarchic appeal of punk and New Wave.

As a political statement, though, *Controversy* is a significant disappointment. The album finds Prince dabbling in various issues on "Ronnie, Talk To Russia," "Annie Christian" (which makes reference to the shootings of Lennon and Reagan), and "Sexuality" (where he declares himself a "new breed leader"). But the incoherence of the ideas in these songs called into question whether Prince had a meaningful agenda. Arguably, his core message of sexual freedom, which rang through so clearly on *Dirty Mind*, was diluted by the excursions into issues like disarmament and gun violence. "Prince is at his most naïve and disturbing when the subject is overtly political," complained the *Village Voice*.

Some were also troubled by the messianic tone of the lyrics. Both "Controversy" and "Sexuality," for instance, focus almost exclusively on Prince himself as an object of public fascination and worship. "Controversy" also includes a chanted version of the Lord's Prayer, highlighting the tension in Prince's work (and in his mind) between lust and morality. These dualities, while in some respects intriguing, demonstrated a self-fascination that would eventually threaten to overwhelm his work.

While "Controversy," the album's lead single, had little impact on the Pop Singles Chart (reaching only No. 70), the album itself sold more strongly than *Dirty Mind*. While not a blockbuster hit, *Controversy* went gold in three months (reaching No. 3 on the Soul Chart and No. 21 on the Pop Chart), stoking the buzz created by *Dirty Mind*. Tastemakers in Europe were now taking notice, and sales spiked upward there as well.

Prince's managers immediately began planning a tour of mid-sized theaters in the United States. Even before this swing started, though, he played two shows that demonstrated the challenges of winning over a mass audience. In fall 1981, his managers received a phone call from representatives of the Rolling Stones, asking if he wanted to open for the band during a three-night stand at the Los Angeles Coliseum. Prince agreed, placing himself before the largest crowds of his career.

The tens of thousands of people who arrived in time for his set on the first night seemed for the most part unsure what to make of Prince. Many of the males sitting closer to the stage (who were in any event impatient to see the Stones) seemed put off by his androgynous image. Catcalls and boos rang out during the first songs and, moments later, paper cups and other debris began to fly, driving the whole band from the stage after just fifteen minutes. Bill Graham, the legendary promoter running the show, came out and chastised the crowd, predicting that they would pay big money to see Prince within a few years.

Frustrated, Prince flew back to Minneapolis immediately after the show, agreeing to return for the second concert only after lengthy phone conversations with Steve Fargnoli and Dez Dickerson. Although there was some hope that the debacle would not be repeated, word of the incident had circulated among Stones fans, and the next night concertgoers came to the show loaded with food to throw. Tension built during the set opener, "Uptown," as Prince and his mates could clearly see the hostility in the faces of Stones fans close to the stage. When Prince signaled the band to start "Jack U Off," bassist Mark Brown, playing his first major show with the group, sensed that things were about to fall apart. Although he knew Prince to be straight, Brown had always detected an unmistakable (though accidental) current of homoeroticism in the song. "When you talk about street lingo, where I come from, guys don't jack girls off," Brown noted. "I don't think he understood that—Prince was in his own world."

"Jack U Off" indeed provided a spark to set off the homophobic, testosterone-and-alcohol fueled audience. Brown was hit by a bag of chicken and a grapefruit, and a Jack Daniels bottle just missed him. A bottle of orange juice narrowly missed Prince, smashing against the drum riser and cascading the liquid across the stage. Frightened, the band again fled the stage, thus concluding the most dramatic public repudiation of Prince's career.

The band quickly left the premises in a limousine and agreed that they would not play with the Stones again. But as horrifying as the experience had been, Prince had steeled himself for the crowd's response and seemed less perturbed than on the previous evening. His priority was consoling Brown, whom he feared might quit the band after experiencing such trauma so early in his tenure.

"Mark," he said, looking seriously at the bassist, "this isn't our audience."

Before long, though, it would be.

CHAPTER FOUR

Pawns

When Prince offered to build a band around Morris Day in exchange for the song "Partyup" in the summer of 1980, it was the latest shift in a long and complex relationship. For years, Day had shadowed Prince along the road to stardom. When they were teenagers, Day joined Prince's first band, Champagne, on drums, replacing Charles Smith. They developed a strong friendship, and Day's mother, LaVonne Daugherty, helped manage the group. Prince, Day, and bassist André Cymone (then using his last name Anderson) functioned as a team, sharing leadership responsibilities as they competed with other Minneapolis groups.

Champagne's unity was fractured when, in the summer of 1976, Minneapolis studio proprietor Chris Moon singled out Prince (who had just graduated from high school) and let him record for free at Moon's facility. The power balance within the group changed irrevocably, with Prince's friends being forced to assume subordinate roles. Cymone chose to stay, while Day withdrew.

Two years later, after receiving a lavish contract from Warner Bros. and releasing his first album, Prince began assembling a touring band. Day, along with several other local drummers, accepted an invitation to audition. In the summer and fall of 1978, he took turns with Charles Smith, Bobby Z. Rivkin, and others in occupying the drummer's chair. Arguably, Day was the most talented candidate; he had a sophisticated sense of musical dynamics, modulating his drumming in a way that guided an entire band. "I loved his playing—very funky, very quick," recalled Rivkin, who, even though he had been jamming with Prince throughout the development of *For You*, felt anything but secure. "At any moment I expected Morris and Prince to get back together, and I'd be out," he said.

In the end, though, Rivkin's phlegmatic personality and sturdy work ethic carried the day. Also, he was white, allowing Prince to attain the racial diversity he wanted in his band. Rivkin would drum with Prince for the better part of a decade, while Day retreated to the local funk circuit, playing with various bands over the next two years.

In the summer of 1980, during the recording of *Dirty Mind*, Day found his way back, albeit in a less glamorous capacity; he became a "runner" for Prince's band, picking up sandwiches and drinks during rehearsals. But Prince continued to respect Day's musicianship, as his interest in "Partyup" showed. When the deal for the song was struck, events finally seemed to have shifted back in Day's favor.

In spring 1981, following the *Dirty Mind* tour, Prince actively began planning a side project for Day to fulfill his side of the bargain. Initially, he wanted Day to play drums while using Alexander O'Neal, a talented Minneapolis soul singer, as the front man. But Prince's initial meeting with O'Neal was rocky—the singer wanted more money and control than Prince would give up. Prince subsequently hatched the plan of Day himself handling the vocal chores.

Prince had already planned every detail of the project, to be dubbed the Time. It would include strong elements of camp, with Day functioning as equal parts singer and comedian. The image he created for Day was quite familiar to Prince's friends: He would play a wisecracking, showboating, jiving hustler very much resembling Prince's "pimp" persona that sometimes emerged in social situations. "Morris Day's whole character came from Prince," noted bassist Mark Brown. Elements were also borrowed from Day's perceptions of Prince's father, who impressed the neighborhood with his flashy clothing when Prince was growing up. When Prince began to record music for the project, he sang the guide vocals (which would later be imitated by Day note-for-note) in a raspy voice that sounded like an old man. "That was him imitating his dad and men of his father's generation—barber shop guys," noted engineer Susan Rogers.

As Day learned the vocal parts, Prince recruited a group of talented Minneapolis musicians for the group's live lineup: Terry Lewis on bass, Jimmy "Jam" Harris and Monte Moir on keyboards, Jellybean Johnson on drums, and Jesse Johnson on guitar. These members also became very much part of the Time's image, preening onstage in vintage suits as they played.

The project was every bit as important to Prince as one of his own albums, and he intended to direct the band from behind the scenes. According to both Rivkin and Owen Husney, he was strongly influenced in this respect by his viewing of the 1980 Taylor Hackford film *The Idolmaker*, about a music impresario who creates and manipulates a series of photogenic performers. Prince came away from the film inspired to create an entire roster of acts that would represent different dimensions of his artistic personality.

Prince recorded almost all of the music for the album, and his goal was to have the Time faithfully execute the songs during live performances. Prince dominated the group's early rehearsals, providing a stream of instructions and pushing the group to exhaustion. His energy left them in awe, Jimmy Jam recalled in a 2002 interview with *Performing Songwriter*. "He'd come to our rehearsals for five or six hours, then go to rehearsals for his own band, then cut all night in the studio, and the next day he'd show up at rehearsal with some new song he wrote," Jam remembered.

Notwithstanding Prince's pervasive involvement, however, something surprising happened: The Time developed a chemistry of its own. As the group stretched out and added its own touches to the music, Prince felt pride that his handpicked lineup had proved so effective. "He could see that we were getting pretty frightening, so he started to leave us alone," recalled Jellybean Johnson.

The group's first album, *The Time*, was released in July 1981. No songwriting credits appeared on the front cover or inner sleeve, but production credit was split between Morris Day and Jamie Starr, who had also received an engineering credit on *Dirty Mind*. Speculation appeared in the Minneapolis press that Jamie Starr was a Prince alias, and that he had been deeply involved in the creation of the album. Although both of these rumors were true, Prince, his managers, and Morris Day all issued denials.

Musically, *The Time* reflected Prince's funk roots more than any of his projects to date. Whereas his first two albums featured mostly poppy R&B, and *Dirty Mind* showed movement toward rock and New Wave, *The Time* was dominated by tight dance grooves. The lyrics were simple and playful, offering Day plenty of opportunity for comic posturing.

The album became a surprise hit, going gold in seven months while reaching No. 7 on the Billboard Soul Chart and No. 50 on the Pop Chart. With sales even stronger than for his own *Dirty Mind*, it was clear that Prince had discovered in the Time a commercially viable project. And the group's first shows, performed in Minneapolis clubs in fall 1981, electrified audiences. Rivkin recalls that Prince, while pleased, had also begun to worry that he had created "a Frankenstein's monster." He feared losing sway over a band that he considered his own.

Three members of the Time were most threatening to Prince: keyboardist Jimmy Jam, bassist Terry Lewis, and guitarist Jesse Johnson. Jam and Lewis were in essence a unit—a songwriting and production team with grand plans for the future. Johnson was a terror on the guitar, playing leads with a ferocity that rivaled Prince's. "Prince frequently intimated that the only guitarist he's really afraid of is Jesse Johnson," recalled Alan Leeds.

november 1981 to march 1982: controversy tour of the united states

Two months after *The Time* became a hit, *Controversy* was released and also generated strong sales. Prince's managers organized a tour that would capitalize on these successes by including the Time as the opening act. The two acts played theaters ranging in capacity from about 2,000 to 8,000 and were joined in some cities by the popular funk group Zapp (also on the Warner Bros. label), led by Roger Troutman.

Commercially, the tour was much more successful than the *Dirty Mind* tour, indicating that a significant cult following was now within Prince's grasp. His popularity remained strongest in markets like Detroit and New York, where large, racially diverse audiences attended the shows. His sets carried forth the sexualized energy of the *Dirty Mind* tour, as he performed all manner of salacious stage moves, including simulating masturbation with his guitar during a lengthy version of "Head." The guitar work of Prince and Dez Dickerson drove the overall sound, which was again much rawer and heavier than on record.

Offstage, Prince and his band at first continued to enjoy the camaraderie that had characterized the *Dirty Mind* tour. Prince traveled with his comrades on a single bus, where they socialized and watched videos of the previous shows. But if Prince's relations with certain band members—most notably Matt Fink, Lisa Coleman, and Mark

Brown—were quite amiable, they were not characterized by any great emotional intimacy. While Prince occasionally lowered his guard, he never did so completely, and everyone was conscious of him more as an authority figure than a friend.

For the African-American members of the band—Brown and Dickerson—life on the road was not without its awkward moments of being stared down by whites, particularly in southern cities. One morning before a show in Tampa, Florida, Dickerson was getting a cup of coffee in the hotel restaurant when he experienced a moment of terror: A huge man who looked like the quintessential redneck biker—long hair, muscles, tattoos—was striding toward him. "I thought I was about to die," the guitarist remembered. Fortunately, the hulking figure passed right by, and may have even grunted a hello.

About an hour later, Dickerson received a phone call summoning him to Prince's room for a band meeting. When he walked in, he was shocked to see the same man he had encountered in the restaurant. Dickerson was introduced to Chick Huntsberry, Prince's new bodyguard.

On the bus the next day, Huntsberry's presence proved intimidating to everyone, and he spent most of the ride to Jacksonville surrounded by empty seats. Finally, Dickerson decided to approach him and found the bodyguard to be a warm, friendly person who had lived a fascinating, if rough, life that had included working security at biker bars.

At six feet six inches and over 300 pounds, the bearded, tattooed Huntsberry really did look like a refugee from a motorcycle gang, and the contrast between him and Prince was stark to the point of absurdity. At first, Prince thought so too; although he agreed with his managers that more security was needed, he couldn't imagine having Huntsberry shadow him. A couple of days later, Prince mentioned to Dickerson that he was going to send the bodyguard home.

"Why?" Dickerson asked.

"He's just too big, he scares me," Prince responded.

Dickerson related the conversation he had had with Huntsberry on the bus and urged Prince to keep him. "I think he's a good guy—you should give him a chance."

Prince thought about it and decided to follow Dickerson's advice. And as the bodyguard began accompanying him almost everywhere, Prince came to feel comforted by having a human barricade against the world. Huntsberry was dedicated enough to do just about anything for his new charge, and Prince began relying on him not only for protection but for a wide variety of personal errands. They soon became almost inseparable.

But for the rest of the band members, Dickerson included, there was a downside to this new arrangement. Huntsberry took his obligation to guard Prince's privacy perhaps too seriously, and everyone else suddenly found their access restricted. "It was a turning point for the closeness we used to have," noted Bennett. The symbolism of Huntsberry's imposing presence at the dressing room door was clear to Prince's colleagues: They were no longer welcome.

As the tour continued, the Time continued to jell as a unit. The group, wanting to prove that they belonged on the same bill with Prince, played with intensity and determination each night. Enthusiastic audience reaction to their sets, however, left Prince worried about being shown up, and both bands became conscious of a growing rivalry. "To a point it was real positive," observed Time keyboardist Moir. "On our side it was, 'Let's kick his ass tonight!' But after a while, it became unhealthy."

As the tour went on, the Time chafed at Prince's attempts to exert control over the band. Jam, Lewis, Day, and other band members wanted to write their own music, which they doubted Prince would ever allow. Then there was the issue of money. *The Time* had taken off commercially, but the band members were living on a small weekly salary. "At one point, Jesse [Johnson] and those guys were eating peanut butter out of a jar in their hotel rooms so they could save what little money they got so they could have something when they got home," said Charles Smith, who remained friendly with the band. "And Morris didn't have any money, either."

Prince provided constant small reminders of his authority. In March, when the tour arrived in Minneapolis, he called the group onstage to perform a song during a show at First Avenue. But he kept his own microphone to interject comments, warning Day that "this is my stage" and jokingly threatening to have Chick Huntsberry remove one of the Time's members.

As the Time's members became increasingly disgruntled, the competition between the two groups became heated and even confrontational. After one show, a Time member hurled a nasty comment at Rivkin; another night, Jesse Johnson said something that Prince interpreted as an insult to his mother.

The hostility burst to the surface during the last show of the tour at Riverfront Stadium in Cincinnati. During their opening set, the Time found themselves being pelted by eggs from offstage. Gradually, they realized that Prince and some of his band members were the culprits. The barrage increased, and, toward the end of the set, Prince and his accomplices abducted Jerome Benton, a dancer for the group, from the stage and poured honey all over him. Then they pelted him with garbage. "They tarred and feathered him, basically," recalled Fink, who did not participate and insisted to the Time members that he wanted no part of the battle.

Then, as the Time's set ended, Chick Huntsberry grabbed Jesse Johnson and hauled him to Prince's dressing room. There, Huntsberry handcuffed Johnson to a horizontal coat rack bolted into a brick wall. Prince came in and began taunting Johnson and tossing Doritos chips and other pieces of food at him. "This is what you get for talking about my mama!" Prince shouted.

The various members of Prince's band and crew in the room looked on with horror as the episode continued. "It was a cruel thing to do," observed Bennett. Fink recalled, "I just sat there and said to myself, this is getting out of hand."

Humiliated and frightened, Johnson writhed in his cuffs. Finally, to the amazement of the onlookers, he managed to rip the entire twelve-foot-long coat rack out of the wall. His hands were still cuffed to the rack, which he began swinging wildly. "Jesse was uncontrollable," Fink said. "He just lost it. Chick had to contain the situation before someone got hurt."

Huntsberry restrained Johnson and then released him. Furious and shook up, Johnson fled the dressing room and breathlessly told the rest of the Time what had happened. They immediately began gathering food to use in retaliation. Prince's managers, upon learning what was afoot, issued the Time a stern admonition: Nothing must be thrown during Prince's set. The Time interpreted this as narrowly as possible; at the end of the show, as Prince and the band left the stage, the Time began hurling eggs and other items at them. Prince's team responded by throwing yet more food as the fight spilled into the backstage area. The road managers, in a bid to help the two groups vent hostility short of real violence, had dozens of cream pies brought in for the combatants to use as ammunition. The Time now had the advantage, having donned plastic bags to avoid having their clothes ruined. "They turned into warriors, literally," remembered Fink.

The battle continued back at the hotel, where the two ensembles threw whatever edibles they could find at each other. In the end, there was significant damage to their hotel rooms; Prince insisted that Morris Day pay for most of it, arguing, incorrectly, that the Time had initiated the fight. Thus, what might have produced a catharsis instead generated another grievance for the Time to nurse. Jesse Johnson, in particular, remained bitter both about the dressing room incident and—just as critically—Prince's stifling domination over the Time, which had in the first place fomented the tensions that erupted during the fight. "Jesse's hostility toward Prince was really bad, it was scary," said Fink. "Jesse had a major ego problem, and issues occur when people with an ego problem are in a subordinate position."

Even as he struggled with the Time, Prince began planning another side project—an all-female group that would, again, perform his music and adopt a persona he created. Prior to the *Controversy* tour, three women were selected, rather arbitrarily: girlfriend Susan Moonsie, wardrobe assistant Brenda Bennett (the wife of set designer Roy), and Jamie Shoop, an employee of Cavallo, Ruffalo & Fargnoli. Only Bennett had any singing experience. Prince planned to have the group, called the Hookers, wear lingerie onstage and sing sexually charged lyrics.

During the tour, plans shifted when Prince one evening at a club noticed an especially sexy young woman; she was copper-skinned, sultry, and had an overall appearance very much like Prince's own. "It's been said that when they met, they both stopped in their tracks; looking at each other, it was like seeing themselves, but of the opposite sex," said Alan Leeds. A scout was sent over to ask if she wanted to meet Prince, and she agreed.

The young woman, Denise Matthews, had show business aspirations and was thrilled when Prince said he wanted to construct a band around her. Prince was also wildly attracted to her, and they quickly became involved. Over the coming weeks, he explained to her the concept for the Hookers. She was taken aback, however, by the stage name he suggested for her: Vagina, albeit with the "i" pronounced as a long "e." She refused, but agreed to the name Vanity.

Work on the project began immediately after the *Controversy* tour. Since Prince wanted only three members, Jamie Shoop, who was more interested in learning the business of music than prancing about in her garters, bowed out, leaving a trio of Vanity, Moonsie, and Bennett. Prince dubbed the group Vanity 6, a sly reference to the number of breasts in the ensemble.

The newly christened Vanity was neither an experienced nor talented singer, but she did have a charismatic stage presence. She also had a tough, sarcastic edge to her personality—seemingly just the trait required for the situation she found herself in.

In truth, Vanity's bravado masked deep feelings of pain and insecurity that had developed over a difficult life—particularly during a childhood when she suffered years of physical abuse from her father. Much more emotionally vulnerable than she seemed on the surface, Vanity tended to become resentful when she felt she was being controlled or manipulated; with Prince, of course, this was the case much of the time. Thus, their romantic relationship, which began amidst a glow of sexual chemistry, soon became combustible. Prince continued to see other women—including her bandmate Susan Moonsie—and Vanity's fits of jealousy left him, in turn, feeling cornered. "His relationship with Vanity wasn't as close as with Susan," said Roy Bennett. "There was no way to have a close relationship with her; she wasn't that kind of person."

Indeed, as Prince got to know Vanity, he enjoyed her company less and less; her forward, abrasive personality annoyed him, as he tended to prefer more demure women. The unreleased song "Wonderful Ass," describing an unhinged nymphomaniac, was about Vanity, engineer Rogers said. "He was in many ways a prude; she offended him in many ways, offended his sensibility," Rogers observed. "He liked good girls."

In musical terms, *Vanity 6*, released in August 1982, finds Prince mining the same upbeat funk territory as on *The Time*. While hardly among his best works, the album does have some strong moments, such as the lubricious "Nasty Girl." The vocals are the project's weak point, as Vanity lacks the musical talent to pull off her role with much credibility. Moonsie and Bennett handle lead chores as well on parts of the album, with neither showing much in the way of vocal chops.

But regardless of its deficiencies, *Vanity 6*, like *The Time* before it, demonstrated Prince's ability to turn side projects into commercial successes. The album reached No. 6 on the Black Chart and No. 45 on the Pop Chart, selling nearly 500,000 units during its initial run and achieving gold status in 1985. The group's titillating image generated media attention and helped pave the way for other female artists who would use cleavage and lacy outfits to help sell records, such as Madonna, Janet Jackson, TLC, and Destiny's Child.

The album's cover credits were for the most part fictional. The so-called Starr Company (ostensibly an enterprise of the elusive Jamie Starr) and Vanity 6 split the credit for production and arrangement, while the songs themselves are credited to one or more members of the group, in collaboration with (on some songs) certain members of the Time. At the ASCAP copyright office, however, seven of the eight songs are registered as Prince compositions. (Dez Dickerson gets full credit for "She's So Dull," and Time members Terry Lewis and Jesse Johnson each get a partial credit on a song.) Still, Prince's team again parroted the party line that Vanity 6 was an independent group and that he had not been involved.

As much as Prince was fascinated by women like Vanity, who presented themselves purely as sex objects, his interest in the opposite gender encompassed more than just his very active libido. In fact, he seemed to feel most comfortable and unrestrained in the company of women, be they lovers, friends, or employees. And in terms of the career opportunities he offered to women in certain male-dominated fields—for example, studio engineering—Prince was genuinely progressive, as he would demonstrate throughout the 1980s.

Peggy McCreary, a staff engineer at Sunset Sound in Los Angeles, first met Prince during the recording of *Controversy* in summer 1981. A former waitress and gofer at Hollywood's legendary Roxy club, McCreary had landed her coveted slot at Sunset after taking night classes in engineering. When she learned that Prince was on his way over from nearby Hollywood Sound, where a malfunction had ended his session, she felt dread. Knowing little about him other than that he sang about oral sex and incest, she envisioned him as boorish and inappropriate, perhaps a crasser version of Barry White, the soul singer known for his vivid evocations of lovemaking.

The first thing that surprised her was Prince's size; he was slight and delicate, more china doll than prowling wolf. He was also shy and hardly spoke. When McCreary asked a question, Prince mumbled unintelligibly without making eye contact.

"Look," she said bluntly as the session continued, "I'm not going to be able to do this unless you talk to me."

Seemingly appreciating her directness, he opened up. Remaining polite and giving little hint of the sex fiend of his songs, Prince chatted amiably about girlfriends, plans for the future, and even his childhood. After the *Controversy* tour he began working frequently at Sunset, using McCreary as his engineer for weeks at a time.

Although McCreary continued to see occasional flashes of Prince's sociable side, his workaholic tendencies took over as he recorded the follow-up to *Controversy* in the spring and summer of 1982. Often it was just the two of them in the studio, and the demands on McCreary became brutal, with sessions often dragging on for as long as twenty-four hours. Basic human needs were seen as distractions; when McCreary would suggest getting something to eat, Prince responded that food made him sleepy and that he preferred to go hungry.

McCreary struggled to match his pace and energy. When he saw her yawning, Prince would offer a brief respite, telling her to step outside while he recorded a vocal. But she wasn't allowed to go home; even after sessions, she was expected to remain and create rough mixes of the songs he had finished. "He had no tolerance for human weakness," she remembered.

Prince was also unpredictable and arbitrary in his scheduling. Not infrequently, McCreary was awakened by late-night or early-morning phone calls ordering her down to the studio. Other times he would fail to show up for previously booked sessions, leaving her waiting anxiously. She would knit sweaters to pass the time, only to learn, late in the day, that Prince had packed his things and returned to Minneapolis. On yet other occasions, he would show up at the studio in a stretch limousine, insisting that they drive to nearby Santa Monica and catch an obscure art film.

During the marathon sessions at Sunset, McCreary marveled at Prince's creativity and productivity. On *Controversy*, Prince's forays into styles ranging from electronica to rockabilly had met with mixed results, but now his ease with different genres increased dramatically. The Linn LM-1 drum machine, which had been used only on *Controversy*'s "Private Joy," became the linchpin of his composing process. He usually started a song with the Linn, sometimes routing the machine through effects boxes typically used for electric guitars. "He always wanted to keep people guessing," noted Don Batts, who remained Prince's primary engineer in Minneapolis. "Clavets were tuned to the point where they sounded like tin cans."

Prince also took a stylistic leap in his use of synthesizers. By recording the same riffs multiple times, he achieved a remarkable tonal thickness on songs like "D.M.S.R.," where the synth line became the melodic focal point. "Let's Pretend We're Married," another model of synth composition, featured a descending, minor-key line (which doubled the vocal melody) floating over another keyboard riff that chugged away underneath like a freight train.

Lyrically, Prince continued to explore sexual taboos. At times, though, a newfound wit and irony leavened the proceedings; "Little Red Corvette," for example, used sports cars and horse jockeys as carnal metaphors, and "Let's Pretend We're Married" was a tongue-in-cheek paean to anonymous sex. Elsewhere, the themes were darker, as "Automatic" and "Lady Cab Driver" touched on domination and submission.

When Prince presented the completed album—a two-record set of lengthy songs—to Bob Cavallo and Steve Fargnoli, they were pleased with the material and delighted to hear an apparent hit single in "Little Red Corvette." After digesting the work, though, the managers felt something was missing: an over-arching, thematic song in the vein of "Controversy," which on that album had provided a conceptual and musical foundation for what was to follow.

Prince, while not pleased to hear he had created anything less than a masterpiece, took their views as a personal challenge. "He yelled at us, and then he went back to Minneapolis and kept recording," remembered Cavallo. What emerged from these additional labors was "1999," which became the title track of the album and a defining song of Prince's career. After tracking the piece, he made a crucial decision during the mixing process. The verse vocals had been recorded as a three-part harmony featuring himself, Dez Dickerson, and Lisa Coleman, but in the final mix, he dropped out two of the voices on each line so that each singer became a lead vocalist—Coleman on the first line, Dickerson on the second, and Prince on the third. The result, evoking Sly & the Family Stone classics like "Sing A Simple Song" and "Hot Fun In The Summertime" (both of which use a similar baton-passing technique), gave "1999" a playfulness that had until then been unrealized.

The album was now complete. Warner Bros. was initially resistant to a two-album set, believing it would be difficult to market. But Fargnoli was again persuasive in presenting Prince's arguments to the label, and Mo Ostin soon threw his pivotal support behind the project. *1999*, released in October 1982, was greeted with fervor by music critics, who found it a much fuller realization of the ideas Prince had explored on his previous two albums. *Rolling Stone* commended Prince for "keeping the songs constantly kinetic with an inventive series of shocks and surprises." The *Los Angeles Herald-Examiner* admired his protean ability to "move[] confidently and effectively back and forth between pulsing funk and artful pop." In the eyes of the rock music establishment—the critics, executives, and musicians atop the industry—*1999* graduated him from a wunderkind into a full-fledged creative force, an iconoclastic figure in the league of the Clash and Lou Reed, if not yet David Bowie or John Lennon.

1999 was certainly Prince's finest album to date, and it remains a consensus choice as one of his three most significant works ever, along with *Purple Rain* and *Sign O' The Times*. The initial point of interest is that *1999* at once is, and is not, a double album; while there are four sides of music, the eleven songs are no more than would appear on most single discs. Throughout, Prince lets the long grooves travel where they will, but few of the songs feel bloated or unconcise; indeed, to hear a number like "1999" in its edited form (as it was released to radio) is to be robbed of the much richer experience that results from discovering all of the song's unexpected twists.

While there are many outstanding tracks, *1999* is also greater than the sum of its parts. Heavy synthesizers dominate throughout, giving the album sonic consistency, but there is also considerable stylistic diversity: "Little Red Corvette" is a nearly perfect pop ballad, "Delirious" incorporates a noticeable tinge of rockabilly, and "Automatic" sounds something like Devo meets Sly Stone.

If one track stands out, it is unquestionably "1999." It begins with a synth riff that (as first observed by the critic Davitt Sigerson) follows the same melody as the backing vocals in the chorus of the Mamas and the Papas' 1966 hit "Monday, Monday." The lyrics, which address fear of nuclear destruction, manage to somehow be haunting, fatalistic, and funny at the same time. Near the end, the song becomes a hedonist's anthem, as a crew of background singers chants "party!" while Prince grunts and shouts. A bass guitar abruptly hiccups its way to the fore, and cascades of synthesizers add to the celebration.

The final trick of "1999" is the ending. As the song reaches its climax, a new sound emerges from the depths of the mix—a long, throaty shriek from Prince. This provides a transition to the coda where, over a drumbeat and a minimalist funk guitar, he sings in an electronically distorted voice of his worries about everyone having a bomb. The song's message, delivered at a time when the U.S. government was engaged in a major arms buildup, convincingly articulated society's growing paranoia about nuclear war. After his clumsy attempts at political commentary on *Controversy*, "1999" again raised hopes that Prince was that rare artist who could capture the public mood.

To promote *1999*, Cavallo and Fargnoli organized a major concert tour that began in November, just weeks after the album's release. In addition to showcasing Prince and his band, the tour featured opening sets by the Time and Vanity 6, making it an extravaganza that revealed Prince's various artistic personae. The Roy Bennett–designed stage set featured props such as motorized Venetian blinds (which served as a backdrop for the entire tableau), an elevated catwalk, and a brass bed. The song list emphasized *Controversy* and *1999*, while also including the more obscure "How Come U Don't Call Me Anymore?," a piano ballad released as a B-side to the single of "1999." Prince's confidence as a performer was in full bloom, and the audiences at the venues, which had capacities ranging from 7,500 to 10,000, were enraptured.

Less pleasant were the offstage dynamics. Prince's bandmates felt increasingly distant from him, as Chick Huntsberry's presence again proved intimidating. The band leader traveled on a separate bus during much of the tour, accompanied usually by Huntsberry, Fargnoli, and a girlfriend. The bus became Prince's private universe; even after arriving in a city, he typically remained there until going onstage, returning afterward to record musical ideas on a portable machine or to enjoy female companionship.

Of Prince's bandmates, Dez Dickerson was the most disgruntled. During the *Dirty Mind* tour, Dickerson had experienced a religious awakening that prompted him to become a born-again Christian. From then on, playing Prince's sexually explicit music before large crowds became a conflicted exercise. Another turning point for him had occurred on the *Controversy* tour, when the band returned to Minneapolis for a homecoming concert at the Met Center. For everyone else this was a joyous occasion, but Dickerson dreaded playing the songs in front of family and friends. At a meeting out of Prince's presence, he asked his bandmates to support his demand that "Head," with Prince's show-stopping guitar masturbation, be dropped from the set. With some reluctance, they agreed to unite behind Dickerson. But when the issue was raised during the sound check, Prince's physical presence proved too intimidating. When the matter was put to a vote, everyone but Dickerson followed Prince's lead and agreed to retain "Head." Feeling betrayed, Dickerson shouted at his bandmates and even came after Matt Fink with a drum stool.

During the 1999 swing, Dickerson voiced his concerns directly to Prince and appealed to his own sense of spirituality. The band leader seemed sympathetic, but only to a point. "There were a few times where I really felt his heart was open, that he was seriously weighing the things I was saying," Dickerson remembered. "But he had consciously built his notoriety on being controversial; there was a conflict between what he knew to be right and what was working in his career."

Indeed, the more famous Prince became, and the more attention he received for his explicit lyrics, the more he wondered whether his own spiritual values were compatible with this path to success. On 1999, as on all of his previous albums, Prince listed "God" first on the liner-note thank-yous. In the songs themselves, though, were intense and graphic descriptions of sexual conduct. The apparent contradiction between conventional Christian morality and his own conduct was hardly lost on Prince — in fact, it sometimes left him genuinely uncomfortable. For the moment, though, he felt there was little he could do to resolve this tension, and he told Dickerson as much.

The guitarist seemed certain to depart after the tour. An heir apparent quickly emerged, though: nineteen-year-old Wendy Melvoin, a friend and lover of Lisa Coleman's whom Coleman had brought along on the tour bus. She grew up with Coleman in the San Fernando Valley, and they had known each other since childhood. Upon learning that Melvoin played guitar, Prince invited her to sit in with the band during sound checks and immediately liked both her sound and her tough, mildly masculine image, which he knew would add to the band's already interesting appearance.

Prince's relationship with the members of the Time, meanwhile, had not improved greatly since the epic food fight. Against the wishes of the group members, who longed to write their own songs, Prince had recorded most of the Time's second album, *What Time Is It?*, on his own. Released in summer 1982, it was another success, reaching No. 2 on the Black Chart and going gold in the process. The single "777-9311," propelled by Prince's skillful bass playing, became a modest hit. (It also created a hassle for Dez Dickerson, who had not known that his phone number was going to be used as the title of the song. When calls from strangers poured in at all hours of the night, he was forced to have it changed and circulate a new number to family and friends.) But the success of the song and album only underscored for the Time's members that they were Prince's puppets, and some began to consider quitting.

Prince, sensing resistance to his rule, tried to assert himself by complaining, without any basis whatsoever, that the Time was not performing strongly enough in concert.

"He would come in and get all over their case," remembered Roy Bennett. "He would ride them heavily, and, obviously, when you're doing a great job and someone's telling you you're screwing up, you wonder, 'What is this guy? What does he want?' It caused major tension."

Jam and Lewis, who unbeknownst to Prince had started doing production work for other groups on the side, wondered how long they could stand having their creativity suppressed. "I'm sure they felt that at some point he would loosen up the reins, but he never did," Bennett observed. "They're two very talented guys, and the last thing they wanted was to be told what to do all the time."

Late in the tour, Alan Leeds, a thirty-three-year-old music industry veteran who had worked extensively with James Brown, was appointed the tour manager in an effort to bring some order to the chaotic swing. Leeds later learned from Steve Fargnoli that Prince, when presented with several candidates for the position and being told about their backgrounds, simply said, "Get the James Brown guy." After quitting college at age twenty-two to do tour promotion for the Godfather of Soul, Leeds became Brown's tour manager and a confidant during a critical stretch of his career in the early 1970s. A thoughtful man with a melancholy handsomeness, Leeds was indefatigable both in terms of handling the complex logistics of running tours and in dealing with larger-than-life personalities like Brown. When he joined up with the 1999 tour, Leeds was at first roundly ignored by Prince and had to communicate through Huntsberry. Soon, though, Prince opened up, and Leeds joined the bodyguard in shadowing him virtually everywhere he went.

While Leeds' arrival brought something of a calming influence to the tour, the rivalry between Prince's band and the Time continued, with the opening act again upstaging Prince in some cities. Finally, in a move that at once outraged the Time and also convinced them that they had in some sense won the war, Prince booted the band from the bill during appearances in cities he considered most important, such as New York and Los Angeles. His fear of being shown up was transparent.

Money also remained a grievance for the Time. Morris Day, believing that his charisma was a substantial reason for the group's success, had several heated discussions with Prince about compensation. The response was always the same: Prince declared that since he wrote all of the music, neither Day nor anyone else in the band deserved anything extra. Adding to the band's chagrin about their small checks, Prince insisted that they serve as backing musicians for Vanity 6 during the tour, playing behind a pink curtain while the women sang.

Vanity herself was not finding life on the road particularly enjoyable. The whiff of stardom generated by *Vanity 6* proved overwhelming for her, and she began to drink to dull her emotions. In addition, her romance with Prince was deteriorating rapidly. While fans thought of her as his leading lady, in truth he gave up on this idea rather quickly; she remained a sexual option for him, but only one of many. Jill Jones, an on-and-off girlfriend since the *Dirty Mind* tour, showed up often on the 1999 swing. "He juggled the affairs on a day-to-day basis—some nights Vanity would disappear with Prince, then some nights Jill would end up on the Prince bus, leaving Vanity in the hotel stewing," said tour manager Leeds. "He seemed unfazed by the resultant drama, but it clearly affected everyone else."

Vanity's bandmate Susan Moonsie, who for several years had been the closest thing to Prince's true girlfriend, refused to tolerate these shenanigans and withdrew from the romantic sweepstakes. Rather than play the wounded ex-lover, she forged a friendship with Vanity, and while her relationship with Prince remained strong, it was of a platonic nature. But in the eyes of some colleagues, the end of his romance with Moonsie eliminated an important grounding influence from his life. "She was never frantic about him," said Bennett. "She knew who he was, what he was up to, and she wouldn't take his shit."

In late 1982 and early 1983, as the tour marched on across the country, Prince achieved a series of breakthroughs that in short order transformed his commercial status. First, the video station MTV began playing "1999," making him one of the few black artists in rotation on a channel that had since its inception emphasized white rock 'n' roll. This introduced Prince to a large new audience, which liked what it saw: His image was hip and rebellious, the music was catchy but original, and his video clips were full of sexy females. MTV had discovered a new star, and so had America. The racial divides that had characterized pop music throughout the seventies and into the early eighties were finally coming down, and Prince became one of the pioneers in introducing African-American styles to vast numbers of white consumers.

Prince's main competitor for pop stardom among African-American artists, Michael Jackson, was more commercially successful, but also in the long run less influential. Jackson's 1982 blockbuster *Thriller*, while it became the best-selling album of all time and also virtually inaugurated the eighties music-video boom, did something less for Jackson's reputation as a bona fide artist. His skills as a singer and dancer were astonishing, but *Thriller*'s radio-friendly grooves owed as much to producer Quincy Jones as to Jackson. Moreover, in terms of blending black and white styles, Jackson accomplished far less than Prince; in fact, Jackson's music from *Thriller* onward in many respects constitutes a repudiation of his R&B heritage. From the standpoint of both musicianship and ability to unify funk and rock, Prince led the way even while Jackson got much of the credit as a result of his unparalleled commercial prowess.

In February 1983, the release of "Little Red Corvette" brought Prince that *sin qua non* of pop success: the Top 10 hit single. The melodic ballad, which shot to No. 6 on the Pop Singles Chart, demonstrated conclusively that he was not simply a funk musician with a cult following, but a budding songwriter capable of working in different styles. The combination of this hit and Prince's presence on MTV, coupled with the fawning media attention that had surrounded him for several years, significantly boosted Prince's visibility. And these developments in turn fueled *1999*, which would sell three million copies in its first year. Additional tour dates were booked, this time into arenas with capacities of over 10,000 people.

After the tour, a calm of sorts settled over the Prince camp. Dez Dickerson quit and was replaced by Wendy Melvoin, eliminating a major source of tension within the band. She moved in with Coleman at the Residence Inn in Eden Prairie, a complex that provided long-term housing primarily to corporate clients. Alan Leeds also relocated to the Minneapolis area and became in essence the chargé d'affaires, maintaining close contact with Cavallo and Fargnoli in Los Angeles as he executed Prince's daily requests.

For his part, Prince worked to rebuild the atmosphere of community within his team that had been eroded by the arrival of Huntsberry and the struggles with the Time. Bandmates and associates were invited over for cookouts and to watch videos. Prince also gathered everyone for bowling nights, basketball games, and afternoons of softball. While these activities were generally pleasant and diverting, Prince's hyper-competitiveness sometimes reared its head; during a game, he would not hesitate to act as referee as well as participant. "In softball, someone would obviously be out, and Prince would say 'No, he was safe!'" Leeds said. "Well, what are you going to do? If you protested, he was gonna take his bats and gloves and go home."

Prince also worked diligently in his home studio, generating new music that showed him on the verge of reaching his tremendous potential. Cavallo, during his visits to the purple house in Minneapolis, was enthralled when Prince would spontaneously sit down at a piano and begin singing. "It was as if he had a direct line to the heavens," Cavallo recalled. Leeds, who had worked previously with James Brown and George Clinton, concluded that in terms of pure songwriting ability, Prince was the most talented figure he had encountered. "The music was just pouring out of him," Leeds recalled.

Prince seemed to realize he was on the verge of even bigger things. Anxious to preserve a sense of mystery about himself as his fame grew, he began refusing requests for interviews. During the last one he would give until 1985, a conversation with Robert Hilburn of the *Los Angeles Times*, he was not especially revealing. He did, however, want to clear up a rumor: He was not the mysterious producer behind the Time and Vanity 6 albums.

"I'm not Jamie Starr," Prince insisted.

CHaPTer FIVe

ajesty

I n late 1982, on the cusp of superstardom, Prince faced a significant challenge. He had broadened his following significantly with the success of
1999, but had not yet joined pop music's elite—the handful of artists who dominate
the charts and the attention of the media. The question was how to join that group
without damaging his status as an innovator. His core following of urban hipsters would
surely embrace another avant-garde album like *1999*, but the casual pop music consumers needed to take his career to the next level might not. Prince was determined to
expand his audience without compromising his art, a dilemma few major groups since
the Beatles had successfully confronted. Still, friends believed that if any contemporary
musician could pull it off, he could. "He had a clear vision—he was vitally interested
in music, but also in success," noted Bob Cavallo. "That's an incredibly powerful combination, someone who wants to be successful but who will not sacrifice quality of
musical vision."

To achieve these twin goals, Prince had to navigate the shoals of a pop marketplace where insipid, formulaic music ruled the day. Very few of the chart toppers of the
early eighties were challenging artists like himself; rather, the likes of Hall & Oates,
Rick Springfield, and Olivia Newton-John dominated the scene. There remained an
apparent racial barrier as well. The two major black pop stars of the early 1980s, Lionel
Richie and Michael Jackson, presented much more wholesome images than the priapic
Prince. By the standards of the times, he remained an improbable superstar.

As *1999*, fueled by the success of "Little Red Corvette," outsold his previous
albums by a wide margin, Prince pondered the tasks facing him. Questions were triggered in his mind when the *1999* tour frequently bumped into Bob Seger and the Silver
Bullet Band, with the two acts sometimes playing the same venue on successive nights.
When keyboardist Matt Fink remarked that the Seger bus seemed to be shadowing
them, Prince asked him to explain the appeal of that artist's classic rock. "I just don't
see what people see in it," Prince said.

Fink replied that Seger's simple, anthemic songs played to Middle America. "Write something like that," Fink told him, "and you'll cross right over." Soon after, Prince taught the band "Purple Rain," a majestic, four-chord rock ballad with a swelling chorus. It seemed to Fink that Prince had again shown how easily he could assimilate aspects of other genres—even genres he did not particularly like—while preserving the originality of his own sound.

After the critical and financial triumph of *1999*, Prince believed the time was ripe to pursue something that could dramatically increase his following: a feature film. His first concrete idea for a movie—a project started and then aborted during the *Controversy* tour—was a concert documentary interspersed with dramatic vignettes. During the *1999* tour, though, Prince conceived a more traditional film where musical numbers would follow a storyline. On the bus, he was often seen scribbling ideas for a screenplay in one of his omnipresent purple notebooks.

Movies had long been among Prince's favorite forms of diversion. When time allowed during tours, his managers arranged private post-concert screenings at local theaters. And he was a frequent visitor to Minneapolis cinemas, entering after the lights went down to avoid detection (usually sitting with a female companion and with a bodyguard and Alan Leeds on either side to create a barrier against bystanders). His taste in cinema was wide-ranging; Leeds recalls seeing everything from art films to *Rambo* movies with Prince. To term him a student of cinema overstates the case; he simply loved going to the movies, as well as viewing selections from a collection of videos that expanded quickly as the home video format became widespread.

But getting a go-ahead for a feature film would be difficult, and Prince knew it. Movies were expensive to make, and his stature as a musician, while increasing, could hardly guarantee success in this new arena. Rather than advancing his fortunes, a film could just as easily derail a promising career; Prince had no acting experience, and his sexualized persona was perhaps too intense for mainstream moviegoers.

Unsurprisingly, Warner Bros. Pictures, the filmmaking arm of the company that released his albums, showed no interest when first approached by Steve Fargnoli. Unwilling to give in, Prince used a key piece of leverage: His contract with Cavallo, Ruffalo & Fargnoli was about to expire, and he bluntly told his managers to secure a movie deal if they wanted to keep him as a client. This surprising bit of hardball demonstrated how badly Prince wanted to make a film.

But even apart from their desire to retain Prince as a client, it took little time for Fargnoli and Cavallo to warm to the idea. Neither had made a movie, making this a chance for a career plum. They pitched Prince's concept in early 1983 to Mo Ostin, seeking his help in selling it to Warner Bros. Pictures. Although Ostin and Prince did not have a close personal relationship—during encounters backstage at concerts or entertainment awards shows, their conversations tended to be short and stilted—on important issues they remained closely in sync. And the usually headstrong Prince was surprisingly open to Ostin's feedback. "Mo could stand up to him, but in a way that was comfortable; he knew when to give and when to pull back," noted Marylou Badeaux.

As Cavallo and Fargnoli had hoped, Ostin was prepared to gamble again. While he couldn't guarantee the support of Warners' film division, Ostin agreed to loan Prince's managers several million dollars for the production, a transaction negotiated by Cavallo. Prince was told that he had a green light to at least create the movie. Securing a distributor would wait for another day, making it doubly important that the film be of high-quality. "It's one thing for a record company to finance you, but they don't release movies," noted Alan Leeds. "There's a point where you've got to deal with a film company, or you're just an amateur making a very expensive home movie."

Why did Ostin line up so quickly behind the film, despite the obvious risks? Even apart from the great talent he perceived in Prince, Ostin, like Cavallo and Fargnoli, understood things about the artist's character that most did not. To the public he was an eccentric, oversexed wunderkind, and to the media he was a figure of great mystery—a musical genius who gave only vague hints of his inner feelings. But around seasoned entertainment industry executives, Prince when necessary dropped both his pretenses and his opacity, becoming level-headed, focused, and cogent. "He knew exactly how to articulate what he wanted—even if it wasn't in a whole lot of words," Cavallo noted. And Ostin, like Prince's managers, knew that he was no rock 'n' roll party animal, but rather a workaholic.

Prince also knew how to cultivate high-ranking executives. "Prince can sell ice to Eskimos," Badeaux noted. "He's done it with me—at the end of a conversation, you're saying, 'Yeah, the sky really is green.'" As he had been towards teachers in the Minneapolis school system, Prince remained respectful of authority figures, treating older, powerful men like Ostin and Cavallo with dignity and politeness. "He never said an unkind word to me during the ten years I worked with him," remembered Cavallo.

The same was not true for Prince's underlings, however. As he became more famous and his entourage grew, his professional relationships were increasingly governed by a sense of class-consciousness. At the opposite end of the caste system from executives like Ostin were technical and other support employees, who were sometimes expected to work as long as thirty-six hours with only short breaks. "He was unmerciful towards engineers and technicians," noted Alan Leeds. "He had absolutely no patience with equipment and its limitations. If a tape had to be rewound, he'd pace for thirty seconds and then sarcastically ask an engineer, 'Aren't you ready yet?' While they frantically tried to repair a problem, he might stand over them with arms folded or begin pacing back and forth."

Leeds, the manager with the most day-to-day contact with Prince, found his job at once exhilarating and jarring. Appreciating Leeds' knowledge of R&B music, Prince sometimes treated him as almost a mentor, and on a few occasions, the bandleader even opened up emotionally to Leeds. But in the end, the tour manager, like everyone else, was expected to serve as a highly efficient functionary and to cater to Prince's every whim. "It was as if he were saying to me, 'OK, now I want Alan the big brother,'" Leeds recalled. "Then it might be, 'Now I want Alan the best friend.' Then it might be 'Now I want Alan the gofer.' I'd better not confuse the three roles, because if he sends me on a mission and I come into rehearsal empty-handed, and I start laughing and joking like we did in front of the TV last night, I'm not going to last very long."

Leeds' job expanded once again as preparations for the film commenced. After moving his family to Minneapolis, Leeds became the overseer of logistics, establishing a base of operations in a cavernous warehouse in the Minneapolis suburb of Saint Louis Park, where acting lessons and dance classes started for Prince and other members of his band. Back in Los Angeles, Cavallo and Fargnoli searched for a screenwriter and director, eventually handing both roles to William Blinn, a television writer who had worked on *Roots* and penned the Emmy-winning *Brian's Song*.

Prince envisioned a quasi-biographical tale of a struggling musician who overcomes the odds to achieve stardom. Blinn, while comfortable with this concept, initially had great difficulty communicating with Prince, finding him at best cryptic and at worst completely unresponsive. When they went to a movie together in an effort to warm things up, Prince left without a word after twenty minutes.

But the relationship gradually improved, and an outline of the story emerged from their discussions at Prince's home in Minneapolis. Prince would play the tortured performer known as "the Kid" (a nickname coined by Cavallo); Morris Day, the leader of the Time, would be the Kid's rival both for musical stardom and the affections of the beautiful Vanity (a.k.a. Prince's girlfriend Denise Matthews). Another key element was the Kid's troubled family life, particularly his relationship with an abusive father. All of this would take place against the backdrop of an incestuous, highly competitive music scene not unlike the one Prince had known during his teen years in Minneapolis.

As Blinn fleshed out his screenplay, titled *Dreams*, Prince composed new songs and taught them to his band, a unit he now formally dubbed the Revolution. The personnel from the 1999 tour remained intact, except for the replacement of Dez Dickerson with Wendy Melvoin, which significantly changed both the sound and social dynamics of the band. Melvoin, just nineteen, had never even played in a band before, but this lack of context, rather than causing intimidation or fear, had a freeing effect. She joked with Prince and treated him with little deference, something he found refreshing, and they quickly developed a close friendship. "Everyone else was more or less intimidated by him, but Wendy came the furthest of anyone I've ever seen at pulling Prince out of his shell," remembered studio engineer Susan Rogers.

Seeing Wendy as a potential star, Prince made her a focal point of the Revolution. Her guitar work, while unspectacular from a technical standpoint, was made distinctive through her use of dense, ethereal chords. Her vaguely masculine appearance—Wendy had short hair and tough features—created an intriguing counterpoint to Prince's more feminine androgyny. Blinn's screenplay included an undercurrent of homoeroticism between Wendy and Lisa, as well as a plot strand involving their efforts to convince the Kid to perform one of their songs.

As the band became immersed in rehearsals and acting classes, Prince constantly reminded everyone how important the movie was to all of their fortunes. "Do you have what it takes to be a star?" Prince asked Matt Fink one day at rehearsal. Fink, taken aback by the blunt query, said that he did, but Prince responded with a sarcastic smirk, indicating that the answer was unconvincing. But gradually, through a combination of cajolery, flattery, and intimidation, Prince persuaded his comrades that the film would rocket their careers into the stratosphere. "Prince would say to me all the time, 'Mark, after this, you're never going to have to work again,'" noted bassist Brown.

These promises were a form of psychological motivation—seeing wonderful things ahead, the Revolution stayed focused through a demanding period of preparations for the movie. When the days of rehearsing at the warehouse began to feel endless, Prince did whatever was necessary keep his young recruits motivated. He insisted that "the

Revolution" meant something more than a group of backing musicians. "He convinced them they were a self-contained band, and he played that to the hilt to get whatever he needed out of them," said Leeds.

Prince succeeded in turning his five-piece band into a powerhouse. The Revolution's debut, on August 15, 1983 in Minneapolis, would be remembered as a turning point in his career. First Avenue, the hometown club that became an important location for *Purple Rain,* was packed with admirers on this sweltering summer night. Six new songs were performed, including "Purple Rain," the raucous "Baby, I'm A Star," and the distortion-drenched rocker "Let's Go Crazy." Prince's songwriting had tightened considerably, showing an increased melodic and structural sophistication. Outside the club, engineer David Rivkin captured the show on tape from a mobile studio; some of the songs would end up on the film soundtrack.

Onstage, the Revolutions's appearance was striking in its racial, sexual, and visual diversity. Matt Fink, the mad scientist–like "Dr. Fink," twirled a stethoscope as he banged on the keyboards; Wendy and Lisa exchanged knowing glances; and Prince danced, preened, and twirled about the stage, giving cues and shifting quickly from guitar to keyboard. The show was both celebratory and cohesive; not only was Prince's sound evolving, but his backing musicians were more prominent than ever before. In fact, they were no longer just sidemen: Prince and the Revolution had become a rock 'n' roll band.

Prince also planned to include music in the film by the Time and Vanity 6. But in actuality, both groups would be — as had been the case on their earlier albums — essentially fictions; Prince would write, perform, and record most of the songs, with vocals being the only major contribution of the groups' supposed captains, Morris Day and Vanity. Both Day and Vanity aspired to their own careers and resented being puppet band leaders. Prince underscored Day's powerlessness by firing Jimmy Jam and Terry Lewis, the Time's most talented members, ostensibly because they were spending too much time producing outside projects. This move effectively tore the group apart, as original members Monte Moir and Jellybean Johnson quit, unwilling to continue without Jam and Lewis. Prince restocked the lineup with relatively unknown Minneapolis musicians, leaving Day and Jesse Johnson with a dramatically different Time.

To make matters worse, Day developed a cocaine problem, making him even more moody and confrontational. As recording of the Time's third record began, and Day again went through the tedious exercise of mimicking Prince's guide vocals note-for-note, it was apparent the end was near for the Time, Prince's first and most successful side project. "It was a very tense situation," recalled Susan Rogers. "Morris was very unhappy and basically non-participating. He was going to get the movie over with, and then it was obvious that he was out of there."

This left Jesse Johnson — who felt underpaid and overworked, and who retained plenty of resentment against Prince over the coatrack incident — as the group's leader. However, Johnson, like Jam and Lewis before him, wanted badly to express his own ideas and succeed on his own merits. Realizing the Time was unlikely to be a forum for this, he began to consider going solo.

The relationship between Prince and Vanity was also disintegrating, and Vanity was already headed down a road that would eventually leave her health in ruins as result of drug use. She drank excessively and had also begun smoking cocaine with Day. (Her drug problems would escalate dramatically in coming years after she became romantically involved with Nikki Sixx of the group Motley Crue, and she would eventually lose a kidney as a result of her partying.)

Initially, much of the public and media were fooled into thinking that both the Time and Vanity 6 were freestanding groups that created their own music. But when Prince finally started dropping public hints that he was in fact Jamie Starr, the alleged producer of these acts, the illusion was shattered. Being unmasked was humiliating for both Day and Vanity. "When people came to realize how big a role he played in some of these projects, they started to lose a little respect," Leeds noted. "When you realized that Vanity 6 was really all his concept, from the lingerie they wore, to the songs they sang, to the music that was played behind them, it wasn't the same."

With the disgruntlement of Vanity and Morris Day threatening to derail the production, another snag arose: William Blinn's television series *Fame* was renewed for a third season, leaving him without time to complete *Dreams*. Cavallo and Fargnoli began seeking a new writer and director, first approaching James Foley, who had recently completed the film *Reckless*. Foley declined but recommended his editor, thirty-year-old Albert Magnoli. At first, Magnoli was uninspired by Blinn's take on *Dreams* and said he would pass. But a brainstorming session with Cavallo left him much more optimistic, and Magnoli agreed to meet with Prince. They connected with surprising ease, and Magnoli took the job and refashioned *Dreams* into a script called *Purple Rain*.

But relations between Prince and his leading lady continued to flag. Partly as a retort to Prince for his womanizing, Vanity flaunted various affairs she was herself involved in. "I tried men, women, everything," she told the magazine *Jet* in 1993. She also developed a close friendship with Alan Leeds, who found Vanity lonely and increasingly upset about Prince's treatment of her. "It didn't take long to realize she was a competitive pistol that hungered for companionship and wasn't about to let Prince's desire for control sentence her to the confines of her hotel room," he remembered.

A turning point in the relationship came when Vanity had an affair with Albert Magnoli, enraging Prince. Just a few months before shooting was to begin, Vanity left *Purple Rain*. She has said she quit over money issues, although other reports indicated she was fired. One knowledgeable source says Vanity was indeed dismissed, and that both her financial demands and the affair with Magnoli were factors.

Prince and his managers agreed that the best course was to find a replacement who could in essence stand in for Vanity. Hundreds of obscure actresses and wannabes answered a call to audition for the vacant role. Prince quickly settled on twenty-two-year-old Patricia Kotero of Santa Monica, California, who had starred in the miniseries *Mystic Warriors*. The reason for the selection was obvious to everyone: Kotero looked very much like Vanity. Prince inauspiciously dubbed her Apollonia, after a character in the first *Godfather* film (played by Simonetta Stefanelli) who is killed by a car bomb after marrying Al Pacino's Michael Corleone.

Shortly after recruiting Apollonia, he took her to a Los Angeles club where he had heard that Vanity would be partying. Vanity, who had not yet learned anything about her replacement, was shocked to see a woman dancing nearby who looked like a mirror image of herself. The message was clear: In Prince's world, anyone was replaceable.

Few of Prince's associates had been impressed with Vanity's musical talents, although she was undeniably charismatic. But Patricia Kotero was something else altogether. Although her appearance—sultry, curvaceous, bodacious—was almost indistinguishable from that of her predecessor, in terms of her personal magnetism, Apollonia was no Vanity. Plucked from obscurity to star in a film and to front a singing group, she was immediately in over her head, displaying little talent in either area. She lacked Vanity's edge; all that remained of the character Prince had created was sexiness. "She was kind of boring—very Cali, girl-next-door type, to tell the truth," said one frequent visitor to the set. "I don't think she was creative or clever enough to hold Prince's interest." Nonetheless, she became the front person of Apollonia 6, with Susan Moonsie and Brenda Bennett reprising their Vanity 6 roles.

Although Prince believed that Apollonia could probably make it through her thin role in *Purple Rain,* he concluded her vocal talents were not worth expending any of his better songs on. A bounty of strong material was considered for her *Apollonia 6* album, only to be reclaimed for other uses. Prince seized "Take Me With U" for the *Purple Rain* soundtrack (where it retains Apollonia's backing vocals), and "Manic Monday" was later given to the Bangles and reached No. 2 on the Pop Singles Chart in 1986. "17 Days," a powerful mid-tempo rocker, was released as a single B-side to "When Doves Cry," one of several successful singles from *Purple Rain.* After this plundering, mostly filler remained for Apollonia to sing. "He was not optimistic about Apollonia 6, so he wasn't going to be really critical about those songs," Rogers noted.

Nonetheless, some of Prince's associates were troubled that sub par material would be used even for this dubious side project. With Vanity and now Apollonia, a pattern was emerging: Prince would expend time, energy, and music on women simply because their beauty fascinated him. Libido, so long a driving force in his life, now seemed to be clouding Prince's judgment. "The Vanities and the Apollonias bothered me," said Matt Fink. "I thought he could be producing extremely talented people, not people who were there for their looks rather than their singing."

As with all female protégées, Prince insisted that Apollonia follow a rigid code of conduct. She was told to eat only what he ate—often just candy and herbal tea—and ordered to break up with boyfriend David Lee Roth, the lead singer of the group Van Halen. "He wanted to make everyone clones of himself," Apollonia told *People* in a 2001 retrospective. "There was a side of him that was just a tyrant...He made me promise I wouldn't date anyone publicly during promotion of the film."

While Apollonia denied in the press that she and Prince became romantically involved, rumors to the contrary flew on the set of *Purple Rain.* "She and Prince did have a brief fling," confirmed one knowledgeable source, "But I don't think he ever had a genuine flame for her. And there's no doubt that part of his attraction to Apollonia was a desire to get Vanity's goat."

With all elements finally in place, shooting began in November 1983 in Minneapolis. The pace was rapid, as Magnoli wanted to finish before the arrival of winter made outdoor scenes impossible. But the young director also tried to keep the atmosphere loose and informal; scenes were shot in as few takes as possible, creating a playful energy between Prince and his associates. Two professional actors, Clarence Williams III and Olga Karlatos, played the Kid's quarrelling parents, adding gravity to the proceedings. Shooting of the musical numbers took place at First Avenue, where hundreds of extras cheered and danced as Prince and the Revolution, as well as the Time, lip-synched to previously recorded material.

A major surprise was the on-screen magnetism of Morris Day, who channeled his frustrations into a bravura performance despite a growing drug problem. "During the making of the movie, more than once he had to be physically dragged out of his house and driven to the set, between the paranoia and exhaustion from all-night freebase binges," said an insider who was sometimes sent to roust Day. Still, Day managed to play his character—a slick, sleazy, self-absorbed womanizer—with the perfect degree of camp, and many critics would credit Day with nearly stealing *Purple Rain*. (Pauline Kael in the *New Yorker*, for instance, called him "a full-fledged young comedian.")

With the Minneapolis scenes complete, the next step was to decamp to Los Angeles to complete outdoor shooting in warmer weather, but the initial funding from Mo Ostin had run out. Cavallo and Fargnoli engaged in intense negotiations with Warner Bros. Pictures, trying to convince the company to pick up the film. "They had their necks out and were out of money," Leeds noted. As the cast and crew enjoyed a wrap party in Bloomington, Minnesota, Cavallo and Fargnoli finally received a commitment from Warners to provide additional financing and distribute the film. *Purple Rain* was going to make it to cinemas, representing the realization of one of Prince's lifelong dreams. Could superstardom be far off? "We were on a pretty exciting ride at that point, and we knew where it was going," said tour set designer Roy Bennett. "There was something big out there for us; we just never knew how big."

With the film largely complete save for editing, Prince, flush with excitement about *Purple Rain* and full of creative inspiration, retreated to Sunset Sound Studios in Hollywood to complete the soundtrack. Among the new tracks he laid down was "When Doves Cry," slated as the first single from the *Purple Rain* soundtrack. The song struck associates as one of his oddest yet, particularly since he decided during the mixing process to omit the bass line, creating an airy, spartan feel. On the chorus, Prince layered multiple vocal tracks into a powerful, gospel-like harmony. Not everyone at Warner Bros. heard a hit—Marylou Badeaux recalls one incredulous colleague asking "What kind of fucking record is this, with a bunch of strange sounds?"—but Prince was adamant, believing he had discovered a signature composition. And he was right again; "When Doves Cry," released in May 1984, heralded the impending arrival of a new ruler of pop music. It shot to No. 1 on the Pop Singles Chart and sold a million units, becoming the best-selling song of the year.

The lyrics, which tell of romantic loss and abandonment, were something of a farewell to Susan Moonsie, Prince's girlfriend of several years. Although it was Prince's infidelity that had prompted her to end the relationship, he still felt wounded and betrayed. But Moonsie stayed in Apollonia 6 and would remain a sister-like confidant for several years, representing an important link to his pre-superstardom life. "He knew she was one girlfriend who didn't date him for his money or his stardom, because she was there before both," observed Leeds.

Meanwhile, a serious new love interest emerged for Prince. Among the guests Wendy Melvoin invited to Minneapolis for her debut with Prince's band was her twin sister, Susannah, who greatly resembled Wendy but had a more feminine style. Prince was delighted to discover that his favorite new band member had a beautiful double, and an instant mutual attraction developed. Well-educated and stylish, Susannah stimulated Prince intellectually as well as physically. But she had a boyfriend in California and was not immediately available for a romance, which infuriated Prince. His jealousy inspired one of his most moving songs ever, the ballad "The Beautiful Ones." It begins with Prince tenderly singing over an interlocking foundation of piano and synthesizer progressions, but in the song's climax he unleashes a torrent of screams, hysterically beseeching his lover to choose him over another man.

Won over by Prince's passion, Susannah put her relationship on hold and moved to Minneapolis to live with him. But she was hardly the only game in town; not only did Prince engage in copious one-night stands, but in early 1984 he also started a romance with Sheila Escovedo, a talented percussionist whom he was planning an album around. He had met Escovedo—whom he now gave the stage name Sheila E.—in 1978, and had followed her career closely. (Her father Pete Escovedo, also a skilled percussionist, played with Santana and other groups.) In early 1984, he invited her to Minneapolis to work on a project featuring her as a vocalist. Escovedo, who saw herself as an instrumentalist rather than a front person reluctantly agreed, and their collaboration quickly became romantic. "He had a great deal of affection for Sheila," added engineer Susan Rogers. "They were not only lovers but they were friends."

But for both Sheila and Susannah—two strangers now linked by their pursuit of the same man—what at first seemed like a storybook romance with a powerful pop star became tumultuous and painful. Howard Bloom, then Prince's press agent, became close with Escovedo and found her often distraught about her relationship with Prince. "Sheila E. wanted to live with him for the rest of her life, and it wasn't going to happen; it was awful for her," Bloom said. "She was in love with Prince, and she was convinced that Prince was in love with her."

For much of the period from 1984 to 1986, Susannah would seem to have the upper hand as Prince's primary girlfriend, but her position was never secure. Singer Jill Jones—another protégée with whom he planned to record an album—remained an on-again, off-again girlfriend, and Prince was generally ready to sleep with virtually any woman who grabbed his attention. Bloom recalls, for example, dispatching a publicist from his company to meet with Prince and getting a call that afternoon asking him to send the woman back for carnal purposes. "He was sexually omnivorous," remembers Bloom, who declined the request. "Life for him was a sexual hors d'oeuvres tray."

summer 1984: release of purple rain

The entire *Purple Rain* mosaic—the film, soundtrack, and various spin-off albums and groups—was now complete, and summertime, when blockbusters are released and new stars created, had arrived. If the 1980s was the defining decade of the "entertainment event"—the blockbuster film or album that transfixes public and media attention in the manner of Michael Jackson's *Thriller* or movies like James Cameron's *The Terminator*—then *Purple Rain* was among the prototypes for this phenomenon. Warner Bros.' carefully staggered release of key elements of the project—the single "When

Doves Cry" in May, the album in June, and the movie in late July—proved a model of marketing. The album, like the single before it, went No. 1, displacing Bruce Springsteen's *Born In The USA* on the Pop Chart, and stayed there for an astonishing twenty-four weeks. Worldwide, it sold 16.3 million copies. And the film, which grossed $70 million and was among the top moneymakers of 1984, made Prince one of the most visible entertainers in the entire world. His persona, as well as his music, riveted public attention. While he was in some ways a divisive figure—oddly dressed, androgynous, cocky—millions viewed Prince as the new embodiment of cool.

Critical response to the album was almost uniformly strong; just as Prince had hoped, *Purple Rain* was praised as simultaneously accessible and experimental. "Like Jimi and Sly, Prince is an original; but apart from that, he's like no one else," wrote Kurt Loder in *Rolling Stone*. Added the *Miami Herald*, "*Purple Rain* serves as an affirmation of his versatility and substance as a performer and composer."

Rather than an overly polished work of pop, *Purple Rain* is an energetic collection that ranges across significant stylistic terrain. Its powerful rock ballads, "The Beautiful Ones" and "Purple Rain," both of which build slowly to monumental climaxes, show as much craft as anything Prince had written to date. The most famous song, "When Doves Cry," is a strange and original pop creation and also a tour de force of studio technique, featuring remarkable vocal multi-tracking that creates a virtual army of Princes singing in harmony. More so than any other Prince album, save perhaps 1987's *Sign O' The Times*, *Purple Rain* is packed with strong material and avoids the filler that would characterize many of his 1990s projects.

The film itself is another matter; as both cinema and pop culture, *Purple Rain* has not aged gracefully. All of the goofiest fashions of the 1980s—puffy hairdos, garish clothing, pancake makeup (none of these things limited to one gender)—permeate the movie, particularly when the camera lingers on the extras that populate the concert sequences. The film's main characters (the Kid included) are lightly drawn and cartoonish, and few of the acting performances—save for that of Morris Day—are creditable. While the film's music is more enduring, in the context of the movie the songs are at times overwhelmed by the eighties imagery and the melodramatic plot.

The film does reveal much about Prince's psychology. Each of its elements—the plot, the characters, and the songs—are expressions of specific parts of his personality and biography. Morris Day's performance received as much attention as any other aspect of *Purple Rain*, but few reviewers were aware how much Day's character echoed the real-life Prince—or at least one version of him. Yet another side is seen in the Kid: a wounded, withdrawn, and vulnerable person not unlike the reticent figure that William Blinn encountered during early script meetings. "Prince is a Sybil character," noted Jon Bream, an early biographer, in a 1985 interview with the *Boston Globe*. "He has many different personalities inside of him."

As planning began for a massive U.S. concert tour, Prince's momentum continued to build. Even as his music gained new popularity among white fans, his status among African-American listeners was reconfirmed by the success of two R&B albums: Sheila E.'s *The Glamorous Life* and the Time's *Ice Cream Castle*, both released in 1984. (The title of the Time album came from a line in the Joni Mitchell song "Both Sides, Now," from her 1969 album *Clouds*.) Although Prince was not credited on either album, word of his involvement quickly became public knowledge. While Sheila E. in press interviews emphatically denied Prince's involvement, her father revealed the truth in an interview with *Rolling Stone*. Sheila's infectious single "The Glamorous Life" was quite successful on urban radio and reached No. 1 on *Billboard*'s Dance/Disco Singles Chart. The Time album was even more successful, reaching No. 3 on the Black Chart on the strength of two funky singles, "Jungle Love" and "The Bird." Whereas *Purple Rain* contained very little straight R&B music, these side projects were full of potent funk. (Ironically, just as the Time reached its peak of popularity, the group suffered its final defection. Unbeknownst to the public, Morris Day's involvement had already ended, and in late summer 1984, Jesse Johnson also quit to seek solo success.)

In addition, Prince released under his own name a new song, "Erotic City," aimed at fans who might have missed the heavy grooves of *1999*. This B-side to the twelve-inch single of "Let's Go Crazy" featured co-lead vocals by Sheila E. as well as Prince's first use of an interesting technique; by slowing the tape down before recording his voice, he created a speeded-up vocal that sounds something like Prince on helium. Elsewhere, his voice was slowed down to a growl. (These tricks did not originate with Prince, however, having been pioneered on songs like George Clinton's "Atomic Dog" and Zapp/Roger Troutman's "More Bounce To The Ounce.") The hypnotic bass line of "Erotic City" made it an instant favorite in dance clubs.

Prince's fingerprints were found elsewhere on the pop charts. Chaka Khan released a cover version of the then-obscure "I Feel For You" from his second album, *Prince*; it rose to No. 3 on the Pop Singles Chart. And Sheena Easton released the Prince-penned single "Sugar Walls" (its lyrics refer to a woman's vagina), which also entered the Top 10. Prince had become a one-man hit factory, leading to more talk in the press that Prince might be a George Gershwin or Duke Ellington of the pop world.

To satisfy all of this hype, the *Purple Rain* tour had to be an extravaganza. The stage set, designed by Roy Bennett, was the most elaborate of Prince's career, costing $300,000 and featuring props like a purple bathtub that rose from below the stage. The compressed tour schedule included ninety concerts in thirty-two cities across the United States.

To pull off the complicated logistics of the swing, Prince's organization had to attain a new level of discipline and efficiency. With Steve Fargnoli continuing to spend most of his time in Los Angeles, the key player on the scene in Minneapolis remained tour manager Alan Leeds. He was joined by Karen Krattinger, an attractive, tough-minded Georgian who had been the road manager for the SOS band. Temperamentally, Leeds and Krattinger were near opposites and complemented each other perfectly; he was a strategic, sometimes lofty thinker with a passion for R&B music, while she was a meticulously organized administrator with almost no interest in artistic issues. Together, they became the linchpins of Prince's team and also served as close personal aides to Prince. With the help of numerous others within Prince's organization, they orchestrated one the most elaborate pop tours of 1984–85.

The opening night, at Joe Louis Arena in the Prince stronghold of Detroit, demonstrated how thoroughly *Purple Rain* had captured the public's attention. The 20,000 fans went into a frenzy the moment the spoken words that begin "Let's Go Crazy" crackled over the speakers. The crowd-pleasing show focused on *Purple Rain* (eight of its nine tracks were played) and *1999*. Although certain vaudevillian touches—the bathtub and other props, as well as Prince's five costume changes—drew objections from some critics, who would have preferred more spontaneity, his fans seemed enraptured. (Less successful was an opening set by Sheila E., who lacked the presence to be a credible front person and—despite her talents as an instrumentalist—came off essentially as a female Prince clone.)

The tour packed arenas everywhere it went, with shows selling out just hours after they were announced. The crowds were not only much larger than any Prince had experienced as a headlining performer, but had a very different flavor; suburban parents brought children who had begged for concert tickets, whites greatly outnumbered blacks—it was, in short, the generic mass audience that gravitates toward any artist of the moment. The days of Prince as an underground phenomenon were gone forever.

Along with casual fans checking out the next big thing, the crowds contained large numbers of zealots who identified—in many cases excessively—with the Prince and the Revolution of *Purple Rain*. Largely as a result of the film, each band member became highly recognizable. "They all had their own very vocal pockets of fans at shows," Leeds recalled. "Wendy and Lisa in particular were instant role models for every aspiring young female musician in the country." The wild desire of fans and groupies to meet and touch their new heroes kept the atmosphere charged with emotion and expectation. "It became a circus," noted drummer Bobby Z. Rivkin. "There were people dressed up in costumes, people dressed up like you. It was extremely exciting, but you had to be careful—it was very powerful."

To satisfy the expectations of new admirers, Prince had created a show in which the visual elements were just as important as the music. But in the process, something was lost: The subversive energy of earlier tours was snuffed out by the props and choreographed routines that Prince felt were integral to a major-market production. Dez Dickerson, watching from the sidelines, felt vaguely nauseated by the spectacle. "It was a big part of why I had left—he wanted the shows to become more and more structured and would often say, 'I want it to be like a Broadway play,'" Dickerson recalled. "For me, it was going in an entirely different direction from what I felt was the heart of what we do as a craft. I didn't want to become Wayne Newton in high heels."

Among the show's stranger elements was an interlude during which Prince had an anguished "conversation with God" against swirls of synthesizers. While largely incomprehensible, this dialogue seemed to reflect Prince's struggle to reconcile his lustful side with more traditional morality. The segment served to inform the audience that he was not unconflicted about having become a national symbol of licentiousness. With the largest crowds of his career looking on, Prince seemed intent on showing that he recognized a higher authority and was, at heart, a God-fearing man.

As he watched the show, publicist Bloom saw that an important, and in many respects unfortunate, transition had occurred in Prince's career and his psyche. From *Dirty Mind* through *1999* he had been a bona fide rebel who rejected prevailing social norms. Now, having achieved the heights of fame, Prince felt an obligation to curtail the more outlandish elements of his character. With so many young people around the world fixated on him, perhaps he even felt the need to become something of a role model. "Prince had been rebelling against God and morality, and now God and morality were taking him over," Bloom observed. "His emphasis was not on sexuality any more, but on God."

The conflict in Prince's mind between lust and spirituality was driven in part by the attention paid to him by self-appointed guardians of social values—politicians, evangelists, and freelance moralists. In late 1984, for example, thirty-six-year-old Tipper Gore, wife of the handsome young senator Albert Gore, discovered her daughter listening to *Purple Rain* and was shocked in particular by the lyrics of "Darling Nikki," which refer to a woman masturbating with magazines. Four months later, Gore and several other well-connected women in Washington (including Susan Baker, wife of Treasury Secretary James Baker) started an organization called the Parents' Music Resource Center (or PMRC) whose self-described mission was to clean up popular music through rating systems and other measures. The PMRC's campaign, which eventually resulted in the placement of warning labels on certain "explicit" albums, cited Prince as a leading offender of cultural decency.

While Prince was hardly unaware of the publicity value of Gore's attacks on him, the charge that his music corrupted the minds of children stung. In many respects, his bedrock value system was conservative, authoritarian, and hierarchical, and it was becoming even more so. Gore of course had no inkling that in mid-1984, while creating a side project called the Family, Prince pulled a song called "Feline" from the project because group member Paul Peterson felt it offended his religious sensibilities and, even more importantly, his mother. "Prince is gonna be the first one to listen when someone says 'My religion doesn't allow me to do this,'" recalled engineer Susan Rogers. "Those words carry a lot of weight for him. He also respects mothers and respects family life even though he didn't have such a good one of his own." While Prince had previously been more reluctant to accommodate band members' concerns— witness his refusal to drop "Head" from the live set at Dez Dickerson's request during the *Controversy* tour—by the mid-1980s, with his fame broadening, he worried more about becoming too offensive.

The downside of all this was that Prince's music and persona gradually became less subversive and arguably less interesting. He became a modern pop icon, but to do so was forced to give up some of his edge and distinctiveness. "First you rebel against something," noted Bloom, "and then you turn into it."

The crushing fame brought on by *Purple Rain* brought on another transition: Prince became more and more cloistered and remote, not only from rabid fans, but even from many of his own associates. He moved everywhere with a phalanx of bodyguards led by Chick Huntsberry. "It was ridiculous—you felt like you were going to be frisked every time you walked backstage," said Marylou Badeaux, who had previously enjoyed ready access to Prince. It was difficult to get near Prince even to discuss important issues. "He just kind of shut himself off—he became a different person at that point," recalled production designer Roy Bennett. "Between Prince and everybody else, a wall came up."

Upon leaving the stage each night, Prince was flanked by bodyguards and whisked away in a limousine, sometimes leaving band members unsure even whether there would be an encore. "There were two or three times where the band felt the response was so amazing that certainly he would come back, but meanwhile he was already in his car halfway back to the hotel," remembered Badeaux. Ensconced in his room, he usually studied a videotape of the previous night's performance or played piano, rarely entertaining guests other than female companions.

One of the few former colleagues who stayed in touch, Dez Dickerson, felt a dramatically different atmosphere when Prince invited him and his wife Becky back to his hotel after a show in Washington, D.C. The large suite housed a grand piano that was trucked from city to city, and various handlers, including a private chef, buzzed about.

As Dickerson and Prince became immersed in a jocular conversation, the rock star pretenses melted away; for a moment it was if they were back in Minneapolis, goofing around after rehearsal. "He was starting to kind of come back to life again, like in the old days," the guitarist recalled. As he and Becky left, Dickerson remarked that they should all get together and go shopping in Georgetown, as they had on previous tours. Prince's eyes lit up with expectation, but then just as quickly a sad look crossed his face. "Nah, I can't do stuff like that anymore," he said. "I can't go out."

Dickerson realized things had changed irrevocably. He said goodbye and left, and although the two men would remain in sporadic contact over the years, their communications usually ran through Prince's intermediaries. "We never really had any quality time together after that," Dickerson said.

Dickerson was hardly alone in feeling a drastic change. Each member of the band had at some point during recent years considered Prince a friend, but now felt they were being treated more as employees. "Prince wanted to keep it all business," Matt Fink remembered. While Prince's friendships with Wendy and Lisa would rekindle once the pressures of the tour abated, the closeness that Fink, drummer Rivkin, and bassist Mark Brown had once enjoyed with him would never quite return.

The sheer craziness of the *Purple Rain* tour gradually took a toll on much of the band. Brown, only in his early twenties and experiencing a heady rush of fame he never could have anticipated, began drinking heavily. "For me, the whole thing was a little too much at a young age," he said. "When life comes to you that easy, you start abusing it, it doesn't matter who you are. If you don't take it in perspective, you will start to burn out, and I believe that's what happened to all of us."

Light recreational use of marijuana and cocaine among some band members and other members of Prince's circle was not unheard of, but never became rampant. (Prince never participated and actually became enraged when he caught Matt Fink and Lisa Coleman doing drugs together, nearly firing them.) But among members of the crew—the men and women who erected stage sets and transported the heavy equipment in trucks—cocaine use became commonplace. Always the first to arrive in a city on the day of the show, the crew undertook the Herculean task of setting up for the band's afternoon soundcheck. When the show finally concluded late at night, they packed up and drove onto the next city to begin the same cycle again; under such conditions, the use of stimulants became perhaps the only means of staying awake. "There were serious amounts of drugs going on within the crew," said Roy Bennett. "It was ridiculous, people wouldn't sleep for days." Added another knowledgeable source: "Almost everyone outside of Prince and the band were using coke. I sometimes think coke kept the buses and trucks afloat for those six or seven months."

Secluded in his hotel room or his private bus, Prince remained oblivious to all of this. Reports of the crew's activities finally reached him near the end of the tour, but by this time it was too late to become outraged; the exhausted crew members would do whatever was necessary to complete the grueling swing and return home.

With the triumph of *Purple Rain*, Prince had become, unquestionably, part of pop music's elite, the handful of stars that define any given decade. His main competitors, in terms of both record sales and sheer visibility, were Michael Jackson, Madonna, and Bruce Springsteen. While Jackson's status was primarily that of a prolific hitmaker, the other members of the quartet had cultural impact as well. Madonna, by exposing her brassieres and singing unapologetically about female sexual gratification, changed fashion and provoked debate about gender issues. Springsteen, whose music reflected his working-class roots in Asbury Park, New Jersey, became a populist hero and symbol of traditional American values.

Prince's impact was more subtle but no less important, and references to him turned up in unexpected places. In Spike Lee's film *Do The Right Thing* the bigoted Pino (John Turturro) reluctantly concedes during an argument that his favorite musician is Prince. The import is clear: Prince was the first authentically African-American star (something the skin-bleaching Jackson cannot fairly be called) since Jimi Hendrix to appeal to huge numbers of whites, including many who had little or no contact with blacks in their day-to-day lives.

At the same time, however, Prince's movement toward rock and pop proved controversial among black fans. It did not go unnoticed that the most prominent members of his band—Wendy, Lisa, and Matt Fink—were all white, while Mark Brown, the sole black member, was pushed to the sidelines beginning with the *Purple Rain* tour. Although the influence of important black artists like James Brown and Sly Stone remained part of Prince's fabric, he had also made some conscious changes in his sound and image to appeal to a broader, whiter audience.

Prince's androgyny was another part of his persona that gained wide attention. Although associates say that he had no interest in the political goals of gays, his gender-bending imagery—like that of Wham!, the Eurythmics, and Culture Club—dovetailed with an increasingly visible homosexual rights movement in America and helped make androgyny and bisexuality hip.

Prince's new fame, however, would not come without a price. Some of his associates felt that he became far too identified with *Purple Rain*. So many stars before him, having achieved similar prominence, were soon reduced to cartoon-like status. Could a similar fate befall Prince? "The tour was the closest thing to 'Beatlemania' for Prince and his group," said Eric Leeds (Alan Leeds' brother), who later joined the Revolution on saxophone. "It was really a phenomenon that was greater than Prince; the vast majority of the fans were enthralled with *Purple Rain* more than with what Prince was about in totality. One of the biggest mistakes he made was to think that *Purple Rain* was going to be the norm rather than the exception."

And just as the main characters in the film represented divisions in his psyche, Prince was split over how to proceed after having become one of the most successful pop stars of his time.

chapter six

Hangover

Well before the circus-like *Purple Rain* tour lurched to a close, the man at the center of this extravaganza was in some respects ready for it all to be over. That part of Prince that craved stardom was, of course, elated by the public frenzy over the film, album, and tour. He had achieved the sort of fame that turns a name into a household word. And to a large extent, this was just what he had sought since starting his professional music career at age eighteen. But another, equally important part of Prince longed for artistic respect—the sort that he worried might be incompatible with indiscriminate public adoration. "I think he really had fears of being typecast as Mr. *Purple Rain*," observed Alan Leeds. "By the time that tour was over, he was so sick of that music and that whole concept."

Also, Prince was no great fan of being on the road for long periods of time, a problem reinforced by his tendency to cloister himself in hotel rooms during off hours. "Six months was his limit; he burned out after that," noted Matt Fink. While some band members wanted to cash in on *Purple Rain* by taking the tour to Europe, Prince's goal was to finish the U.S. swing and get back into the studio.

The frenetic pace of the tour allowed little time for reflection. But during those brief moments when Prince did pause to consider his next move, he resolved that his next albums would demonstrate musical growth and travel in a radically different direction. To help achieve this goal, he convened a school of sorts—an informal but intensive survey of important rock and jazz musicians of the twentieth century. As a youth, Prince had been exposed only to Minneapolis' very limited menu of radio stations, and by the time he reached his late teen years, he was too immersed in his own music to make learning about other artists a priority. To make up for this gap in his education, Prince in mid-1984 began encouraging members of his inner circle to share with him their extensive knowledge of various musical forms.

His friends were well-suited to the task. Bandmates Wendy and Lisa, and his girlfriend Susannah Melvoin (Wendy's sister), all steeped in the music of the sixties and seventies, played him records by the Beatles, Rolling Stones, Led Zeppelin, and others. Saxophonist Eric Leeds and his brother Alan, both jazz aficionados, exposed Prince to the canons of Miles Davis, Duke Ellington, and Charles Mingus. And percussionist-drummer Sheila E. introduced him to contemporary jazz-fusion artists like Weather Report. "I always enjoyed eavesdropping on whatever Prince might be listening to in his dressing room," recalled Alan Leeds, who would hear everything from classic Al Green to Miles' *Sketches Of Spain* to early Little Richard.

Prince's inner circle was beginning to resemble a salon, as the 1984–86 period found him surrounded by stimulating, creative, and sophisticated people who were themselves bound together by musical affinities, friendship, and family ties. Both Leeds brothers at times served as mentor or older-brother figures to him, and twins Susannah and Wendy, so similar in temperament and appearance, also enjoyed deep personal bonds with Prince. The creative synergy among Prince, Wendy, and Lisa strengthened almost by the day. Lisa's brother, David Coleman, and Wendy and Susannah's brother, Jonathan Melvoin, both talented musicians, occasionally passed through the creative circuit as well and played on various songs.

Prince absorbed voraciously the information offered by his friends, and immediately applied this knowledge in the studio. Still, his innate impatience gave his studies a rushed quality, as he rarely focused on any subject in detail. During conversations with friends, Prince would not hesitate to abruptly and rudely cut someone off the moment he began to lose interest. "There was a certain submission to the friendship, even when you were sitting around talking about Duke Ellington or Miles Davis," recalled Alan Leeds. "He wanted to hear what you had to say, but he wanted to hear it in response to his specific questions. He didn't want a lot of editorializing."

Still, Prince's approach to songwriting became at least marginally more collaborative, as he sometimes let his bandmates, and especially Wendy and Lisa, add their voices to the composing process. While Prince had in the past never been averse to "borrowing" musical ideas from his associates—for instance, taking someone else's riff and then, in isolation, fashioning it into his own full-fledged song—he now opened himself more to genuine exchanges of ideas.

A turning point in this respect was the song "Around The World In A Day," the first draft of which was written and recorded not by Prince, but by David Coleman, Lisa's brother. For a birthday present in June 1984, Coleman received from Prince three days of "lock-out" recording at Hollywood's Sunset Sound, giving him exclusive access to the expensive facility for this seventy-two-hour period.

Coleman was himself a sophisticated musician with an unusual palette of influences. Like his sister, he was impacted by his musical parents, and, when he was just ten he formed a band with Lisa (called Waldorf Salad) that was signed to A&M Records. But his interests even then extended well beyond kiddy pop. After being trained in cello, he taught himself a variety of instruments, including guitar. Through a close friendship during high school with a young woman from Beirut, he became fascinated with Middle Eastern culture, studying Arabic and learning a variety of international instruments. This influence emerged during his Sunset Sound sessions, where Coleman recorded a song using (along with more conventional instruments) a fretless Arabic guitar called an oud, an Arabic drum known as a darbouka, and finger cymbals.

Coleman circulated "Around The World In A Day" among family members and friends, and via Lisa the song soon made its way to Prince. Both its sing-song melody and exotic instrumentation intrigued him, and the song's psychedelic feel echoed the 1960s music he had discovered through Wendy, Lisa, and Susannah. When Coleman bumped into him at a concert in Los Angeles, Prince effused about the song and said this was exactly the sort of thing he was interested in exploring—not on the next album, but the one after that.

The timetable quickly accelerated. Coleman had expected little more to come of Prince's interest, but shortly after the Los Angeles encounter he received a phone call from Steve Fargnoli's office asking him to bring tapes of the song and all of his Middle Eastern instruments to Minneapolis. Thus, in mid-September 1984, Coleman and his musical partner Jonathan Melvoin (who would later, after joining the live lineup of the Smashing Pumpkins, tragically die of a heroin overdose in 1996 at age 34) met Prince at a Minneapolis warehouse to rerecord the song. As Prince explored the array of exotic instruments Coleman and Melvoin had on hand, the session quickly took on a playful energy. When Coleman broke out Saudi Arabian "fireman cymbals," Prince got into the spirit by exuberantly banging on them while blowing a police whistle. Coleman recalled Prince—who had over that same summer become one of the biggest stars in the world—as an engaging, unpretentious collaborator with an almost boyish enthusiasm. "He was just so charming and unassuming," Coleman remembered.

The finished song did not differ greatly in feel or sound from Coleman's original demo, save for Prince's singing and a drum pattern he developed on his Linn LM-1 machine. Prince altered Coleman's lyrics but retained the title and chorus phrase. "Around The World In A Day" set the tone for Prince's next project: It would have a decidedly experimental tinge and would showcase new influences, particularly sixties-oriented psychedelic rock. It would seemingly also make some allowance for collaborative songwriting.

Exactly how group-oriented the project would be, however, remained an issue of great concern to his bandmates. As Prince focused his energies on his own songwriting, an undercurrent of tension developed between him and the rest of the Revolution, who had a number of simmering grievances. In one sense, it was the headiest of times for Wendy and Lisa, Matt Fink, Mark Brown, and Bobby Z. Rivkin—they were in the midst of a major U.S. tour and awash in popular adoration. Seeing themselves on movie screens and televisions was the stuff of childhood fantasies come true.

Still, less pleasant realities also intruded. First, there was money: Prince had become a multi-millionaire almost overnight, and they had not. Mark Brown recalls that he and the others were making about $2,200 a week, and that at the end of the tour, each Revolution member received a mere $15,000 bonus. "It was a slap in the face. We had grossed him over $80 million," said Brown, who nonetheless says he blames Prince's accountants and managers more than the bandleader himself. (Prince would later give band members a much larger bonus—said to have been in the range of $1 million each—as a thank-you for *Purple Rain*, but by that point Brown had left the group.)

The band members also felt that Prince, by stealing away to recording studios without them (as he often did during the tour), slighted their contributions. The one thing they had to hang onto was that they were part of the Revolution—an entity that

Prince, throughout the making of *Purple Rain,* had insisted was an integral part of his identity. The band members considered themselves part of perhaps the most distinctive and influential pop group of their time. "They pretty much felt they were the second coming of the Beatles as a band," said Alan Leeds. "They had an enormously inflated sense of their importance to the project."

But to Prince—regardless of what he had told his bandmates to motivate them during preparations for the film—the Revolution was nothing more than his backing group, and could be changed at will. Midway through the tour, the band members were surprised when saxophonist Eric Leeds (Alan's brother), who had previously done some studio work with Prince, showed up backstage. On the second evening of a three-night stand in Greenville, South Carolina, Prince asked Eric if he had brought along his saxophone. Having rarely played anywhere larger than a nightclub, Eric jumped onstage for the climactic "Baby, I'm A Star." At one point during the lengthy jam, Prince cut off the band and let Eric solo in front of the 15,000-person crowd.

Prince liked what he heard, and invited Eric to join the tour. He began taking prominent solos, which diluted other members' time in the spotlight. The affable saxophonist was hard to dislike on a personal level, but other band members resented his intrusion into their private fraternity.

Eric's time in the spotlight was particularly difficult to swallow for Wendy, who throughout the tour had felt her star rising as female fans, in particular, reacted wildly to her presence onstage. Wendy's time to shine was "Purple Rain"; she began the song with shimmering guitar chords and, after the rest of the band joined in, was usually given several minutes to solo before Prince began singing. But at a show in Santa Monica, California, just before the band came out for an encore, Prince gathered them and issued a last-minute change—this time, Eric would play the solo. In an instant, Wendy's signature moment had been stolen from her, and it showed in her eyes the moment she left stage. "Wendy was whiter and paler than I've ever seen her before," said Alan Leeds. "Just crushed."

Prince was hardly unaware of his band members' frustrations and their desire for more stability and creative input. Yet, such matters were not of great concern to him; no one was going to leave the band in the middle of a tour like this, and the band members were in any event under contract. Adding new members and deciding who took solos were his prerogatives alone. No one could be allowed to get too comfortable. Prince had a new album to worry about, and viewed occasional backstage carping as a small matter next to his broad creative vision.

Prince recorded several other songs for his next project in early 1984, again emphasizing an entirely different style from the guitar- and rock-oriented sound of *Purple Rain.* "Pop Life," with Sheila E. on drums, was a languid, agreeable funk number with an overlay of psychedelia, including sampled crowd noise reminiscent of the Beatles' "A Day In The Life." Another new number, "Paisley Park," also relied on a slow tempo and utopian lyrics recalling songs like Jimi Hendrix's "Electric Ladyland" and the Beatles' "Magical Mystery Tour." This new material found Prince stretching, albeit with mixed results, to find new directions.

To Prince's credit, the explosion of *Purple Rain* mania throughout the United States and Europe did nothing to dampen his desire to experiment, and during the tour he darted into recording studios whenever breaks in the schedule allowed. Even before the tour reached its peak—a grueling stretch of sixty-seven shows between December 26, 1984, and April 7, 1985—Prince managed to complete his new album, entitled *Around The World In A Day*, by flying to studios in Minneapolis and Los Angeles during breaks, and also by relying on mobile trucks that contained full recording setups.

The final song for the project, a ballad called "The Ladder," was created in a typical frenzy of activity. During a five-night stand of concerts at Minnesota's Saint Paul Civic Center, Prince taught the band the tune during a sound check and recorded it with them the next day at a Minneapolis warehouse. And as the homecoming concerts continued, Prince used every free moment to complete the album. On Christmas Eve 1984, while he and the band played a matinee show, engineer Susan Rogers gathered all of the tapes for the new album and drove a mobile truck to Prince's purple house on Kiowa Drive. She waited in the driveway until he arrived after the concert, when he recorded a final vocal and then sequenced the album with Rogers' help. They finished work after four a.m. on Christmas morning. "He had nobody over there at Christmas, which is fairly typical of him," Rogers said. "He was mainly interested in getting his record cut together."

Prince previewed the album for Warner Bros. during a ceremonious "listening party" for about twenty company officials in early February 1985 in Los Angeles. Joni Mitchell and Prince's father, John L. Nelson, were among the special guests present. Attendees were seated on the floor of a large conference room, and as the high-pitched flute that begins "Around The World In A Day" lilted from the speakers, Prince and Lisa walked in holding flowers; the whole scene was, according to one attendee, "very Haight-Ashbury."

After each song, the assembled executives applauded heartily. But in truth, many were surprised by the subdued, languorous feel of the disc's first three songs: "Around The World In A Day," "Paisley Park," and the protracted ballad "Condition Of The Heart." Not until the fourth cut, the infectiously melodic "Raspberry Beret" (featuring a very Beatles-esque string section composed by Wendy and Lisa) did anything resembling a Top 40 hit emerge. All told, it was a strange follow-up to the hyper-kinetic *Purple Rain*. "He told me he could see on the faces of the Warner Bros. people that it wasn't really working," remembered Eric Leeds.

The album's cover carried forth the ambiance of affable whimsy reflected in the lyrics of its songs and indicated a shift in image. An elaborate painting by Doug Henders shows Prince along with various band members and other characters in a color-drenched landscape. Prince, no more prominent than anyone else in the scene, holds in his hand a tiny ladder. His shoulder-length hair is gray and his face is partly obscured by a white wrapping. The cover presents Prince as wiser and somewhat world-weary, a radically different figure than the young, cocksure rock star astride a motorbike on the cover of *Purple Rain*.

Prince's associates realized this rather downbeat album was unlikely to sell nearly as many copies as *Purple Rain*. Having reached the pinnacle of fame, his strategy seemingly was to trade in some of that success for enhanced artistic credibility. And, to his friends and bandmates, he seemed at peace with that decision—even if not everyone agreed with it. "I felt it was a mistake timing-wise to put something else out so soon after *Purple Rain*," keyboardist Matt Fink said, a view shared by many officials at Warner Bros., who believed that Prince was saturating the market with his music. But Prince, who saw *Around The World In A Day* as reaffirming his commitment to artistry, was relatively unconcerned with marketing issues. For at least the moment (and his feelings would certainly change in coming years) he had accepted that there would never be another year like 1984 for him. He had attained a level of fame that was neither possible to perpetuate nor, in the end, particularly worth saving.

And he reached this conclusion at just the right time, for the backlash that so often accompanies global superstardom was about to begin.

january 28, 1985: downtown los angeles

The American Music Awards at the Shrine Auditorium served as yet another commemoration of Prince's remarkable 1984. Surrounded by his peers and competitors in the music industry, from Michael Jackson to Bruce Springsteen, Prince performed "Purple Rain" with his band and then collected three awards—Favorite Album for *Purple Rain* in the black music and pop music categories, and Favorite Single for "When Doves Cry." He was, in many respects, the very center of attention at this key music industry fete. The only sour note was Prince's obsession with security; many eyebrows were raised when, each time he was called to the podium, he brought along bodyguard Chick Huntsberry.

After the show, Prince was scheduled to participate in an event that threatened to overshadow the awards ceremony itself. He, along with more than forty other pop stars, had been invited to A&M studios to participate in the recording of the song "We Are The World" for a charitable relief effort called USA for Africa. This campaign to relieve African famine was inspired by a similar effort in Britain led by musician Bob Geldoff. The main creative forces behind the song were its producer, the legendary bandleader Quincy Jones, and Michael Jackson, who wrote the music with Lionel Richie. The session was planned for the evening of the American Music Awards to maximize the number of participants. Bruce Springsteen, Ray Charles, Stevie Wonder, Bob Dylan, Tina Turner, Diana Ross, Cindy Lauper, and many others were present.

A line of the song had been written for Prince to sing and a space in the studio blocked out for him to stand next to Michael Jackson. But at some point during the course of the evening, he decided not to show up, and instead took a limousine to the restaurant Carlos & Charlie's on Sunset Boulevard with Jill Jones and several bodyguards. (Primary bodyguard Huntsberry was not present.) While he has never explained the suddenness of his decision not to attend, Prince later said in interviews that he would have felt uncomfortable around so many entertainment luminaries, and that he preferred to work with close friends. This rings true; Prince in any situation needed to feel in control, something that would have been impossible at a session dominated by his arch rival, Michael Jackson.

Recording of "We Are The World" proceeded without Prince. Across town, as Prince and his entourage exited the Mexican restaurant at about two a.m., several paparazzi descended on him. One particularly audacious photographer jumped into his limousine. Prince and his friends were justifiably frightened and outraged, and the bodyguards reacted by seizing the photographer's camera and forcefully ejecting him from the car. The police were summoned, and one bodyguard—six-foot-nine-inch, 300-pound Lawrence Gibson—was arrested for battery, and the other, Prince's friend Wally Safford, for robbery.

Predictably, the confluence of these back-to-back events—Prince's no-show at a high-profile charitable event, and a violent incident involving his security staff—brought down a hail of negative publicity. Any nuances in either story were blurred, and Prince came off as self-centered, security-obsessed, and—most damningly—unwilling to drop his rock star pretenses for a charitable cause.

Seeking damage control, Prince agreed to contribute a song to the *We Are The World* album. He cut "4 The Tears In Your Eyes," during a rare day off on the *Purple Rain* tour; the exhausted duo of Prince and Susan Rogers worked in the vast, empty Louisiana Superdome, which the day before had been filled with 70,000 screaming fans. Unable to find any food, Rogers finally scrounged up some warm cokes and stale salami sandwiches that served as their only sustenance during a long day of recording. "He put in his time for the cause in a very noble and gracious way although no one was there to see it," Rogers said.

Unfortunately, the symbolism of Prince's absence from the "We Are The World" session proved more powerful and obscured his own considerable charitable efforts. During the *Purple Rain* tour Prince held various benefit concerts and food drives, including concerts for the hearing-impaired. Yet the incident involving his bodyguards, along with the aloof, ultra-cool image he presented through the media, solidified public perceptions of him as an eccentric egomaniac. And matters were not helped when the *National Enquirer* published an article, based on an interview with Huntsberry (who had recently quit his post) entitled "The Real Prince—He's Trapped in a Bizarre Secret World of Terror." It described Prince as (among other things) a cloistered weirdo with an obsession for Marilyn Monroe.

Prince poured some of his frustration about these developments into a pair of songs—"Hello" and "Old Friends 4 Sale"—recorded in the spring of 1985. "Hello" is essentially a blow-by-blow description of the evening of the "We Are the World" session. Musically, the song pulsates with energy and features special touches such as a sped-up guitar solo and a harpsichord-like keyboard riff. "Old Friends 4 Sale" lies on the border of blues and jazz and incorporates strings by Clare Fischer, a well-known orchestral composer to whom Prince began sending songs for input in 1985. The song's title seems a direct reference to Huntsberry's selling of his story to the *National Enquirer,* and the lyrics also address the cocaine problem that prompted the bodyguard to sell his account. The unusually personal words also mention Prince's manager, Steve Fargnoli, by name and allude to the angst of the post–*Purple Rain* period. These two strong songs, however, were deemed too personal for prominent release: "Hello" would become a B-side to "Pop Life," the second single from *Around The World In A Day,* and "Old Friends" would end up, in essence, consigned to oblivion. (A version of the song would finally be released in 1999 on *The Vault . . . Old Friends 4 Sale,* but by that time Prince had changed many of the lyrics, making them far less revealing.)

Recording these songs seemed to help Prince put his recent media imbroglios behind him, at least from an emotional standpoint. Still, he recognized that the controversies over "We Are The World," the bodyguard incident, and the *National Enquirer* article threatened to detract from the release of *Around The World In A Day*. Facing the media scrutiny and sensationalism that accompanies superstardom, Prince redoubled his efforts to recast himself as an artist, rather than a celebrity to be packaged, sold, and exposed. As the album was readied for distribution in spring 1985, Prince handed Warner Bros.' publicity department a series of directives that left label officials perplexed about how to market the album. Intent on the project being viewed as an integrated artistic statement, he ordered that neither singles nor videos accompany the release. Nor did Prince want a high-octane publicity campaign; in fact, he forbade the label even from running advertisements in leading trade publications. Warners officials, unable to say no after *Purple Rain*, reluctantly acceded to every demand and simply hoped for the best. "Everybody was having a heart attack," observed Marylou Badeaux. "But we ended up doing it his way."

april 1985: release of around the world in a day

Despite Prince's unorthodox approach to publicity, his new album debuted at No. 1 on the Billboard Pop Chart, displacing the *We Are The World* album from this position. Yet this magnificent start was in essence an aftershock from *Purple Rain*; just as Warners had feared, sales of the album tapered off quickly, and *Around The World In A Day* exited the No. 1 slot after just three weeks. *Purple Rain*, by contrast, had topped the charts for twenty-four weeks.

Although it had seemed that Prince was prepared for a return to a more modest level of fame, the reality of seeing *Around The World In A Day* fade so quickly proved disconcerting. Suddenly ambivalent about his minimalist promotional strategy, he agreed to rush out a single and video of "Raspberry Beret," both of which performed strongly on their own but failed to turn *Around The World In A Day* into any sort of blockbuster. (The single's B-side, the blistering rock cut "She's Always In My Hair," written about Jill Jones, had more sheer power than anything on the album itself.) With the album stalling, Warners searched the album in vain for an instantly accessible pop hook that might turn things around; the second single, "Pop Life" (backed with "Hello") reached No. 7 but failed to boost album sales significantly.

Adding to Prince's frustration was that the album was not universally greeted as a masterpiece by music critics. While some applauded his efforts to incorporate new influences into his sound, many in the same breath concluded that he had fallen somewhat short of the mark. In comments that must have seemed particularly biting, some critics ridiculed his efforts to emulate the spirit and style of the 1960s, finding these excursions strained and overly literal; Jim Miller of *Newsweek*, for example, called the record "an eerie attempt to recapture the utopian whimsy that characterized the Beatles' *Sgt. Pepper*."

Prince, who had not given an interview since 1983, undertook efforts to repair his image following the "We Are The World" fiasco and the underwhelming performance of *Around The World In A Day*. An extensive conversation with him appeared in the September 1985 issue of *Rolling Stone,* and his image graced the cover with the headline "Prince Talks." He used this platform to defend *Around The World In A Day* and to argue that he had made a conscious choice to target the album at serious fans, rather than the millions who casually purchased *Purple Rain.* "You know how easy it would have been to open *Around The World In A Day* with the guitar solo that's on the end of 'Let's Go Crazy?'" he said. "That would have shut everybody up who said the album wasn't half as powerful." Implausibly, Prince denied that the music or styles of the 1960s had swayed him. "The influence wasn't the Beatles," he asserted. "They were great for what they did, but I don't know how that would hang today."

Prince also made a deliberate effort to soften and demystify his persona, inviting *Rolling Stone* into his purple house. The reporter, Neil Karlen, was only too happy to assist in image rehabilitation, portraying the digs as surprisingly modest and issuing an almost point-by-point rebuttal of the *National Enquirer* article: "No," Karlen wrote, "The man does not live in an armed fortress with only a food taster and wall-to-wall, life-size murals of Marilyn Monroe to talk to."

Notwithstanding Prince's belated publicity campaign, which also included broadcast interviews with MTV and a Detroit radio station, the commercial fortunes of *Around The World In A Day* did not improve. The multi-platinum album cannot be called a failure (it sold three million copies in the United States alone), and appears as such only next to the unrealistic benchmark of *Purple Rain,* which moved more than 11 million units in the States. Yet something fundamental had changed; Prince could no longer claim the mantle as the most commercially successful artist in popular music. In fact, after 1984, he would never again enjoy that status.

In many respects, Prince made a bold and laudable decision by creating such an offbeat album in the aftermath of *Purple Rain,* and by resisting pressure to make a *Purple Rain II.* The largest failing of *Around The World In A Day* is that Prince simply did not put enough time or care into either the creation of the album or his study of the sixties influences that emerged so obviously. He took an important step by exposing himself to the Beatles and others, but his explorations were in the end rushed and superficial.

Further, the album was in essence tossed off during breaks in a grueling tour. Some of the tracks have a murky, almost unprofessional sound, an unfortunate result of the haste with which they were recorded and the frequent use of mobile trucks as studios. And the predominance of slow- and mid-tempo songs also drags things down. After the lively *Purple Rain,* the album seems indicative of a post-*Purple* hangover, a depletion of energy and confidence.

The strongest portions of *Around The World In A Day* occur when Prince's creativity melds with those of his collaborators, as on "Raspberry Beret," where his strong pop melody is given wings by Wendy and Lisa's orchestral additions. The title track, a David Coleman–Prince composition, is one of the clearest examples of shared songwriting in the entire Prince canon and is also, not coincidentally, an engaging and fresh-sounding piece of music. (John L. Nelson, receives a songwriting credit as well, but no one has been able to pinpoint his contribution, and associates believe this was simply an attempt by Prince to reach out to his father and to help him financially.) The session during which Prince, Coleman, and Jonathan Melvoin cut the song is a rare instance of Prince letting his guard down and enjoying the flow of creativity without trying to control the process.

By contrast, some of the solo performances on *Around The World In A Day* sound underdeveloped, including the plodding "The Ladder" and "Tambourine," a sparse, claustrophobic outing dominated by Prince's frenetic drumming. One associate observed that his prominent use of live drums on this track was a competitive response to the presence in his life of Sheila E., someone clearly more skilled on that instrument.

Lyrically, songs like the title track, "Paisley Park," and "The Ladder" are bogged down by loopy imagery and psychedelic utopianism. Meanwhile, "America," a rather blatant anti-Communist diatribe, and "Pop Life," which cautions against drug use, show Prince's conservative, moralistic side. And both songs contain rather dismissive references to people living in poverty, wholly consistent with the anti-welfare, individualistic philosophy of the Reagan administration. (The album cover has similar touches, including a naked black child waving an American flag and a jet fighter plane streaking across the sky.) All told, *Around The World In A Day* seems an awkward mixture of late-sixties imagery and mid-eighties morality.

"America" also makes reference to something that continued to haunt Prince— his fears of a nuclear holocaust. He had previously addressed this topic in "Ronnie, Talk To Russia" and in "1999." In "America," he equates a young student's lack of patriotic spirit with increased risk of war. Prince's worries about annihilation would remain a recurrent theme in his music throughout much of his career, particularly during his happiest times, such the immediate post–*Purple Rain* period. "Nuclear destruction is something that can really, really frighten you if you are having the time of your life," engineer Rogers observed. "It was very important to him to feel safe and protected."

But while the odd lyrical messages and inconsistent music of *Around The World In A Day* failed to redefine Prince as completely as he had hoped following *Purple Rain*, it did not undermine his status as an important artistic figure. Although some critics were dissatisfied with the album as a whole, they also applauded Prince for trying to challenge himself and his audience. The *New York Times*' Robert Palmer, in a review that captured perfectly the sense of excitement many rock scribes felt about Prince in the mid-1980s, struck a cautionary note about the artist's seemingly boundless ambition, but also expressed considerable admiration:

> Prince is risking charges of imitation and excessive eclecticism by deliberately invoking so many icons of 60's rock. He is also asking, perhaps demanding, to be taken seriously. If the Beatles' *Sgt. Pepper* is the one rock album almost universally revered as a work of art, Prince clearly would like *Around The World In A Day* to be No. 2, at least . . . Overall, whether one approaches it as a concept album or simply a collection of superb pop songs, it is an instrumental and stylistic tour de force, Prince's finest hour—for now.

Clearly, in the eyes of Palmer—and even many critics who were less enthusiastic about the album—Prince remained singular among 1980s stars like Michael Jackson, Bruce Springsteen, and Madonna, whose music, however well-crafted, at that point rarely reached beyond set boundaries of commercialism. *Around The World In A Day* was an important step in Prince's development as a musician and composer, if also an uncomfortable and hesitant one.

Much had changed for Prince in a short time. Certainly, the fall-off in sales from *Purple Rain*, along with the controversies that surrounded him in early to mid-1985, did much to derail his superstardom and fostered a popular image of him as a remote, eccentric figure. Meanwhile, the ambitions and frustrations of his band members—especially Wendy and Lisa—threatened to destabilize the chemistry that had helped make *Purple Rain* a worldwide phenomenon.

But Prince had more important things to worry about. Having achieved what he considered an artistic breakthrough with *Around The World In A Day*, he wasn't about to let public opinion or band politics interfere with his development. For now, at least, he was prepared to continue—and indeed, to accelerate—his artistic growth.

chapter seven

Counter-Revolution

As the 1980s continued, the sound Prince had perfected with records like *1999* and *Purple Rain* became the most influential (and for that matter, the most openly imitated) style of the entire decade. His artistic calling cards—minimalist production, taut funk rhythms, and salacious lyrics—were appropriated by dozens of pop artists, often with potent results. Even as important musicians like Miles Davis, Eric Clapton, and Robert Plant hailed Prince as a pop pioneer, the most convincing evidence of his influence was on the radio: It was almost impossible to spin the dial without encountering something that sounded very much like him.

The floodgates opened in October 1985—just over a year after *Purple Rain* swept across America—with the No. 1 hit "Oh Sheila" by the Flint, Michigan, group Ready for the World. The remarkable thing about the song was not its melody or the band's musical performances (both of which were marginal), but rather how much it sounded like Prince. Indeed, the whole Ready for the World enterprise seems to have been conceived as a knockoff. The band's androgynous, makeup-heavy image, the posing of lead vocalist Melvin Riley, Jr., and the music's synth-dominated feel were all openly purloined from Prince.

Over the next three or four years, Prince's influence would show up in the work of more significant artists. George Michael, former leader of the teenybop group Wham!, matured into a skillful songwriter on the 1987 album *Faith*, which incorporated aspects of the Prince lexicon in almost every song. The album's two biggest hits, "I Want Your Sex" and "Father Figure," paid homage to "When Doves Cry" and "Little Red Corvette," respectively. And Michael's yelps and growls were an obvious, if misguided, attempt to echo Prince's singing style. But *Faith* contained enough songwriting panache to elevate it far above the level of imitators like Ready for the World.

The same is true of the stunning 1987 debut by the eclectic soul artist Terence Trent D'Arby, *Introduction To The Hardline According To Terence Trent D'Arby*. While the album contained some clever pop music, such as the elegiac "Wishing Well" (which hit No. 1 in 1988), D'Arby's true model was not Prince the pop star, but Prince the avant-garde experimentalist. Indeed, in subsequent years D'Arby frequently invoked Prince's example in defense of his own right to make increasingly obscure, inaccessible music—a course that eventually all but doomed a promising career.

And there were numerous other examples. The producers who crafted Paula Abdul's 1988 smash debut *Forever Your Girl* consciously evoked Prince's compact dance-floor aesthetic, and the album's frequent use of synth lines as principal song hooks also echoed his work. The same can be said of Janet Jackson's 1986 breakthrough *Control*, which was produced by Prince's former confederates Jimmy Jam, Terry Lewis, and Monte Moir.

Prince's style became known in the music press and among musicians as "the Minneapolis sound." Among its distinguishing characteristics—along with sheer funk-iness—was the striking absence of horns, usually a standard element in R&B and funk music. Since his first album, Prince had used synthesizers for melodic lines that other-wise would have been handled by trumpets or saxophones. On *Controversy* and *1999* he had perfected this technique by constructing in many songs an intricate, intersecting latticework of synth lines, giving the music a tense, heavily electronic feel. This, more than anything else, was the common thread in songs like Janet Jackson's "What Have You Done For Me Lately?," George Michael's "Father Figure," Paula Abdul's "Straight Up," and Ready for the World's "Oh Sheila."

Interestingly, no sooner had he constructed a musical paradigm that influenced countless artists, than Prince struck off in new directions. After completing *Purple Rain* and *Around The World In A Day*, the next step of Prince's musical evolution was a tentative movement in the direction of jazz that included his first use of horns. While the Beatles and other sixties rock bands were the primary influence on *Around The World In A Day*, Prince soon began exploring other genres, including the jazz-fusion compositions of Miles Davis and others. Influenced by Miles' rich textures and by the ethnic allusions in the music of Duke Ellington, Prince continued to move in new stylistic directions, for the first time in his career integrating saxophone and trumpet into his music.

The first signs of his interest in jazz were seen as far back as early summer 1984 as he planned a side project called the Family. Like the recently disbanded Time, the group would be nominally independent from Prince, although he planned to record the bulk of the Family's music on his own and then piece together a band from his friends and associates. Three former Time members were recruited, including sideman Paul Peterson as the lead singer, and Prince's girlfriend Susannah Melvoin was added as the second vocalist.

In a significant departure from his previous work, Prince asked an outsider to add strings to his music. After learning of the respected orchestral composer Clare Fischer, who had worked with R&B artists such as Rufus, Prince sent him several of the Family tracks for his input even before meeting him. "Prince said, 'I want movie music,'" noted engineer David Rivkin, who contacted Fischer. "Fischer's arrangements cut across the track like there was a movie going on, and that's what [Prince] wanted. Something dis-sonant, something weird—the guy just sliced across the tracks sideways, independent of the music almost." Delighted with the outcome, Prince became superstitious about the relationship and insisted upon never seeing Fischer in person, preferring to simply forward him tapes.

The Family project also commenced Prince's fruitful studio association with saxophonist Eric Leeds, who was brought into the fold by his brother Alan, Prince's tour manager. After recording several songs, Prince invited Leeds to Minneapolis to add saxophone overdubs and then quickly folded Leeds into the group. Leeds, with his sophisticated knowledge of jazz and vast record collection, also contributed significantly to Prince's ongoing musical education. "I talked up Miles [Davis] a lot to Prince," Leeds noted. And Prince recruited Leeds' friend Matt "Atlanta Bliss" Blistan on trumpet, creating a full horn section.

Prince also began work on a new album (ultimately titled *Parade*) that melded the various sounds and styles he had been exploring—psychedelia, string arrangements, and the jazzier textures made possible by Leeds' presence. Just ten days after the conclusion of the exhausting *Purple Rain* tour, Prince decamped to Sunset Sound studios and commenced a series of prolific and adventurous sessions. For the next several months, each of Sunset Sound's three studios was typically in use by either Prince or his associates. The atmosphere was festive, as musicians popped from one studio to another to check on each other's progress, also playing Ping-Pong in the recreation room and shooting baskets on a court that sat between Studios 2 and 3. (By all accounts, Prince was among the most competitive and skilled at both games.) When Prince needed privacy, Studio 3, a self-contained building with a bathroom and kitchen, provided him a hermetic work environment, which he decorated with scarves, Christmas lights, candles, and a queen-sized bed with purple sheets, where he would lie and write lyrics.

Along with the planned use of horns (which were overdubbed by Leeds after Prince recorded basic tracks), the first day of the *Parade* sessions found other changes afoot. Rather than programming patterns on his Linn LM-1 drum machine, which had been a signature of his sound on *1999*, *Purple Rain*, and *Around The World In A Day*, Prince returned to the use of live drums that marked his earlier albums. As the session got underway, he settled in behind the drum kit, taped lyrics to a music stand in front of him, and signaled engineer Susan Rogers to start the tape. He instructed her not to stop it if he stopped playing, and then ripped off four songs in a row, with brief pauses between them. Each composition was fully mapped out in his head, and he used the taped-up lyric sheets as a guide to the structures.

After finishing, Prince returned to the control booth, bristling with energy and enthusiasm. "Alright, here we go! Where's my bass?" he said to Rogers. Following the same process, he laid down bass guitar parts on each of the songs. Whereas many musicians can spend days on a single piece, Prince was sketching the better part of an album's side in an afternoon. When *Parade* was released, these four songs— "Christopher Tracy's Parade," "New Position," "I Wonder U," and "Under The Cherry Moon"—would appear in the same sequence Prince recorded them.

The manic pace continued as Prince stayed in Studio 3 virtually around the clock, catching brief respites of sleep at a rented home in nearby Beverly Hills. In short order, nine new songs were recorded. The chaotic "Life Can Be So Nice," with Sheila E. adding cowbells, was recorded at the tail end of a twenty-four-hour marathon session. Just as the exhausted engineers began to clean up, Prince barked out, "Fresh tapes!"

Although Prince often worked alone, Wendy and Lisa were frequent visitors to Sunset Sound, adding their own instrumental ideas to songs he had already recorded. Rapidly, the personal and creative chemistry of the troika of Prince, Wendy, and Lisa developed to the point where they virtually became a band within a band. "He was more comfortable with giving them a tape and saying, 'Put whatever you want on it and give it back to me,'" noted Rogers.

But inevitably, the ascendancy of Wendy and Lisa as Prince's closest friends and musical partners left the other members of the Revolution feeling excluded, and the band's tight chemistry began to erode. Matt Fink, who had been Prince's keyboardist since 1978 and had made modest contributions to *Dirty Mind* and *Purple Rain*, now felt a growing chill in the air. "I got married, and you kind of get cut out of the picture [by Prince] when that happens," he recalled. Bobby Z. Rivkin also felt underutilized; Prince was now playing live drums in the studio and also jamming more and more often with Sheila E. Mark Brown, dissatisfied with his role as a sideman, on several occasions almost quit before being dissuaded by Chick Huntsberry, with whom he developed a tight friendship.

In truth, the sense of mission and esprit de corps that the Revolution members had felt during the recording of *Purple Rain* and the shooting of the movie had all but dissipated by the time the tour ended. The addition of Leeds as a virtual member on the tour let other members know that Prince's plans and visions might not always include them in prominent roles—or include them at all.

Following the tour, Prince began spending more time both socially and in the studio with Wendy and Lisa. Not only lovers but lifelong friends, the two women had been composing together for years and in combination created a sound that struck listeners as unusually emotionally expressive. Lisa, with her classical training, was the superior musician, but their artistic symbiosis went far beyond instrumental chops. Their ideas proved a perfect complement to Prince's work; in places where his music threatened to become sterile or harshly minimalistic, the women would lend lushness and feeling. New songs like "Our Destiny" and "Roadhouse Garden," both composed with Wendy and Lisa, demonstrated the melodic sophistication and pop-rock flavor that they brought to his sound. (Neither has been released, although live versions circulate among collectors.)

Given Prince's general resistance to surrendering creative space, his relationship with Wendy and Lisa would have been unstable even if strictly professional in nature. But there were other potential flashpoints as well—most notably, his tumultuous and passionate relationship with Susannah Melvoin, Wendy's twin sister. When Susannah emerged as Prince's main (though hardly only) girlfriend, Wendy suddenly found herself again sharing a large part of her life with the same person with whom she had shared a womb. Moreover, Susannah was a skilled vocalist, and Prince added her as a kind of adjunct member of the Revolution, making her part of the musical equation as well. Prince frequently socialized with Susannah, Wendy, and Lisa as a group. He enjoyed their company, and did not mind the pimp daddy–like ritual of entering restaurants and nightclubs with three beautiful women in tow. At times, though, the lack of privacy in his romantic life became frustrating. "He soon realized that dating Susannah was like dating all three, because Susannah shared things with her sister and Lisa that

Prince was unaccustomed to his band being privy to—his private life," said a confidant who watched the relationship unfold.

The purely musical part of the Prince-Wendy-Lisa relationship was also marked by rapidly shifting dynamics. For the moment, Wendy and Lisa found themselves contributing more to Prince's music than ever before. They added musical embellishments to most of the new tracks he recorded at Sunset, and Wendy even took the lead vocal on the psychedelic oddity "I Wonder U." Yet, the notion that he needed any kind of ongoing help in the studio was anathema to Prince. From *For You* through *1999*, absolute self-sufficiency defined his career, and he was extremely reluctant to continue down any path towards collaborative or, even worse, democratic songwriting. As such, Wendy and Lisa could never be sure when Prince would reclaim his territory. And Prince wanted it both ways; he appreciated what Wendy and Lisa brought to his sound, but was unwilling to give them what they wanted most—some measure of equality and stability.

Of all of Prince's band members, the one most ripe for defection was Mark Brown, a prospect that troubled Prince. He appreciated what Brown's unique, percussive style of playing brought to the Revolution's live sound and even asserted, in an interview with *Rolling Stone*, that if Brown were not in the band, he would not even use bass in his music. But Brown's true ambition—like that of André Cymone before him—was to become a figure not unlike Prince himself, a respected songwriter and producer of other bands. In 1984, unbeknownst to Prince, Brown took under his wing a seven-piece rock-funk outfit called Mazarati that he had discovered in the Minneapolis clubs. Soon he became essentially a member of the group, regularly jamming with them onstage. Because he worried that Prince would frown upon such extracurricular activities, Brown performed wearing a mask and identified himself onstage as "The Shadow." "I thought he was going to be pissed at me because I had kept it a secret from him," Brown recalled.

But as this double life became more stressful, Mazarati guitarist Terry Christian urged Brown to let Prince know about the project. "Just tell him," Christian advised one evening as the two musicians were driving around Los Angeles. "The worst he can do is want a piece of it or tell you to stop."

Brown did approach Prince, who was more curious than angry. After taking in a Mazarati concert, Prince realized he might even have a new side project on his hands. He urged Brown not to take the group to another label, but to release its first album on Paisley Park Records. Brown agreed despite his concerns about retaining creative control over the project. And as rehearsals for the album proceeded, Prince sometimes arrived unannounced, with his presence proving distracting and inhibiting. At gigs, he often jumped onstage to jam with Mazarati, and soon he even began telling group members how to dress. Gradually, the group lost its sense of identity.

When Mazarati began recording at Sunset Sound, Prince gave the group two songs for possible inclusion on its album. The group used "100 MPH" but passed on a number called "Jerk Out" because some members were offended by its explicit lyrics. Brown functioned as the producer of the sessions, but Prince, too busy with *Parade* to oversee the sessions himself, wanted a more veteran presence in the studio, and placed a call to engineer David Rivkin in Minneapolis.

"Can you come out to L.A. for the weekend?" Prince asked. "I've got some stuff for you to do." Rivkin agreed, packed two pairs of pants, and booked a flight. When he arrived the next day, Prince greeted him boisterously. "Oh, by the way, you've got to be here for a couple of months!" he exclaimed. "We have a Mazarati album to do."

A few days after Rivkin's arrival, Prince took a break from his own work and poked his head into Studio 2, where Mazarati was working. When one of the band members asked off-handedly if he had any more songs for them, Prince paged Susan Rogers over a studio loudspeaker; when she arrived a few moments later, they disappeared into a room with an acoustic guitar and a four-track cassette recorder.

As he waited for Rogers to prepare the equipment, Prince tapped impatiently on the body of the acoustic guitar. "Rolling?" he asked. She quickly responded affirmatively, and Prince began briskly strumming a basic twelve-bar blues pattern and singing mournfully in his lower register. The song, "Kiss," was completed in just minutes, and Prince emerged with the tape. "Here, finish this off," he said to Rivkin and Brown. "Do what you want with this song!"

After Prince left, the group caucused. Tony Christian, Mazarati's rhythm guitarist, was not impressed. "Nobody liked the song," he recalled. Rivkin wasn't enthralled by "Kiss" either, but the song's blues orientation triggered ideas in his mind. He and Mark began reconstructing it, first creating a foundation of drums that made the piece peppier and more danceable. Rivkin added an infectious piano riff borrowed from an obscure Bo Diddley song called "Hey Man." He and Coke Johnson, another engineer present, used a studio trick that linked the acoustic guitar part to the hi-hat cymbal, making it follow the same jagged rhythm. Singer Terry Casey then added his own rendition of Prince's words, and Rivkin came up with an idea for a backing vocal part based on the song "Sweet Nothings" by pop singer Brenda Lee.

Working through the night, they completed the song by about nine a.m., when the band members went home as Rivkin and Johnson prepared a mix. When Prince stopped by around noon, Rivkin gave him a cassette. Intrigued, he took a portable boom box out to the basketball court in the center of the complex and blasted it. "He went ballistic," remembered Johnson. Prince could not believe that his languid blues number had been changed into something so funky and energetic. "This is too good for you guys!" Prince shouted. "I'm taking it back."

But after this initial reaction, Prince felt guilty about poaching the band's work. Huddling with engineers Rogers and Peggy McCreary, he asked their opinions. Although McCreary felt Mazarati should keep the song, Rogers cast the tie-breaking vote in favor of Prince because she felt "Kiss" would get more exposure on his album.

With this resolved, Prince took the master tape and cut his own vocal (this time using his falsetto), replacing Terry Casey's. He also added a James Brown–style guitar lick at the beginning of the song and during pauses that recurred at the end of each chorus. Finally, he tweaked the mix, dropping out the bass guitar. He was finished in a little over an hour; "Kiss" had completed its transformation from a Prince song, to a Mazarati song, and back to a Prince song. It would eventually reach No. 1 on *Billboard*'s Pop Singles Chart as the first single from *Parade*.

Not surprisingly, given its genesis, credit for the song was contested. Although Prince gave David Rivkin an "arrangement" credit for the song, the rest of the credit states that "Kiss" was "produced, composed and written by Prince and the Revolution." In an apologetic call to Rivkin, Prince said that Warner Bros. would not allow him to give anyone other than himself a producer's billing. Rivkin—while he certainly didn't accept this flimsy explanation—remained philosophical about the episode and concluded, in the end, that Prince's modest additions to the piece made it much better.

Mark Brown also claims that he was in essence the producer of "Kiss," and remains chagrined that Rivkin, rather than he, received the arrangement credit. Brown says he gave Prince and his managers numerous opportunities to compensate him for his contributions to the song, but no action was ever taken.

Even as he worked on *Parade*, Prince was planning *Under The Cherry Moon*, his follow-up film project to *Purple Rain*. Success in the world of film remained a priority for him, and of all the laurels he had received for *Purple Rain*, the most meaningful had been his Academy Award for Best Original Song Score. At the ceremony, when he reached his backstage dressing room he handed his award to bodyguard Chick Huntsberry and was immediately grabbed in a bear hug by Steve Fargnoli. Although various associates have attested that Prince typically resists such contact, this time he succumbed to the emotion of the moment and earnestly reciprocated Fargnoli's hug. "I never found Prince to be a touchy-feely person who easily expressed any kind of physical affection, particularly towards men," noted Alan Leeds, who was surprised as anyone to witness the embrace between Prince and Fargnoli. "Even his handshake was wishy-washy, soft, and seemingly reluctant—this was the one-and-only exception I saw." The moment reflected Prince's spontaneous, heartfelt joy over receiving Hollywood's highest honor.

The stunning success of *Purple Rain* virtually guaranteed Prince the right to make whatever sort of film he wanted, within certain budgetary constraints. Just as he sought to enhance his status as a songwriter through the more challenging music of *Around The World In A Day*, Prince now wanted to create a movie that would be taken more seriously by critics than the shallow and melodramatic *Purple Rain*. He had a tentative idea for a wry comedy that would be shot in black and white. Prince also proved receptive to the concept, advanced by Steve Fargnoli, of filming in France.

As a means of selecting locations for the film and exposing Prince to European culture, Fargnoli took him (along with Alan Leeds) to Paris in June 1985; they stayed at the Nova Park Hotel near the Champs-Elysées. Hoping that Prince would share his passion for Paris, Fargnoli proposed a variety of outings. But on the second day of the visit, Prince ducked into a music store and became enamored with several new pieces of equipment, including several cutting-edge synthesizers. He asked Leeds to arrange for a line of credit through Warner Bros.' local office, and, by that evening, Prince had a makeshift studio running in his hotel. "At that point we lost our mate to the gear," Leeds recalled. "Getting Prince away from his new toys was like pulling teeth." While Prince later agreed to visit the Louvre, he backed out at the last minute. And an evening drive past the Arc de Triomphe and the Eiffel Tower found Prince with no inclination to get out of the car to view these historic monuments.

Prince did show some willingness to visit restaurants and nightclubs, but in a curious reversal of rock star stereotypes, it was Fargnoli and Leeds who more often prowled

the town. One night at a club, the men ended up so inebriated that they failed to recognize two friendly women who joined their table as prostitutes, resulting in a bill of
over $1,000 even though no physical contact occurred. A drunken Fargnoli shouted
obscenities on the street as he and Leeds reached their hotel at about six a.m. As
Fargnoli tried to steady himself using a street sign, Leeds heard a familiar sarcastic voice
calling from a balcony above the street. "Look, Paris! That down there is my management!" shouted Prince, who was still fiddling with his new equipment. "Hey, down
there on the street, can you bums quiet down and let a rock star get some work done?"
Leeds, who was almost as drunk as Fargnoli, could do nothing but sit down on the side-
walk and start laughing.

Yet despite his resistance to sightseeing or partying, Prince was sold on the idea of
filming overseas; he decided to shoot *Under The Cherry Moon* in Nice on the French
Riviera, which he had visited on a side trip from Paris. A writer named Becky Johnson
was commissioned to write the screenplay from Prince's basic idea about a poor piano
player who meets a rich socialite.

Although Warners' film division in essence greenlighted Prince's next picture without even seeing a script, objections were raised when it was learned that he wanted to
film in black-and-white. Prince held firm, and a compromise of sorts was reached — it
would be shot in color, but transferred to black-and-white (which presumably kept alive
the possibility of reversing Prince's decision). Michael Balhaus, who had worked with
Martin Scorcese on several movies, was recruited as the cinematographer.

For *Purple Rain*, Prince had relied on friends and associates as the principle cast
members, and he planned to do the same in *Under The Cherry Moon*. But the
Revolution, after being a focal point of the previous movie, would not play a major role
this time; instead, he cast friend Jerome Benton (also a member of the Family) as his
comic foil and sidekick. Prince initially wanted Susannah Melvoin to play the female
lead, but the studio prevailed on him to accept the casting of Kristin Scott-Thomas.
Selected as director was Mary Lambert, who had helmed various MTV videos.

A modest budget was approved, and Prince's team got the go-ahead to begin filming in Nice in fall 1985. Warner Bros.' film division had doubts about the project from
the very beginning, but the die was cast — Prince was going get an opportunity to build
upon the tremendous success of *Purple Rain*.

mid-september 1986: somewhere over the atlantic ocean

At least among Prince and his entourage, optimism reigned about *Under The
Cherry Moon*. As he and several close advisors flew to Nice to start the project,
Prince's recent setbacks — the bodyguard/"We Are the World" controversy and the
rapid fall-off in sales of *Around The World In A Day* — seemed far away. And there was
apparently another reason for cheer: Among those accompanying Prince on the flight
was Susannah Melvoin, wearing something that looked very much like an engagement
ring. Shortly before the team had left Minneapolis, an article appeared in *USA Today*
reporting that Prince, one of the entertainment industry's most eligible bachelors, had
proposed to Susannah.

In truth, he hadn't, exactly; Prince had given Susannah the ring, and she had chosen to interpret this as a marriage proposal, which perhaps it was. The article's origins were unclear—it was based upon anonymous sources—but Prince was incensed over this intrusion into his personal life. In truth, he remained deeply ambivalent about committing to Susannah, and now the whole matter was spilled out before the public.

The group cleared immigration and customs and arrived at the Beach Regency Hotel to a beautiful day—eighty degrees and sunny with a relaxing sea breeze. The penthouse suite, where Prince, Susannah, and bodyguard Gilbert Davison would be staying, occupied the majority of the top floor and had a wraparound balcony that afforded startling views of the ocean to the front, and the towering hills of Saint Paul de Vence to the rear.

Moments after being escorted to the penthouse, Prince silently steered Alan Leeds into the bedroom and out of earshot of the rest of the group. He ordered Leeds to immediately take Susannah home. More specifically, he wanted her brought to Prince's residence in Minnesota. "I don't want her going to L.A. and crying on Wendy and Lisa's shoulders," Prince insisted.

Reluctantly (and realizing that his job would be in jeopardy if he refused) Leeds agreed. But his wife, Gwen, upset with Prince's treatment of both Susannah and her husband, had to be restrained from going upstairs to confront Prince when she learned the news. Gwen was left alone for two days as Leeds flew Susannah home to Minneapolis and then immediately turned around and jumped on his third transatlantic flight in a week back to Nice. A perplexed flight attendant who had encountered him flying in the same direction a few days earlier wondered why he was traveling back and forth across the Atlantic.

With Susannah removed from the scene, Nice became a sexual playground for Prince. He met women at local nightclubs, and during the two-month shoot, he would also enjoy visits from girlfriends Sheila E. and Jill Jones. He also had an affair with Scott-Thomas, according to a knowledgeable source. "Prince and Kristin were definitely an item during the making of the film," the source said. "It was hardly an enduring relationship, but they spent an awful lot of private time together in Nice while filming."

The production itself, though, was far less of a lark. Director Lambert quickly alienated much of Prince's team with what they perceived as a haughty attitude, and the decision was made to dump her. Then, the inevitable happened: Prince himself took the helm, just four days into shooting. This action ratcheted up the pressure on Prince and immediately led to predictions in the media that *Under The Cherry Moon* was a doomed vanity project.

The initial fallout from Prince's takeover was mixed. It certainly created resentment within the larger Hollywood film community. Veteran actor Terrence Stamp quit the movie, unhappy with what he perceived as Prince's imperious manner. But Stamp's replacement, Steven Berkoff, developed a grudging respect for his novice director, and everyone seemed to agree that Prince, in contrast to Lambert, brought a highly disciplined and focused atmosphere to the set.

Yet there were more fundamental problems with *Under The Cherry Moon*, most notably its script—a confused, tone-deaf mixture of slapstick comedy and Princely preening. The movie would obviously rise or fall on the acting ability of Prince and

Jerome Benton—a dubious proposition at best, since it had been Morris Day, not Prince, who carried much of *Purple Rain*. And with his very limited experience in directing (he had previously helmed only the "Raspberry Beret" video), the project ultimately proved too much even for Prince. By the time the filming was halfway completed, everyone involved, including Prince, seemed to realize that the wheels were coming off. "What it came down to, I think was a case of the idea being more ambitious than the skills," observed Leeds. "There were some casting problems, scripting problems, and directing problems. You ain't gonna fix them with a night of conversation around the fireplace."

Other signs were mounting that Prince, for all his energy and ideas, had finally spread himself too thin. Shortly before he departed Minneapolis for Nice, his Paisley Park Records released the eponymous debut by the Family. Initially, enthusiasm was high that the Family would be a worthy successor to the Time, Prince's most successful side project to date. But while the Time was oriented principally toward black R&B listeners, the Family was tailored to white New Wave and pop fans. "We've got to go after some of that Duran Duran money," Prince exclaimed to engineer David Rivkin during the sessions, referring to one of the slickest and most successful synth-pop groups of the 1980s.

While Prince recorded all of the basic tracks, including guide vocals for singer Paul Peterson, in a matter of days, the next step proved much more difficult. Listening to the guide, Peterson struggled as ordered to imitate every nuance of Prince's vocals; Rivkin recalled one session where twelve hours were required to complete three lines. By the time Peterson finally finished the album, much of his enthusiasm for the project had disappeared.

Much of the material on the album was strong, showing the focus and experimental flare Prince brought to his music in the mid-eighties. (Standouts included "Nothing Compares 2 U," a ballad that would become a No. 1 hit in 1990 for Sinead O'Connor.) Most of the instruments on the album were played by Prince himself, with Eric Leeds' saxophone and Clare Fischer's strings prominent on several tracks. "I consider it as much a Prince album as anything else he's done," noted Eric.

The lead single, "The Screams Of Passion," generated some interest from radio, but the project as a whole faced a fundamental problem: No one was available to promote it. Band members Jerome Benton and Susannah Melvoin were in Nice (she was eventually summoned back after having been temporarily banished to Minneapolis), meaning that the band could not play concerts. At Prince's Paisley Park Records (which released *The Family*), no one was really in charge, and in truth there was little to be in charge of, as the vanity label was lightly staffed and poorly organized. "Paisley certainly was an unfocused label in its very gestation at that time, and didn't even have a single employee, really," recalled Leeds. And although the label was a subsidiary of Warner Bros., its relationship with the parent company was too poorly defined to make a difference in terms of promotional muscle.

Further, like so many of Prince's satellite projects before and since, the Family represented a futile attempt to have another vocalist imitate his singing style. While the album as a whole has many virtues, Paul Peterson's undistinguished and affected vocals undermine songs like the airy "Screams Of Passion" and the propulsive "High Fashion."

Ultimately, the Family existed only as a front; the album would have been more successful if released (and sung) by Prince himself, rather than through a bogus band. "You cannot put somebody in a certain costume and automatically have them assume that role," said engineer Susan Rogers regarding Paul Peterson's failure to emerge as a credible front man. "It was an impossible task."

As *The Family* quickly faltered, failing to crack the Top 50 of the Pop Chart, a frustrated Paul Peterson called Prince in Nice and announced he was quitting the group. "If you're gonna be in charge of this band, you can't do four million other things at the same time," Peterson shouted. "Yes, I can!" Prince shot back. "I did it with the Time, didn't I? I did it with Sheila E. I did it with Vanity 6." But although Prince and other members of the Family still believed that the project held promise, Peterson could not be convinced to stay. The group came to a quick end with the exit of its designated star. Soon after, a frustrated Prince complained to David Rivkin, "I shouldn't have let him go so far away from me and out of my control."

november 1985: nice

Back in France, the shooting of *Under The Cherry Moon* limped to a close. Even as it became apparent from dailies that the film was not working, Prince composed music for the soundtrack. He involved Wendy and Lisa in this process, renting them an apartment across the English Channel in London, where they recorded frequently at Advision Studios. The duo developed, among other things, an instrumental piece that would become the song "Mountains" on *Parade*. On weekends, Prince frequently joined them for recording sessions, socializing, and clothes-shopping sprees.

On the set in Nice, Prince seemed conflicted about Christopher Tracy, the character he had created for himself to play in the film. This charismatic, sexy, and somewhat snide piano player was hardly a sympathetic figure, and Prince's plan all along had been for Tracy to die at the end of the film, representing his own symbolic transcendence of these character flaws. But Warner Bros., preferring (as film studios invariably do) a happy ending, pushed him to conclude with Tracy reforming and heading off into the sunset with love interest Mary (Scott-Thomas).

The alternative ending was shot, and publicist Howard Bloom, viewing a cut of the film where Tracy survives, found himself believing in the character's redemptive journey. "Warner Bros. insisted on him getting the girl at the end, and it really worked," Bloom remembered. "This little asshole character that was so hard to identify with, you bonded with by the end."

But Prince favored the original ending. In the final cut, Tracy died (the victim of an assassination) with the result, in Bloom's view, that any meaning in the film was also destroyed. From the publicist's perspective, this was another powerful indication that Prince could no longer tolerate his own dark side, the part of his persona most responsible for making him a musical and cultural rebel. "It was a turning point for Prince—he was killing off this character who was part of himself," Bloom observed. "His instincts were with God now—he had created this character who was such a scamp, and he had to kill him."

As work on *Under The Cherry Moon* concluded, Prince also made a fateful decision about the future of his band. At a November wrap party, Susannah Melvoin and Eric Leeds again joined him in Nice, accompanied by guitarist Miko Weaver and bodyguards/dancers Greg Brooks and Wally Safford. All of these confederates had been slated for the live lineup of the Family and after the band's demise had nothing to do. Eric had lunch with Prince and Susannah at the film studio commissary to discuss plans. "Well, what do we do now?" Eric asked Prince.

"Why don't you just come on with us?" he responded, which Eric took to be a formal invitation to join the Revolution. "Sounds good to me!" he said quickly.

Prince's overture, it turned out, extended to all of the ex-Family members, representing a dramatic expansion of the band. Weaver became the third guitarist, joining Prince and Wendy; Susannah was added as a backing vocalist; and Brooks, Safford, and Jerome Benton signed on as dancers. Finally, Leeds' friend Matt Blistan was drafted on trumpet, completing the Revolution's transition from a lean rock outfit into a full-scale, eleven-member R&B ensemble.

Wendy, Lisa, and the other members of the Revolution learned of these changes when they arrived in Nice to shoot a video for "Girls & Boys," a song for *Parade* and the movie. Wendy and Lisa in particular were stunned by this further dilution of their own roles. The Revolution—which they viewed, in significant part, as "their" band—had been commandeered by outside forces and transformed into something radically different than the group that had captured the public's imagination in *Purple Rain*.

During a break in choreography rehearsals for the video, Wendy's emotions bubbled forth in a tirade in the commissary. Sitting at a table with Bobby Z. Rivkin, Matt Fink, Eric Leeds, and Matt Blistan—and with Brooks, Safford, and Benton within easy earshot—she began attacking her boss and, by extension, her new comrades. "Prince is out of his mind, he's ruined everything," she said. Looking at Leeds and Blistan, she said, "At least you guys are musicians, but now we're just an everyday funk band. We look like a circus. Doesn't he know what an ass his fans will think he is?"

Wendy's verbal slaps were clearly directed at the three dancers, who avoided a direct confrontation by ignoring her, but went on ogling female extras in the commissary—behavior that Wendy doubtlessly saw as symbolic of what had changed in the Revolution.

Wendy and Lisa's arrival in Nice also led to another troubling discovery—Sheila E., Susannah's principal rival for Prince's affections, was there for a romantic visit. Wendy and Lisa resented her presence, especially in light of the way Susannah had earlier been sent home from Nice, and they worried that Sheila also coveted Rivkin's position as drummer in the band.

Numerous factors influenced Prince's restructuring of his band. According to Susan Rogers, he had a nebulous concept that the expanded Revolution would embody various groups of "twin" or "triplet" figures—Wendy and Susannah; himself and Miko Weaver; Eric Leeds and Matt Blistan; and the dancers. More concretely, Prince wanted to make productive use of the personnel he had recruited for the Family. Finally, he felt some obligation to reconnect with his R&B roots; after two rock-oriented albums, there were whispers in the media and among fans that Prince had become too "white" in his approach. The presence of dancers and a full horn section made Prince's group reminiscent of classic funk outfits like James Brown's Fabulous Flames.

But whatever the rationale behind his decisions, the swelling of the Revolution changed things irrevocably and placed additional emotional stresses on his core band members. The new arrivals, by contrast, felt they represented the wave of the future. "I started calling the band the counter-Revolution," remembered Eric Leeds. "The name 'Revolution' did not have the same meaning to [Prince] after he expanded the band." The unit that had been so tightly knit during *Purple Rain* was now separated into feuding camps—and even more disturbingly, these factions were to a significant extent broken down along racial lines.

As *Parade* and *Under The Cherry Moon* were completed, matters were proceeding on two tracks—one toward collaboration, the other toward confrontation. Wendy and Lisa, just as they seemed to be making progress toward being accepted as true songwriting partners, found their roles in the live band diminished by the ill-considered expansion of the Revolution. There were also indications that Prince, even as he stretched his songwriting in intriguing new directions, had become dangerously unfocused. *Parade* was in danger of being overshadowed by the boondoggle of *Under The Cherry Moon*, and the implosion of the Family destabilized the Revolution. Plus, he had more girlfriends than he could keep track of and was pitting them against each other. Surrounded by an increasingly large group of band members, lovers, and confidants, Prince was, in many respects, choosing to isolate himself, ignoring mounting signs of trouble and insistently keeping his own counsel—whatever the cost.

CHAPTER EIGHT

Factory

Prince loved being in the Minneapolis area during the springtime, and in 1986 there was something special to celebrate: he was moving into his new home, a ranch-style property in the suburb of Chanhassen. (He gave his previous residence, the famous purple house on Kiowa Trail, to his father, John L. Nelson.) And just a few miles away, construction began on Prince's Paisley Park Studio complex, envisioned as the seat of an expanding musical empire.

Prince's new three-level home (including a basement) sat on a verdant lot that afforded plenty of privacy. A long, circuitous driveway led from a security booth to the home, and the entire thirty-acre property was surrounded with a black fence. The residence itself sat about 200 yards back from the rural street it faced, with the trees that masked the main home adding another layer of protection from the outside world. The exterior was painted yellow with purple balconies and window trim. Inside, the living room (home to Prince's purple piano) extended two stories up to a loft-like roof with exposed wooden beams. His master bedroom included a sitting area overlooking the living room. The rear of the house opened onto a small lake surrounded by woods, and the backyard sported a tennis court, basketball court, and swimming pool.

With its modest size, exposed wood, and lack of high-tech amenities, Prince's new abode felt perhaps more like an upscale ski lodge than a haven for the rich and famous. Indeed, far more money was poured into Paisley Park than his residence. "When I first visited the house, he saw my reaction and said, 'I know, it's kind of small, isn't it?'" remembered Mark Brown. "I said I had expected some marble pillars or something, but he said he didn't go in for that gaudy stuff."

Susannah Melvoin, Prince's primary girlfriend, was going to move in to the new home, representing his first real attempt at cohabitation. She and her close friend Karen Krattinger, now general manager of Prince's organization, took charge of decorating and organizing. Susannah added artsy touches throughout the residence, such as hanging large nude canvasses she had painted. The two women were also given free rein to shop for furnishings. And in what had been a wine cellar, Krattinger meticu-lously organized thousands of videotapes Prince had made of shows and rehearsals. "It became this amazing history of his entire career," she noted.

Prince enjoyed hosting barbecues, sports, and video nights at home. Among the frequent guests were Wendy and Lisa; Alan Leeds, along with his wife, Gwen, and son Tristan; Eric Leeds; and bodyguard/friend Gilbert Davison. During the spring and sum-mer, Prince also gathered friends for softball games and bowling nights throughout Minneapolis. "It was nice for him to be able to incorporate his social life into his home," said Susan Rogers. "He had what he'd always wanted: people around him. They would go upstairs and watch TV or sit in the kitchen for hours telling jokes."

Although $10 million was being poured into the construction of Paisley Park, scheduled for completion in 1987, Prince also had a costly, state-of-the-art studio built in his home and insisted that it be large enough to accommodate group performances, something that had been impossible in his previous home. In the studio control room, Susannah installed stained-glass windows that were illuminated by the morning sun, giving the studio a church-like serenity. Completion of the studio's technical elements fell to Rogers. Working with Westlake Audio of Los Angeles, the contractor designing the facility, she divided the basement of the Chanhassen mansion into a warren of "iso-lation" rooms where band members would set up during sessions. Prince's purple piano, too large for the basement, sat upstairs in the living room and was wired downstairs.

By mid-March, with Rogers still working out the studio's kinks, Prince without warning informed her that the Revolution was coming over to test the facility. They planned to record "Power Fantastic," a song based on a composition by Lisa Coleman called "Carousel." She was reluctant to share the idea—according to Rogers, she and Wendy may have been considering it for a solo project—but after weeks of Prince's cajoling, she had finally let him work with it. Using her chordal melody, he arranged a jazz-like piece full of somber majesty that evoked Miles Davis' *Kind Of Blue*.

As the session began, Rogers discovered the studio was one pair of headphones short and concluded the only person who could spare them was herself. Since Prince was singing in the control room, the main speakers had to be shut off so that the playback would not be picked up by his microphone. Prince preferred to vocalize alone, but allowed Rogers to remain so she could monitor the song's progress. He sang in a corner of the room, his back turned away from her. As the band played, Rogers could hear noth-ing but Prince's falsetto vocal, disembodied from the rest of the song. It was one of the most intimate experiences of her career; she felt at the very center of artistic creation.

Even with Prince's last-minute hatching of a new introduction, the band nailed "Power Fantastic" in one take. Eric Leeds, who played a lilting flute solo, walked out of the studio feeling goosebumps. "That's one of the greatest things we ever did," he remarked; no one disagreed.

"Power Fantastic" was to be one of the cornerstones of Prince's next project, *The Dream Factory*. For the moment, at least, he had decided to carry forward and even amplify the collaborative tenor of *Parade*. As work began, he let everyone stretch out a bit. He composed the lullaby-like ballad "A Place In Heaven" for Lisa to sing and took a day off while she completed the vocals on her own. When Lisa composed a solo piano piece, entitled "Visions," Prince surprised everyone by slotting it as the opening cut of *The Dream Factory*. Two quirky pop songs, "Teacher, Teacher" and "It's A Wonderful Day," included prominent vocal and songwriting contributions by Wendy and Lisa. "In A Large Room With No Light," a dense and busy jazz-fusion piece, featured live playing by most of the Revolution and drumming by Sheila E., whom Prince favored over Rivkin for such complex numbers. Susannah was put in charge of the album's cover art, which had a homemade look and included contributions from everyone in the band, with each member scrawling pictures and words that would appear on the front or back cover.

The collaborative ethos carried over to rehearsal sessions, which were often dominated by sweaty jams. Mark Brown recalls one improvisation lasting so long that he made a sandwich and snacked on it even as he kept thwacking away at his instrument to keep the groove going. No one could seem to get enough of playing. "I think that my greatest memories of my musical career are of rehearsals that were spectacular, not shows," Rivkin recalled. "It was an exciting, exciting time."

For Wendy and Lisa in particular, things had moved back in a direction they preferred. Prince's frustrating expansion of the band into the unit that Eric Leeds wryly dubbed "the counter-Revolution" hadn't diminished their roles in the recording studio; in fact, they were being given more latitude than ever before. While Eric Leeds was a new and important contributor to Prince's music, the other added members of the band guitarist Miko Weaver and the three dancers, Jerome Benton, Wally Safford, and Greg Brooks—rarely contributed to new recordings. Wendy's power within the group increased, as Prince made her the de facto second in-command, letting her run rehearsals on days he did not attend. "Her musical discipline, articulate assertiveness, and work ethic clearly made her the logical and most effective candidate, and deep down the whole band knew that," noted Alan Leeds.

Prince's openness to the influence of others also extended to his continued study of jazz. Eric Leeds, who often lent Prince albums, found him fascinated with John Coltrane's *Love Supreme* and classics from Duke Ellington's *Live At Newport*, such as "Diminuendo And Crescendo In Blue." Miles Davis remained a growing inspiration; when Leeds mentioned one day at rehearsal that the great horn player had complimented Prince in a recent interview, Prince was deeply touched. "You know, Eric, that's what makes it worthwhile, when someone like that says something," he said.

Given the apparent mutual admiration, associates of both musicians were hopeful that a collaboration might materialize. When Miles moved from Columbia to Warner Bros. Records in 1985, the idea seemed even more possible, and a meeting between him and Prince was arranged.

After completing *Parade*, Prince recorded "Can I Play With U?," which he sent to Miles along with a note urging him to add whatever he liked. Miles cut a horn part but didn't seem particularly inspired by the pedestrian song, and after receiving it back, Prince decided not to release it. Still, their affection for each other's work remained strong. "Prince does so many things, it's almost like he can do it all," Miles would write in his 1989 autobiography, *Miles*. "Plus he plays his ass off as well as sings and writes...For me, he can be the new Duke Ellington of our time if he just keeps at it." They would appear together onstage once, in a performance at Paisley Park in 1987, and Prince would continue to send Miles tracks from time to time, some of which were performed live. (For example, Miles and his band performed an instrumental take on "Movie Star," a then-unreleased Prince number, during his 1987 tour.)

Still, according to Alan Leeds, who helped arrange the initial meeting between the two musicians, Miles would have preferred a face-to-face collaboration over Prince's favored practice of sending tapes through the mail. As would often be the case when Prince worked with prominent musicians, he seemed reluctant to proceed in a fashion that might have required artistic compromise. "Up until his illness and death, Miles continued romancing the idea of an eventual album collaboration with Prince— an idea Prince never rejected but never brought himself to take seriously enough to commence writing or recording together," Leeds said. "Instead, Prince made periodic offers of various tracks. Miles held out, wishing for the opportunity to actually work together. Alas, it never happened."

A few days after recording "Can I Play With U?," Prince undertook a series of jazz-like jams at Sunset Sound with Eric Leeds, Sheila E. on drums, and Levi Seacer, Jr. (a member of Sheila's own band), on bass. These sessions represented one of the few examples of genuinely democratic collaboration in Prince's career, as he, and everyone else present, threw out ideas that straddled the border of jazz and funk. "He was dealing with musicians of a very high caliber," recalled Eric. "Water seeks its own level, and I think he was finding the better quality of water." Various instrumental numbers were recorded, and Prince seriously considered releasing some of them under the anonymous banner of a group called the Flesh.

Sadly, this interesting project was tabled, and Prince began to turn inward with respect to his jazz excursions. Playing all the basic instruments by himself, he recorded an album of instrumentals and had Eric Leeds overdub saxophone parts. Eric, while pleased to be involved in the new project, had found the Flesh sessions much more galvanizing. "What had been a dialogue between musicians now became a script," he remarked later.

The album, released under the name of the fictional group Madhouse and called simply 8 (it contained eight songs, with each identified by a number rather than a name), was released in January 1987 without any credits. While Prince's involvement was at first denied by his management, eventually word leaked out that he and Leeds were the sole players. Considering the absence of vocals, the album did quite well, reaching No. 25 on the Black Chart. The single "6" even became a hit on the Black Singles Chart, climbing to No. 5. Still, 8, while in some respects a tribute to Prince's instrumental virtuosity, demonstrates a rather superficial understanding of jazz. "While the record might have a certain charm, I personally never thought much of it," said Eric Leeds. "I never felt that it was a real jazz LP, but more like 'play-acting' as a jazz LP."

The initial concealment of his involvement in 8, according to Susan Rogers, stemmed from Prince's desire to avoid being seen as obsessed with music, which, of course, he was. "He created this Prince character, and he doesn't want the public to think of him as just a workaholic," she observed. "It was important to his image that he not be seen as somebody who was in the studio all of the time."

As work continued on *The Dream Factory* during spring 1986, the jovial, collaborative atmosphere that had at first surrounded the project gradually dissipated. Of the various ways that Prince reminded Wendy and Lisa that he was still in charge, perhaps the most hurtful was his failure to fully credit their songwriting contributions. The most recent example of song pilfering occurred on the album *Parade*; when Wendy and Lisa reviewed the album's cover art, they discovered that Prince withheld individual songwriting credit for them on "Mountains" and "Sometimes It Snows In April," pieces for which they had composed much of the music. As a result of such incidents, they became increasingly reluctant to share their ideas with Prince, and began stockpiling material for a possible solo career.

Another of their concerns was the emotional health of Susannah. After the painful incident in which Prince had sent her home from France during the filming of *Under The Cherry Moon*, the couple were trying to repair their fragile relationship. Although she agreed to move into the new home, Prince's resistance to monogamy remained a consistent problem; Susannah had been made aware of his dalliances in Nice, and her patience was diminishing. Back in Minnesota, Prince continued to sleep with, among others, Sheila E., Jill Jones, and actress Troy Beyer, whom he had met in Los Angeles.

On some level, Prince felt threatened by Susannah's education and worldliness; when he recorded a song called "The Ballad Of Dorothy Parker," for example, it fell to Susannah to tell him that Dorothy Parker was a renowned American poet. The name "Dorothy Parker" had apparently reached him as a snippet of popular culture, and he penned the song without knowing exactly who she was. "Crystal Ball," recorded by Prince on his own for *The Dream Factory*, contains the lines "My baby draws pictures of sex/All over the walls in graphic detail—sex!" a reference to the large nudes Susannah had hung in his home. With little knowledge of art, Prince had trouble understanding nakedness outside a sexual context, and the song finds him struggling to relate to his lover and her work.

Although Prince bought Susannah an engagement ring, the notion of lifelong commitment frightened him, leading to his wildly inconsistent behavior toward her. It was widely felt among Prince's associates that he did love Susannah deeply, but nonetheless felt unprepared for a more conventional relationship. He privately told production designer Roy Bennett that he felt overwhelmed by his feelings for her and worried that the relationship could cause him to quit playing music.

Susannah, despite the oscillations in the relationship, struggled to make it work. "She loved him unconditionally," observed her friend Karen Krattinger. But cohabitation did not agree with Prince, and after just a few months of living together, he told Susannah he wanted her out. But, riddled with ambivalence (or to put it less kindly, wanting to have it both ways), he convinced her to rent an apartment a short drive away. "He wanted her in his life, but he couldn't go to sleep and wake up with the same person everyday," Rogers recalled.

Although he refused to be faithful, the idea of Susannah with another man nonetheless outraged Prince. Shortly after she moved into his home, he recorded "Big Tall Wall" (which remains unreleased) describing a relationship in which Prince wants to effectively imprison his lover. The song's description of a "stone circle so you can't get out" refers to the apartment complex where Prince installed Susannah, a development of converted silos in Minneapolis' Lake Calhoun district.

The twists in the relationship left Susannah angry and exhausted, and she wrestled with leaving Prince and Minneapolis altogether. The lovers' conflicts also placed stress on Prince's relationship with Wendy and Lisa. When he arrived at the studio in a foul mood, they could tell he had been fighting with Susannah the night before. They also knew that even as Prince demanded loyalty from Susannah, he was dating other women, and they saw him as a hypocrite. Susannah's pain became difficult for Wendy and Lisa to ignore, even as they struggled to separate the personal and professional elements of the conflict.

There were other clouds on the horizon as well, most notably the release of *Under The Cherry Moon*. Advance word about the film among Hollywood insiders was uniformly negative, and Prince knew that his parallel career as an actor/filmmaker stood to suffer serious damage if the movie flopped, as now seemed likely. One evening at his new home, the notoriously controlled Prince exploded with emotion, laying down on the floor and screaming at Susannah that he hated the movie.

As rehearsals began for upcoming tours in support of *Parade*, Wendy and Lisa again became frustrated about Prince's augmentation of the Revolution. "We've gone from being the Beatles to being an overblown R&B band," Wendy blurted out during one session. The vision that she and Lisa had of a small, intimate ensemble where they shared the spotlight with Prince seemed to have been obliterated. Things got even worse as, over roughly a month between June and July 1986, Prince unilaterally made changes to *The Dream Factory*, replacing collaborative efforts (including "Power Fantastic," "It's A Wonderful Day," and "Teacher, Teacher") with solo compositions. Seemingly less invested in the project, he also booked a series of live engagements dubbed The Hit and Run Tour, which took the band to Detroit, Louisville, and elsewhere. He periodically flew alone to Los Angeles, recording songs for side projects at Sunset Sound Studios in Hollywood and seeing girlfriends, including actress Sherilyn Fenn, who would later become famous for her work on the television series *Twin Peaks*. He was not always missed; when he disappeared to the West Coast after instructing Wendy, Lisa, and Susannah to complete the song "Witness For The Prosecution," the atmosphere in the studio suddenly felt light and breezy.

When he returned, the fighting continued, particularly with Wendy; according to Susan Rogers, spats between the bandleader and guitarist were a "weekly if not daily occurrence." One rehearsal at the Washington Avenue warehouse degenerated into a shouting match between Prince and Wendy and Lisa, according to Matt Fink. "You fucking lesbians, you're gonna rot in hell for your lifestyle!" Prince screamed. "You're a fucking womanizer," retorted Wendy. "You're such a prick and a control freak. You're just a womanizing pig."

The ongoing pattern of lacerating incidents—the fights, his withholding of song credits, his cruelty towards Susannah—had finally driven Wendy and Lisa to the edge. Fed up, they visited the mansion and demanded that things change and that they be treated as creative equals. Prince refused them point-blank. Not surprisingly, it seemed that his notion of making *The Dream Factory* a genuinely group-oriented project had simply been another short-lived whim.

What happened to cause Prince to back away so forcefully and abruptly from what was shaping up as the most group-oriented (and not coincidentally one of the most interesting) records of his career? Simply put, the ascendancy of the Revolution threatened him. For several years—since the commencement of the *Purple Rain* project—Prince had struggled with how best to draw on the talents of his band members without allowing his career to become dependent on them.

march 31, 1986: release of parade

After the somewhat disappointing sales performance of *Around The World In A Day*, Prince and his management were hungry for a hit, and the success of the single "Kiss" (which reached No. 1 on the Pop Singles Chart) gave them hope that *Parade: Music From Under The Cherry Moon* would also take off. At the same time, Warner Bros. worried that the album's sheer eclecticism and many experimental touches might hinder its commercial potential.

Indeed, coming from an artist who just two years earlier had been the most commercially successful figure in all of pop music, *Parade* is a remarkably challenging album. While this prevented it from becoming a massive success, it was also key in helping Prince build a sophisticated and loyal following. Like only a handful of other major pop artists in the mid-eighties, he sold enough records to keep him on the airwaves and television screens while at the same time demonstrating consistent artistic growth. Other artists in this category—who not coincidentally would also enjoy long and fruitful careers—included the Police, U2, Bruce Springsteen, and Madonna. The Police, led by the prolific Sting, blended reggae, rock, and New Wave into a unique sound, while U2, relying on the adventurous guitar work of Bono, took basic pop songs in sonically intriguing directions. Springsteen, despite being in a hit-making period that was one of the least interesting of his long career, continued to pen lyrics that showed rare honesty and integrity. And Madonna—while she had yet to convincingly remake herself into the more serious artist she would be recognized as following 1987's *Like A Prayer*—remained arguably the most disciplined and focused entertainer in pop.

These were Prince's competitors, in part for record sales but also for the unofficial title of the most influential and relevant figure in contemporary music. And that he so convincingly matched them (and often bested them) was a major reason why his stature among critics and other musicians continued to rise even as his record sales declined. *Parade* was an equally convincing artistic statement as recent important records like U2's *The Unforgettable Fire* (1984) or the Police's *Synchronicity* (1983). In popular music—a field where vapidity and commercial artifice usually proved more saleable than genuine art—he remained that rare figure who refused to compromise.

Demonstrating Prince's interest in jazz and psychedelia, *Parade* is one of the most collaborative albums of his career and features important contributions from Wendy, Lisa, and others. Although inconsistent, its patchiness is part of the album's charm. It is a pleasure to see Prince exploring new directions, even where these excursions fall a bit short. In addition to the stunning "Kiss," classic tracks from *Parade* include the relaxed funk workout "Girls & Boys" (featuring playful horn work by Eric Leeds) and the ultra-catchy rock number "Anotherloverholeinyohead." "New Position" is a spare piece of funk, and the dense "Mountains" finds Prince's stylings melding with the sixties influences introduced by Wendy and Lisa. *Parade* is among Prince's most interesting records and documents his quest to understand himself and the musicians then most important in his life, Wendy and Lisa.

Critics, while noting its inconsistency, generally praised *Parade* and saw in the album continuing signs that Prince's talents might be boundless. "Who but Prince fills us today with the kind of anticipation we once reserved for new work by Bob Dylan, the Beatles and the Rolling Stones?" began Davitt Sigerson's review in *Rolling Stone*, again making clear how much hope the critical establishment had invested in Prince's success. The *Detroit Free Press* called the album "a confirmation of Prince's place as a superior melodist, arranger and player as well as a celebration of his creativity."

As some at Warner Bros. had feared, sales in the United States were rather disappointing, topping out at just under two million. But as Prince's reputation as an innovator grew, so did his commercial success in Europe and other places more open to challenging artists; *Parade* sold another two million abroad. The album's overall performance showed that while Prince had fallen a long way from the stratospheric height of *Purple Rain*, he was building a rock-solid base of fans across the globe.

july 1, 1986: sheridan, wyoming

Finally, the day arrived that Prince had been dreading: the premiere of *Under The Cherry Moon*. For a musician who claimed to be driven more by art than commerce, the event was a reminder of the sometimes crass promotional activities that must accompany endeavors like a feature film. Warner Bros.' movie division and MTV sponsored a bizarre contest, the winner of which would have the film's premiere held in his or her hometown and be escorted to the event by Prince himself. The winning entrant—the ten-thousandth caller to an MTV hotline—was Lisa Barber, a twenty-year-old hotel chambermaid in Sheridan, Wyoming, a city of about 10,000 people, where entertainment generally meant hunting or fishing.

For its corporate sponsors, the selection of Sheridan provided an opportunity to demonstrate that Prince could still captivate fans in America's heartland. But despite the marketing hype—or perhaps because of it—the band's mood was anything but festive as they arrived for the event. No one really wanted to be in Sheridan, and certainly not at the drab Holiday Inn where the post-screening party was to be held. On the day of the premiere, a seemingly minor incident occurred that led to a meltdown. Wendy cracked open a beer in her room at the hotel and, upon exiting, bumped into Prince in the hallway. Outraged that any band member would drink in this quasi-public setting, he informed Wendy that she would be fined $500. Wendy said nothing, but something snapped for her, and this infantilizing incident became a metaphor for Prince's insistence on controlling not only their music and image, but even their personal behavior. On the spot, she resolved to leave the band.

The film's premiere went forward that afternoon at Centennial Theatre in Sheridan's modest downtown. Prince showed up in the same outfit he had worn on the cover of *Parade*—tight black pants with large white buttons, and a matching black half-shirt that left his small, flat belly exposed. True to his promise, he served as Lisa Barber's date. Before picking her up in a limousine, he sent over a clothier and make-up artist to package her for the event.

Those in attendance at the theater, a peculiar mixture of several hundred of Barber's Wyoming friends and celebrities flown in by Prince on two Lear jets, found common ground in their distaste for the film. "I couldn't figure out what was going on," said one Sheridan resident afterward, speaking for many. During the screening, Prince briefly put his arm around Lisa Barber, but otherwise interacted little with either her or the crowd.

By the time the band was on a plane headed back to Minneapolis, early reviews had arrived, plunging Prince into gloom and casting a pall over the flight. The notices were negative, often laceratingly so: The *New York Times,* for example, called his character in the film "a self-caressing twerp of dubious provenance." Wrote Glen Lovell in the *San Jose Mercury News:* "The last time I can remember such an outrageous, unmitigated display of narcissism was when Barbra Streisand discovered she could do it all, and cranked out celluloid monuments to herself, like *A Star Is Born.*"

A distressed Prince continued obsessing about *Cherry Moon,* so much so that he failed to heed signals that his band was falling apart. Assessing their situation once more, Wendy and Lisa concluded that the downsides of remaining with Prince simply outweighed the benefits. His repeated failures to credit their songwriting contributions, the transformation of the Revolution, the cruel treatment of Susannah, and, finally, the $500 that indeed turned up missing from Wendy's weekly paycheck as a result of her "public drinking" added up to a disturbing picture. Still, they knew that a decision to leave Prince was not without serious consequences, given that *The Dream Factory* had just been completed and mastered. Despite Prince's late excision of some of the more collaborative material, the record remained a showcase for their influence on his music. Lisa's "Visions" commenced the album, and her lead vocal on "A Place In Heaven" remained intact. Wendy demonstrated her talents on a solo guitar interlude. They understood that their departure could lead to the suppression of this material and that an uncertain professional life lay in their post-Prince future. Just the same, they were ready to walk away and begin planning a solo career.

Later in July, Wendy and Lisa showed up at Prince's home and said they wanted out. While aware of their growing dissatisfaction, Prince never believed that they might actually quit, and now faced a logistical problem, as a tour of Europe and Japan was about to begin in support of *Parade.* With *Cherry Moon* failing at the box office, postponing the tour would likely doom the album's commercial prospects.

The entire situation was coming unglued. Mark Brown felt woefully underpaid and was troubled by his ever-shrinking role in the band; even at the height of the *Dream Factory* sessions, he had felt a bit like an outsider, as Prince never considered him a contributor on the level of Wendy and Lisa. He also still smarted over his lack of credit for the hit "Kiss." Finally, the setup for the *Parade* show confined him to the very back of the stage, hidden by the rest of the group and the dancers. "I was behind the piano, next to [drummer] Bobby Z., and behind three guys that used to be the bodyguards," Brown noted. "I started feeling a little unappreciated." He had just been offered $3,500 a week to tour with Stevie Nicks (Prince was paying about a third of that), and told Prince he might forego the *Parade* tour in favor of this opportunity.

Alan Leeds moved quickly to save the tour. Although he sympathized with Wendy and Lisa, professional considerations dictated that he try to convince them to stay. After learning of their plans to quit from Rivkin, he drove to their rented Minneapolis apartment and persuaded them to rejoin the Revolution. Just the same, everyone was aware that a Rubicon had been crossed, making a long-term reconciliation between Prince and his two best friends unlikely. Brown also agreed to stay for the tour only after Prince pleaded with him.

As the tour got underway, Rivkin also felt a distance growing between himself and Prince. Sheila E., whose band was the opening act on the Japanese leg of the *Parade* tour, often sat in with the Revolution on drums during sound checks. Despite being the longest-serving member of the band, Rivkin had never really bonded with Prince on a personal level the way Sheila E. did, and now sensed his job might be in jeopardy.

Most of the band found the *Parade* tour highly satisfying, at least from a purely musical perspective. A fifteen-date European swing put the band before a total of 120,000 people in London, Paris, Rotterdam, Stockholm, Hamburg, and other cities, and, in contrast to the regimented *Purple Rain* tour, these shows allowed for improvisation and variation of the set. Some of the songs took on a jazzy orientation, such as "Anotherloverholeinyohead," which became a forum for Lisa's radiant piano soloing and the intersecting horn lines of Eric Leeds and Blistan. The feelings of artistic connection made Wendy and Lisa wonder whether their relationship with Prince might be worth rescuing after all. Offstage, though, Prince's treatment of the women was aloof, making it clear that their abortive departure before the tour had wounded him. Other people did not leave him, he told them when the relationship was over.

Beyond the music, other elements of the show—particularly the three dancers—were more controversial among Prince's brain trust. Manager Steve Fargnoli, like Wendy and Lisa, had reservations about the change in focus from a basic pop-rock group to a sprawling funk revue. The entire visual thrust of Prince's live act had changed, going from a quirky, androgynous scene dominated by him and Wendy to a more traditional spectacle of R&B showmanship. Fargnoli believed something had been lost.

In London, Prince encountered a fifteen-year-old girl named Anna Garcia who very much fit his paradigm of female beauty—she was part Hispanic and had a seductive beauty not unlike that of Vanity and Apollonia. The attraction between Prince and Garcia was immediate, and they spent a long night talking together in a hotel room. But Prince, seemingly mindful of the potential consequences, made no sexual advances whatsoever. He did, however, leave his contact information with her and promised to stay in touch. Her bubbly energy intrigued him, and he began to formulate ideas for a side project based around Garcia.

After completing the European leg of the tour, the band headed for Japan, where ticket sales and audience responses were also strong. From all outward appearances, Prince and the Revolution were at the top of their game and remained a tightly knit unit. In truth, arguably the most interesting backing group of Prince's career was about to come to an end.

They concluded the tour before a raucous crowd of 50,000 people at Yokohama Stadium on September 9, 1986. Wendy, Lisa, Rivkin, and Mark Brown would never again perform in front of such a huge audience. The band finished the set with an encore of "Sometimes It Snows In April," the ballad which Wendy and Lisa had helped compose, but received no credit for on *Parade*. As Prince and the band rode back to their hotel, the atmosphere in the limousine was tense and freighted with finality. Prince, a towel wrapped around his neck, appeared exhausted and said nothing. Alan Leeds, who had managed to keep the band together long enough to complete the tour, looked over and knew there was nothing more he could do.

october 7, 1986: beverly hills

Following the tour, Prince and select members of his entourage fled the coming Minnesota winter and headed for southern California. Just days after the move, he invited Wendy and Lisa to his rented home in Beverly Hills for an evening of dinner and shooting pool. Recreation was the last thing on his mind, however. After dinner, Prince excused himself and placed a phone call to Rivkin in Minneapolis, where it was two-thirty in the morning. Prince quickly came to the point: The drummer was being replaced by Sheila E. "You're the man and you've done a great job," Prince said, trying to soften the blow. "We're gonna be friends forever. I'm gonna honor your contract." Rivkin, tired after years of non stop touring and recording and aware that Sheila E. was better suited to Prince's increasingly complicated music, accepted the decision with equanimity. "[Sheila E.] was one of the five best drummers in the world, in my opinion," he said later. "I was replaced by someone who was one of a kind." Rivkin describes Prince's firing of him as "totally admirable, totally kosher, totally man-to-man."

After hanging up, Prince returned to Wendy and Lisa at the dinner table and told them that he was disbanding the Revolution and that they too were being fired. He said he wanted to return to recording music on his own as a "one-man band." They were surprised, if not entirely shocked; in the previous months, it had become clear that their bond with Prince was broken beyond repair.

Although Rivkin appreciated the rationale behind his own dismissal, the ousting of Wendy and Lisa seemed less explicable, given their central importance in Prince's personal and professional lives (which have never truly been separate). "I really don't understand, to this day, what happened when he let Wendy and Lisa go," Rivkin said. "It's the old expression of getting too close, I think. I always knew how to maintain a distance, to keep a job and keep Prince happy. But they got really close, and probably made music too much together or something. He wanted to take it back, so he let them go." Matt Fink, whom Prince invited to remain in the band, also considered the decision to dismiss Wendy and Lisa a mistake, believing that Lisa's evocative piano style, in particular, would prove irreplaceable.

Alan Leeds, while mindful of the musical consequences, was less surprised by Prince's decision. He knew that Prince associated particular projects with the personalities involved, and that his feelings about Wendy and Lisa had become completely negative. By disbanding the Revolution, Prince sought to purge these emotions, and after Wendy and Lisa departed, friends and colleagues who remained were told not even to mention their names.

Brown departed voluntarily to seek solo success despite being asked by Prince to stay. Aside from Fink, Prince had lost or exiled a group of musicians that had been a part of his identity from *Purple Rain* onward, and the repercussions were immediate. He canceled release of *The Dream Factory* and shelved other material he had developed with the Revolution, arguably his most creative colleagues ever. Most of this music remains unreleased.

Complete copies of the final, mastered version of *The Dream Factory* are available on the bootleg market (much to the chagrin of Prince, who resents circulation of his outtakes). Had the record been officially released, it might have been greeted with even greater critical fervor than *Sign O' The Times*, the album that supplanted it. (The two records share several cuts in common.) *The Dream Factory* is Prince's loopiest, most eclectic album by a significant margin, and shows him continuing to stake out remarkably inventive turf for a major pop star. Following "Visions," Lisa's reflective piano instrumental, the album kicks into the title track, a raucous slice of funk-rock featuring multiple vocal tracks by Prince, some speeded up, others slowed down. The album includes hybrids of blues and psychedelia ("Strange Relationship" and "Train"); a complex, suite-like composition with no less than twenty-four distinct musical sections ("Crystal Ball"); a waltz in 3/4 time ("A Place In Heaven"); and a blistering, Rolling Stones–like rock number ("Witness For The Prosecution"). The concluding piece, "All My Dreams," is the aural equivalent of a day at Disneyland, with carnivalesque organs, all manner of electronically treated vocals and sound effects, and references to Cap'n Crunch and submarines. Perhaps most surprising is that *The Dream Factory* remains coherent despite ranging across so much territory; while its musical scope brings to mind the Beatles' *White Album*, it is a more unified work. As brilliant as *Sign O' The Times* would prove to be, *The Dream Factory* is equally impressive, and its shelving was one of many unfortunate consequences of the Revolution's demise.

Prince's home studio fell into disuse shortly after he disbanded the group. He completed *Sign O' The Times* in Los Angeles, and afterward began using almost exclusively the Paisley Park complex, which became operational in late 1987. He eventually converted the control booth of the home studio into a pool room.

Although many of the musicians Prince would employ in the future were more accomplished instrumentalists than Wendy, Lisa, Brown, and Rivkin, the creative triumphs of the Revolution illustrate the axiom that in pop and rock music, passion counts for more than musical chops. As musicians (and people), Wendy and Lisa were playful, open-minded, and opinionated—qualities that would be missing in many of Prince's future band members, notwithstanding their technical proficiency. "The songs we did with Wendy and Lisa," Eric Leeds noted, "included some of the most wonderful stuff we ever did."

CHAPTER NINE

ALONE

A s the post-Revolution era began, Prince found himself with a host of problems, both personal and professional, to address. *Under The Cherry Moon* had tanked, calling into question whether the promise he had shown with *Purple Rain* would ever be realized. The Family had disintegrated after Paul Peterson's defection, leaving Prince without a meaningful side project. And by firing Wendy and Lisa, he had excised from his life his closest friends and principal creative collaborators. These departing bandmates had become fixed in the public mind as a part of his image, with the two of them together providing an intriguing musical and visual counterpoint to Prince. Now, as their absence sunk in, Prince felt a growing loneliness as well as a compulsion to prove to the world he could thrive without them.

The bar was high. Prince's previous two albums, *Around The World In A Day* and *Parade*, both featuring important contributions from Wendy and Lisa, had engendered critical fervor and solidified a passionate international following. True, his record sales had fallen off significantly since *Purple Rain*—something that began to concern Prince and his management team, especially after the *Under the Cherry Moon* debacle—but as a pioneering musician and songwriter, his star was still on the rise. Not just a multi-platinum-selling celebrity, he was recognized as a bona fide artist capable of reinventing himself with each successive album. But with Wendy and Lisa gone and the Revolution disbanded, could the run keep going?

Prince wanted to answer this question unequivocally by creating a landmark album that would silence all doubters. Not two weeks after dismissing Wendy and Lisa, Prince in October 1986 returned to the familiar surroundings of Sunset Sound's Studio 3 and resumed writing with an intensity that was unusual even for him. The atmosphere was austere and distraction-free. A year earlier, during the recording of *Parade*, the Sunset complex had percolated with the activities of his associates. But now, the core group had shrunk down to just Prince and engineer Susan Rogers. When they weren't in Los Angeles, the duo spent most of their time working in Prince's studio in the basement of his new home in Chanhassen, Minnesota. To Rogers, who worked with Prince almost around the clock, it seemed that he was avoiding feelings of isolation through compulsive activity.

But whatever his motivation—genuine inspiration, a need to escape reality, or the competitive desire to top his recent work with Wendy Melvoin and Lisa Coleman— Prince continued to create some of his most imaginative and galvanizing music ever. In fact, the period from March 1986, when he embarked on *The Dream Factory* project, through the end of the year, when he completed the landmark album *Sign O' The Times*, arguably constitutes the very peak of Prince's career. Not only focused and primed, he was also—to an extent that would rarely be the case during his wilderness period from 1990 to 2000—concerned more with artistry than commercial success.

Various tributaries were flowing into Prince's river of creativity. For several years he had been encouraging friends and associates to expose him to musical forms outside of his funk-pop vocabulary, including jazz and psychedelic rock. He had enthusiastically explored such styles, albeit with mixed results, on his two most recent albums. But now that Prince had assimilated most of what interested him, his excursions into different genres became more assured, his experimentation more natural. He had always been confident in his ability to incorporate new ideas—in his mind, it was but a short step from listening to Miles Davis to actually composing with him— but now, the influence of precursors like Miles and the Beatles began to affect his music in a way that sounded less strained and more organic.

Like the material from *Around The World In A Day* and *Parade*, Prince's recordings from fall 1986 incorporated new approaches—the funky cut "Hot Thing" used a recurring keyboard embellishment that sounded simultaneously psychedelic and Middle Eastern, while the rocker "I Could Never Take The Place Of Your Man" echoed sixties surf pop—and yet, this music was unmistakably Prince, bearing his trademarks of minimalism and unresolved tension. He also became even more adept at using the recording studio as an instrument in itself, and sometimes new sounds and textures emerged in the studio by happenstance, as he proved willing to follow wherever "mistakes" brought him. For instance, "The Ballad Of Dorothy Parker," the first song recorded in his new home studio, got its mid-range-dominated sound as a result of a technical glitch. While Prince and engineer Susan Rogers were working, a snowstorm caused a power outage. When the lights came back on and work resumed, the playbacks seemed to Rogers dull and murky; Prince, in a creative trance, did not notice, and Rogers was hesitant to interrupt the session. But when she checked the equipment after he went to bed, Rogers found that, as a result of the blackout, the soundboard had been running on half of its recommended wattage, robbing "Dorothy Parker" of its high end and giving the song a distant and subdued feel. Learning of the problem the next day, Prince treated it as serendipity, deciding that the offbeat sound added character.

Later, at Sunset Sound during the recording of the avant-garde funk number "If I Was Your Girlfriend," Rogers committed a rare technical error that caused Prince's vocal to distort on certain words. "I thought he was going to rip my head off," Rogers remembers. But when Prince came into the control booth to hear the playback, he seemed to like the effect, which is present on the released version. The song would become yet another memorable cut on *Sign O' The Times*.

Yet another studio accident shaped "Forever In My Life," a ballad comprising nothing more than several tracks of vocals, a percussion pattern composed on the Linn LM-1, and sprinkles of acoustic guitar. Before singing, Prince asked Rogers to mute his previously recorded backing vocal; upon playback, it was apparent that he had begun late, and that his lead vocal thus lagged behind the rest of the music. Again, Prince found the results of the blunder worth keeping.

Along with the new material he was developing at Sunset Sound and in his home studio, Prince had a cache of strong songs culled from the shelved *Dream Factory* album. Although Prince wanted to avoid releasing numbers that featured input from Wendy and Lisa or other band members, he planned to use several of his solo compositions from the discarded album. The arsenal was full for the career-defining masterpiece Prince wanted to uncork.

Audacity defined Prince's most influential works, and he wanted his next album to be every bit as controversial as earlier classics like *1999* and *Purple Rain*. And—perhaps seeking an even clearer break with the music and identity developed with the Revolution—he became obsessed with the notion of redefining himself. After discovering a production gimmick that sped up his voice, Prince conceived of an alter-ego named "Camille" based around this technique. During a nine-day period at Sunset Sound, he recorded five songs for an album called *Camille*. And over cocktails at Tramps, a Los Angeles nightclub, Prince told saxophonist Eric Leeds of an idea for a film in which Prince would play two characters, one being the "evil Camille." At the end of the film it would be revealed that the two were one and the same, and that the protagonist had a split personality.

If the film concept (which was never pursued) was just a glimmer in Prince's mind, the notion of a "Camille" album was more concrete, and he rapidly sequenced a record that included only tracks using the speeded-up vocal sound. But he soon discarded that idea and planned something even more outlandish: a three-album set. Very few major artists had ever released three records at once, with George Harrison's *All Things Must Pass* and the Clash's *Sandinista* being among the handful of examples at the time. Prince found a worthy challenge in the creation of such a magnum opus, recalled Alan Leeds, who remained one of Prince's closest confidants after the departure of Wendy and Lisa. "He knew that just having the balls to do three records would create a big bang," Leeds said. And he would do it as a one-man band, playing nearly every instrument on one of the longest albums of all time.

Prince remained in virtual lockdown mode at Sunset Sound as he worked to complete the project. Among his next efforts were "Adore," a gospel ballad comparable to the best of Al Green, and the punkish-but-quirky "Play In The Sunshine." As he worked, other intriguing new influences emerged in his music. Prince had been listening to the ethereal, highly melodic compositions of Kate Bush and Peter Gabriel, becoming particularly enthralled by Bush's brilliant "Cloudbusting." As always, he remained influenced by Joni Mitchell and made a lyrical reference to her song "Help Me" in his own song "The Ballad Of Dorothy Parker." When he played new cuts for associates, they immediately realized they were hearing some of his strongest material ever; Prince's legendary work habits and discipline were melding with an increasingly deeper understanding of other strains of pop music.

The three-album set was entitled *Crystal Ball*, after a complex, suite-like song that he considered one of the most profound lyrical and musical statements of his career. The lyrics addressed a recurring theme in Prince's work—his worries about war. The inspiration for "Crystal Ball" came from the U.S. bombing of Libya in Spring 1986, an event that prompted Prince to cut short a trip to Europe. The song's reference to "little babies in makeup [who] terrorize the Western world" seems a direct allusion to the Libyan dictator Muammar el-Qaddafi. As he did in "1999," Prince argues in the song that unrestrained hedonism is the only reasonable response to worries about death.

As with *The Family* project in 1984, Prince sent "Crystal Ball" to orchestral composer Clare Fischer for extensive overdubbing. He included a note explaining the importance of the song, which Fischer and his son and writing partner, Brett, took as license to indulge themselves fully. After transcribing the music of the sprawling piece, which featured excursions into reggae, syncopated jazz, and various strains of funk, the Fischers added horns, strings, and percussion. The sixty-piece orchestra included eight French horns.

As his bold new album took shape, Prince began previewing it for friends. "He just loved playing music for people when he had their undivided attention," recalled Leeds. "You would get in his car with him, maybe drive to a Dairy Queen and get an ice cream, and then just sit and listen to the sequence of a new album." In the past, Prince often seemed open to feedback on minor issues like track sequence, but not in the case of *Crystal Ball*. "His attitude was, 'Don't mess with me, this is it!'" Leeds recalled.

With the album nearly finished, Prince took a rare night off to celebrate Thanksgiving with Susannah Melvoin, with whom he continued a turbulent romance even after firing Wendy and Lisa. Susan Rogers, whom Prince also invited, arrived at his rented Beverly Hills house expecting a large, festive crowd; she found no one but a tired Prince and his girlfriend. "After dinner we watched some videos, and he fell asleep on the couch," Rogers remembered. "That was Thanksgiving."

A number of the songs slated for *Crystal Ball* had been directly inspired by Susannah. "The Ballad Of Dorothy Parker," recorded after a fight between the couple, relates how Prince consoled himself through an anonymous affair with a waitress. "If I Was Your Girlfriend" finds Prince wishing for the relaxed intimacy enjoyed by female friends, flowing from his observations of Susannah and Wendy, twins who shared emotional as well as physical similarities. And "Forever In My Life" captures his relationship with Susannah at a pivotal moment, with Prince promising that he is tired of meaningless sexual encounters.

Notwithstanding such sentiments, Prince's relationship with Susannah continued to be poisoned by his voracious appetite for other women. His callous treatment of Susannah was also upsetting to Karen Krattinger, who by now had become general manager of Prince's production company. Susannah was one of her best friends, and still Krattinger was ordered to perform odious tasks like installing her in an apartment after Prince banished her from his new home. After years of backbreaking hours (which included almost single-handedly organizing Prince's sprawling business files into a functional state), Krattinger began to wonder how long she could continue. "Prince put me in the middle of his relationship way too much," she said. "I saw him throwing away and hurting the most wonderful woman I felt he would ever know."

Prince made little secret of his dalliances with numerous other women. While one-night stands were a frequent occurrence, steady companions were singer Jill Jones and Sheila E., who was also emerging as an important musical collaborator. A tense and unpleasant dynamic developed between Susannah and Sheila, who encountered each other not infrequently as a result of their intersecting musical and personal relationships with Prince. And Sheila's emotions, like Susannah's, were affected by her shifting fortunes. Krattinger, who dealt with frequent requests from all members of Prince's entourage, recalls Sheila as humble and cordial when on the outs with Prince, but haughty and disdainful when the romance was flourishing. "It was as if she thought that when she was going out with him, she should be treated exactly like him," Krattinger said.

Each of Prince's "girlfriends" had something in common—their willingness to accept (although not always entirely without protest) his insistence on maintaining multiple relationships. And while few of his serious romantic interests were complete pushovers or airheads—Sheila E. was a stunningly talented musician, and Susannah hailed from a sophisticated, musically inclined family—they were nonetheless submissive in their relationships with him. Conversely, his affairs with more headstrong women, such as Madonna, Sinead O'Connor, and the New York artist-singer Carole Davis, tended to be very short-lived. "I don't think he actually wanted to be around anyone more worldly or knowledgeable than himself for very long," observed Leeds. "He gravitated to more simple women who'd settle for staying in his house, sharing popcorn and movies and not challenging his comings and goings."

Despite his bountiful romantic life, Prince's focus remained on his music. With *Crystal Ball* complete, the next step was for Prince's management team to present the project to Warner Bros. The modus operandi in dealing with Warners was to have Steve Fargnoli handle meetings with top executives, an arrangement that suited everyone well. Mo Ostin and Lenny Waronker still viewed Prince as an unstoppable creative force, but had in the post–*Purple Rain* years developed concerns about his business judgments, believing in particular that he released albums too frequently. Fargnoli was the perfect middleman in this relationship; he understood Prince's personality and was a forceful, articulate advocate for his client, and yet was also well-respected and liked by the Warners chiefs.

Time and time again Fargnoli had convinced Warners to support commercially risky ideas, such as releasing the demo version of *Dirty Mind*, making *1999* a double album, financing the *Purple Rain* film, and selecting the controversial "When Doves Cry" as the lead single from *Purple Rain*. Because such schemes had in the past been accepted, Prince came to believe that the company's support was unconditional, and he had great faith in Fargnoli's ability to elicit Warners' enthusiastic backing.

By late 1986, however, the dynamics in the Prince-Fargnoli-Warner Bros. triangle had started to shift. Prince, while unquestionably a favorite of critics and a signature artist on Warners' roster, was no longer an ascendant commercial force. Since *Purple Rain*, his album sales had tapered off consistently. Warners officials began to view his behavior as erratic; he recorded far more material than the label could release and then damaged his own public image through incidents like the "We Are The World" fiasco and the firing of Wendy and Lisa. Mo Ostin and Lenny Waronker had no doubts about Prince's talent, but began to see him as self-thwarting.

With *Crystal Ball*, Prince faced an additional problem: No one in his inner circle, including Fargnoli, was entirely supportive of the concept of a triple-album. Alan Leeds, while enthusiastic about much of the material, feared that such a sprawling release could be perceived as a display of arrogance rather than a defining accomplishment. "A backlash among fans and critics was certainly possible," he noted. "Besides die-hard fans bathing in an orgy of new material, there were few upsides."

Even Fargnoli, charged with convincing Warners to release the record, was lukewarm and had started to harbor doubts about Prince's career. "Man, they're not going to buy this," Farngoli told Prince as discussions with Warners continued. Prince was not pleased. "You work for me—you make 'em buy it," he responded.

Cracks thus developed in one of Prince's most important relationships. "I think Steve was getting to the point where he started to feel like he didn't need this," said Warners' Marylou Badeaux. "It's not unusual for an artist to make demands of his management, but some of Prince's demands were getting more and more out in left field."

The dispute also marked a turning point in the relationship between Prince and Ostin, who was deeply concerned about the economics of a triple-album set. How many consumers would shell out up to thirty dollars for it? It would be expensive to produce and distribute and might not turn a profit even if, as Prince hoped, critics declared it a masterpiece. Shortly after learning of the project, Ostin visited Sunset Sound to hear the record and meet with Prince and Fargnoli. His response shocked Prince. "I respect your vision, but it just won't fly," he said, insisting that Prince pare *Crystal Ball* to a double album.

Bitterly disappointed, Prince refused to back down, and the battle over the album continued for several weeks. "There were a lot of meetings, a lot of loud hollering, a lot of frustration," recalled Leeds. "It was very, very ugly." On several occasions, Prince stormed out of conference rooms after exploding at Warners officials, according to Marylou Badeaux.

Faced with the reality of his diminished commercial clout, Prince finally agreed to trim the set as Warners had asked. But he would never forget that the company had taken a meat cleaver to his meticulously constructed masterwork. "Prince lost interest beginning with editing it into two albums," observed Leeds. "He had allowed himself to see it only as a three-record set, and as such it seemed to him an incomplete work— not the true vision he had set out."

Needing to edit *Crystal Ball*, Prince reluctantly scrapped the lengthy title track, which took up nearly half an album side. Clare and Brett Fischer, after putting so much effort into it, were disappointed to learn the song might never be released. Prince also discarded strong cuts like "Good Love," an exuberant pop song that used the "Camille" vocal technique, and "Joy In Repetition," a hypnotic ballad that showed the influence of Kate Bush and Peter Gabriel.

The dispute over *Crystal Ball* left Prince frustrated and depressed, and to make matters worse, his relationship with Susannah Melvoin was spinning out of control for the last time. In the months since the couple had concluded their brief attempt at cohabitation in Prince's Chanhassen home, their fighting had continued, taking an emotional toll on both of them. In December 1986, Susannah finally decided she had had enough; she packed her things and returned to Los Angeles' San Fernando Valley, joining Wendy and Lisa. "You can only subject yourself to so much, unless you're self-abusive, and she had a lot of respect for herself," observed Karen Krattinger. "He probably would have kept her back and forth on a yo-yo forever."

One evening shortly after Susannah's departure, Susan Rogers could tell something was very wrong when Prince came down to the basement studio. Looking disconsolate and barely speaking, he began constructing a song around a melancholy piano pattern. His spoken lyrics portrayed a fictional dialogue between himself and Wally Safford, a dancer in the band. Sounding sad and lost, Prince asks Wally to borrow fifty dollars and some sunglasses so he can impress his lover, but then changes his mind and returns the items, telling Wally that since he is alone now, he has no one to spend the money on. Prince was accompanied only by piano throughout the verse, but guitar, bass, and drums enter as the song built into a chorus on which he sings the phrase, "o-ma-la-di-da."

Watching Prince construct the song, which he called "Wally," Rogers was stunned by the honest emotion and wistful resignation it conveyed. She saw the song both as a farewell to Susannah and a means of expelling the poison of a failed relationship.

"Do you know that malady means sickness, illness in French?" Prince asked Rogers, referring to the phrase he sings in the chorus. "It's almost like the word melody, isn't it?" Prince, who rarely exposed his inner feelings, even in his music, was groping for a metaphor that would convey his feelings of loss. Rogers felt it was a turning point in his songwriting.

But as the session continued, Prince started to distance himself from the creation. He added extraneous instruments that diminished the song's clarity. A percussion part cluttered the verse, detracting from the lyrics.

"Don't you think it was better before, Prince?" Rogers said. "Maybe we should stop." He ignored her, adding a synthesizer riff. Soon it became clear to her: He was intentionally destroying the song. After larding the piece with additional instruments, he finally spoke.

"Now put all twenty-four channels on record and erase it," he told Rogers.

"No, you can't do this!" Rogers said, dismayed by the prospect of losing the statement at the core of the song.

"If you don't, I will," Prince responded.

Rogers stood her ground, and Prince was forced to operate the soundboard himself as he destroyed his own music. "Wally," like his relationship with Susannah, Wendy, and Lisa, involved more emotional intensity than Prince was willing to accept. "I thought it was the greatest thing he had done," says Rogers. "I had waited years to hear a Prince song like this. I ached to hear him be this honest."

Yet, Prince's refusal to explore his feelings was not altogether surprising. Rogers had discussed the topic of depression with him before and found Prince contemptuous of the very notion. "He thought it was practically a sin to be depressed," she remembered. Many other associates have observed that Prince—not only in his relationships, but even in his music—is cryptic and unrevealing of his deepest feelings. "His music is very passionate, but he doesn't let himself open up emotionally," observed Marylou Badeaux. "And look at the way he's dealt with women in his life—he's not able to get emotional, he just keeps it on the level of sex play."

Though Susannah had never formally been part of the Revolution, her personal and creative influence on Prince from 1983 to 1986 rivaled that of Wendy and Lisa. With her exit from the scene, the Revolution period ended irrevocably. The epitaph of this time would be "Wally," a song no one would hear.

march 1987: release of sign o' the times

After being forced to pare down *Crystal Ball* to a double album, Prince retitled it *Sign O' The Times*. The striking cover art shows a cluttered background of debris, most of it with a faint peach color—shabby musical equipment, wilting flowers, broken toys, and faux-neon signs advertising "girls, girls, girls," "arcade," and other diversions. On the far right, in the foreground, a blurry image of half of Prince's face is seen. Unlike most Prince album covers before and since, which generally lack either subtext or subtlety, this one suggested some broader meaning; both cover and title indicated an intent to address the urban decay and class divisions of the Reagan era.

The first single, "Sign O' The Times," did indeed tackle social and political issues, referencing the explosion of the space shuttle Challenger, the spread of AIDS, and Reagan's "Star Wars" missile defense program. This brilliant song became another prime example of Prince's ability to mix artistry and commercialism. Sung somberly in his lower register, "Sign O' The Times" sounded subdued, almost withdrawn, yet bristled with an underlying tension and angst. Far more challenging than most Top 40 fare, it nonetheless reached No. 3 on the Billboard Pop Singles Chart, an auspicious beginning for the project.

Notwithstanding Prince's disappointment over having to trim *Crystal Ball*, *Sign O' The Times* was greeted, essentially, as just the crowning achievement he had wanted the triple album to be. Critical reaction was almost uniformly strong, as it was compared to masterpiece double albums like the Rolling Stones' *Exile On Main Street* and the Beatles' *White Album*. "Truly this man is a genius," wrote Ted Mico in *Melody Maker*. "There are hints of the Temptations, slices of Isaac Hayes, traces of Sly Stone, even footprints of Robert Palmer." *Q* magazine lauded Prince's "sophistication and chops" and commended him for creating a "funk...edge that slices straight into the soft white gut of pop."

The experimental elements he had been wrestling with since *Around The World In A Day* jelled perfectly on the album, and numerous new Prince classics emerged, including the title track, "Hot Thing," "Adore," "I Could Never Take The Place Of Your Man," and "Housequake." The album as a whole did not turn out to be the work of social commentary that the title track suggested; instead, *Sign O' The Times* was at heart a very offbeat party album. Only "The Cross," a raw, guitar-driven track, returned to the theme of urban misery addressed in "Sign O' The Times." Generally, the album's lyrics covered familiar Prince topics while sometimes giving them an idiosyncratic spin;

"If I Was Your Girlfriend" constitutes perhaps his most penetrating exploration of gender confusion, and "The Ballad Of Dorothy Parker" is a backhanded tale of infidelity that recalls the wit of the Beatles' "Norwegian Wood." Several of the songs employed Prince's speeded-up vocal technique, including "If I Was Your Girlfriend," "Housequake," and a rock-funk duet with Sheena Easton, "U Got The Look." These vocal performances were in the liner notes credited to "Camille." (Of the cuts originally slated for the *Camille* album only one, a powerful rock number called "Rebirth Of The Flesh," remains in Prince's unreleased, the others having turned up on *Sign O' The Times* or elsewhere.)

All told, the album was a stunning effort. If *Around The World In A Day* and *Parade* had established Prince as that rare pop superstar who treats artistic growth as more important than commercial considerations, *Sign O' The Times* confirmed him as the single most adventurous figure of the decade. And its reputation would only grow, as it turned up on many best-of-the-century lists during 1999 and 2000.

The triumph of *Sign* owes to many factors, among them his focus and drive following the exit of Wendy and Lisa, his facility with musical technologies like the Linn LM-1, and also the many new influences he had assimilated so rapidly. "To my ears, the better of the material seemed the artistic culmination of all the things he had been exposed to and absorbed from Wendy, Lisa, Sheila, and Eric [Leeds] over the previous couple of years," said Alan Leeds. "It showed musical growth and maturity, while taking him back to his R&B roots like no record of his since *1999*."

Oddly, Prince was not entirely cognizant that the music world felt he had delivered a masterpiece. For him, *Sign O' The Times* would always have an asterisk next to it, simply because it wasn't *Crystal Ball*. His enthusiasm for the album was diluted from the start, and as a result the promotional campaign was less effective than it could have been. Despite the critical praise for the album and the chart success of the first single, sales figures began to taper off rather quickly after an initial burst of purchases by serious fans. *Sign O' The Times* peaked at No. 6 on the Pop Chart but sank rather quickly. (Ultimately, it sold about 3.2 million copies, with half of these overseas, where his popularity continued to build.) A key misstep accelerating this trend was Prince's selection of the laid-back "If I Was Your Girlfriend" as the second single; the song proved simply too quirky for radio.

Still, optimism remained high at Warner Bros. and among Prince's bandmates that the album could be revived on the charts when a two-month European tour in support of *Sign O' The Times* began in May. Prince's popularity in Europe was still increasing (in contrast to his declining commercial status in the United States), and the well-designed show proved to be one of the most exciting of his career. The absence of Wendy and Lisa was filled to some extent by the kinetic Sheila E., whose ability to play complex, jazzy figures added a new dimension to Prince's live sound. Her soloing also electrified crowds. The other members of the revamped band included Levi Seacer, Jr., on bass, Boni Boyer on keyboards and vocals, Matt Fink on keyboards, and Miko Weaver on guitar. Another new member was dancer Cat Glover, who became a visual focal point. The holdovers from the *Parade* tour, along with Fink and Weaver, were Eric Leeds on saxophone and Matt Blistan on trumpet. Dancers Jerome Benton, Greg Brooks, and Wally Safford also remained onstage, but were less prominent than on the

Parade tour. The evenly paced set emphasized the strong *Sign O' The Times* material and gave the band ample opportunity to jam, particularly on the lengthy set-closer, "It's Gonna Be A Beautiful Night," during which Leeds and Blistan inserted phrases from the Duke Ellington–Billy Strayhorn classic "Take The A Train" and James Brown's "Cold Sweat."

The tour was a success in every respect, convincing Warner Bros. and Prince's management that a U.S. tour could reinvigorate sales of *Sign O' The Times* in the United States. But Prince had other plans. Frustrated by the reaction of American consumers, and already impatient to move onto his next project, he opted instead to have the final shows of the European tour filmed and packaged into a concert film for American audiences. "To put it very bluntly, the film was Prince's way of getting out of doing the tour," said Alan Leeds. "Nobody was in favor of the film idea." Warner Bros.' film division, leery about Prince's filmmaking after the abysmal *Under The Cherry Moon*, declined to get involved, forcing him to find another distributor.

Once he completed the film, Prince frantically rushed it into theaters against the judgment of his advisors; the November 1987 release guaranteed it would be lost in the swirl of Oscar-contenders that typically grace screens at year's end. "A number of us told him that the release date was a mistake, but in his mind, we were just trying to undermine him," Marylou Badeaux said.

Worse, the *Sign O' The Times* movie failed to capture the ambiance of the electrifying European shows. Although the music was culled from the concert tour, the video footage was too grainy for professional use, and Prince decided to reshoot the visuals on a soundstage at Paisley Park. The band was thus forced to lip-synch to previously recorded live material, giving the film a rather sterile feel despite its powerful music. Only at one point does it soar, during the melancholy love song "Forever In My Life." Prince, center stage with only an acoustic guitar, riffs playfully and then delivers a blistering vocal as Boni Boyer, Sheila E., and other band members contribute gospel-like backup singing over a simple drum-machine riff. Simultaneously assured and vulnerable, "Forever In My Life" represents one the truest documents of Prince as a compelling and original live performer.

The film, while critically praised, was a commercial flop and failed to boost sales for the album. Prince, having already skipped the U.S. tour, largely withdrew from promotional activities for *Sign O' The Times*, much to the dismay of Warner Bros. "We needed more time with the record, but he was done with *Sign O' The Times* in every way," Marylou Badeaux recalled. "Once he's done with something, he considers it old and tired."

The *Sign O' The Times* enterprise effectively concluded on New Year's Eve, 1987, just nine months after the album had been released. Prince and the band performed a rousing version of the European tour show for a benefit concert at Paisley Park. Miles Davis, whom Prince had invited, joined the band and soloed on a thirty-four-minute, jam-filled "It's Gonna Be A Beautiful Night." Miles' presence added a novel and even comic element, as some members of Prince's band—particularly Eric Leeds and Matt Blistan—seemed to forget exactly whose band they were in. "We were just so absorbed with Miles that the whole band missed a cue that Prince gave," recalled Eric. "And Prince kind of yelled at us, like 'Hey, remember me?' We all had a laugh."

But while this show gave an outward impression of good cheer in the Prince camp, the bandleader was in reality becoming angry and morose. He viewed *Sign O' The Times*, for all the praise lavished on it, as a disappointment, and blamed the less-than-spectacular sales not on his own decisions but on Warners' promotional efforts. And Susannah Melvoin's departure from Minneapolis—just two months after the exit of Wendy and Lisa—left him lonely. Associates saw the intermittent playfulness that usually leavened his personality disappear. Karen Krattinger found that his incessant demands took on an increasing air of unreasonableness, such as when he asked her to cancel Thanksgiving plans with her family. She refused the request. "You are not my family," she bluntly told Prince.

Engineer Susan Rogers also felt things getting worse than they had ever been. "He was in such a bad mood all the time and a lot of us were reaching a burnout phase with him," said Rogers, who after four years with Prince began to think about leaving. "It just wasn't a good feeling in the air."

CHAPTER TEN

BLACK

M
arylou Badeaux arrived at Sunset Sound one morning for a familiar and pleasant ritual: Prince wanted to play her a new song. He had been up all night working, and he wanted Badeaux—one of the few Warner Bros. officials with whom he still felt comfortable after the *Crystal Ball* debacle—to be first to hear it.

The experience was always a heady one, entering the hallowed studio to spend time with the most prolific artist in popular music. Still, upon hearing this latest creation, Badeaux was again struck by a thought that had been running through her head in recent months: Prince's creativity was waning. After years of stunningly inventive music, he was starting to repeat himself. What Badeaux heard that morning was just another song—there was very little that was fresh or interesting about it.

"That's really cool," she offered weakly. Prince picked up on no part of her ambivalence, and a triumphant gleam came into his eyes.

"See, Marylou, I just can't help it—this stuff just comes through me!" he said proudly. "You tell those people at Warner Bros., I can't stop this, it just has to come out!"

Gently, Badeaux tried to explain the label's position. "Consumers have the ability to absorb only so much," she offered. "The label is just trying to protect your exposure."

"I'll decide if my exposure is too much," Prince shot back.

Badeaux realized that in all likelihood, relations between Prince and Warner Bros. would get much worse before they got better. "New stuff was just coming out of him like crazy, but this time it wasn't coming out as good," Badeaux recalled later. "For every great song, there were ten kind-of-okay songs."

Other associates were developing similar views. Engineer Susan Rogers, who spent countless nights with Prince in windowless studios, began to see some of the sessions as exercises, rather than explorations of genuine inspiration. "It may have been better if he had recorded about one-fourth as much as he did," she said. "For every song that was put on an album, three more were recorded that weren't. If he had restrained himself, spent more nights bowling or watching TV..."

For better or worse, Warner Bros. had on its hands a seemingly inexhaustible song-writing machine. It did not satisfy him merely to record reams of material; he insisted that the label release, and enthusiastically market, each and every album that he deemed ready for the public. And this was the crux of the problem: Releasing an incessant stream of music by Prince (or any artist) was not a sound business proposition. And this was especially true if his output was becoming more notable for its quantity than quality.

On the surface, Prince seemed as much a ball of energy as ever, bouncing effortlessly from stage to studio. But on some deeper level he was fatigued. In just a few short years, he had experienced the heady rise of *Purple Rain,* the crash-and-burn of *Under The Cherry Moon,* the disbanding of the Revolution, and countless other highs and lows, and he had barely taken a moment to reflect upon any of it. After a run of creativity that had culminated in *Sign O' The Times,* Prince was, at least for the moment, running out of inspiration.

Adding to this problem was his decision to cease his active study of other musical artists and genres. After several years of exposure to various forms of rock and jazz through friends like Wendy and Lisa, and Eric and Alan Leeds, he had simply had enough. "Prince shut down the school," Alan Leeds noted. "He had the education in Ellington, Miles, and Joni Mitchell, and he was ready to move on. He felt he had gotten out of us what he needed." But Prince was mistaken in the belief that he had nothing more to learn. In actuality, he had never become a serious student of musical forms outside of funk—he was precocious and brilliant, but lacked focus in his apprehension of new influences. And after Prince decided to stop learning, the lack of continued stimulus, coupled with the absence of strong personalities like Wendy and Lisa from his band, quickly became apparent in his work.

Having reached a point of deep frustration over *Sign O' The Times,* in the fall of 1987 Prince began assembling a new album that he hoped would put the bitter taste of that project behind him. Consisting of dark, uncommercial, and often hostile songs, it was entitled, appropriately enough, *The Black Album.* For the most part, the music had been recorded over the past few years, and the only brand new track was a ballad, "When 2 R In Love." The songs were not top-drawer material, and engineer Susan Rogers remembers most of *The Black Album* as being cut during what were supposed to have been days off. Three of the cuts—"Bob George," "2 Nigs United 4 West Compton," and "Le Grind"—were created in late 1986 for Sheila E.'s December 12 birthday party. The vast majority of the instruments on the album were played by Prince, with Eric Leeds and Matt Blistan contributing horns and other band members adding brief raps, shouts, and backing vocals.

After completing the album, Prince presented it to Warner Bros. along with a unique marketing plan: it would have no cover art or identifying markings, other than a stark black front and back. The name "Prince" would not appear. When Warners officials listened to the album, they found lascivious funk jams, anarchic jazz-rock instrumentals, and nothing resembling a radio-friendly single. On "Bob George," Prince's voice is slowed down to a Barry White–like growl (the inverse of the "Camille" technique used to speed up his voice) and he plays a vicious character prone to domestic violence; "Superfunkycalifragisexy," is an uptempo funk number where he sings about bondage, masturbation, and a ritual involving "squirrel meat." After the commercial disappointment of *Sign O' The Times, The Black Album* was clearly conceived as a thumb in the eye of both Warners and the record-buying public.

Another major catalyst behind the album was Prince's desire to reconnect with his African-American fan base. His various excursions into rock, along with the fawning attention he received from the largely white critical establishment, left him worried about perceptions that he had strayed from his roots; *The Black Album's* emphasis on funk was designed in part to compensate for "whiter" records like *Purple Rain* and *Around The World In A Day*.

Still, Prince's vision for the album was otherwise not particularly clear, and the "dark" nature of the music was more reflective of his mood—his anger at Warner Bros. and his loneliness after his breakup with Susannah Melvoin—than indicative of a grand plan to redefine his sound and image. In contrast to the carefully constructed *Sign O' The Times*, the project was essentially thrown together, and shows his desire to do something—anything—to move beyond *Crystal Ball/Sign O' The Times*.

From the perspective of Warner Bros., *The Black Album* was emblematic of the label's concerns about Prince's career. Increasingly, his marketing decisions seemed designed to alienate the public rather than to increase his record sales; meanwhile, his material was becoming consistently less accessible. The company desperately wanted Prince to come up with catchy songs that would re-establish him as a potent hit-maker and guide him back towards *Purple Rain*–like levels of fame. What it got instead was *The Black Album*.

Despite Warners' trepidation, plans for the release went forward and hundreds of thousands of vinyl albums, cassettes, and compact discs were pressed for distribution. As he often did just before putting out new albums, Prince went to a nightclub to audition it for an unsuspecting public. On December 1, 1987—a little more than a week before its scheduled release—Prince went to Rupert's, a Minneapolis dance club. Entering undetected by the crowd, he made his way to the deejay booth and played songs without fanfare to see how club-goers would react.

As the music played over the sound system, Prince mingled with the crowd and eventually became involved in a detailed conversation with a singer-songwriter-poet in her early twenties named Ingrid Chavez. An attractive brunette with a serious and reflective air, Chavez had moved to Minneapolis several years earlier to work on music with a friend. But that collaboration had soured, and since then she had been working alone on her poetry and spoken-word pieces. Like Prince, Chavez had grown up in a strictly religious home (in her case, Baptist), but as an adult she too sought spiritual answers outside the confines of any specific religion.

Prince and Chavez seemed fascinated by each other despite an apparent lack of sexual chemistry, and, after a while, they drove back to the recently completed Paisley Park studio complex. They continued a lengthy and intense conversation about religious issues, love, and life fulfillment, but Prince eventually excused himself, saying he had a stomachache. Waiting to see where the strange night would go next, Chavez stayed put while Prince disappeared elsewhere in the complex.

At about one-thirty a.m., Karen Krattinger received a strange phone call. Speaking with uncharacteristic emotion, Prince apologized for having been so hard on her, said he had trouble expressing his feelings, and that he loved her.

At about the same time that night, Susan Rogers also got a phone call from Prince, asking her to come to Paisley Park. After four years as Prince's engineer, she had resigned that post shortly after the completion of *The Black Album* in October 1987. But she agreed to go to the studio. Arriving in the rehearsal room, she found it dark, save for a few red candles that cast ominous shadows across the walls. Out of the gloom, she heard a woman's voice.

"Are you looking for Prince?"

Rogers, who would later learn this was Chavez, answered, "Yes."

"Well, he's here somewhere," Chavez replied.

Abruptly, Prince emerged out of the darkness, looking unlike she had ever seen him before. "I'm certain he was high," Rogers said. "His pupils were really dilated. He looked like he was tripping."

As he had with Krattinger, Prince struggled to connect emotionally with Rogers. "I just want to know one thing. Do you still love me?" Rogers, startled, said she did, and that she knew he loved her.

"Will you stay?" Prince asked.

"No, I won't," she said, and left the complex.

"It was really scary," she recalled of the evening.

Matt Fink confirmed the sequence of events, saying he was told by bodyguard Gilbert Davison, who was present at Paisley Park that evening, that Prince had taken the drug Ecstasy. "He had a bad trip, and felt that [*The Black Album*] was the devil working through him," Fink said. Chavez has also said that in the course of the evening Prince decided that *The Black Album* represented an evil force.

The next morning when Prince encountered Krattinger, he appeared embarrassed and made no reference to the phone call of the night before. "He never said anything like that again," she said. Prince's sudden and fleeting expressions of emotions are consistent with an Ecstasy trip; the drug is known for producing short-lived feelings of well-being and connectedness.

But something had changed. Prince believed that he had experienced a spiritual and moral epiphany, and that Chavez, serving as a guide, had shown him the way to greater connection with God and other people. *The Black Album*, he decided, represented the anger and licentiousness that he must leave behind. After casting about for months for a way to truly put the Revolution era behind him, he had found one.

Days after the Ecstasy trip, Prince contacted Warner Bros. chairman Mo Ostin and insisted that *The Black Album*, with its release just days away, be canceled. "Prince was very adamant and pleaded with Mo," recalled Marylou Badeaux. Although Ostin ultimately agreed, halting the release was a logistical nightmare for Warners. Five-hundred-thousand LPs—which now needed to be destroyed—had been pressed, and were on loading docks ready for shipment to stores. A small number of vinyl records and CDs escaped destruction, and *The Black Album* quickly became available on the bootleg market, with fans selling and trading cassette duplicates of widely varying fidelity.

Prince has never given a clear public explanation of the decision to shelve the album, but the program from his next tour included a cryptic discussion of *The Black Album*'s "evil" nature, and refers to December 1, 1987 (the night he spent with Chavez at Paisley Park), as "Blue Tuesday."

Had Prince experienced a spiritual rebirth? Associates weren't sure. At the very least, when employees bumped into their boss at the now-complete Paisley Park complex, they found him trying hard to be cheery. "This was a guy who had an awakening and made a major decision that he was going to change his focus, be it temporarily or permanently," said Alan Leeds. But Prince was still Prince, and in some respects the notion of a personal transformation seemed strained and inaccurate. "It was a facade," said Karen Krattinger. "It was evident to me that he still wasn't happy with his life."

january 1988: paisley park studios, chanhassen, minnesota

Having shelved *The Black Album*, Prince immediately threw himself into the recording of his next LP, *Lovesexy*, which he conceived as a document of his epiphany. While the tension between carnality and spirituality had always been a feature of Prince's music, his new lyrics presented these two forces as working in tandem and harmony. Lust and religious rapture were described, in essence, as identical; the title track describes a feeling of mystical enlightenment and also contains lines about sexual emissions. Prince worked mostly by himself, although Sheila E. played drums on several tracks. During breaks from the *Lovesexy* sessions he worked on songs for a planned solo release by Ingrid Chavez, whom he continued to view as a muse and spiritual guide.

Prince slated a song called "The Line," a stately mid-tempo rocker with religious lyrics inspired by a Chavez poem, for the album's centerpiece. Prince, Boni Boyer, and Sheila E. shared vocal chores for the complex song and, during the coda, Boyer sang a portion of the lyrics to "Take My Hand, Precious Lord," the gospel standard by Thomas A. Dorsey. Prince was surprised, however, when associates seemed lukewarm about the song. "Prince felt he was really onto something with 'The Line,' but he wasn't getting the reaction he wanted from the people he played it for," recalled Joe Blaney, who engineered the session. "He kept retouching the song, adding more overdubs."

Prince eventually discarded "The Line" but continued to emphasize religious themes as he developed material. He retooled a *Crystal Ball* castaway called "The Ball" into the pious "Eye No." The ballad "I Wish U Heaven" covered similar territory. The songs had another thing in common: Prince was concentrating more on musical embellishments and labyrinthine arrangements than melody. At times, associates felt, the songs threatened to sink under their own weight. "I thought *Lovesexy* was going to be a great album, but when I heard the final mixes, I was very disappointed," said Eric Leeds, who added saxophone to various songs.

Moreover, very few of Prince's associates related to the lyrical messages, and also wondered why Ingrid Chavez, who seemed to some a bit odd, was playing such a huge role. When band members seemed confused by the lyrics of the title track, he rerecorded it to make the meaning ring out more clearly. It still didn't work. "I did not understand what the term 'lovesexy' was supposed to mean," Eric Leeds said. "People weren't getting it."

But neither Eric nor any other band member confronted Prince about the failings of the new material. Without Wendy and Lisa around, there was no really no one left to question his creative direction; talented band members like Eric, Sheila E., and Levi Seacer, Jr., showed up to play parts and sometimes offered ideas, but had little inclination to directly challenge Prince.

Prince's marketing plan for *Lovesexy*, like much of the music, left associates perplexed. First, when he presented the completed album to Warner Bros., concerns were immediately raised about his planned cover art. Based upon a photo by Jean Baptiste Mondino that had been touched up to look like a painting, it showed a nude Prince sitting with his hand on his heart, his right leg raised slightly to cover his genital area. The background of oversized flowers and ferns included a flower stamen that looks suspiciously like a semi-erect phallus.

When members of Warners' marketing department passed around the cover during a meeting (Prince was not present), several worried aloud that shopping malls and other outlets would refuse to carry the album. Warners requested alternative art from Prince, but he refused; he believed the cover to be an integral part of a carefully constructed personal and religious statement. His conception of *Lovesexy* as a unified whole also prompted his refusal to "index" the compact disc version, meaning that consumers who bought the CD could not flip from song to song, but had to listen to the album in its entirety. The CD medium was just becoming widespread when *Lovesexy* was released, and Warners rightly worried that consumers would find the inability to play their favorite songs maddening.

Then Prince dropped another bombshell: He didn't want to shoot any videos for the album. He boldly claimed to Warners' incredulous marketing team that the absence of a video would distinguish him from other pop stars, as well as create a sense of mystery about the album. No one accepted the argument, but the label couldn't force an artist of his stature to go in front of a camera. There would be no videos.

Just a year after *Sign O' The Times* markedly elevated his artistic stature, frustration was mounting among Prince's management team and those at Warner Bros. Steve Fargnoli increasingly felt unable to sell Prince's schemes to Warner Bros. And Prince's strange decisions—his premature bailout on *Sign O' The Times*, the abrupt shelving of *The Black Album*, and now his hamstringing of the *Lovesexy* promotional campaign—were undermining a career that had seemed so promising. Lost in a reverie over his discovery of the concept of "lovesexy," Prince seemed neither to notice nor care.

march 20, 1988: alan leeds' residence, eden prairie, minnesota

Alan Leeds was among those beginning to harbor doubts about the direction of Prince's career. After working for many years with James Brown, Leeds accepted inconsistent behavior, arbitrary demands, and frequent bouts of hubris as part and parcel of a brilliant artist's character. And yet, Prince's actions were in some respects even more erratic and unpredictable than Brown's.

On a gray late-winter day, as a snowstorm gained force and began coating the Minneapolis suburb of Eden Prairie, Leeds was happy to have a day off from the hectic and exhausting routine of catering to Prince's every whim. It was warm inside, an NFL game was on, and Leeds was home with his family.

Then the phone rang.

As always, there were no pleasantries, no introductions. "I want to shoot a video," Prince said in a quiet, clipped voice. Leeds had to press to find out exactly what this meant. Did he want to make a clip for "Alphabet Street," after all? Prince said yes, and Leeds asked if he had spoken to Fargnoli about this. No, Prince responded, he wanted to shoot without meddling from the managers or Warner Bros. They would just screw things up. Leeds cautioned that this meant the budget for the video would come out of Prince's pocket—didn't it make more sense to contact Warners, which would readily approve financing for the video?

No, Prince said. He wanted to do it on his own.

"OK, when?" Leeds asked.

"Today."

Incredulous, Leeds did everything he could to dissuade Prince from making the video. It was mid-afternoon on a stormy Sunday. No respectable team of filmmakers could be assembled, particularly in Minneapolis where, as Leeds reminded Prince, there was not a film crew on every block as in Los Angeles. Even if a crew agreed to do the shoot, it was unlikely that adequate equipment could be rented and that everyone would make it through the snow to the set. How could this possibly be pulled off?

"Sounds to me like that's your problem, not mine," Prince retorted.

Leeds realized that, at the very least, he would have to placate Prince by placing some phone calls. Although the local community was not large, Leeds knew several skilled directors. Predictably, they refused the assignment. Working through his Rolodex, Leeds called filmmakers whom he considered "B-list," and began to worry that even if someone agreed to take the job, the end result wouldn't be worth the time, effort, or money. As Leeds waited for callbacks, Prince continued to hector him by phone. "When are we shooting?" he asked repeatedly, undeterred by Leeds' warnings that no top-flight filmmakers were available. Prince told him to keep trying.

Frustrated that a rare day off was being spoiled, Leeds continued his efforts and finally found a director, Michael Barnard, who was eager for the assignment. But the question remained: Could Barnard locate a facility and equipment? The afternoon dragged into evening, and the snow kept falling. Prince kept barraging Leeds with phone calls. Finally, Barnard called: The shoot was a go. He had located a facility owned by a cable television company, as well as a truck full of basic equipment typically used to cover city council meetings for local access channels. Leeds, not surprised that matters had come to this, called Prince and told him the shoot was on.

By eleven p.m., with most of the city under snow, film was rolling. Prince had rounded up Sheila E. and Cat Glover to participate. The video was shot against a blue screen, with the result that the footage looked startlingly amateurish and homemade. During the post-production process, Prince had Barnard jazz up the video by having various textual phrases dart across the screen, including "Don't buy *The Black Album*, I'm sorry," and "Ecstasy."

Unfortunately, the hastily made video of "Alphabet Street" resembled an episode of *Sesame Street* more than a professional music production. Of course, Warner Bros. was pleased to have a video—any video—and promptly released the clip to television channels. But as Leeds had feared, it was too late to boost the single. "All this, for a song that was probably beyond saving," he remembered ruefully.

may 10, 1988: release of lovesexy

The first voice heard on Prince's new album belonged not to him, but to Ingrid Chavez, completing her role as the Virgil who guided Prince through his dark night of reflection. (She is identified in the album's credits as "the spirit child.") She speaks several lines over ponderous synthesizer tones, after which Prince and the band rip into "Eye No," a song that, despite its bouncy rhythm, sounds cluttered and lacks a potent hook.

Clearly, Prince's intent with *Lovesexy* was to create a powerful religious/creative statement akin to the work of Marvin Gaye or Al Green. *Lovesexy* has many surface similarities to Gaye's *What's Goin' On*, a landmark album in pop history. Gaye, when he recorded the album, became influenced by the notion of a personal connection with God outside of the structures of organized religion, and he also embarked on a fitness campaign to purify his body after years of drug abuse. According to *Trouble Man*, Steve Turner's 1998 biography of the singer, Gaye described *What's Goin' On* as "a very divine project and God guided me all the way."

On *Lovesexy*, Prince groped for a similarly profound explication of religious connection. The climax of the song "Anna Stesia" uses the repeated phrase "God is love, love is God/Girls and boys, love God above," a direct reference to the *What's Goin' On* track "God Is Love." And just as Gaye tackles political and social issues on tracks like "Inner City Blues (Makes Me Wanna Holler)" and "Mercy Me, The Ecology," Prince does the same on *Lovesexy*, referencing urban blight and gang violence in the songs "Dance On" and "Positivity." But while *What's Goin' On* became a classic, *Lovesexy* is recalled fondly only by hardcore Prince fans. Lyrically, Prince's religious references often come across as overwrought, and his allusions to ghetto life, coming from such a cloistered artist, seem manifestly inauthentic.

Lovesexy contains little reflection about the traumas and personal schisms Prince had recently experienced, the notable exception being "Anna Stesia," in which Prince sings openly about his feelings of loneliness. The title, an apparent play on the word "anesthesia," again indicates that Prince, feeling great pain over the absence of Wendy, Lisa, and Susannah, craved an escape from his feelings of isolation. A more emotionally honest work than most in the Prince canon, "Anna Stesia" is not coincidentally the strongest song on *Lovesexy*.

Critical reaction to the album was divided, but tended toward the negative. Some saw *Lovesexy* as both heartfelt and experimental, and a logical extension of *Sign O' The Times* in terms of its musical complexity. Others found it musically and lyrically overbearing. "Prince's chaff is inevitably more interesting than most artists' wheat," commented *Rolling Stone*, "[But] some of the songs are uncharacteristically ordinary."

Added David Hiltbrand in *People:* "There's too much autoerotic noodling going on . . . There is virtually no evidence of Prince's patented fine-boned funk."

U.S. consumers were also underwhelmed; the record sold only 750,000 copies, Prince's worst commercial showing since his debut record. For the first time in years, Prince had failed to deliver a record that achieved platinum status, indicating that his superstardom was slipping away. Critical and consumer reaction was much stronger in Europe, where Prince's popularity had continued to grow and was now comparable to his standing in America during the *Purple Rain* period; *Lovesexy* sold about 1.9 million copies overseas. But Prince, assessing the album's commercial performance, focused on his weak sales at home and grew increasingly frustrated that his spiritual breakthrough had not been recognized as a milestone. And in truth, he had reason to be concerned; less than four years after releasing *Purple Rain,* one of the most successful albums in history, he was being ignored by the average music consumer.

Among serious Prince fans, an immediate debate sprung up following the album's release: Should *The Black Album* have been released instead of *Lovesexy*? Typically, listeners heard *The Black Album* (probably the most widely traded bootleg in history) on cassette tapes that were third- and fourth-generation duplicates, which gave the music even more of a gritty, authentic feeling. *Lovesexy,* by contrast, seemed glossy and overproduced, and many concluded *The Black Album* better represented the sweaty, funky spirit at the core of Prince's best work.

Had *The Black Album* been released in *Lovesexy*'s stead, it probably could not have done any worse commercially, despite its lack of radio-friendly material. It also could have become a notorious work not unlike The Stooges' *Raw Power* or Lou Reed's *Metal Machine Music,* records that have gained a place in music history for their audacity and shock value. "It would have been a kind of marker in a career, a turning point, for better or worse, at a time when arguably he needed one," observed Alan Leeds. "It would have had a bigger impact than either *Parade, Sign O' The Times,* or *Lovesexy* did. That doesn't mean it would have sold more, but to the people who bought it, it would have meant more."

While the wide circulation of *The Black Album* as a bootleg if anything enhanced his status with hardcore fans, the tamer *Lovesexy,* by contrast, contributed to Prince losing a measure of his hipness. In the mid-1980s, Prince had seemed rebellious and threatening, due in part to the targeting of his music by Tipper Gore's Parents' Music Resource Center and other self-appointed watchdogs. Toward the end of the decade, though, albums such as NWA's *Straight Outta Compton* and Guns N' Roses' *Appetite For Destruction* would set a new standard for explicitness and intensity. *Sign O' The Times* was the last Prince album that would seem bold or ahead of its time.

"I can't think of anything new to play," John Coltrane told a fellow saxophonist toward the end of his life. This poignant comment indicates a problem faced by nearly all artists at some point: The flow of ideas becomes less free, and eventually may even stop.

Sign O' The Times is generally acknowledged to be the peak of Prince's career, and to a degree *The Black Album* and *Lovesexy* projects represent the beginnings of his creative decline. Both records have dense and elaborate arrangements, but the hooks and melodies at the core of the songs are generally not on par with his earlier work. Together, the records indicate that a certain artistic sclerosis began to set in for Prince not long after the departure of Wendy and Lisa. Prince, who had centered his entire life around music, was facing his own diminishing creativity. In the realm of pop music, this phenomenon often emerges on second albums—whereas an artist may have years to contemplate his or her first record, the follow-up must be prepared relatively quickly, and often the vision that led to the debut cannot be sustained. Important first albums such as Elvis Costello's *My Aim Is True*, Patti Smith's *Horses*, the Pretenders' eponymous debut, Television's *Marquee Moon*, Liz Phair's *Exile In Guyville*, and the Doors' debut have ended up as the high-water mark for such artists. Prince was the rare artist whose initial creative burst lasted much longer than one album; in fact, it lasted a full ten years, from 1977 to 1987. (This period of fertility is comparable to that enjoyed by Coltrane; Miles Davis' biographer Ian Carr argues that "Coltrane's truly creative life spanned only about twelve years.")

Because *Lovesexy* does contain "Anna Stesia," "Alphabet Street," and a few other strong songs, there is some disagreement among Prince aficionados over whether the album represented the beginning of his decline, or rather something of a last gasp of his 1980s greatness. The truth is that *Lovesexy*, despite many strong moments, did represent a turning point of sorts. His output from *Dirty Mind* through *Sign O' The Times* constituted a run of brilliant, innovative, and ever-evolving music. Like the Beatles from *Meet The Beatles* through *Abbey Road* and the Rolling Stones from *Aftermath* through *Exile On Main Street*, Prince had managed to surprise the music world with each succeeding release.

With *Lovesexy*, though, Prince finally created an album that failed to reveal new dimensions of his talent. Previously, listeners were able to buy a Prince album with the confidence that they would experience the uncommon pleasure of discovering something they had never heard before. Now, that certainty was gone. Noted Eric Leeds, "Every artist has a creative arc, and Prince had gone through his by *Lovesexy*, in my opinion. His vocabulary had pretty much been completed."

But while Eric's observation about artists completing their creative cycles is doubtlessly true of the vast majority of musicians, it is also a fact that a few giants— Miles Davis and Duke Ellington come to mind—were able to reinvent themselves again and again, including late in their careers. Arguably, Prince's talents could have allowed him to compile a similar record of achievement. But while he would write plenty of memorable songs after 1987, he would rarely rise to the same level of craft and adventurousness, and as a result his ability to blaze new musical trails faded.

Prince, unlike Coltrane, would continue to play long after his initial run of ideas expired. He did not, like so many brilliant musicians before and after him, dissipate his talents through drugs and alcohol. He did not sink into indolence. He continued to compose, perform, and record as compulsively as ever. But perhaps that, more than anything else, was the problem—throughout the 1990s and beyond, he mistook motion for creative development, and frenetic activity for genuine achievement. He failed to realize that being prolific and being brilliant are not the same thing.

For Prince, the basic problem of finding something new to play would challenge and frustrate him, along with his followers and associates, for many years to come.

A 19-year-old Prince immerses himself in the recording of his first album at Sound 80 in Minneapolis. © Larry Falk

With Marylou Badeaux, a vice president of Warner Bros. Records, in 1979. Before signing with Warners, Prince insisted to label officials that he did not want to be pigeonholed as an R&B artist. © Marylou Badeaux

Prince's debut concert at the Capri Theatre in Minneapolis in January 1979. Based on his somewhat awkward and shy performance, Warner Bros. concluded that Prince was not yet ready to tour.
© Greg Helgeson

Flanked by André Cymone (left) and Dez Dickerson (right) on the Prince tour. In part due to the energy provided by his sidemen, the songs from Prince's first two albums took on a more intense, rock-oriented flavor in concert. © Greg Helgeson

The 1980 Prince tour.
Prince's onstage confidence
had increased dramatically.
© Greg Helgeson

On the 1984–85 Purple Rain tour, Prince had anguished "conversations with God" that reflected
his genuine confusion about the contradictions between lust and spirituality. © PN Collection

Prince's majestic solos on the Purple Rain tour showed the masses that he was not just a pop star, but also a brilliant musician. © Dennis Roszkowski

From the Purple Rain tour in December 1984. Prince's intense stage presence often made him look like a man possessed. © Greg Helgeson

The so-called Graffiti Bridge in Eden Prairie, Minnesota, which inspired the 1990 film of the same name. The mural shows Prince in the famous cover pose from Purple Rain. The bridge was ripped down in the 1990s. © Greg Helgeson

Playing an intimate show at
First Avenue in Minneapolis
in 1987, the year that
arguably marked the peak
of Prince's career.
© Greg Helgeson

On the 1988 Lovesexy tour. While
tripping on Ecstasy in late 1987,
Prince experienced an epiphany that
prompted him to shelve the lascivious
Black Album in favor of the more
spiritual Lovesexy. © PN Collection

The 1990 Nude Tour was a
greatest hits show intended
to shore up Prince's finances.
© Marcus Schmidt

On the 1992 Diamonds And Pearls *tour with sidekicks* "Diamond" *and* "Pearl." *The album restored Prince to commercial prominence but also inflicted damage to his critical reputation, which would never completely recover.* © Marta Arias-Salgado

With Mayte Garcia on the 1993 Act II tour. In 1996, Mayte would become Prince's first wife.
© Lena Garnold

On the Jam of the Year tour in 1997, using a microphone in the shape of a gun, one of Prince's various capitulations to "gangsta" rap.
© Russell Hollifield

Morris Day (center) and the Time at a Minneapolis awards show. After creating this side project, Prince started feeling threatened when the group developed into a dynamic funk ensemble. © Greg Helgeson

Bassist André Cymone in his Minneapolis apartment in 1982. Cymone was unable to accept playing second fiddle to his former childhood roommate. © Greg Helgeson

Mayte, in handcuffs, simulating fellatio on Prince onstage. © Big Pictures/Star File

Dez Dickerson, the guitarist in Prince's first touring band. Dickerson exposed Prince to hard rock and other styles. © Greg Helgeson

Alan Leeds, Prince's longtime tour manager and later president of Paisley Park Records. Leeds, who had worked with James Brown and George Clinton, felt that Prince was the greatest songwriter he had ever encountered. © Alan Leeds Collection

Bassist/guitarist Levi Seacer, Jr., who for a time during the early 1990s became Prince's most important studio collaborator. In 1994, frustrated about being relegated to an administrative role in Prince's empire, Seacer abruptly vacated his Paisley Park office, leaving no forwarding address. © Per Nilsen

Miko Weaver, Prince's guitarist from 1986 through 1991. Prince resented Weaver's success with women; during one rehearsal, the two men nearly came to blows. © Per Nilsen

Michael Bland, the powerful drummer of the New Power Generation, Prince's backing band during much of the 1990s. © Per Nilsen

Vocalist/keyboardist Rosie Gaines, who played a key role in the commercial success of Diamonds And Pearls. Although she worked with Prince again on several occasions during the 1990s, Gaines felt she was never given fair financial compensation or songwriting credit. © Per Nilsen

Lisa Coleman (left) and Wendy Melvoin (center) with their band. The duo's departure from Prince's fold took away an element that would ultimately prove irreplaceable. © Vinnie Zuffante/Star File

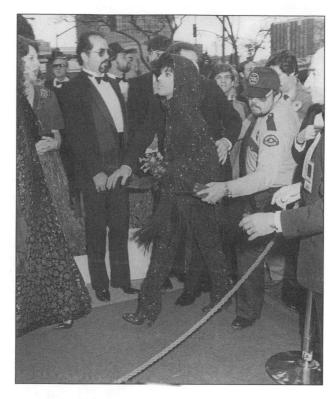

Prince arriving at the 1985 Academy Awards ceremony. He would pick up an Oscar for Best Original Song Score for Purple Rain. © Vinnie Zuffante/Star File

With Kristin Scott-Thomas, costar of the ill-fated Under The Cherry Moon. Although the two stars failed to generate any on-screen sparks, they did enjoy a brief off-stage romance. © Photofest

With Sheila E. (left) and Cat Glover (right) in the Sign O' The Times film, another box-office flop. Offscreen, Sheila and Cat were rivals for Prince's romantic attentions. © Photofest

With Ingrid Chavez in Graffiti Bridge, the big-screen bomb that doomed Prince's career as a film-maker. © Photofest

Prince performing with two longtime heroes, Larry Graham and Chaka Khan, on the Today Show, May 1997. © Mark Karlan/Star File

The image from Purple Rain that made Prince an icon. Nearly a decade later, his "name" change made him a national joke. And nearly twenty years after Purple Rain, he labors in obscurity, his albums purchased only by hardcore fans. © Photofest

PART TWO

Fall: 1988-2002

CHAPTER ELEVEN

antastic

Shortly before she left her position as Prince's primary studio engineer in late 1987, Susan Rogers experienced what felt like a rare moment of tenderness. During a recording session at Sunset Sound, Rogers excused herself to make a phone call. When she returned, she apologized for her absence and mentioned that she had just closed on a new house in Minneapolis. Prince asked where.

"Lake Harriet," Rogers responded, referring to a picturesque body of water surrounded by well-appointed homes.

Prince waxed rhapsodic. "When I was a kid, I always dreamed that someday I'd grow up, be rich, and live on Lake Harriet," he said. "And now I've got people working for me who live on Lake Harriet." Rogers was touched when, a few minutes later, Prince had bottles of champagne brought in to toast her triumph.

Prince's dreams had indeed expanded beyond anything he considered growing up in lower-middle-class North Minneapolis. Then, he had longed to succeed as a musician. Now, having achieved this on a global scale, he aimed for a loftier goal: establishing an entertainment empire from which he could launch projects in music, film, and other media. More than just a star, he would become a mogul.

By early 1988, the seat of the kingdom was finally ready. Paisley Park Studios—located in the Minneapolis suburb of Chanhassen, just a ten-minute drive from Prince's home—comprised three recording studios, a 12,400-foot soundstage for live performances and film productions, and various business offices for a growing staff. Below was a garage Prince entered in his purple BMW, and from where he took a private elevator to the ground floor. Studio A, his main workplace, boasted a forty-eight-track console, an array of high-tech equipment, and an isolation room with granite walls to generate brilliantly clear reverb sounds. For this musician who had spent much of his career recording in relatively primitive home studios, Paisley Park was nirvana.

Prince enjoyed all of the perks of success, including a private chef and a coterie of other handlers to meet his round-the-clock demands. As had been the case as far back as 1978, when he clashed with then-manager Owen Husney over this issue, Prince was insistent on having day-to-day chores handled by others. With his operations expanding, more and more people had to be hired to handle the workload.

Along with having high expectations, Prince often treated his employees harshly; not only was he prone to waking people in the middle of the night, but he issued his demands with pomposity and entitlement. During a conversation in mid-1988 with Anna Garcia (who was now 17 and with whom he continued a flirtatious but nonsexual relationship) he said that he had achieved a lifelong ambition to be a magician. "I do it all the time—I snap my fingers and food appears," he said smugly. "Whatever I want to happen happens."

Garcia, while not on the payroll, was another one of Prince's minions. He placed a premium on docility and preferred to have her just listen to him create music or brainstorm plans for the future; her opinions were not welcome. But whatever her doubts about this arrangement, Garcia remained very much smitten with Prince and was hopeful that she would, with her eighteenth birthday approaching, emerge as his primary romantic interest. He remained enchanted with her as well, largely because she remained something of a blank template on which to sketch his fantasies. He particularly delighted in playing mind games with Garcia where he would describe a hypothetical situation and ask how she would handle it. When she responded in a way that he perceived as "wrong," he assumed a disapproving air; when he liked the answer, he was encouraging and affectionate. Garcia resented the manipulations and felt as if Prince were trying to turn her into a different person.

She was also anxiously waiting for the materialization of the side project he had promised her. One evening when they were relaxing in an Amsterdam hotel room, Prince posed an odd query, asking what Garcia's name was. Realizing that Prince was about to choose her stage name, she responded that he must know. He then sat down at a piano and began playing.

"Of course I know your name," he said. "It's Joy Fantastic."

The song he wrote, "Rave Un2 The Joy Fantastic," was recorded in summer 1988 at Paisley. (It would not be released until 1999, when it became the title track of *Rave Un2 The Joy Fantastic*.) He and Garcia settled on adding the "Fantastic" appellation to her own name, making her "Anna Fantastic." Clothes were tailored for her with this logo labeled on them, and Prince wrote a song called "Pink Cashmere" that described a coat given to Garcia.

On December 31, 1988, the very day she turned eighteen, Garcia flew to Minneapolis and moved in with Prince in Chanhassen. Their long-delayed sexual coupling finally occurred. Quickly, she fell very much in love with him. Garcia often found herself longing, though, for a life in which he was not famous and in which she (not coincidentally) could play a more substantive role. Invariably, she found that his friends and associates in Minneapolis viewed her just as another "Prince girlfriend," rather than an individual.

The couple spent most of their social time together at home watching videos, very rarely going out. Prince frequently brought her to Paisley Park, where she would sit for hours and watch him work. Among the stranger aspects of the relationship was how astonishingly competitive he was with her. One afternoon in the studio, to relieve

Garcia's boredom for a moment he brought her into the drum booth and showed her how to bang the sticks against the skins. When he left for a few minutes, she continued to play and added rhythmic embellishments to her rudimentary beat. Abruptly, a stern-faced Prince walked in. "All right, that's enough," he said. It seemed he was worried Garcia was already becoming too good a drummer, and that this interfered with his concept of a demure, submissive girlfriend.

His passion for winning emerged especially around family members. When John Nelson, then seventy-two, visited the Chanhassen home for a game of pool with his son, Prince was a picture of intensity behind the cue stick. Mostly out of politeness, Garcia offered encouraging comments about Nelson's playing. Prince shot her a dirty look. After the game, he confronted her angrily, saying he couldn't believe that she had rooted for someone other than him; his sense of betrayal appeared genuine. The same vibe characterized games of basketball with the taller Duane Nelson, Prince's half brother, who also visited from time to time. Prince, still showing the bitterness he accumulated during high school when Duane was more successful at sports and with girls, clawed and scraped for every advantage in the one-on-one contests.

When Prince and Garcia were alone, the topic of winning—whether in recreational sports or in the entertainment world—came up over and over. "He always talked about how important it was to be the best at something," she remembered. "He seemed obsessed with that—being the best."

Paisley Park represented the most tangible expression of Prince's desire to be "the best" not only as a musician, but as an industry kingpin. From the beginning, though, a major question for Prince's advisors was whether the enterprise would really be profitable. The large facility was expensive to run and maintain, and it was feared that if Prince used it only as a private playground, costs would escalate. To prevent this, Steve Fargnoli prevailed upon Prince to rent time to artists from outside his circle. An obscure band called Limited Warranty was first to use Studio A; Prince noticed their master tapes on a console during his tour of the finished complex. "The place was beautiful—he was grinning ear-to-ear," recalled engineer Susan Rogers. Curious about what was going on in his new haven, Prince opened up the boxes containing Limited Warranty's music and smirked at Rogers. "Wouldn't it be funny," he asked, "If we stayed up all night and did overdubs on their tape?" Rogers gave him a worried look—such a prank could doom the idea of renting time at Paisley. Prince kept smiling, but put the boxes down and resumed wandering about the facility.

Even as his advisors fretted about the strain Paisley Park might place on his coffers, Prince began planning an elaborate summer tour in support of *Lovesexy*. The album's weak sales made a major swing a risk in the first place. But Prince, who believed *Lovesexy* a profound expression of the spiritual rebirth that had prompted him to shelve *The Black Album*, was insistent that his plans be followed to the letter. Bursting with ideas, he conceived a stage set that would be the most costly of his entire career.

At first, Steve Fargnoli was warm to the idea of an epic-scale tour, believing that it could boost the album up the charts. Excited by the creative possibilities of a lavish show, Fargnoli joined in the planning, and some of his suggestions were incorporated into the set by designer Roy Bennett. But as costs escalated, the manager's business sense took over, and he argued for scaling the production back. Fargnoli's counsel was roundly ignored. For the *Lovesexy* set, Prince created another opulent playground, one that would have to be trucked from city to city. The $2-million set included a minia- ture basketball court, a swing set, and a hydraulic brass bed. The pièce de résistance was a Thunderbird automobile that would circle the stage at the beginning of the show, from which Prince would exit to manic applause. This element alone cost $250,000— more than the entire set for the European *Sign O' The Times* tour. "Prince kept adding things and saying, 'Can I have this?'" Bennett recalled. "The car was a big deal, but Prince wanted to have this car."

When Prince insisted on yet another pricey element—a massive water fountain that would sit in front of the stage, creating a Vegas-like spectacle—Fargnoli objected. He argued to Prince that the tour could not be profitable with so many visual elements, and urged him to at least drop the waterfall. Prince refused, and Bennett (who at vari- ous times also tried, unsuccessfully, to serve as a voice of fiscal restraint) was ordered to build it. Later, Prince changed his mind, concluding that the presence of cascading water near so much electrical equipment constituted a safety hazard. The waterfall was sent to storage and never used for anything.

Fargnoli was miffed that his advice had been so blatantly disregarded, and his phone conversations with Prince started degenerating into spats. Soon, they ceased to communicate directly, and Alan Leeds was squeezed into the uncomfortable role of middleman between his bosses, who both relied on him to deliver heated messages. Already feeling burned out after the *Sign O' The Times* European trek, Leeds faced the complex task of planning the tour. Struggling to meet deadlines, he and his deputies rented vans, buses, and lighting equipment, hired road crews, and booked the show and entourage into arenas and hotels across America. These meticulous efforts left the managers hopeful that, despite the huge overhead, the tour might somehow break even. "This was one of the most logically, economically routed tours I have ever seen," Leeds recalled. "Everything made sense."

Just over a month before the tour, Prince summoned Leeds and Fargnoli to Paisley Park for a meeting about the tour. His manner—as it had been since his supposed spir- itual rebirth at the end of 1987—was serene but resolute. Quietly, Prince insisted that his managers postpone the U.S. swing and instead set up a tour of Europe. Displeased by the response of American consumers and radio stations to *Lovesexy*, he would visit U.S. venues only after enthusiasm for the record increased.

Shaken, Prince's advisors explained the potential consequences. *Lovesexy*, already fading on the charts, might be beyond rescue by the time Europe was done; a prompt U.S. campaign was the only way to boost the album. Moreover, the switch would wreak logistical havoc. Both Michael Jackson and Madonna had already planned summer swings through Europe, meaning that the prime dates at most major venues were gone, and most of the high-quality sound and lighting equipment on the continent had been rented. Finally, all of the work Leeds' team had just put into booking the U.S. swing would go to waste.

Prince ignored the chorus of dissent. He had already hurt *Lovesexy*'s chances by insisting on a controversial cover, refusing to index the CD (preventing consumers from flipping from song to song) and by initially resisting Warners' requests to make videos. Now he had seriously damaged any hopes for a successful tour. "Every decision he made about *Lovesexy* was arguably wrong," Leeds said. "And the worst one was flipping the tour at the last minute."

summer 1988: lovesexy tour

The European *Lovesexy* swing began in Paris in July and drew strong crowds despite the hurdles Prince's managers had faced in arranging it. Prince's popularity in Europe was at its peak, nearing the level of hysteria present in the United States during *Purple Rain*. Motivated by his deep beliefs about the spiritual messages of *Lovesexy*, he performed passionately night after night. The show was divided into two segments separated by an intermission; the first emphasized darker material (including two songs from the aborted *Black Album*), while the second showcased material from *Lovesexy*.

Prince's live band included many carryovers from the strong European *Sign O' The Times* tour, including Sheila E. on drums and the horn section of Eric Leeds and Matt Blistan, offering ample opportunities for instrumental flourishes. Often, though, the musicians became lost in the swirl of props and scantily clad dancers. (Cat Glover, the dancer and Prince girlfriend who had joined the band for the *Sign O' The Times* swing, was a prominent part of the show; offstage, her presence as a romantic rival led to tensions with Sheila E.) And the rigid choreography required by the complex stage design left little room for improvisation, making the experience unsatisfying for some band members. Only rarely, such as when Prince sat down for a solo piano segment, did spontaneity reign. The heavy-handed messages also became distracting, such as during "Anna Stesia," when Prince sermonized for as long as ten minutes as band members noodled on their instruments. "It was overkill," said keyboardist Matt Fink. "I thought it was a big waste of time, and the audience didn't get it."

Offstage, things remained tense between Prince and his management as *Lovesexy* slid down the U.S. charts. After an August 21 concert in Copenhagen, Alan Leeds received an early-morning call in his hotel room from Prince, who had just seen the latest *Billboard* numbers recording the album's free fall. He beseeched his tour manager to return to the United States and fix whatever had gone wrong. "He was almost in tears," Leeds said. "It was almost as if he were saying, 'How can you sit here and fiddle while Rome is burning?'" But Leeds parried the request, arguing that if he were suddenly to abandon his post, the complex *Lovesexy* jaunt could descend into chaos. "It was a total case of miscasting—I was one of the least expendable people at the time and place, and I was one of the least likely people to be able to help things in the States," Leeds noted. "But that was his level of desperation."

By the time the tour finally reached America, the concert swing had lost its rationale. While tickets sold out quickly in Prince strongholds like Chicago, Detroit, and New York, he no longer had huge numbers of fans throughout Middle America. "In some places, he was playing to half-empty houses," recalled Warner Bros.' Marylou Badeaux, who attended about sixty of the *Lovesexy* concerts.

In Boston, a tragedy further dimmed the mood. An automobile accident plunged a car into a line of fans waiting in front of a Tower Records store to purchase tickets for the show in Worcester, Massachusetts; a Berklee College of Music freshman named Frederick Weber was killed, and several other fans were seriously injured. "Prince was devastated," Leeds recalled. "He didn't like what it represented, and he was genuinely upset about the tragic element. The last thing he wanted to do was draw people into an unsafe situation."

When the tour arrived in Massachusetts in October, Prince scheduled a late-night benefit concert in honor of the deceased student at a Boston nightclub. This performance, like other "aftershows" during the tour, was charged with excitement, as Prince and the band, shorn of props, tore into a series of funky jams and cover versions, including James Brown's "Cold Sweat," which backing vocalist Boni Boyer sang as Prince drummed. In this setting, the energy that had been stifled by the *Lovesexy* show's elaborate staging was released.

But the U.S tour as a whole was a disappointment. The sight of blocks of empty seats in arenas spooked Prince, and for years afterward, he remained wary about mounting future large-scale tours of America. He attributed the slow sales to the failure of consumers to understand his new music, but his advisors believed that Prince's own strategic blunders were a large part of the problem. Both within his own management team and at Warner Bros., important people were losing confidence in his judgment.

The commercial failure of *Lovesexy* did nothing to dissuade Prince from pursuing another spiritually themed project, a film musical (and sequel to *Purple Rain*) called *Graffiti Bridge*. Even after his poor decision to postpone the U.S. leg of the *Lovesexy* tour, Prince told Steve Fargnoli to cancel an early-1989 swing through Japan so that he could work on preparations for *Graffiti Bridge*. In a series of contentious conversations, Fargnoli told Prince that he would be sued and stood to lose tens of millions of dollars if he breached his contracts for the shows. Finally Prince relented, but he again felt that his managers were hindering his career plans.

Prince resumed work on his screenplay as soon as he got home from Japan. In the new film the Kid, his character from *Purple Rain,* would again do battle with his rival Morris (played by Morris Day of the Time). The key, though, was finding an appropriate female lead, since Prince had already decided against bringing back Apollonia (Patricia Kotero).

His first choice—one that he had pursued in late 1987 prior to embarking on *Lovesexy*—was Madonna. The parallels between the lives and careers of Prince and Madonna Louise Ciccone had long fascinated the public and the media. She was born just two months later than Prince, and in the mid-1980s, they had become direct competitors for the pop music throne. Both grew up in the Midwest (Prince in Minneapolis, Madonna in Bay City, Michigan) and endured difficult childhoods—Madonna losing her mother at age five and Prince enduring the breakup of his nuclear family at age ten. Both sang unabashedly and graphically about sex and thrived on creating controversy to advance their careers.

Back in 1984, as Prince's popularity peaked with *Purple Rain* and Madonna's *Like A Virgin* ascended the charts, the two stars watched each other with interest and curiosity. Madonna, who like Prince had acting ambitions, wanted to know how he had pulled off the trick of simultaneously scoring a No. 1 record and No. 1 movie. For his part, Prince was intrigued by Madonna's sexualized persona and catchy songs.

Their first meeting came backstage at the American Music Awards in January 1985 and, over the next several months, a romance unfolded. While both were involved in other, more serious relationships—Prince with Susannah Melvoin and Sheila E., and Madonna with the mercurial actor Sean Penn—this celebrity coupling generated scads of gossip and publicity. They were seen at restaurants and clubs in Los Angeles and also turned up at each other's concerts, sometimes briefly performing together, such as during a February 1985 show at the Los Angeles Forum, where she banged a tambourine during "Baby, I'm A Star."

But while the tabloids spoke breathlessly of a red-hot affair between the Material Girl and His Royal Badness (as they were respectively sometimes called in the press), their personal chemistry was at best awkward. While Madonna was mesmerized by Prince's pure musical talent, something about his personality was too fey, delicate, and self-conscious for her—a man's man like Sean Penn was more likely to stir her passions. "They were like oil and water," recalled Alan Leeds. Where Prince was demure and cryptic, she was boisterous and rowdy; where he was mystical, she was concrete; and where he was sometimes remote and haughty, she was generally down-to-earth and relaxed. Karen Krattinger, one of Prince's key business aides in the mid- to late 1980s, was startled to learn that Madonna treated her own staff in essence as friends. "She would say to her assistant, 'Hey, I'm hungry—should we get some food?'" Krattinger remembered. Prince, by contrast, would simply issue orders. While being called to his house late at night to make him a salad was in some ways a heady experience, it was, in the end, a task rather than an interaction.

The romance between Prince and Madonna petered out in late 1985, but they continued to discuss collaborating on music. In 1986, Madonna visited Paisley Park, where they generated a handful of embryonic ideas. Later that year, when Madonna was acting in the David Mamet play *Speed-The-Plow* on Broadway, Prince approached her backstage with a mix of "Love Song," one of the numbers they had taped; Madonna found it more exciting than she had remembered, and she expressed interest in including it on her next album. Rather than working together in the studio, they instead added parts in isolation, using couriers to send the master tape back and forth across the country. The song, a plodding, static composition enlivened somewhat by Prince's skillful vocal harmonies (the entire song, in fact, sounds much more like Prince than Madonna), later appeared on her acclaimed 1989 album *Like A Prayer*.

In 1987, Madonna agreed to return to Minneapolis to discuss *Graffiti Bridge*. Prince, anxious to begin the film and hopeful that he had found the perfect costar, had an apartment lavishly furnished for her. "He thought she would fall in love with the screenplay and stay a month," noted Krattinger, who was in charge of Madonna's arrangements. But she left the unit after one night, preferring the amenities offered by an upscale hotel. Her reaction to *Graffiti Bridge* was much more disturbing—she brazenly told Prince the screenplay was awful and then split town.

By the end of the eighties—the decade they had jointly dominated as the two most visible sex symbols in pop music—Prince and Madonna were drifting apart as both struggled with preserving their superstardom. Over time, Madonna proved a shrewder strategist and evolved more gracefully; by the end of the 1990s, she would re-emerge with the critically praised albums *Ray Of Light* and *Music*, which updated her sound and image. She would also (despite some stumbles) fare much better than Prince as an actor, winning acclaim for her performances in *A League Of Their Own* (1992) and *Evita* (1996). And through her Maverick Records label, she enjoyed great success in breaking new acts. Rather than portraying herself as synonymous with the label or trying to control the output of its artists (as Prince generally did with Paisley Park Records), Madonna gave those she signed significant latitude and freedom, leading to hits by Alanis Morrisette, Candlebox, Michelle Branch, and others.

While Madonna and Prince continued to share mutual respect, they did not collaborate again after "Love Song," and her rejection of *Graffiti Bridge* marked the end of any closeness they had enjoyed.

After Madonna left, Prince put the movie on hold and turned his attentions first to *The Black Album* (which was cancelled at the last minute) and then to *Lovesexy*. But following the *Lovesexy* tour, Prince was anxious to revive *Graffiti Bridge* and scheduled a meeting with manager Bob Cavallo in Los Angeles to discuss the project. Prince's major concern was securing financing from Warner Bros. Pictures, which was leery about his film ambitions after the flop of *Under The Cherry Moon*.

Cavallo arrived for a meeting with Prince in Los Angeles knowing that his firm's once-strong relationship with Prince was in jeopardy. During the *Lovesexy* swing, Prince had actually tried to fire Steve Fargnoli, forcing Cavallo himself (who usually remained in Los Angeles to run his firm) to join the tour to patch things up. It was clear to Cavallo and Fargnoli that Prince had little interest in their advice (or anyone else's) and that he was edging towards self-management. Still, Cavallo, a key supporter of *Purple Rain*, would not reject the notion of a sequel to that movie out of hand, and held out some hope that Prince's once-promising career as an actor could be revived by whatever was about to be discussed.

Prince arrived at the meeting with a twenty-page draft of the screenplay, which he passed to Cavallo to read. The concept (which reprised various elements from *Purple Rain*) seemed saleable enough, even if the execution was hardly perfect. After examining it, Cavallo looked up brightly. "This is a good idea," he said. "Let's get you with some hip young screenwriters and make this happen."

Prince looked at him quizzically. "We don't need any screenplay," he said. "This is all we need."

Cavallo responded that this was at best a treatment for a script and that the idea needed to be fleshed out. But Prince was unmovable. The conversation went nowhere, and Cavallo got up and shook Prince's hand.

"I don't think I can do it," Cavallo said.

Undaunted by Cavallo's reaction, Prince sought others who could help him sell *Graffiti Bridge*. During the *Lovesexy* swing, Albert Magnoli, the director of *Purple Rain*, arrived to shoot a documentary of the tour. Although the film was never finished, Magnoli socialized frequently with Prince offstage, replacing Steve Fargnoli as his closest confidant. Magnoli, with his Hollywood ties, seemed a perfect choice to secure backing for *Graffiti Bridge*.

Karen Krattinger learned that something major was afoot when she received a call asking her to have some packages picked up at the Minneapolis airport. Inside, she found letters dismissing Cavallo, Ruffalo & Fargnoli and appointing Magnoli as manager. Shocked, she phoned Prince. "Do you have something to tell me?" she asked.

She found him in an exuberant mood. "Don't worry, it'll be great," he assured her. "Albert understands me!"

It was only the beginning of a major purge of Prince's business apparatus. In the coming weeks, he fired business lawyer Lee Phillips, financial consultant Fred Moultrie, and others. Finally, Krattinger herself was canned, in large part because of clashes with Magnoli, whom she considered a chauvinist pig. Alan Leeds, another member of the old guard, heard nothing about his own fate for weeks and worried the axe was about to swing his way. Eventually, the tour manager inferred that he was being kept on, but felt frustrated by the way the message was delivered; after years of service and friendship, Prince never even called to assure him that his job was safe.

Prince's appointment of Magnoli surprised many entertainment industry veterans. Fargnoli and Cavallo had been seen by many as the perfect managers for Prince, and through a combination of creativity and savvy, they had, over a period of ten years, guided him to the very heights of fame. Magnoli, for all of his success as a filmmaker, brought little to the table in terms of business acumen; his greatest qualification, it seemed, was that he unconditionally supported *Graffiti Bridge*.

Moreover, Magnoli was entering a situation far more chaotic than he could have imagined. Prince was several million dollars in debt, owing to many factors—the fiscal debacle that was the *Lovesexy* tour, his bloated payroll, and also the legal fees that began to mount in the aftermath of firing most of his business team. (Both Cavallo and Fargnoli brought suits against Prince and eventually settled out of court.) After being one of pop music's biggest money-makers for the better part of a decade, Prince had spent himself into a deep hole. The *Los Angeles Times,* in an article on the management shake-ups, examined the financial disarray. "He spends and spends, but he's not making anywhere near the money he used to," the paper quoted a record executive as saying. "I've heard estimates of his overhead that run more than $500,000 a month."

At first, though, it seemed Prince had made a shrewd decision by tapping a Hollywood insider as his manager. Shortly after assuming his new job, Magnoli was contacted by the acclaimed director Tim Burton (*Beetlejuice, Edward Scissorhands*), who was shooting the movie *Batman* with Jack Nicholson in the role of the Joker. While assembling a rough cut, Nicholson and Burton placed two Prince songs—"1999" and "Baby, I'm A Star"—into scenes as background music. Pleased with the effect, they hatched the idea of asking Prince for new material to add to the film's soundtrack.

Prince flew with Magnoli to the movie's production site in London in January 1989 and was mesmerized by Burton's elaborate and haunting vision of Gotham City. Burton requested just two songs, since the composer Danny Elfman (responsible for the *Simpsons* theme and numerous film scores) had been hired for the soundtrack. But Prince, suddenly inspired about the project, offered an entire album. Warner Bros. Pictures, emboldened by wild audience response to early trailers for *Batman,* decided that the film could sustain two soundtrack records—one a traditional score by Elfman and the other a collection of Prince songs.

Immediately after wrapping up the *Lovesexy* tour, Prince returned to Paisley Park and set to work on *Batman*. Becoming fascinated with the characters (and especially the Joker), he sampled portions of the dialogue and synced his songs directly to scenes. Prince seemed convinced that his contributions would permeate the entire film. "This is going to be my movie!" he exclaimed to studio engineer Femi Jiya.

Prince created the whole album virtually on his own, a rare exception being a visit from Sheena Easton, who dueted on the ballad "The Arms Of Orion." But for the most part, his labors were marked more by haste than by inspiration; on many of the songs, he quickly programmed drumbeats and then layered instruments with little attention to structure or melody. Some previously recorded numbers were revamped to fit the movie, such as "Anna Waiting" (about Anna Garcia), which morphed into "Vicki Waiting" after the character Vicki Vale (played by Kim Basinger).

Only rarely did any genuine experimentation occur during the sessions. "Batdance," slated as the first single, was an intriguing collage of samples, jarringly different musical sections, and searing guitar work. The project's other major compositional effort was "Dance With The Devil," an eerie-sounding piece with Prince singing a descending minor-key melody over a drum-machine pattern. Unfortunately, he shelved the song and it remains unreleased.

Batman arrived in theaters in mid-June 1989 and quickly became one of the most successful movies of all time, grossing $40 million on its opening weekend and eventually taking in $250 million at the box office. The marketing division of Warner Bros. Pictures deftly exploited the film's simple poster image—a black bat against a gold background—for tie-ins of products ranging from toys to cereals. Prince's soundtrack, released at the same time as the movie, benefited significantly from this hype and became his biggest hit in years, selling 4.4 million copies worldwide and reaching No. 1 on the Billboard Pop Chart. Although hardly a *Purple Rain*–scale success, the album reconfirmed his status as a major star.

Critical response to the album, however, was mixed. "It's hard to avoid the suspicion that some of the songs on *Batman* were already sitting around Paisley Park as part of Prince's vast outpouring of music," wrote John Parales in *Rolling Stone*. David Sinclair of the *London Times* observed that "there is a distinctly throwaway quality to much of this material."

The nine-song album contains three high-quality pieces: the idiosyncratic "Batdance," along with "The Future" and "Electric Chair," two songs Prince recorded before being recruited by Burton to work on the soundtrack, and neither having any thematic relationship to the movie. "The Future" blends a propulsive dance beat with a New Age–like synth figure; "Electric Chair" mixes funk and heavy metal and features a compelling multi-tracked chorus.

The remainder of the album is at best passable. "The Arms Of Orion" is schmaltzy, and "Partyman," "Lemon Crush," and "Trust" are by-the-numbers songs with perfunctory (and highly similar) drum-machine patterns as well as anemic melodies. The album as a whole, while hardly devoid of indications of Prince's talent, pales next to his 1980s' classics. The artistic depth of *Parade*, *Sign O' The Times*, and even *Lovesexy* left many of Prince's fans and critical supporters unprepared for a work with so little inspiration or craft.

Nor was Prince's impact on the film as great as he had hoped, as Burton and Nicholson incorporated little of his music. Their plan had never been to build the film around Prince's contributions, and the songs he submitted did nothing to change their mind. His music was most prominent, in fact, in the two sequences where Burton had originally inserted "Baby, I'm A Star" and "1999."

Ultimately, *Batman* was a paradox for Prince. It replenished his capital with Warner Bros., making the company more apt to support *Graffiti Bridge*, and it put him back in the public eye with a No. 1 album. He also received a much-needed infusion of cash. But from a purely artistic standpoint, the album did not approach the brilliance routinely expected from him. Among critics and hardcore fans, suspicion continued to grow that Prince's creativity was waning.

For Anna Garcia, life in Minneapolis with Prince had started to feel confining and dull. Prince's mind games—the taunting hypotheticals and his ceaseless competitiveness—grated on her, particularly when he used these manipulations to prevent Garcia from pursuing her own interests. When she told him she had been offered a film role in Europe, for instance, he began treating her coldly. "Well, I guess you'll have to be there, not here," he said. Convinced by his oblique behavior that she might lose him if she left, she turned down the role.

Prince also urged Garcia to repress her emotions, refusing to hear anything that he felt smacked of negativity. If she complained about an unpleasant plane flight (she frequently flew back to England to visit her family), for example, he would hush her immediately. "Let's pretend that you just appeared," he said. Nor did he want to talk to Garcia about experiences that had shaped her own life, such as her childhood. "Don't talk about your past, because you don't have one," he said on more than one occasion.

Garcia also learned, like so many of Prince's girlfriends before her, that he had little interest in monogamy. On the set of *Batman*, he struck up a relationship with actress Kim Basinger and invited her to Minneapolis to work on music. She agreed, and the relationship developed into a passionate romance in summer and fall 1989. In October, the two celebrities had a steamy session at Paisley Park during which they recorded a lengthy remix of *Batman*'s ballad "Scandalous"; Basinger's contribution is a series of moans interspersed throughout the song.

Garcia had had enough and moved back to London in early 1990. Prince stayed in touch by phone, but Garcia found herself less and less interested in his musings, which rarely touched her interests. Little had been accomplished on the Anna Fantastic project during her stay in Minneapolis; Prince had too much else to do and seemed unable to focus on it. They did collaborate on a song called "Fantasia Erotica," which Prince would later use for an album featuring Carmen Electra. But when the song was released, Garcia's contributions were not acknowledged. "He should have been fair about it and given me my credit," she said. "But I was young, so I guess you live and learn."

The commercial comeback of *Batman* reinvigorated the project Prince most wanted to pursue: *Graffiti Bridge*. Even better, his coupling with Kim Basinger gave him a new, potentially even more bankable, costar than Madonna. To Prince's delight, she tentatively agreed to appear in the film, and he resumed working actively on the script.

But just as Basinger arrived, Albert Magnoli, Prince's handpicked manager, began to lose faith in the project. He felt pessimistic both about the screenplay and also Prince's low-budget approach, which called for using cheap sets at Paisley Park. Believing that the film was unlikely to be a worthy sequel to *Purple Rain*, he voiced his concerns to Prince, who remained unwilling to entertain any dissent on the subject of *Graffiti Bridge*. Their discussions quickly broke down, and a disillusioned Magnoli left Prince's employ after less than a year, confirming the doubts of those who had questioned his suitability for the post.

Prince next turned to the Los Angeles firm of Arnold Stiefel and Randy Phillips, who had worked with Rod Stewart, Guns N' Roses, and Simple Minds. Several Prince associates say that Stiefel & Phillips' pitch was that they could secure the backing of Warner Bros. Pictures for *Graffiti Bridge*, something other potential managers were not willing to promise. "Prince signed with them only because they promised that they would get him the deal—no one else wanted to touch it," said Marylou Badeaux. "He had no respect for them—he was beginning, more and more, to not listen to anyone and was shedding himself of anyone around him who was not a 'yes' man." Arnold Stiefel denies, however, that there was any such quid pro quo, and says that Prince directed him to seek funding for *Graffiti Bridge* only after his firm was hired.

In any case, Stiefel & Phillips did convince Warners to greenlight the picture at a modest $8 million budget. While Stiefel hoped this victory would inaugurate a productive relationship with Prince, he quickly found the opposite; in fact, his client was unwilling even to communicate with him. A pattern developed: Stiefel would phone to discuss strategy, and Prince would just listen, saying nothing. At some point, Prince would abruptly end the conversation by saying "later" and hanging up.

Despite this lack of rapport, Stiefel remained hopeful that *Graffiti Bridge*, with Kim Basinger involved, could be a hit. But in Minneapolis, Prince's colleagues wondered if the Prince-Basinger relationship would last until the shoot began. One day, when longtime engineer David Z. Rivkin was recording alone at Paisley Park, he was surprised to see Prince and Basinger arrive in the studio, hand-in-hand but soporifically silent.

"What are you doing?" Prince asked nonchalantly, to which Rivkin replied that he was writing a song.

"Well, we have nothing to do," Prince responded quietly.

Rivkin looked at the celebrity couple and realized that Prince was bored and looking for a way to spend his day off. When Rivkin played his rudimentary composition, Prince came to life.

"That's great, let's write something!" he said.

For the next eight hours, he and Rivkin composed and recorded while Basinger watched from a couch. Periodically, she got up to make popcorn. After the drum and bass parts were completed, Prince spent ten minutes frantically scribbling lyrics with pencil and paper and then began recording vocals. By the end of the day, a song called "I Am" was complete.

For Basinger, the tedium of sitting around Paisley Park quickly became intolerable. In early 1990, as abruptly as she had arrived in Minneapolis, she left. They were last seen together in public in January at Chaya Brasserie, a Los Angeles restaurant; just weeks later, Basinger's publicist issued a statement saying, "Kim is definitely not involved in [*Graffiti Bridge*]." The publicist also denied that her client had done any recording with Prince.

Basinger's departure sent Prince into a tailspin. Despondent, he called Anna Garcia in England and told her he needed help, which she interpreted as an offer to star in the movie. Uninterested in being a backup option, she bluntly told him he should get on with his life. He seemed hurt but continued to vent about his problems, looking for some expression of support.

"Kim let me down," Prince said. "It's too bad. *Graffiti Bridge* could have been a big hit for her."

Garcia, no longer willing to serve as a security blanket, told him she had friends waiting outside and had to go.

"That was quick," he said, disappointed and surprised that she wouldn't drop her plans to listen to his moaning.

They never spoke again.

With Madonna, Basinger, and Anna Garcia having passed on his movie, Prince's fourth-string option became Ingrid Chavez, the young poet whom he had met in a Minneapolis club shortly before shelving *The Black Album* and embarking on *Lovesexy*. Despite her complete lack of acting experience, Chavez was handed the pivotal role of Aura, the angelic muse who helps the Kid discover his true passions.

The remainder of the cast was picked from Prince's circle of friends, few of whom had any acting experience—only Morris Day, reprising his role from *Purple Rain*, seemed likely to generate any on-screen sparks. And Prince assembled a motley collection of musical guests, including the child singer Tevin Campbell and aging veterans Mavis Staples and George Clinton. He had planned to include the hit-making diva Patti LaBelle in the project, but this never materialized. As Arnold Stiefel learned of these changes, his confidence about the film rapidly disappeared. "Kim Basinger had become Ingrid Chavez, and Patti LaBelle had become Mavis Staples," he recalled.

Shooting began in February 1990 on the Paisley Park soundstage. Stiefel, who flew in from Los Angeles, visited Prince's dressing room minutes before cameras were to roll. Oddly, the star was still in casual clothes, including an oversized sweater cut on one side to expose a shoulder. It reminded Stiefel of Jennifer Beals' outfit in the film *Flashdance*.

"When are you going to change?" Stiefel asked offhandedly.

Prince looked at him darkly. "I'm not—this is what I'm wearing," he responded. "What's wrong with it?"

"What's wrong with it?" replied Stiefel incredulously. "Everything."

Moments later, Stiefel was approached by one of Prince's bodyguards.

"He'd be more comfortable if you weren't here," Stiefel was told coolly.

"You mean here on the set?" he responded.

"No," Stiefel was told, "Here in Minneapolis." Not wanting to stir up trouble, Stiefel caught a flight back to Los Angeles, never to return to the set of *Graffiti Bridge*. (He and partner Randy Phillips would, nonetheless, be credited as the producers of the movie for having helped secure financing.)

Prince ran the shoot with an iron hand, accomplishing takes efficiently and bringing the film in under its modest budget. He also wrote new music, including songs for the Time, whose members had agreed to re-form for the movie. But when a rough cut of *Graffiti Bridge* was presented to Warner Bros. Pictures in April, label executives were dismayed; the film looked amateurish, and the story was nearly incomprehensible. A test screening in a Pasadena, California, theater that had produced some of the highest grosses in the country for *Purple Rain* confirmed Warners' judgment, as the audience scored the film harshly.

Warners decided that substantial editing was required to save the project. But a European tour booked by Stiefel & Phillips was scheduled to begin in June, meaning the film could not be ready for a summer release. *Graffiti Bridge* thus had to be delayed yet again.

As rehearsals for the tour commenced, Prince's mood was sour and conflicts increased between him and certain band members, particularly guitarist Miko Weaver. According to several members of the group, Prince felt threatened by Weaver's good looks and popularity among female fans. "Prince didn't like the fact that Miko was getting women as much as he was," said one musician. "On the road, Miko would have five or six women in his room, and some of them would want to go with Miko instead of Prince."

The tensions boiled over at a rehearsal where a sullen Prince kept asking Weaver to turn his instrument down. Weaver complied, but the bandleader kept picking on his guitarist. Finally, Prince bellowed into the microphone: "I said, 'Why don't you turn your fucking guitar down!'"

Weaver stopped playing, as did the rest of the band.

"Man, you don't talk to me like that," he snarled at Prince.

"You want to take this shit outside?" Prince responded.

"Yeah like I'm gonna come outside with you and your bodyguards," Weaver retorted.

With Prince's protectors and the other band members looking on nervously, the two men continued to stare each other down. Finally, Weaver dropped his guitar and walked out. He temporarily quit after the incident, agreeing only at the last minute to rejoin for the tour.

august 20, 1990: release of graffiti bridge album

Featuring a potpourri of different musical styles ranging from quasi-rockabilly ("Can't Stop This Feeling I Got") to stripped-down funk ("Release It") to straightforward pop (the strong single "Thieves In The Temple"), the eclecticism of *Graffiti Bridge* gave it surface similarities to Prince's previous double albums *1999* and *Sign O' The Times*. But closer examination revealed that Prince's songwriting had slackened considerably, and the album's diversity at times sounded more like incoherence. For every effective song, such as the brilliant "Joy In Repetition" (resurrected from the aborted triple-album set *Crystal Ball*) and the soaring "Elephants And Flowers," there were three or four cuts that served as filler.

Critical reaction was mixed, but surprisingly positive overall. *Rolling Stone* called the album "a tour de force that reclaims Prince's rare stature as a pop Picasso—an experimentalist with enough mass appeal to make his experiments matter." But the public's response was less enthusiastic: Like *Lovesexy*, *Graffiti Bridge* sold under a million copies in the United States, taking him even further in the direction of a cult artist rather than back towards superstardom.

Things got much worse with the release of the film itself in November 1990. Film critics feasted on *Graffiti Bridge*, contributing to a disastrous opening weekend at the box office. "To call *Graffiti Bridge* a feature-length rock video would be an insult to videos: The movie can barely muster the energy to get from one shot to the next," wrote Owen Glieberman in the magazine *Entertainment Weekly*. Richard Harrington in the *Washington Post* urged that "*Graffiti Bridge* should be bronzed immediately and delivered to Hollywood's Hall of Shamelessness, where it might draw bigger crowds than it's likely to at movie theaters once word gets out about how thoroughly execrable it is." Rapidly, the movie was ushered from theaters and into obscurity after grossing just $4.2 million.

The stakes had been high with *Graffiti Bridge*; after two big-screen flops in a row, Prince's film career was effectively over. And as mediocre as *Under The Cherry Moon* had been, *Graffiti Bridge* was a step backwards in every respect. Its production values were shoddy, the script both maudlin and unconvincing, and the acting profoundly amateurish. The movie is an undiluted expression of Prince's vision—a vision that, notwithstanding his talents as a musician, was inchoate and mawkish. The plot, which features the Kid and Morris fighting over ownership of a nightclub, lacks any dramatic tension. The film's spiritual message, the part that mattered most to Prince, resonated with almost no one. In the end, it turned out that those who had questioned the project's viability, a list that included Madonna, Bob Cavallo, Albert Magnoli, and Kim Basinger, had all been right.

Notwithstanding the scathing reactions to the movie, Prince refused to acknowledge *Graffiti Bridge* as a failure. "It was one of the purest, most spiritual, uplifting things I've ever done," he told *USA Today*. "Maybe it will take people thirty years to get it. They trashed *The Wizard Of Oz* at first, too."

chapter twelve

HIT

The disappointment of *Graffiti Bridge* left Prince in a precarious position, both commercially and artistically. Not only could his albums no longer be counted on to soar up the charts, but he had lost some of his reputation as a musical pioneer, partly because of his own declining creativity but also because of what was happening around him. As the 1980s gave way to the 1990s, major changes gripped popular music, and for once, Prince was not leading the way.

For much of the decade, Prince's bold lyrics, his blending of musical styles, and androgynous, biracial persona had helped erode social divisions of race, gender, and sexual orientation. When Tipper Gore in 1985 made him a poster child for her campaign to place warning stickers on explicit albums, she helped define him as an insurrectionist. From the standpoint of various self-appointed cultural guardians—Gore's group, television evangelists, right-wing politicians—Prince was dangerous and irresponsible. After all, his songs advocated not only self-gratification, but also oral sex ("Head," "Let's Pretend We're Married"), and even incest ("Sister"). However, to the youth of America (and many people in their twenties and thirties) he was fun, exciting, and outrageous—a rebel's rebel.

But between 1985 and 1990, a seismic shift occurred in the music world with the emergence of rap and hip-hop. As tough-talkers with cartoonish names like Dr. Dre, Snoop Doggy Dogg, and Ice Cube began to dominate the charts, Prince was no longer controversial or subversive, and he knew it. A major part of what had defined him— his ability to shock—was slipping away.

At first, Prince dismissed rap as a fad. He (along with many music critics) questioned whether rap could even rightly be characterized as a form of music, since rappers did not play instruments but instead rhymed over rhythm tracks borrowed from other sources. To Prince, pioneering rap groups like Run-DMC and Grandmaster Flash, with their boastful lyrics, simplistic drum-machine beats, and buffoonish costumes, were at best mere performers, not musicians, and he was incredulous that they were enjoying any degree of success. "Do you know what it's like," Prince complained one day to Alan Leeds, "to sit here and see these people on the charts who do nothing but *talk?*"

Prince had expected rap to quickly fade away. Instead, by the late 1980s the style had matured into a new and vital form of African-American folk music, something music critics and cultural commentators began to acknowledge. Rap also became a potent political force, as the lyrics of Grandmaster Flash and the Furious Five, Public Enemy, and others convincingly articulated the grievances of African-Americans in America's blighted cities. Musically, rap groups began taking "sampling"—the practice of using a groove or lick from another artist's work in a different context—to new heights of sophistication, layering snippets of music into stunning sonic collages. At its most rudimentary level, sampling means simply using the instrumental tracks of a song as the background for a rap, as on the Sugarhill Gang's "Rappers Delight" (which relies on Chic's "Good Times") and MC Hammer's "U Can't Touch This" (a reinterpretation of Rick James' "Super Freak"). The more creative end of the spectrum, though, is seen in complex numbers like Public Enemy's "Brothers Gonna Work It Out" (from *Fear Of A Black Planet*, 1990), which blends a funky bass-and-drum groove with a distorted sample of Sly Stone screaming (from "Sing A Simple Song") and, deep in the mix, Prince's wailing guitar solo that concludes "Let's Go Crazy."

As rap's popularity spread beyond its initial base of African-American fans to young suburban white males, radio stations began embracing the style, and record companies that had once snubbed rap artists started signing them in droves. Then, at the very end of the 1980s, a subgenre called "gangsta" rap emerged from the crime-plagued ghettos of Los Angeles, New York, and other cities. Taking rap's sheer intensity to another level, gangsta artists like NWA (Niggas Wit' Attitude), Ice-T, and Schooly D created music that was angry, aggressive, and, to many ears, distasteful in its graphic depictions of gang violence and sexual conquest. The defining moment for gangsta rap was the release of NWA's *Straight Outta Compton* (1989), a harrowing portrait of life in South Central Los Angeles. With its vivid scenes of police brutality and black-on-black crime, the album forecasted both the beating of Rodney King in 1991 and the riots that tore through Los Angeles the following year.

As songs like NWA's "Fuck Tha Police" and Ice-T's "Cop Killa" prompted a national debate over rap lyrics, all Prince needed to do was look at a newspaper to learn he had been supplanted as a rebel. Gangsta rap raised the bar of outrageousness to the point where his music and image, along with much else that had been "cutting-edge" during the 1980s, suddenly seemed tame and irrelevant.

Moreover, as a result of the emergence of rap and other marketplace factors, Prince's commercial clout continued to wane. Two of his previous three albums, *Lovesexy* and *Graffiti Bridge*, had stiffed on the charts. Only his *Batman* soundtrack, buoyed by the immense success of the film, had been a hit. And the relative dearth of outstanding music on these three albums prompted the critical establishment to turn its attention toward fresher artists. At thirty-one—hardly a tender age in the world of popular music—Prince already seemed on his way to becoming an elder statesman known largely for past victories. Landmark albums like *1999*, *Purple Rain*, and *Sign O' The Times* had secured him a place in music history, but the question remained: Could he remain relevant to younger listeners and compete with the rappers whose presence on the pop charts so infuriated him?

Prince's fading superstardom, of course, was only as significant a problem as he chose to make it. True, his releases could not compete sales-wise either with gangsta rappers or with syrupy divas like Mariah Carey. But his core constituency remained quite large both in the United States and Europe, as perhaps two million fans world-wide would purchase virtually anything he put out. A great many of these followers pre-ferred Prince's experimental, idiosyncratic side and were unconcerned about his absence from the upper echelons of the Top 40. Notwithstanding the weak points of *Lovesexy*, *Graffiti Bridge*, and *Batman*, Prince—like Bob Dylan, Miles Davis, and David Bowie at comparable points in their careers—retained the virtually unwavering sup-port of a sophisticated group of loyalists around the world. This intrepid following imposed only one requirement—that he display the artistic integrity and adventurous-ness that had characterized his career to date.

But for Prince, the status of a cult artist, even a very successful one, was not enough. The dizzying fame he had achieved through *Purple Rain* was too fresh in his mind, and the failure of *Graffiti Bridge* (particularly the film) had been intensely frus-trating. Unwilling to accept his diminished position on the charts, he elected to try to reclaim his status as one of pop's major commercial successes, regardless of the cost to his reputation.

Truth be told, Prince had already made modest forays into the rap style during the mid-1980s, but in a fashion that drew little attention to itself. The funk classic "Girls & Boys" from *Parade* contains a brief section of playful rapping by Prince. And on *Sign O' The Times'* "It's Gonna Be A Beautiful Night" and *Lovesexy's* "Alphabet Street," female band members rap during short portions of songs. But these initial explorations were rare, unobtrusive, and quite distinguishable from the work of music's leading rap-pers, most of whom were males. Rather than mimicking a trend, Prince effectively and originally integrated it into his own work.

Prince's first direct commentary on rap was "Dead On It," recorded in 1986 and later slated for *The Black Album*; the song was a scathing parody that attacked what he perceived as the genre's musical shallowness. Over a booming drumbeat and a heavy-metal guitar riff like those often used by Run-DMC and others, Prince vocalizes in a stuttering fashion that mocks the genre.

Some of Prince's associates were surprised that he would so openly criticize an exciting new musical movement, especially one led by African-Americans. Susan Rogers, the studio engineer on the session, found "Dead On It" emblematic of Prince's inability to understand rap. "In his earlier years he had a wisdom that connected him with people who were young and fresh out of school, but he didn't get it anymore," she observed. "'Dead On It' was an embarrassment and proof positive that he didn't get it. It was very disappointing for me."

Although "Dead On It" was shelved along with the rest of *The Black Album*, the record's wide circulation as a bootleg left fans quite aware of Prince's views: He would use sprinklings of rap when it suited his needs, but he would never embrace the style wholeheartedly, and he questioned the value of rap as a freestanding genre. Although a brief rap by T.C. Ellis (another one of his Minneapolis protégés) was included on the reprise of *Graffiti Bridge*'s "New Power Generation," this was seemingly the furthest he would go toward embracing the style.

summer 1990: nude tour of australia, japan, and europe

Prince's first concert swing since *Lovesexy*, and the first organized by his new managers, Arnold Stiefel and Randy Phillips, was not tied to any album—by this time, there was little point in promoting *Graffiti Bridge*—but was instead simply an attempt to cash in on his popularity in foreign markets and shore up his finances. It was a stripped-down affair (hence the moniker the Nude Tour) with few props— another means of maximizing profits. Marketing considerations also dictated the content of the show; in particular, Prince was re-examining his views regarding rap. He added to the band a dance troupe known as the Game Boyz, a trio of African-American men who brought a distinctly hip-hop-oriented visual flavor to the show. In another move designed to foster a more youth-friendly image (as well as to cut costs after the *Lovesexy* boondoggle), Prince jettisoned the veteran horn section of Eric Leeds and Matt Blistan.

An important addition to the band was Rosie Gaines, a full-throated vocalist who belted out bluesy screams just as passionately as her predecessor, Boni Boyer. Prince loved Gaines' singing but was wary about her commitment, given that she had enjoyed some solo success before joining his band. "I hope you're not like Boni," Prince cautioned, which Gaines took to mean that she should not harbor any ambitions beyond serving him.

Behind the drum kit, Sheila E. was replaced by nineteen-year-old Michael Bland, a highly skilled and energetic player from the Minneapolis music scene whose style was closer to straight-ahead rock and lacked Sheila E.'s jazz and Latin flavorings. Sonny Thompson, a longtime fixture on the local funk circuit, became the new bassist as Levi Seacer switched to guitar. Seacer also emerged as a key Prince collaborator in the recording studio and became the group's second-in-command.

From the standpoint of pure musical chops, Prince had upgraded in every single position, with the possible exception of drums. Still, almost to a person, these musicians were more practiced than interesting. Aside from Rosie Gaines and possibly the muscular Michael Bland, who often sounded as if he were pummeling his drums, no one had a distinct voice on their chosen instrument. Largely absent from the group, which Prince dubbed the New Power Generation (or NPG) was the personality and verve that musicians like Wendy, Lisa, Dez Dickerson, and Mark Brown brought to the Revolution, and that Escovedo and Eric Leeds added to his *Sign O' The Times* and *Lovesexy* troupes. But Prince had soured on musicians with their own artistic agendas, and he deliberately selected players who were young (other than the veteran Thompson), malleable, and happy just to be playing with a star of his stature.

The senior member of the band was now Matt Fink, the last remaining link to the original Revolution. A key figure in Prince's history, Fink had a speaking role in *Purple Rain*, cowrote the title track of *Dirty Mind*, and played a memorable synthesizer solo on

Dirty Mind's "Head." His onstage persona of "Dr. Fink," complete with lab jacket and stethoscope, had been an important part of the Revolution's punkish image. But his once-strong personal relationship with Prince had cooled, and he began to feel like an outsider. "I felt like he was favoring the black side of the group," Fink said. "He wasn't coming to me for anything, like he did in the past. It was like, 'Do your job, I'm gonna hang with my black buddies now, my gang.'" And Prince, so often caustic during rehearsals, became particularly hard on Fink, going so far as to belittle him during a sound check where Fink's parents were present. "Fink's the kind of guy you want to put in a locker and keep him there for awhile," Prince bellowed into the microphone as the keyboardist's shocked bandmates and family members looked on.

The ongoing barbs had an underlying message: Fink, who had gained weight and was showing other signs of aging, couldn't provide the hip, youthful image required for this gig. The Game Boyz, with their visual flare and "street" toughness, represented the future of the band.

The next piece fell into place by accident. Unbeknownst to Prince, Game Boyz dancer Tony Mosley occasionally practiced raps he had written during sound checks. One afternoon, midway through the tour, Prince overheard him and experienced an epiphany: Mosley had a tough, streetwise image, a powerful baritone voice, and witty rhymes. Quickly, a delighted Mosley was integrated into the live act not merely as one member of the dance troupe, but as a rapper who sometimes took center stage. And when the European swing concluded, Prince called him into Paisley Park Studios to add raps to several songs, including a remix of the song "New Power Generation" from *Graffiti Bridge*. Rapidly, this inexperienced young rapper emerged as a key member of the New Power Generation.

From the very beginning, though, Prince saw talents in Tony Mosley that no one else could detect. "I thought he was a Dr. Dre wannabe," said Rosie Gaines in a typical appraisal. Throughout Mosley's tenure, reactions to his contributions—from fans, critics, and Prince's associates—would be almost monolithically negative, and with good reason: Mosley's delivery was sloppy and dull, his image contrived and generic. His sudden prominence in Prince's music had little to do with Mosley himself—it was instead a historical accident explained only by Prince's haste to exploit the commercial appeal of rap. Because Prince had never understood rap, and in fact disliked it, he failed to perceive the vast gulf between his new recruit and much more skilled rappers, like Chuck D. and Ice-T, to whom Mosley's stylings bore a superficial resemblance.

But Mosley had the boss' ear, and he knew it. Several band members recall that Mosley exclaimed one day to his colleagues regarding Prince (who was not present): "I'm gonna shove black down that nigga's throat if it kills me." This declaration was a rallying cry to bring Prince back to his roots in African-American music.

And Mosley's impact quickly became apparent. Prince, in a visual emulation of "gangsta" rap, began singing into a microphone shaped like a gun and also began favoring more masculine clothing. Quite consciously, he was updating himself to attract younger consumers and to reconnect with African-American fans who might have been turned off by his movement toward rock and pop in the mid-1980s. "He wanted other black artists to look at him as 'hard' and as 'street' as they were," studio engineer Michael Koppelman said. "I remember he kept using the word 'hard.'"

To be fair, Prince's intent was never to embrace the violent nihilism of gangsta rap, but merely to borrow aspects of its imagery. With Mosley, Prince hoped to present the world a tough urban rapper whose lyrical messages, in contrast to those of groups like NWA, emphasized self-improvement; Mosley was a "gangsta," perhaps, but a benign one. But in any case, the notion of Prince as "hard" was preposterous. The massive appeal of gangsta rap stemmed from its authenticity; rappers like Dr. Dre, Ice Cube, and others had indeed been ghetto gangbangers, and in some cases continued to have run-ins with the law long after becoming famous. Prince, by contrast, was a cloistered, insular figure with no real connection to life on the streets. "He was as believable as a 'gangsta' as Snoop Dogg would be in a polka band," observed Alan Leeds.

Prince even engaged in revisionist history regarding his own views of rap music. He began identifying himself as a supporter of rap artists and claimed to associates that his own music—going as far back as the spoken-word, "people call me rude" interlude in his 1981 song "Controversy"—profoundly influenced the genre. "I remember Prince saying something to the effect that he had invented rap," Koppelman recalled.

Along with exploring new musical styles, Prince was also—as always—on the lookout for new romantic possibilities, and an opportunity would soon emerge on this front. In July 1990, a sixteen-year-old dancer named Mayte Garcia was dragged by her mother to Prince's concert in Barcelona, Spain. The child of Puerto Rican parents, Mayte spent much of her childhood in foreign countries due to her father being in the military. Home base was usually Germany. She had gravitated toward dancing since age three, showing skill in ballet and other forms, and in her mid-teens she picked up belly dancing and became interested in Middle Eastern music. One of her favorite tricks was to flip a coin using her belly button.

Mayte hadn't wanted to attend the concert because she was feeling under the weather and was not a Prince fan, but her mother convinced her to come along. She enjoyed the show and was particularly intrigued by the Middle Eastern undertones in the song "Thieves In The Temple." After the show, her mother encouraged Mayte to undertake an ambitious career move: sending Prince's organization a tape of her dancing. Not expecting anything to come of it, she agreed. About a month later, though, she received a call asking her to bring another tape to a show in Germany. She did, and was surprised to find herself called backstage for a meeting with Prince.

The chemistry between the rock star and the teenage beauty was immediate. As Prince told *Ebony* in 1996, he was enraptured even by the photo on her video case. "She was sixteen. I fell in love," he said. After Mayte left the dressing room, Rosie Gaines looked at him and said, "There's your future wife."

Prince stayed in touch through phone and mail, and Mayte continued to send him videos. As had been the case with Anna Garcia, Prince gave no overt signs of his sexual attraction to Mayte while she was underage. Still, a courtship was occurring, and both parties knew it. Prince told Garcia he wanted her to dance in his band and also sing on albums of music that he would write.

But even with Mayte waiting in the wings, Prince began pursuing another young protégée. Also in 1990, while visiting the Los Angeles nightclub Spice, Prince noticed a short, buxom blonde on the dance floor and sent over one of his handlers to approach her. The woman—a naive eighteen-year-old from Ohio named Tara Leigh Patrick, who had moved to Hollywood to follow her dream of breaking into the entertainment industry—was invited to Prince's rented home in Beverly Hills to audition for him. Nervous that she was being played for a fool, Patrick nonetheless agreed and ended up dancing and singing before a silent and expressionless Prince. He remained chilly afterwards, and Patrick left thinking she had blown her first big opportunity. About a month later, though, she received a phone call from Prince saying that he had written a song for her and wanted to sign her to a record deal.

From the start, Prince felt a strong sexual attraction to the busty Patrick, and a romance quickly commenced. Unlike so many teenagers who travel to Hollywood seeking fame, Patrick seemed to have stumbled upon the real deal, a powerful entertainer who wanted to shepherd her career and also be her boyfriend. Recasting her as a rapper, he developed rhythm tracks for Patrick to vocalize over. Soon, he asked her to move in with him in Chanhassen.

One evening while the couple watched a videocassette of the 1954 Otto Preminger musical *Carmen Jones,* Prince mentioned to Patrick that she "looked like a Carmen" and that this would be a perfect stage name for her. She agreed, and came up with the idea of adding "Electra"—the name of a Greek goddess—to the title. Thus was born Carmen Electra.

Associates recall Prince being quite taken with Electra, but not to the point where he was willing to cease dating other women. Just the same, reports filtered out to Electra's friends that Prince treated her in a highly domineering manner, insisting, for example, that she be immaculately dressed and groomed even when doing errands. Also, Electra soon found that being Prince's girlfriend was hardly all glamour and glitz, and that he was more of a workhorse than a party animal. "She hung around a lot; she would just sit there in the studio for hours and hours, and then he would take her home and come back and keep working," engineer Koppelman remembered.

Although Electra's voice was weak and her rapping imprecise, Prince took her seriously and spent long hours laboring on her album. As a result, more promising projects involving Rosie Gaines, Ingrid Chavez, and others suffered from inattention. Many of Prince's associates were flabbergasted that any serious musician, let alone a figure like Prince, would have professional interest in someone like Electra. But as in the case of Tony Mosley, Prince ignored any criticisms of his latest discovery.

With the arrival of Mosley and Electra, a major transition in Prince's career was nearly complete. During the mid-1980s, he had surrounded himself with a sophisticated group of friends and associates who had shown him new musical and cultural vistas. Eric and Alan Leeds exposed him to jazz, Wendy and Lisa taught him about sixties rock, and girlfriend Susannah Melvoin introduced him to art and high fashion. Now, virtually all of these people were gone from his life. (Only Alan Leeds, who would soon leave his post as president of Paisley Park Records, remained, and his personal relationship with Prince had already cooled.) Their replacements had little or nothing to teach him. NPG members like Michael Bland, Sonny Thompson, and Levi Seacer, while diverse and interesting people (Bland read Nietzsche during breaks in rehearsals, for example) and skilled musicians, were nonetheless conscious that Prince placed a premium on loyalty and docility. "My goal was to keep him out of my face, and I knew that to do it, I'd have to be brilliant, and I'd have to be able to learn the parts right as he was teaching them to me," one band member recalled.

Additionally, the prominent roles enjoyed by Mosley and Electra demonstrated the troubling extent to which Prince now valued style over substance. "Previously, he had enjoyed having people around like Sheila and Eric who kept him on his toes," observed Alan Leeds, "but after a while, he started surrounding himself with people who weren't a threat."

In terms of romantic interests, Prince was gravitating almost exclusively toward young models and actresses. During the 1980s he had explored more challenging romances with Susannah and (briefly) the New York artist Carole Davis, but these relationships—not unlike his friendships with older, more sophisticated musicians like Eric Leeds—on some level made Prince uncomfortable. Carmen Electra, who would later gain fame not as a rapper but as a *Baywatch* babe and *Playboy* centerfold, fit the new prototype for his girlfriends.

The final step in Prince's transition from the Revolution to the New Power Generation came with the dismissal of Matt Fink. When Prince decided on very short notice to perform at the "Rock In Rio" festival in Brazil, Fink, busy producing another project that could not be postponed, asked Prince's management to find a temporary replacement. Tommy Elm, a young keyboardist from Minneapolis, was drafted for the show, and much to Fink's surprise the switch ended up being permanent. "Prince never once called me to ask me why I couldn't do the gig," Fink recalled. "There was no personal phone call, no loyalty. His attitude was 'You didn't drop everything you were doing for me, so seeya!'" After offering Elm a slot in the New Power Generation, Prince rechristened him Tommy Barbarella, after the 1967 film *Barbarella*.

The collective image of the band was far less diverse than the face Prince presented to the world during the Revolution years. Barbarella was the only white member and Gaines the only woman. "We were his first black band, and our thing was to help him get his black audience back, because he had lost that," observed Gaines. Prince, once the apparent successor to Sly Stone and Jimi Hendrix in terms of his ability to blend black and white styles, was focusing more and more attention on a single market segment.

Another shift was that Prince allowed the NPG to play a significant role in the composing process. For most of his career, he had functioned in the studio primarily as a one-man band, playing most of the instruments on his first twelve albums. While *Purple Rain*, *Around The World In A Day*, and *Parade* had included input from members of the Revolution (especially Wendy and Lisa), these contributions usually came after Prince recorded the basic tracks. Only rarely (such as on "Purple Rain" and "Baby, I'm A Star" from *Purple Rain* and "America" and "The Ladder" from *Around The World In A Day*) did Prince record to tape with a full ensemble.

But with the New Power Generation's lineup now complete, Prince began relying extensively on the band in the studio, where songs were recorded live. Band members were encouraged to bring in their own ideas, and rehearsals became a primary forum for song creation. Levi Seacer, an aspiring songwriter and producer, was often deputized to create bass-and-drum grooves for presentation to Prince.

The impact of these changes was immediate: Prince's music became more ordinary and less edgy, and his songwriting essentially went on autopilot. Where his 1980s work had been characterized by, alternatively, minimalist funk and dense orchestration, his early 1990s output was much closer to straightforward rock and R&B. Prince's new band had plenty of competency but lacked a musical ideology, and the ideas that emerged from his sessions with the NPG were rarely distinctive.

But Prince was quite pleased with his group and hustled them into the studio in late 1990 to record three new songs: "Cream," "Live 4 Love," and "The Flow" (the latter song based on a Tony Mosley rap). Each was very much a collective effort. "The Flow," built on a shuffling funk-rock groove, showcases the intersecting vocals of Gaines and Mosley. "Cream" is powered by Bland's pile-driving drumming and Prince's blues-rock guitar riffing. Although over time the New Power Generation would cohere into an overly slick ensemble, these early recordings were engagingly raw, largely because the players were still getting to know each other. Michael Koppelman, one of the principal engineers on the project, would, later on, watch with dismay as songs like "Live 4 Love" were overhauled, becoming overproduced and glossy where they had once been powerful and energetic. "The first version of the album that we cut together was great," recalled Koppelman of the record that became *Diamonds And Pearls*. "Over the course of the year that we worked on it, it deteriorated."

Two of the songs that would end up on the album—"Money Don't Matter 2Night" and "Live 4 Love," addressed the 1990–91 Gulf War, the latter song being written from the perspective of a fighter pilot. Marylou Badeaux, who attended various dates on the Nude Tour, recalls visiting with Prince in his hotel room as he watched reports on CNN of Iraq's invasion of Kuwait. "He was concerned, not just about his safety, but about war in general," Badeaux remembered. According to Koppelman, the first version of "Live 4 Love," recorded in November 1990, took a critical stance on U.S. plans for intervention, which were at that time being considered by the Bush administration and Congress. But after the United States entered the war with air strikes against Iraq in January 1991, Prince—not unlike millions of other Americans who felt a moral obligation to support the country's troops in the field once combat began—shifted his position and altered the lyrics of "Live 4 Love" to make the pilot in the song a more sympathetic character.

In March, as work continued on *Diamonds And Pearls,* Prince received a phone call from Kate Bush, whom he had met in person backstage at a Wembley Stadium concert on the Nude Tour. The two musicians admired each other greatly and had discussed working together. Bush was now working on a song called "Why Should I Love You?" and wanted Prince to contribute backing vocals. Pleased at the request, he asked her to send the master tape of the song to Paisley Park.

Also excited about Bush's interest was Michael Koppelman, who had long been a huge fan of her music. He received Bush's tape and set it up for Prince to add his parts. Upon hearing "Why Should I Love You?," though, Prince developed other ideas. Instead of recording the vocal part Bush had requested, he transferred portions of the song to a blank master tape and began adding his own instruments. Koppelman watched in horror as Bush's song was transformed. "It was heartbreaking for me, because it was a beautiful Kate Bush song that we were just butchering," said Koppelman.

Further, Prince misinterpreted a line of Bush's lyrics on the chorus; instead of singing her line, "Of all the people in the world/Why should I love you?," Prince sang the first portion as "All of the people in the world." When Koppelman pointed out the apparent error, Prince smugly said that he and Bush had had "a little talk about that"; he seemed to be implying that she had agreed to the change. The next day, though, Koppelman learned that Prince had come back into the studio (without informing Koppelman, who in the past had always been contacted before sessions) to recut the vocal and correct the mistake.

After placing countless vocal and instrumental parts on the song, Prince sent it back to Bush. Both she and her engineer, Del Palmer, were shocked at the musical carnage and unsure what to do with it. "It basically took two years to put back together," Palmer said. "I made a general mix of the whole thing, gave it to Kate, and she puzzled over it for months. We tried to turn it back into a Kate Bush song."

"Why Should I Love You?" was finally released in 1993 on Bush's *The Red Shoes*, where it retains some of Prince's instrumental and vocal contributions. The song, while not without intriguing passages, shows the scars from the torturous process leading to its creation and sounds for the most part strained and inorganic. Palmer said that while he views the song as interesting, "In a lot of ways it didn't turn out as we'd hoped."

In early March, Prince presented an initial configuration of songs for *Diamonds And Pearls* to Mo Ostin and Lenny Waronker at Warner Bros. The company had wanted to hold off on a new Prince album, favoring instead a "greatest hits" collection that would cleanse the poor aftertaste of *Graffiti Bridge*. Concern was growing within Warner Bros. that Prince's insistence on releasing new material so rapidly was overwhelming consumers and saturating the market. But he held firm, and once the material sank in, Ostin and Waronker realized that it was the most commercially promising effort he had delivered in years. Although some at Warner Bros. felt ambivalent about his use of rap, the fact remained that this music, unlike the complex, spiritually oriented material of *Lovesexy* and *Graffiti Bridge*, might reach the vital youth market.

Ostin and Waronker became strongly invested in the project and participated in a number of meetings with Prince where they urged him to write additional commercial material. "Mo and Lenny had decided they were going to get Prince to make a great album, and not just a good album," noted Jeff Gold, who became senior vice president for creative services at Warner Bros. in 1990. "They felt his career needed a boost again." And Prince, after the disappointment of *Graffiti Bridge*, was to some extent open to their input.

Despite his newfound affection for group recordings, Prince continued to work alone on some of the material for *Diamonds And Pearls*, including the brilliant "Schoolyard," a funk-pop offering based on a percolating drum-machine pattern. Unfortunately, the song (which also includes effective backing vocals by Rosie

Gaines), represents the endpoint of the explorations that Prince had been undertaking for years with his LM-1 rhythm machine. Throughout the 1980s, Prince made the relatively primitive device a staple of his songwriting, running it through Boss effects pedals to achieve a drum sound unlike anything else in pop music. But beginning with *Lovesexy*, Prince began to lose interest not only in the Linn but, more generally, with rhythmic experimentation. With some exceptions, the beats he created on *Lovesexy*, *Graffiti Bridge*, and *Batman*—whether the product of rhythm machines or live drums— were less propulsive, less angular, and, ultimately, less interesting. "Schoolyard" represents one of the last times during the 1990s that Prince used the Linn before briefly resurrecting it on 1999's *Rave Un2 The Joy Fantastic*.

Another solo effort for *Diamonds And Pearls*, one far less interesting than "Schoolyard," was "Gett Off," a song that represented the heights of Prince's efforts to achieve a rap feel. Featuring ample contributions by Mosley and Gaines, the plodding number (based on a sampled rhythm pattern created by Levi Seacer) is awash in electronic noises and snippets of rapping and includes remarkably unsubtle and strained lyrics about anonymous sexual gratification. But both Prince and Warner Bros. were pleased with "Gett Off," believing it might break through to hip-hop fans, and the song was slated as the first single from *Diamonds And Pearls*. Meanwhile, "Schoolyard" was discarded and remains unreleased.

As Prince became absorbed in mixing and sequencing the album, some of the New Power Generation's camaraderie began to dissipate. Virtually every member of Prince's camp, from band members to studio engineers, found that his mood could shift rapidly and unexpectedly—one day in the studio he might be jocular and talkative, but the next would arrive wearing dark sunglasses (a sign he had slept very little or not at all) and treat people with remarkable coldness. "This was a guy who could host you for basketball and barbecue on Sunday at his house, and then jump all over you on Monday morning as if you were two different people in his life," noted Alan Leeds. There were also emerging concerns among band members about songwriting credit; although the recording of *Diamonds And Pearls* had been a fairly collaborative process, it seemed that most of the numbers were going to be credited on the album only to Prince. And Rosie Gaines became even more disappointed when Prince failed to fulfill a promise to help her solo career; after completing only a few songs with Gaines, Prince turned to Carmen Electra's album and a project for Elisa Fiorillo, another attractive but negligibly talented singer.

Prince pushed both himself and his band members relentlessly, and it wasn't uncommon for people to come down with flu and colds. "You had to get used to sleeping three hours, having nine hour rehearsals, and you were lucky if you got lunch," Gaines remembered. She recalls Prince (like everyone else) looking haggard some days, and she often encouraged him both to eat more and to take vitamins. "I think he needed someone to care for him, to care how he felt," she said.

But Prince demanded so much of himself and the band for one simple reason: He wanted a hit. After his recent chart setbacks, Prince believed he had reached a crucial crossroads in his career that would lead him either back to superstardom or toward musical obscurity. After peaking with *Purple Rain* in 1984, Prince had for several years emphasized artistic growth over commercial considerations. The result was a series of adventurous, sometimes erratic, rarely uninteresting albums that confirmed him as the most creative pop musician of his time. But despite the loyal fan base he developed between 1985 and 1990, the side of Prince that craved fame—the part of his psyche from which "Baby, I'm A Star" had sprung—became dissatisfied. His records weren't selling the way he wanted, he was no longer one of the world's most prominent superstars, and his financial situation remained shaky. *Diamonds And Pearls* became the means of rectifying all of this.

Despite the prominence of the New Power Generation on *Diamonds And Pearls,* Prince decided that he alone would grace the album cover, and he presented Warner Bros. with an odd photo of himself holding his mouth open and sticking out his tongue. Jeff Gold, the newly appointed senior vice president whose responsibilities included overseeing album covers, was mortified. Benny Medina, a veteran senior vice president who enjoyed significant contact with Prince, set up a meeting about the cover with Prince and Gold. It was Gold's first face-to-face contact with Prince, who was heavily made-up and wore a strange fluorescent green outfit. "He looked like he was ready for a photo shoot, and of course I learned later that he always looks like that," Gold remembered.

After introductions were concluded, the three men sat down and Medina came to the point: Gold didn't like the cover Prince had proposed. A moment later, a knock came at the door. Medina's lawyer needed to urgently speak with him, and the vice president excused himself. Gold sat uncomfortably as Prince glared across the table at him.

"So, what didn't you like about the cover?" Prince probed.

Gold gently explained that he thought something more distinctive was needed, and Prince asked for some examples of covers he liked. When Gold mentioned a project by REM, Prince went into a mini-tirade, saying that the group looked like a bunch of farm boys.

"What do you expect me to do, wear blue jeans and a T-shirt?" Prince asked incredulously.

"Well, it would be different," Gold ventured.

Prince looked at Gold as if he were insane. "You know what, I ought to go and have a set of clothes made for you," Prince said sarcastically. "I could make you look good."

Gold began to feel as if his first meeting with arguably the most important artist on the Warners roster was going very badly. When was Medina coming back?

Prince kept honing in on Gold. "What have you ever done, anyway? Show me something you've done that you think is good."

Gold, happy to have a break but wondering how much worse things might get, hustled upstairs to his office and grabbed a stack of album covers he had helped design. He brought them back to Prince, who flipped through them grimly. "Nah," he grunted as he blazed through the pile. "Well, this one's okay, but nah."

Finally, he reached the last record in the stack—a special edition of Susanne Vega's 1990 album *Days of Open Hands.* It featured a hologram on the cover.

"Now this is cool," Prince said. It was the first positive comment Gold had heard in an hour. "Why can't I have something like this?"

"Well, maybe you can," Gold responded.

"Nah, it'll cost too much money; they won't let me have something like this," Prince griped.

Fortuitously, Gold had just a couple of months before met a holographer with a technology that made these specialized visual images much cheaper to make. Gold told Prince that there might be hope after all.

Medina soon returned, and the meeting ended on an inconclusive but upbeat note. In the coming days, Gold determined that the holograms could indeed be produced fairly cheaply, and a photo shoot took place with Prince and two young women he had dubbed "Diamond" and "Pearl." Gold tried to socialize with Prince during the long equipment-related breaks during the session, but made no headway. Gold, a knowledgeable record collector and student of many musical genres, mentioned he had heard about Prince's work with Miles Davis. "Nah, I never worked with Miles Davis," Prince responded tersely, and stalked away to another corner of the set.

But when the developed photos came back, Prince was mesmerized by the results, which caused the image to change in appearance when tilted. After the holographic cover came out, Gold even received a thank-you note—something Prince's assistant told him was a true rarity. "The more [I] look, the more [I] love," Prince wrote in purple ink, using a picture of an eye in place of the word "I." "Thank U 4 the cool cover— Prince." Gold, who had felt like persona non grata during the first meeting with Prince, instead emerged as a hero.

On September 28, 1991—just a few days before the release of *Diamonds And Pearls*—the jazz giant Miles Davis passed away. Even in the last months of Miles' life, associates of both men had been encouraging further collaboration between them. In January 1991, Prince sent Miles three instrumental tracks that had been recorded back in 1988 for a possible third Madhouse album. Rather than adding horn parts, Miles and his band completely rerecorded the songs ("Penetration," "A Girl And Her Puppy," and "Jailbait"). He had tentatively planned to include them on what became his last solo album, *Doo-bop* (1992). But after Miles' death, neither his nor Prince's versions of the songs were released.

Gordon Meltzer, Miles' tour manager, contacted Alan Leeds to invite Prince to speak at a memorial service in New York. Prince instructed Leeds to tell Meltzer that he would prefer to send a written message to be read by someone else. This statement was delivered at the ceremony by Leeds, who added some of his own words about Miles.

It is difficult to view Prince's decision not to attend—like his longtime reluctance to engage in a full-fledged collaboration with Miles—as stemming from anything other than his fear of being in situations that he cannot fully control. The notion of being a speaker at an event that included the likes of Jesse Jackson and New York City Mayor David Dinkins likely intimidated him to the extent that his presence became impossible.

Prince chose a more solitary means of saying goodbye. Two days after Miles' death, he recorded an instrumental song at Paisley Park called "Letter 4 Miles," featuring Michael Bland on drums. It remains unreleased.

* * *

october 1991: release of diamonds and pearls

A major media blitz commenced with the release of the new record. To orchestrate the campaign, Prince hired Frank DiLeo, who had done promotional work for Michael Jackson. From the perspective of Warner Bros., DiLeo's arrival sent a signal that Prince lacked complete faith in the record label's promotional efforts. "He never felt we did our best," noted Marylou Badeaux. "He always felt that all success was because of him, not the company." And Prince's resentment toward the label continued to grow over Warners' complaints that he needed to slow down his output.

The *Diamonds And Pearls* push included high-profile performance showcases, and Prince and his band played energetic versions of "Cream" and "Daddy Pop" on the *Arsenio Hall* show and then "Gett Off" at the MTV Video Music Awards several nights later. For the MTV show, Prince appeared in a pair of pants cut so as to expose his buttocks, which generated significant media attention and water-cooler gossip. Clearly, Prince was trying to regain the element of shock that had fueled his initial rise to fame, but this time, there was a definite hint of ridicule in reactions to the stunt.

Still, the music itself was powerful, as Prince's young band members threw themselves into the performances. After the visit with Arsenio Hall, Prince and select associates retreated to his Beverly Hills home to watch a video of the show, and they came away elated. "We were all just in awe—shit, it was so good," said keyboardist Tommy Barbarella of the performance, which is recalled by some fans as one of Prince's strongest television appearances. The second single from the album, "Cream," reached No. 1 on the Pop Singles Chart, helping make *Diamonds And Pearls* a significant hit.

Prince also did a handful of interviews to promote the album, praising his band members, and in particular Rosie Gaines. "Rosie is like a tornado," he gushed to *Details*. "There's never enough hours in the day for her voice. There's never enough tape for her voice." But during these interviews, some reporters were openly skeptical of Prince's movement towards rap, putting him on the defensive. "Well, first, I never said I didn't like rap," he lamely told the British magazine *Sky*. "Anyway, everybody has the right to change their mind."

Prince's bedrock support among critics was weakening, as reactions to *Diamonds And Pearls*, while hardly hostile, were muted. The giddiness with which rock scribes greeted Prince's mid-1980s records like *Sign O' The Times* and *Parade* was absent. In the eyes of many critics and tastemakers, Prince was becoming just another pop/rock star— and even one willing to embrace current trends to achieve commercial success. "The imp continues spinning his wheels, the hole in the road growing a little deeper with each new record," wrote David Browne in *Entertainment Weekly*. Prince's hometown *Saint Paul Pioneer Press* called the album "long on eclecticism but short on originality." And Tom Moon of the *Philadelphia Inquirer* wrote that "[a]fter years as pop's closest thing to a Miles Davis–style innovator, [Prince] has compromised his artistic vision to sell some records."

Prince's excursion into rap was found wanting by most critics and serious fans of the style. Much bile was spewed at Tony Mosley, whom many saw as a pale imitation of a gangsta rapper. The consensus was that Prince had committed a spectacular error in judgment by making him a focal point of the NPG. (On the album's liner notes,

Prince even called Mosley "the wittiest pen the Twin Cities has ever seen.") And Prince's new streetwise image seemed an implausible reach.

But Mosley's slipshod rapping was only the most glaring deficiency on an album that represented an almost wholesale retreat from Prince's experimental pop-funk of the 1980s. Most of the music on *Diamonds And Pearls* is pedestrian, rarely straying from well-worn templates. The title track, despite its surplus of pop hooks, sinks under the weight of its over-production. "Cream," which borrows heavily from the classic rock hit "Bang A Gong" (by T Rex), is catchy but insubstantial. "Money Don't Matter 2night," which models the relaxed sound of late-period Stevie Wonder, breezes by without impact. "Willing And Able" is one of the few standout tracks, featuring a hypnotic bass guitar figure and a bluesy falsetto vocal by Prince. But this cut, like so much of the album, suffers from excessive instrumentation, as a needless sitar-like guitar riff drains the intensity.

But whatever its deficiencies, the album achieved Prince's goal of restoring him to prominence on radio, television, and in the print media, reaching No. 3 on the Pop Chart and No. 1 on the R&B Chart. Elated with his comeback, Prince mounted a massive tour of Japan, Australia, and Europe that proved every bit as successful as the album. Showcasing Tony Mosley and Rosie Gaines, the shows also relied heavily on meticulous choreography that left little room for musical improvisation. The New Power Generation's lineup was augmented by three female dancers (in addition to the Game Boyz), a rap-style deejay, and a five-piece horn section. Even more than the *Lovesexy* show, the production was a visual and aural carnival. "It was a freak show," remembered Tommy Barbarella. The concert began with Prince emerging from what looked like a space capsule amidst a flourish of lights. The set emphasized *Diamonds And Pearls* while also including crowd-pleasing favorites like "Purple Rain," "Let's Go Crazy," and "Kiss."

A scantily clad Carmen Electra served as an opening act during the European portion of the tour; she struggled gamely to project her warbly vocals over a band that Prince had assembled, but the twenty-minute sets invariably left audience members cold. Prince, scrambling for a solution, began replacing her band members one-by-one as the tour continued. "He couldn't put the blame on her, so he put it on the band—it was kind of a joke," recalled Barbarella. "The problem wasn't the band, it was that her squeaky little rap vocals did not carry in an arena or auditorium."

Electra's act was mercifully shelved after a June concert in London, although Prince assured her that her album would go forward. In any case, Electra seemed unperturbed by the apparent setback, and perhaps had already concluded that her talents lay elsewhere than rapping. Rather quickly, she had matured from an unsophisticated Midwestern teenager into an extremely ambitious young woman, and her looks and charisma began attracting the interest of entertainment industry impresarios.

Prince's romance with Electra continued in an on-and-off fashion during the tour. Another girlfriend, actress Troy Beyer, also visited him on the road, and he spent time with Mayte Garcia, although their relationship for the moment remained platonic.

As the *Diamonds And Pearls* tour received frenetic receptions in Australia and Japan, band members were caught up in an almost overwhelming fame that they had never expected. "By the time we got to the tour, the band felt invincible," drummer

Michael Bland said. "I would be flipping through television channels and see myself—few feelings can match that. I felt prosperous, but also very focused. We sounded as good as any bootleg of Sly & the Family Stone that I had ever heard." But the heady excitement also had less pleasant effects, as band members felt an increasing separation between themselves and Prince. Most members of the ensemble rode together on one bus, while Prince traveled in a limousine with several female companions and bodyguards. The atmosphere on the bus began to resemble an out-of-control fraternity, as the Game Boyz and other members of the male-dominated entourage engaged in rampant womanizing and generally crude behavior. "Tony M. and [Game Boyz dancer] Damon [Dickson] seemed determined to make life miserable for many around them," noted one observer.

Most unhappy was Rosie Gaines, the only woman on the bus. Several band members, resentful of her prominent role onstage, taunted her for being overweight and generally created an environment where few women would have felt comfortable. Gaines voiced concerns to Gilbert Davison (Prince's former bodyguard who was appointed manager after the rapid departure of Stiefel & Phillips) but nothing changed. Finally, she went directly to Prince, who seemed annoyed by the assertion that anything was wrong on his tour bus. "He didn't want anyone to complain to him, ever," Gaines recalled. Only when she threatened to leave the tour and told Prince that he might ultimately face legal trouble for some of the shenanigans on the bus did he act—not by intervening, but simply by transferring Gaines to another bus with Mavis Staples, one of the opening acts on the tour. For the remainder of the tour, Gaines felt a deep schism between herself and much of the band, and she spent almost all of her offstage time alone. "That tour was the worse time of my life," she said. "What was happening on the bus had nothing to do with Prince, but he didn't do anything to protect me, either."

His behavior towards Gaines showed Prince's moody, divided personality. Occasionally, he treated her almost as a confidant, as when the two enjoyed late-night conversations about spiritual issues. But around his male entourage, Prince would often echo the misogynistic tone set by some band members. "When he was with the boys, then I was just another woman to him," Gaines said. "He was kind of a male-chauvinist at that point; he would say things like, 'Oh, she must have her period.'"

With multiple family members depending on her, Gaines sent much of her weekly wage (about $2,200) home, and had only $800 to her name when the tour ended. Just the same, she put her belongings in a truck and drove from Minneapolis to her home in Pittsburg, California, quitting the band for good. Although she would later work with Prince in the studio on several occasions, she would long harbor resentment about what she considers an absence of complete credit for her songwriting contributions on *Diamonds And Pearls*. "A lot of those were ideas the band came up with," Gaines asserted. "He had told us before doing [*Diamonds And Pearls*] that we were going to be like a family, we're all going to do it together, and we're going to share in it together, and we all trusted him. That's our fault for not getting it on paper."

When Gaines approached Prince about songwriting credit, he made clear that he considered *Diamonds And Pearls* his work, and he disagreed that she deserved more money. "I told him, 'You want us here twenty-four hours a day, but you don't pay us enough money to look after our families,'" she remembered. "I don't think it really clicked with him that people have lives, they have children. He would always say to me, 'People have to look out for themselves.'"

Life on the road was also sometimes hard for young Mayte Garcia. Although Prince continued to treat her as a girlfriend-in-waiting, he took no steps to insulate Mayte from the rambunctious, male-dominated atmosphere that surrounded the tour. Gaines recalls on several occasions seeing Mayte in tears on the bus and in dressing rooms, apparently overwhelmed by feelings of homesickness. When Mayte was summoned to the inner sanctum and felt the glow of Prince's attention, it felt magical. But at other times, left to her own devices, she was simply a confused teenager with no one to talk to.

As Gaines watched the Prince-Mayte courtship unfold, she marveled at how much this young woman resembled his previous girlfriends, both in looks and temperament. She was another young woman who could not have been easier to manipulate. This would likely be another relationship that would persist only until Mayte—like Kim Upsher, Susan Moonsie, Susannah Melvoin, and Anna Garcia before her—grew up enough to object. "She was too young to have her own thoughts yet, and Prince liked that," Gaines remembered. "But I knew that would change."

Commercially, *Diamonds And Pearls* turned out to be exactly the comeback Prince had hoped for; it was, other than the stratospheric *Purple Rain*, the biggest seller of his career to date, moving 2.9 million units in the United States and 6.3 million worldwide. The intense publicity campaign raised Prince's profile and did much to remind younger record buyers of his existence. Yet it was in many ways a Pyrrhic victory. He had traded in his status as an experimentalist and critics' darling for an uptick on the charts—one that would prove quite short-lived. After his awkward embrace of rap music, Tony Mosley, and gangsta imagery, it was much harder to take Prince seriously as the Ellington-like figure he had seemed on the verge of becoming.

Prince, while at least conscious of a potential backlash among critics and hardcore fans caused by *Diamonds And Pearls*, did not seem overly concerned. With his fame reinvigorated, he turned back to his core concern—making as much music as possible. He was filled with ideas—far too many, in fact, to suit Warner Bros., which wished he would slow his output. But his hand had been strengthened by *Diamonds And Pearls*, and he believed the album's success gave him renewed license to release whatever he wished, whenever he wished. The fundamental tension between him and Warners on this issue would soon blow up.

CHAPTER THIRTEEN

ames

With good reason, Warner Bros. expected that Paisley Park Records, its joint venture with Prince, would be a cash cow. In the early and mid-1980s, he had created successful projects such as the Time, Vanity 6, and the Family out of whole cloth by writing and recording all of their music. He had been a one-man hit factory, churning out chart-topping songs like "When Doves Cry" and "Kiss" under his own name while crafting hit singles for the Bangles ("Manic Monday"), Sheena Easton ("Sugar Walls"), and others. By giving Prince the perk of his own label, Warners hoped to gather all of his future triumphs under its umbrella.

Prince's own plans for Paisley Park Records were even grander. He envisioned the label as a contemporary successor to the legendary Motown Records, through which founder Berry Gordy placed a personal stamp on the careers of R&B giants like Smokey Robinson, the Supremes, Stevie Wonder, and Marvin Gaye. Gordy's control was pervasive, to the point where artists were told how to dress onstage and what to say in interviews, and Prince's conceptualization of side projects like the Family and the Time showed a similar obsession with detail. (Lost on Prince was that Gordy's tyrannical and smothering management style alienated some of his most important artists, causing bitter clashes with Marvin Gaye and others, in some cases driving artists from the label.) And although Paisley was technically a partnership with Warner Bros., Prince expected free rein—and a blank check—to do what he wished with the label.

Another model of what Prince sought to achieve, at least in terms of commercial success, was no further away than the neighboring suburb of Edina, Minnesota, the home of Flyte Tyme Productions. This flourishing concern of former associates Jimmy Jam and Terry Lewis—members of the Time until Prince fired them for branching out to produce other groups—was a mecca for Top 40 artists. Jam and Lewis were by the mid-1990s arguably the most successful production team in popular music, having created multi-platinum records with Janet Jackson (*Control* in 1986 and *Rhythm Nation 1814* in 1989), Alexander O'Neal (*Hearsay* in 1994), and others; Prince considered them competitors and saw Paisley as a way to even the score.

There was, however, a fundamental difference between the skills of Prince and those of the Flyte Tyme team. Jam and Lewis, while not Prince's equals as musicians or songwriters, were more adept at collaboration, an essential skill for a producer. Prince, by contrast, functioned as an auteur even when working on side projects with other musicians; his presence tended to stifle, rather than enhance the creativity of others. "Invariably, no matter who the artist was, he tried to force them into his thing," noted Alan Leeds, who in 1989 surrendered his post as Prince's tour manager to become president of Paisley Park Records. "He never displayed the ability to park his own agenda. When he produced Patti LaBelle, it sounded like a Prince record. It became his vision, not the artist's."

There was another basic problem: In the mid-1980s, with his songwriting powers at their peak, Prince generated enough strong music for a variety of spin-offs. But by the end of the decade, with his creativity tapering off, there wasn't enough quality material to go around. Increasingly, recording and composing became a rushed exercise for Prince; with his attention diffused across as many as a dozen different projects at once, he lacked the focus that had animated his best work.

Recognizing the need to diversify the label, Prince did sign some artists from outside of his circle and gave them the freedom to develop their own albums. (In such instances, he typically contributed a song or two but would otherwise stay out of the way.) These signings, though, were not particularly astute. Two New Wave–oriented acts, the neo-psychedelic group the Three O'Clock and the chirpy singer Dale Bozzio (formerly of Missing Persons), released forgettable albums on Paisley Park in the late 1980s. Prince also signed two aging R&B veterans, George Clinton and Mavis Staples, whose best work was well behind them and whose Paisley releases (Clinton's *The Cinderella Theory* and *Hey Man . . . Smell My Finger* and Staples' *Time Waits For No One* and *The Voice*) had little commercial or critical impact.

The Paisley Park label became not an incubator for new stars but rather a scrap yard for aborted projects. In the early 1990s, albums by Rosie Gaines, Jill Jones, Robin Power (a marginal rapper whom Prince met at an L.A. nightclub), and Margie Cox (a singer who had previously worked with Prince's drummer Michael Bland) were undertaken but ultimately dropped. Moreover, Prince paid little attention to the purely business aspects of the label and refused to operate with any sense of fiscal restraint. Believing that it was Warner Bros.' responsibility to generate sales, he was nonplussed by what he perceived as a lack of promotional support. Indeed, Prince was skeptical about the parent company's sincerity, as were some of his associates. "Paisley Park was not really a priority with Warner Bros.; I don't know if their commitment was so real," said studio engineer David Rivkin. "I believe it was kind of a carrot they held in front of him to keep him on Warner Bros." A source who then worked at Warners concurs in this view: "Paisley was superficial, just a way to placate Prince."

It is also true, however, that Prince gave Warners little to work with and did a poor job of running Paisley Park. Leeds, for one, believes that Prince could have done more to forge a harmonious relationship with the parent label. "He refused to accept the premise that once you take someone's money, they're a partner," Leeds observed.

A project featuring Ingrid Chavez, Prince's sometime spiritual muse and the costar of *Graffiti Bridge*, came to symbolize many of the problems with the label. The long road to Chavez' solo debut began in December 1987, when Prince, aglow over the spiritual epiphany that inspired *Lovesexy*, began working with her. Initially, he seemed enthusiastic about the project, which featured Chavez reading her poetry over restrained, atmospheric grooves. Songs like "Elephant Box" and "Heaven Must Near" sounded like a mixture of Princely funk and New Age ambient music.

But when Prince was waylaid by the *Lovesexy* tour, the *Batman* soundtrack, and then *Graffiti Bridge*, the Chavez project fell into limbo. It may have remained there absent the intervention in 1990 of Michael Koppelman, the talented engineer who had worked on *Diamonds And Pearls*. After bumping into Chavez on several occasions at Paisley Park, he began collaborating with her on material that deviated somewhat from Prince's initial template. The music retained a subdued, ethereal ambiance, but Koppelman made greater use of melody and dynamics. Most notably, Chavez actually began singing (as opposed to just speaking) on songs like the catchy "Hippy Blood."

When the duo in 1991 finally completed the album—now about evenly split between the Chavez-Koppelman collaborations and the original Prince songs—the question was how to get it before the public. Prince had seemingly lost interest. Chavez, while hopeful that he might still release it on Paisley Park, feared that Warner Bros., after so many flops from the subsidiary label, would fail to get behind the project. Seeing "Hippy Blood" as a potential hit single that could fuel the success of the entire album, Chavez met with Warners officials to play them cuts and, hopefully, to drum up support. "We had dollar signs in our eyes," recalled Koppelman.

But Prince, upon learning of these activities, felt blindsided—partly by Chavez' overtures to Warners, but also because work on the album had proceeded without him. He and Chavez had an angry confrontation in a Paisley Park control room as Koppelman watched from outside. In the course of this clash, the once-promising project was derailed. The album's ultimate fate was just what Chavez feared—Prince agreed to release it but did nothing to make it succeed. Warners made nothing more than a perfunctory effort at promotion. Chavez' oddly titled *May 19, 1992* (released on September 24, 1991) was barely acknowledged by the music press and failed to enter the Billboard Pop Chart.

A few weeks after the Prince-Chavez row that consigned the Chavez' album to oblivion, Koppelman found himself alone with Prince in the studio. Although he did not want to spark another disagreement, he couldn't help but ask why Prince had been so upset about the project. "If it's good music, what's the big deal if the label hears it before you do?" Koppelman asked. "I mean, did you like it? Do you think 'Hippy Blood' is any good?"

Prince gave Koppelman a strange look. Without a tinge of sarcasm or anger, he said, "Yeah, it's good. It's so good it's going to change music."

Koppelman suddenly understood. For all of his swagger, Prince was at his core vulnerable and insecure. Even though he had been too busy to complete the Chavez project, he was hurt that it went on without him. He also feared that he had been shown up. Prince's insistence on control, it seemed, stemmed at least in part from deep-seated worries that others might outdo him.

*   *   *

The lack of attention that bedeviled the Chavez project impacted various other Prince efforts in the early 1990s as well. Between December 1991, when he began recording ⚥, his follow-up to *Diamonds And Pearls*, and October 1992, when it was released, Prince labored on numerous other efforts, including an album featuring his backing band, the New Power Generation; a collection of songs for a film musical; and the planned solo debut by Carmen Electra. He also contributed songs to albums by Celine Dion ("With This Tear"), Joe Cocker ("Five Women"), Howard Hewitt ("Allegiance"), and other artists. And he found time to shoot a short film featuring his newest protégée, Mayte Garcia. Unfortunately, very little of note would emerge from all of this harried activity.

As on *Diamonds And Pearls*, The NPG remained an integral part of Prince's composing process, often cutting songs live in the studio with him. But the feel of the band had changed. Although *Diamonds And Pearls*, recorded shortly after the NPG's formation, captured some of the energy and rawness of a still-jelling unit, by late 1991 the group became ultra-polished. Three new songs recorded in December all gave the band a chance to show off its chops, with Michael Bland leading the way with his heavily accented drumming. "Sexy MF" blended rap and James Brown–style funk, "Love 2 The 9's" veered toward jazz-fusion, and "The Morning Papers" was a slice of middle-of-the-road rock. But for all the stylistic ground covered, there was a troubling commonality—a sense of creative lethargy and missing inspiration. The topflight musicianship could not hide (and sometimes highlighted) the inherent weakness of the songs. A number like "Sexy MF," for all its danceability, sounded more like an unfinished idea than a completed cut.

Elsewhere, Prince became overly fascinated with structural complexity and instrumental embellishments, resulting in songs with all the life and spontaneity squeezed out of them. The sprawling, heavily orchestrated "3 Chains O' Gold" meandered through its Byzantine arrangement and seemed to almost drown in overdubs. As the band members worked on the song during a long, tedious recording session, more than one was reminded of the Queen song "Bohemian Rhapsody," a highwater mark of rock 'n' roll excess.

Even as they worked on ⚥, Prince and the NPG began developing an entire project called *Gold Nigga* around Tony Mosley's rapping. The songs, penned by Prince but featuring heavy instrumental input from the band, were essentially funk jams and employed titles like "Black MF In The House" and "Goldnigga." A direct response to the profanity-laced work of gangsta rappers like NWA, this project again found Prince struggling to achieve "street" credibility. But like the rap forays on *Diamonds And Pearls*, the results seemed strained and inauthentic.

The New Power Generation also emerged in the early 1990s as the center of Prince's social life. With Rosie Gaines gone, the ambience surrounding the band became ever more like a boys' club, as Prince reveled in the bawdy, Richard Pryor–like humor offered up by Levi Seacer and other members of the ensemble. When Seacer took to greeting colleagues in the halls at Paisley Park by bellowing "You sexy motherfucker!," Prince found this hilarious and built "Sexy MF" around this phrase. Whereas earlier in his career, friends found Prince to have a strong feminine presence, he was now quite consciously exploring his masculine energies. There remained few if any strong female confidants in his life (a role that Rosie Gaines briefly fulfilled), as young companions like Anna Garcia, Mayte Garcia, and Carmen Electra were discouraged from offering their opinions and served primarily as pretty muses.

Even as he worked with the NPG on 🎵 and *Gold Nigga,*Prince pursued a variety of other projects on his own. During the *Diamonds And Pearls* tour, he jumped at a chance to re-enter the world of film when James Brooks, the director of *Broadcast News* and *Terms Of Endearment,* asked him to contribute a song for the movie musical *I'll Do Anything* starring Nick Nolte and Albert Brooks. During a meeting with James Brooks in March 1992, Prince was so enthusiastic about the endeavor that he offered to write the entire soundtrack. The director agreed, and Prince began creating material to be sung by the actors in the film. Most of the numbers were hastily written and recorded at 301 Studios in Sydney, where Prince retreated between his Australian shows and even late on the evenings of the concert themselves. Songs like "Make Believe" and "Be My Mirror" had a sing-songy, whimsical feel appropriate to a musical, but offered little in the way of melodic or rhythmic appeal.

Brooks' film quickly ran into trouble. Test screenings with the characters singing received scathing reviews from audiences, prompting the director to radically rework the project. He scrapped the notion of a musical and turned *I'll Do Anything* into a standard romantic comedy. (The film opened to mediocre reviews in 1994.) There was no need for Prince's compositions, and his involvement ended. Three of the songs, "The Rest Of My Life," "There Is Lonely," and "My Little Pill" later turned up on his album *The Vault . . . Old Friends 4 Sale* in 1999; the rest remain unreleased.

With 🎵 ready and awaiting its late-1992 release, Prince and Warner Bros. had an important piece of business to take care of: signing a new agreement. Their existing pact was about to expire at a fortuitous time for Prince. The success of *Diamonds And Pearls* boosted his commercial status, and changes in the music industry strengthened his hand even further.

The 1980s, like any decade, had seen its share of one-hit wonders—marginally talented artists who managed to rise from obscurity to the top of the pop charts. But to the record labels that backed them, acts like Tiffany, Exposé, the Escape Club, Michael Damian, and Mike and the Mechanics—all of whom scored No. 1 hits as the decade wound down, only to quickly disappear—were money-makers only in a very short-term sense. And they did nothing for the reputations of the companies they made music for. By 1990, when the saccharine group Milli Vanilli was exposed as a fraud (the members of the ensemble had neither sung nor played on their albums), the industry took a collective deep breath and re-examined its priorities.

In the early 1990s, executives at major companies like Warner Bros. made an important shift in their approach. Although continuous efforts were made to discover and develop new acts, the labels also tried to identify artists already on their rosters with the potential for longevity. Executives began to place even more of a premium on stars not only with proven hit-making ability, but who also enjoyed loyal fan support and artistic credibility. This rarified club included Aerosmith, which reinvented itself in the late 1980s after years of drug addiction and artistic dormancy; Michael Jackson, for years the hottest-selling artist in popular music; Janet Jackson, whose name had become a trademark every bit as powerful as her brother's; Madonna, someone with an unfailing flare for creating publicity who had also begun to demonstrate genuine musical talent; and the alternative rock band REM, which built a large and committed following through a series of strong albums.

Beginning with a $40 million, three-album deal negotiated between Janet Jackson's management and Virgin Records in March 1991, labels extended a series of dramatic long-term pacts to such artists. Financially, these were the most staggering packages the industry had ever seen. Sony signed Michael Jackson to a $60 million, six-album deal and then Aerosmith to a $37 million, four-album agreement. Madonna brokered a complex $60 million deal with Time-Warner that included funding for her own record label, Maverick.

Prince in many respects fit the paradigm of the flagship artist. When his lawyer, Gary Stiffleman (who had negotiated blockbuster deals for the Rolling Stones, ZZ Top, and Aerosmith), sat down with Warner Bros.' officials in summer 1992, he knew that they had little choice but to offer a lucrative long-term contract. The company was not likely to let one of the most successful artists in its history defect to a competitor. Still, Mo Ostin and the other Warners executives across the table from Stiffleman knew that Prince was far more mercurial, in terms of his artistic and personal temperament, than Madonna, Janet Jackson, or even Steven Tyler and Joe Perry of Aerosmith (who shed their party-boy images after entering drug rehab). Whether his next effort would be a well-crafted, commercially oriented work like *Diamonds And Pearls* or a self-indulgent quirk-fest like *Graffiti Bridge* was impossible to predict.

The agreement reached between Prince and Warner Bros. in late August was, like most large-scale entertainment industry pacts, extremely complex and not susceptible to easy interpretation. Nonetheless, his in-house publicists beat Warners to the media, and they trumpeted the deal in simple, dramatic terms: a six-record pact worth $100 million. On its face, this seemed to dwarf all of the recent deals that had altered the record industry's economic landscape. Prince's team, led by Paisley Park vice president Jill Willis, claimed that the deal gave him an advance of $10 million per album in addition to new funding for Paisley Park Records and perks like an office suite in Los Angeles' Century City.

At Warners, there was immediate shock over this characterization of the accord. The $100 million figure that appeared so prominently in media accounts had a profligate ring, making the company appear irresponsible. It seemed inconceivable that Prince had landed a better deal than Madonna, also part of the Time-Warner family. Since 1983, she had released eight albums, which sold a collective 76 million worldwide—an average of 9.5 million each. Prince's sales during the same period averaged four million an album.

Follow-up media articles questioned whether Prince had indeed misled the press about the lavishness of the deal. The $10 million per-album advance, it was reported in *Time*, kicked in only if his previous album had sold five million copies or more; if sales fell below that number, a new figure would have to be negotiated. Since he rarely sold this many copies (*Purple Rain* and *Diamonds And Pearls* being rare exceptions), the

$10 million figure was inherently speculative. An article in *Billboard* quoted several entertainment industry insiders saying that Warners would never have agreed to the deal on the terms described by Prince.

Although these accounts gave Warner Bros. some cover, officials there continued to feel snookered by Prince's hyperbolic portrayal of the deal. He, in turn, was distressed to read stories questioning whether he really was the highest-paid artist in pop music. With Prince and Warners at odds over what the contract meant, the latest chapter in their relationship began under a cloud of tension and mutual suspicion.

Adding to the tension was that there was no longer an effective, day-to-day inter- mediary between them. (Gary Stiffleman, who handled legal rather than managerial affairs for Prince, stepped back after the contract was inked.) For years, Steve Fargnoli had been effective in smoothing over cracks in the relationship. But with the firing of Cavallo, Ruffalo & Fargnoli, Prince abandoned the notion of placing his business affairs in the hands of a strong executive. After ending his brief relationship with Stiefel & Phillips, he installed as the nominal manager his longtime bodyguard, Gilbert Davison, who also became president of Paisley Park Enterprises, the umbrella corporation for Prince's various activities. To say that Davison was a lunkhead with no business experience overstates the case, but nor was he a first-tier manager, and his authority was extremely limited. "Prince was becoming paranoid and less trusting of the people around him," noted one Warners official.

With no buffer between himself and the label, Prince began to have a level of direct contact with Warners officials that was extremely unusual for a major star. Those who dealt frequently with Prince found him haughty, imperious, and wildly unrealistic in his expectations. Meetings over promotional issues became strange and unproduc- tive exercises. Marylou Badeaux recalls a session where as many as thirty staffers and executives gathered at a huge conference table to talk strategy with Prince, who came alone. As is typical for such affairs, attendees piped up with enthusiastic predictions about record sales; Prince quickly became impatient and started rolling his eyes as he looked across the table at Badeaux. "He was like, 'I can't believe that these people are saying these things,'" she said.

Then he began interrupting with pointed questions, giving the meeting the air of an adversarial proceeding. When one attendee mentioned international sales projec- tions, Prince interjected sarcastically, "So, what happened in Spain with the last record?" An uncomfortable silence followed.

"He was letting people know that he knew his business," Badeaux recalled. "He was saying, 'I'm not going to just be the docile artist sitting there, and you're not going to put anything past me.'" But if Prince was skillful at cutting through blather, he was less effective as a business partner. Always quick to criticize Warners' efforts, he recog- nized no responsibility on his part to help; once he delivered an album, he believed his work was done.

The promotional campaign for ♀ got off to a poor start over a dispute regarding the choice of a lead single. While Prince favored "My Name Is Prince" (an abrasive, rather hookless number that seemed to offer little chart potential), Warners' pop music department argued for "7," a melodic, acoustic-guitar driven song with soaring har- monies and Middle Eastern inflections. "'7' just blew me away," recalled vice president

Jeff Gold. But Prince, believing this dialogue was a sequel to his arguments with Warners over "When Doves Cry" and "Kiss," insisted on having his way. Why he believed so strongly in "My Name Is Prince" is unclear, but he may have felt that the song's hip-hoppery would appeal to the same audience that had eagerly purchased *Diamonds And Pearls*. This time, however, he was wrong. "My Name Is Prince," released on September 29, reached only No. 36 on the Pop Singles Chart and No. 25 on the R&B Singles Chart.

It was an inauspicious beginning for ♀, which hit the streets in mid-October 1992. The album is in many respects a companion piece to *Diamonds And Pearls*, again featuring prominent contributions from the NPG and Tony Mosley. The most ambitious— and controversial—aspect of the album was Prince's attempt to construct what he termed a "rock soap opera," a musical story with segues spoken by a narrator (the actress Kirstie Ally). The narrative had initially been more coherent, but when Prince at the last minute added a song called "I Wanna Melt With U," many of the explanatory segues were excised so the lengthy album could fit on a single compact disc. As far as could be discerned, the plot focused on Prince's attempts to woo the teenage princess of a Middle Eastern country (played by Mayte Garcia). But the story made little sense, and the narration offered little more than a distraction from the music.

Like *Diamonds And Pearls*, ♀ divided fans and critics. Many were perturbed by the rapping, the orchestral production, and the confusing rock opera concept. Others admired the stylistic scope of the album, which included sentimental ballads, techno-pop, and dance-floor funk, amongst other styles. But the general consensus was that ♀ broke no new ground, and certainly did not stand among Prince's best works. " ♀ is the prolific Prince's most derivative-sounding album," complained Jon Bream in the *Minneapolis Star Tribune*. J.D. Considine in *Rolling Stone* praised much of the album, but felt that the ideas at its core were murky. "As usual, ambition gets the better of him, and Prince ends up turning what might have been simple fun into a high-concept muddle," he wrote.

♀ finds Prince in the same creative malaise that had characterized his work since at least *Batman*. Like *Diamonds And Pearls*, the album is glossy and overproduced, but it is even less enjoyable due to the inclusion of slackly written songs like "My Name Is Prince," "Sexy MF," another drony funk number called "The Max," and the gossamer-thin ballad "Sweet Baby." Several numbers are remarkably conventional and unoriginal, such as the reggae-flavored "Blue Light" and "The Morning Papers," which would not sound out of place on a Billy Joel album. The only notable accomplishment to emerge from the murk is "7," an assured piece of songwriting with many fascinating production touches, including acoustic guitar, a jaunty drum-machine pattern, and sitar-like overdubs. (Notably, the song is a Prince solo recording.)

Sales were reasonably strong at first, but the album was a commercial disappointment in comparison to *Diamonds And Pearls*. ♀ reached No. 5 on the Pop Chart and sold 2.8 million copies worldwide, a respectable showing but far short of the smash Prince expected. He became furious about the sales figures, which he blamed on slack promotion by Warner Bros.

If Prince's poor decisions about ♀—the choice of a first single and the rock opera concept among them—were not enough to give label officials pause about the contract they had just signed, there were other disquieting signals as well. During 1992, he presented the label with various configurations of *On Top*, the planned solo debut by Carmen Electra. The consensus among label officials was that the material was not nearly ready for release—the backing tracks that Prince created were not especially effective, and Electra's vocals were amateurish. As diplomatically as they could, executives voiced their misgivings. Undeterred, Prince kept writing songs and even had an expensive video shot for the song "Go Go Dancer."

Finally, the album, now called *Carmen Electra*, was released in February 1993. In many respects—like so many of his side projects before it—it was another Prince album. But despite the funky beats and other trademark touches, the most prominent element was the vocal work of the former Tara Patrick, and studio trickery could mask neither the weakness of her voice nor her lack of precision as a rapper. On fast-paced songs like "Step To The Mic," she seemed to be struggling simply to keep up.

The record sold very poorly and failed to even enter the Pop Chart. From the perspective of Warners, which had sunk $1 million into promoting *Carmen Electra*, the entire effort was nothing short of a boondoggle. For all of the work Prince invested in it, the album was unmistakably a slipshod effort and another sign that his creativity— to say nothing of his ability to judge talent—had gone missing.

In May 1992, Alan Leeds, one of the very last members of Prince's inner circle with a truly independent voice, resigned his post as president of Paisley Park Records. This concluded an association with Prince that began nearly a decade earlier on the *1999* tour. For many years Leeds was a trusted friend and confidant, but he and Prince had drifted apart in the early 1990s. As he prepared to leave, Leeds felt a deep sense of disillusionment about an artist whose career had just recently seemed so promising. The rapping and other commercial capitulations, the pseudo-gangsta imagery, and the attention lavished on protégées like Electra all seemed to Leeds a betrayal of Prince's astonishing potential. "I don't think he took his gift seriously," said Leeds, looking back at Prince's work from this period.

At Warner Bros. and other labels, there was no retreat from the gigantic deals given to major artists in the early part of the decade. In 1996, a bidding war with Dreamworks Records prompted Warners to enter an $80 million, five-album pact with REM. This agreement (like some of the other mega deals before it) generated plenty of second-guessing, especially when the group's subsequent album sold poorly.

For the industry as a whole, this new way of doing business ended up a hit-or-miss proposition. While REM failed to justify the millions spent on it, Janet Jackson scored one success after another. Her brother, by contrast, lost his commercial rhythm and became embroiled in various legal and public relations battles. Aerosmith, meanwhile, despite the advancing age of its members (which had prompted some industry insiders to question the group's deal) continued to be a market leader for years to come.

But if some of the huge contracts proved more prescient than others, no deal would create more angst for any record label—and indeed, the entire industry—than the one given by Warner Bros. to Prince.

arfare

P rince was outraged by the poor commercial performance of ♀. He placed the blame wholly on Warner Bros., believing that its publicity campaign had been slack. That his own decisions contributed to its failure—such as the poor choice of a lead single and the album's confusing storyline—did not enter Prince's thinking.

Prince's misplaced griping helped generate a pervasive gloom about his career at the label. Among the mid-level staff, whose efforts and enthusiasm were essential to the success of any project, there was growing impatience with his arrogance, eccentricity, and inflexibility. "The mood was that people had had it," recalled Marylou Badeaux. "People were saying to me, 'This guy is out of control.'"

Major concerns also developed within the company's executive offices. Having so recently signed him to an expensive contract, Mo Ostin and Lenny Waronker were worried about Prince's commercial performance as well as an inherently related issue: the brisk pace at which he insisted on releasing albums. They understood well that successful marketing of a pop release depends on building a sense of mystery. When albums are issued relatively infrequently—perhaps every couple of years—a new project is greeted as a major event and a rare glimpse into the world of an elusive figure. By generating records more frequently than once a year and touring almost as often, Prince turned this premise on its head, and the release of ♀ so soon after *Diamonds And Pearls* halted his commercial comeback. He had become seriously overexposed—another point Prince would not think of conceding.

His ubiquity highlighted another problem: His identity as an artist had become ill-defined at best. Was he still an innovator and synthesizer of genres? The clumsy rapping on *Diamonds And Pearls* and ♀ called this into question. Cultural rebel? Not with gangsta rappers and young alt-rockers like Kurt Cobain capturing the imagination of America's youth. Pop hitmaker? *Diamonds And Pearls* hinted at this possibility, but in truth he could not compete with multi-platinum perennials like Mariah Carey, Janet

Jackson, and Boyz II Men. No longer an instantly bankable superstar nor an acknowledged creative revolutionary, Prince offered fans no compelling reason to buy his albums, and his following was eroding.

And he insisted, over Warner Bros.' objections, on pushing album after album on the public. This fundamental conflict led to the gradual deterioration of relations between Prince and Mo Ostin, the single most important figure at the company. Through roughly the first half of the 1980s, Prince and Ostin enjoyed a cordial and productive partnership, but with Warners' refusal to green-light the three-album set *Crystal Ball* in 1987, Prince came to feel he could no longer depend on Ostin's support. Still, in the years that followed the chairman remained as flexible as he could—approving the controversial cover art for *Lovesexy*, pulling *The Black Album* at the last possible moment, and supporting dubious Paisley Park releases like *Carmen Electra*. But by mid-1993, the chairman's fiduciary duty to the corporation he ran forced him to inject some reality into the relationship; no longer could Prince be given carte blanche to pursue his whims.

Just as Ostin and others at Warner Bros. feared, however, Prince's remedy for the disappointing showing of ⚥ was to quickly release another album. In early 1993, he continued work on *Gold Nigga*, the jam-filled, heavy funk album showcasing Tony Mosley's rapping. Prince's plan was to release the record under the aegis of his backing band, the New Power Generation, by summertime, only about eight months after the release of ⚥.

For Warners, the time had arrived to draw the line. Already reluctant to release another album so quickly, Ostin and Waronker heard nothing to change their minds in the abrasive, pseudo-gangsta rap of *Gold Nigga*. They told Prince that the company had no interest in the album but instead wanted a reasonable pause in new music to allow for the release of a greatest hits package.

Prince felt censored. Far more important even than his financial compensation from Warners was what he considered his absolute right to expose his work to the public. To him, marketing considerations were subsidiary to this fundamental act. And while only a fraction of his recorded output was on vinyl—by 1993, the locked room at Paisley Park that housed his master tapes (universally known among his associates as "the Vault") contained about 300 unreleased songs—the decision had to be his alone. Denying him the right to release music equaled creative oppression.

Not even the band members who had helped create the album, however, believed that *Gold Nigga* was worth fighting very hard over. Most of the group was perplexed that after being critically lambasted for his concessions to the rap marketplace on *Diamonds And Pearls* and ⚥, Prince would build an entire record around Tony Mosley. "Prince really did believe in Tony M., even if no one else did," recalled keyboardist Tommy Barbarella.

Sadly, most of the NPG, like so many of Prince's fans, had lost their confidence that this once-vibrant artist had much more to offer in the way of groundbreaking work; the whole endeavor of working for him had lost its raison d'être. "After 1992, we really did nothing to contribute to raising the bar," conceded drummer Michael Bland. "What did we stand for? Was there a reason for what we were doing other than just good entertainment?"

The clash over *Gold Nigga* reawakened Prince's long-held distrust of the music industry establishment. Even as a teenager signing with Warners, Prince had, not without good cause, viewed the major labels as faceless corporations with a long history of exploiting artists—especially African-Americans. From the very beginning, he worried about his own creative freedom, fearing that he would be pigeonholed as a "black" artist and that the label would try to control his sound and style. Now, many of the worst fears he harbored about Warners and its ilk seemed to be coming true.

Unfortunately, there was no one left within Prince's camp to advise him that, in many respects, Warner Bros. had the better of the various arguments separating them. With the departure of Alan Leeds from his post as Paisley Park Records president in 1992, Prince's inner circle was stripped of its last truly independent voice. At a time when he badly needed a fresh perspective, Prince had no one who would dare stand up to him, and he was about to make a series of decisions that would irrevocably damage his career.

april 27, 1993: warner bros. records, burbank, california

A phone call came into Mo Ostin and Lenny Waronker from Gilbert Davison, Prince's manager. Over the course of a tense conversation, they were informed that Prince was "retiring" from recording and would deliver no additional new music to the label. Instead, he would fulfill the remainder of his lucrative contract with material from "the Vault."

Later that day, Paisley Park issued a press release that tracked what Davison had said: Prince was ending his traditional recording career to pursue "alternative media projects, including live theater, interactive media, nightclubs and motion pictures."

The strange statement was greeted with widespread skepticism throughout the music industry. In *Rolling Stone*, various of his former associates expressed incredulity that the most prolific artist in pop would stop recording music. "Prince is a very mercurial fellow," Eric Leeds said. "He could change his mind tomorrow. I just kind of chuckle when I hear those things. I say, 'Okay, here he goes again.'"

But there was more to come.

On June 7, Prince's 35th birthday, an even more perplexing release emerged from Paisley Park. It announced that he was legally changing his name to ♀, the same unpronounceable symbol that graced his new album. No explanation was given.

The media avalanche that followed was filled with derision and mockery. The "name change" (which was not legally sanctioned) was portrayed alternatively as a publicity stunt or compelling evidence that Prince had come unhinged. Tongue-in-cheek speculation raged about how he should be addressed; several publications, noting that the symbol seemed to be a combination of the signs representing masculinity and femininity, suggested that he be called "Pat," after an androgynous character from *Saturday Night Live*. Cheryl Johnson, a columnist for his hometown *Minneapolis Star Tribune*, began calling him "Symbolina." Gradually, most publications adopted the neutral but unwieldy moniker "The Artist Formerly Known As Prince"; this generated yet more ridicule. Shock jock Howard Stern mocked him as "the artist people formerly cared about." When Prince's own publicists started using the pretentious appellation "the Artist," the whole episode had become a national joke.

Prince's own band and management team learned about Prince's decision at the same time as the general public. They also had no idea what to call him, and Prince offered no guidance other than to emphasize that the symbol was unpronounceable. "After a while, everyone settled on 'boss,'" recalled Barbarella.

Why had he done it? Among fans and in some media articles there was speculation that Prince was seeking to escape his contract with Warner Bros. by changing his identity and then arguing that the label's agreement was with "Prince." Or maybe this was just a new artistic persona, like "Camille" of the *Sign O' The Times* era. Perhaps there really was no explanation, and this simply confirmed that Prince was the most eccentric star of his generation.

In interviews, it seemed that Prince really believed he had experienced a personal transformation. He seemed intent on convincing the world that "Prince" was gone and that "the Artist" had taken his place. His public statements took on a schizophrenic quality. "Prince never used to do interviews," he told *Time Out* magazine. "You'd have to ask Prince why he never used to do interviews, but you're not talking to Prince now. You're talking to me."

At Warners, "Everyone was baffled and upset," recalled Marylou Badeaux. "On top of everything else, now there was this. I couldn't see how it would be a positive." Ostin, Waronker, and other top executives huddled with lawyers to discuss the various turns—the "retirement" announcement, the refusal to give the company new music, and the name change. One thing seemed apparent: Prince was retaliating against the company over its refusal to release *Gold Nigga*. In all likelihood, he would use the subterfuge of "alternative media" to pursue projects on his own while stiffing the label with material from the Vault. It sounded like a breach of contract, albeit a creative one.

Nonetheless, a consensus emerged within the executive suite against immediate legal action. In one sense, Prince had actually relieved pressure on Warners; for the moment, he was not agitating for the release of more albums, giving the company an opportunity to release a greatest hits collection. They presented the best-of concept to Prince, who with some reluctance agreed to support it.

Thus, in summer 1993, both sides pulled back from what might have become a cataclysmic legal battle. A multi-disc set was assembled that covered career high points like "When Doves Cry" and "1999" along with rare songs previously released only as single B-sides. Prince also contributed four unreleased numbers: the pretty ballad "Pink Cashmere" (inspired by Anna Garcia), the hip-hop influenced "Pope" (with backing vocals by Mayte Garcia), the blues-rocker "Peach" (based around a recorded moan from Kim Basinger), and the Revolution-era track "Power Fantastic." Other points of interest included a live version of "Nothing Compares 2 U"—a song originally recorded for the Family side project in 1985 and turned into a No. 1 hit in 1990 by Sinead O'Connor—with Rosie Gaines sharing the lead vocal.

Released in September 1993, the three-volume set entitled *The Hits/The B-Sides* (which could be purchased as a complete work or in separate albums) was a powerful retrospective of some of Prince's finest work, although perhaps not the complete document some fans would have preferred. ("Kiss" was missing, along with the funk classics

"Girls & Boys" from *Parade* and "Housequake" from *Sign O' The Times*.) It sold well, yet not quite as strongly as might have been expected, peaking at No. 19 on the Pop Chart and moving about three million units in the United States.

Warners' ineffective promotion of the package stirred up the already tense relationship with Prince. In a maladroit attempt at humor, the company took out an advertisement in *Billboard* that was filled with smiley faces, dollar signs, and other symbols (including the by now infamous ♀). Concluding with the line "Just don't call him Prince, OK?," it seemed to ridicule rather than endorse his name change.

Offended, Prince struck back with his own *Billboard* ad the following week. Mocking Warners' statement by again using an array of symbols, the ad made caustic references to the label's restraint of Prince's artistic output. It was a strange sight—a promotional campaign that degenerated into sniping between label and artist. A very public battle had been joined.

august 21, 1993: downtown los angeles

On August 21, Prince's first foray into "alternative media" took place at a nightclub he had recently purchased and renamed "Glam Slam," after a song on *Lovesexy*. Dubbed *Glam Slam Ulysses*, the musical-theatrical production (ostensibly an adaptation of Homer's play) featured Carmen Electra in the dual lead role of Penelope and Calypso. While Prince did not appear onstage, the show (which he also cowrote with playwright Kenneth Robbins) relied heavily on his music. Unfortunately, the songs were arguably his weakest of the 1990s, and Electra's onstage work was little better than her rapping. The bombastic production was savaged by the critics and closed after just two weeks. Even Prince realized it was a failure and scrapped a tour of U.S. nightclubs.

While Prince and Electra continued their on-and-off romance for about another year, *Glam Slam Ulysses* effectively marked the end of their artistic collaborations. And Prince had recently discovered a new love interest and protégée: singer Nona Gaye, the talented daughter of Marvin Gaye. Their courtship began in summer 1993, when Gaye, then 18, was invited to a concert at Prince's Minneapolis night club (another part of the growing Glam Slam chain). She was seated at a private table along with Mayte Garcia (who had by then turned 19). As these two young rivals for his attentions watched, Prince tore through songs like "She's Always In My Hair" and "Irresistible Bitch."

In coming months, Prince and Gaye began dating and working together in the studio, where they recorded the ballad "Snow Man" (it remains unreleased and is one of the more intriguing Prince outtakes). But while they continued to see each other sporadically for several years, the relationship lacked emotional intimacy. "It was very strange, a whirlwind of head trips and mind screws," Gaye told *Esquire*. "Three years I dated him and I didn't know him and never really let him know me, either."

Gaye also became part of another alternative media project, a film called *The Undertaker* (shot on the Paisley Park soundstage) that featured music interspersed with dramatic footage. Acting in the film along with Gaye was Vanessa Marcil of the daytime soap *General Hospital*. Using a stripped-down version of the New Power Generation that included only drummer Michael Bland and bassist Sonny Thompson,

Prince performed live versions of previously released songs like "Bambi" and "Peach" along with newer numbers like the bluesy "The Ride" and the strong mid-tempo rocker "Dolphin." But while Prince initially planned a full-length feature film, he changed course midway through the project and turned it into a forty-five-minute short that focused on music rather than the storyline. A limited edition home video was released in England and Japan in 1995 and became a collector's item.

In the end, projects like *The Undertaker* were the musical equivalent of busy work, representing nothing more than brief flights of fancy. Bland recalls that the music for *The Undertaker* was recorded "out of sheer boredom." With little practical use, these high-cost, low-return endeavors placed a tremendous strain on Prince's finances. After recovering from near-bankruptcy in the late 1980s, Prince had replenished his coffers to some degree, but was now back in trouble. For several years, some advisors had been meekly mentioning to him that costs were outstripping revenues, but he ignored the warnings. By late 1994, though, rumors began to circulate throughout the Twin Cities area that local film and wardrobe companies could not get Paisley Park to pay its debts.

Bruce Orwall, a reporter for the *Saint Paul Pioneer Press*, investigated the reports and discovered numerous indications that Prince was unwilling—or maybe unable—to meet his financial obligations. Orwall's exposé, published as "Purple Drain" in January 1995, chronicled horror stories of local businesspeople who had been stiffed by Paisley Park. A young filmmaker named Rob Borm, hired to shoot a video for "Gett Off" in 1992, was forced into bankruptcy when the shoot went more than $1 million over budget. After several years of letters and phone calls to Paisley, Borm finally got a portion of the money, but too late to satisfy his own creditors.

There were numerous other examples. Jim Mulligan, owner of a Minneapolis video company, spent six weeks sending letters and faxes to Paisley Park before he was able to collect a mere $1,400. A business run by Saint Paul couple Gary and Suzy Zahradka, which made canes that Prince toted to fashion shows to make him look stylish, sued Paisley Park for $4,500. The problem was not confined to local businesses; the Record Plant, a Los Angeles studio, spent five months seeking a $150,000 payment, which it finally received only after threatening to keep a master tape that Prince had forgotten to take with him.

Attempting to communicate with his organization about such problems was an exercise in futility. No one answered the phones, and middle managers who had made commitments to vendors suddenly disappeared. The lines of authority were murky at best. Nominally, Paisley Park Enterprises president Gilbert Davison was in charge. Prince's half brother Duane Nelson, who often provided security for concerts at Paisley Park, seemed to play a major, if ill-defined role. And Jill Willis, who held the lofty title of vice president also (and who later claimed to have been a key figure in negotiating the 1992 deal with Warners) enjoyed day-to-day contact with Prince. Yet none of these people had any meaningful authority. "He made the worst selection of people making executive decisions—people that didn't have a clue," recalled Prince's tour production designer, Roy Bennett. "These were people who had come from nowhere, and none of them would say anything to him—they just did whatever he wanted." Sometimes, Prince undermined his executives by reversing their decisions; on other occasions he insisted that they refrain from pestering him about any business issues. In any case, he retained ultimate control over the purse strings, and as a result his operations were descending into chaos.

In February 1994, Warner Bros. took steps to protect itself from Prince's poor financial decisions: It terminated Paisley Park Records, its joint venture with him. Warners had lost millions on the label, and Prince had never even set foot in the lavish Century City office suite given to him as part of his 1992 deal. Almost overnight, the vanity label was shut down. Albums in the works by new acts Belize and Tyler Collins were shelved, and Rosie Gaines' long-postponed *Concrete Jungle*, slated for a March release, was again put on hold.

Oddly, Prince seemed unperturbed; in fact, he seemed emotionally disconnected from much of what was occurring in his life. "I did not get the feeling that it even mattered to him," Badeaux recalled. To replace the label as a new outlet for side projects, Prince formed NPG Records under his Paisley Park Enterprises umbrella. That he would lack the promotion and distribution machinery of a major label seemed not to bother him.

He rushed out his first independent release almost immediately—a single called "The Most Beautiful Girl In The World." (Warners, still wanting to hold off on new releases, passed on the song but let him issue it through NPG Records.) It became the first record under his new name. Issued in February and distributed in the United States by the small Bellmark Records label, "Beautiful Girl" provided another twist in the feud between Prince and Warners. To the surprise of many in the record industry who thought Prince's career might be in permanent decline, it became a major hit. Echoing the production approach of Philadelphia soul groups like the Delfonics, the song was a shimmering slice of pop with an instantly recognizable falsetto vocal. A seeming return to Prince's halcyon days, "Beautiful Girl" sold a remarkable 700,000 copies, attaining gold status and reaching No. 3 on the Billboard Pop Singles Chart.

For Prince, this was irrefutable evidence that the naysayers—especially Warner Bros.—were wrong. His name change represented not vain silliness, but instead heralded a creative renaissance. Most importantly, the record's worldwide success proved what he had been arguing all along—Warner Bros. had botched the promotion of his recent albums. "Beautiful Girl" demonstrated that Warners was utterly superfluous to his success.

His hand thus strengthened, Prince prepared his next salvo against his nemesis.

On March 11, Prince presented Warner Bros. with his next album, entitled *Come*. It was everything the label had feared. Most of the songs were mediocrities that had been recycled from *Glam Slam Ulysses*—the frenetic, tuneless "Loose!," the languid, barely there "Space," and others—underscoring Prince's refusal to give Warners new music. The rest sounded like hastily written curiosities, and even one of the more interesting numbers, the haunting, stripped-down "Papa" (a seemingly autobiographical piece which addressed the theme of child abuse) seemed intentionally obscure. There was nothing in the collection that could be released to radio as a single. "The company was so upset with that album—people said it was a piece of shit," remembered Badeaux. "There was a feeling that he was dumping garbage on us."

Ostin and Waronker bluntly told Prince that the album was unacceptable. Again stepping back from the precipice of a possible legal confrontation, Prince agreed to add several more songs, including "Beautiful Girl." He returned to Warners in mid-May, armed with a revamped version of *Come*. But it was, if anything, worse than before; "Beautiful Girl" was not added, and one of the stronger numbers, the distortion-drenched "Endorphinmachine," had been excised. "Mo and Lenny were dismayed that 'Beautiful Girl' wasn't on the album," Badeaux recalled. "There was definitely a sense he was giving the label anything to fill out his contract."

Muddying the picture further, Prince also presented Warners with another full album, called *The Gold Experience*. It contained his most exciting work in years—the brilliant folk-funk hybrid "Shy," the kinetic funk jam "Days Of Wild," and "Gold," a rock ballad that was perhaps his best effort in this vein since "Purple Rain." "Beautiful Girl" was also present.

Prince's proposal was to release two albums simultaneously—*Come* under the name Prince and *The Gold Experience* under ♀. And he wanted both to count toward the fulfillment of his Warners contract—an obligation that he sought to escape as quickly as possible.

Flooding the market with material, however, was exactly what the executives wanted to avoid. Nor were they optimistic about releasing music with an unpronounceable symbol, rather than the powerful "Prince" trademark on the front cover. They agreed to release *Come*; *The Gold Experience* would have to wait.

Again, Prince was furious and complained that the label was censoring him. The Prince-Warners relationship again started coming unglued, and any faint hopes of healing the breach were dispelled by Prince's next stunt: He began making all public appearances with the word "slave" scrawled on his cheek with black makeup. As he told interviewers, his situation was indeed analogous to that of a slave—Warners owned his master tapes, the fruits of his labor. "If you don't own your masters, the master owns you," he told *Ebony*, claming that this was just another example of white corporate America exploiting people of color.

It was a bold claim to make. By raising the banner of racial struggle (a point also made implicitly when, in interviews, he compared his name change to that of Muhammad Ali), he seemed to grossly overstate the import of a business dispute that was, after all, about music rather than life or liberty. Moreover, his contention that musicians should retain ownership of their master tapes, which on its face sounded reasonable, was in truth a call for overhauling the music industry. Under such a scenario, record companies would pay large sums of money to artists but receive only one-time rights to the music. And even if the system of ownership were so changed, it did not seem reasonable for artists to argue—as Prince was doing—that they should retroactively gain ownership of tapes governed by existing contracts.

Moreover, Prince's assertions of racial aggrievement came out of thin air. Here was an artist who (in interviews and in songs like "Controversy") had consciously downplayed his African-American heritage, preferring instead to come across as a pan-ethnic figure. On issues of racial relations and politics, he had remained largely silent, offering no comment, for example, on Jesse Jackson's campaigns for the presidency in 1984 and 1988. The notion of writing a song about events like the 1992 Los

Angeles riots seems not to have crossed his mind. And yet here was Prince, taking on the white power structure.

Even Prince's band members, most of whom were young African-Americans, were largely unsympathetic to his arguments and were troubled that he was letting the fight with Warners dictate artistic decisions. They felt more like Prince's pawns than his comrades-in-arms. "The saga was building every day, but it really had nothing to do with us," recalled Bland. "Mostly, I rolled my eyes. There were some valid points he was making, but to me business is business, and it's important to follow through on your obligations."

Prince, though, believed that he was being exploited by Warners in any number of ways. That he was a multimillionaire pop star with vastly greater freedom and opportunity than most people on the planet seemed not to matter. As he told *Q* magazine, "If you're shackled and restricted, it doesn't matter how much money you got."

As he had throughout his career, Prince was pushing himself relentlessly. He continued to sleep as little as three hours a night and consumed very little food. After years of this lifestyle, he had become disturbingly thin and gaunt. His appearance, along with his string of bizarre actions—the retirement announcement, the name change, the "slave" message—left some associates convinced that Prince was using stimulants, perhaps cocaine. They wondered if his workaholism prompted him to dispense with his own longstanding (and very rarely violated) prohibition on illegal substances. "My assumption, and I know that this was a lot of people's opinion, was that he was on drugs," said Roy Bennett. "There was a lot of turmoil in his head, from the fight with Warner Bros. and his financial problems."

Bennett's supposition is supported by a member of the New Power Generation who claims to have been told by bandmate Miko Weaver that Weaver regularly shared cocaine with Prince on the *Diamonds And Pearls* tour. (Weaver did not respond to several requests for interviews.) There is other anecdotal evidence of drug use by Prince; former studio engineer Chuck Zwicky, for example, claims knowledge that Prince actually entered drug rehab during the 1990s.

Still, if Prince did become a regular cocaine user, he effectively concealed direct evidence from his associates. And not everyone believes that Prince, so long a devotee of a clean lifestyle, would make such a radical change. For example, Alan Leeds—although he did receive a report from a former Prince girlfriend of a one-time experiment with cocaine in the eighties—strongly doubts that Prince ever developed what he would term a drug problem. "Cocaine abuse rumors ran hot and heavy during the 1990s, but I never heard anything credible enough to accept it without question," Leeds said. And Leeds is clear that when he was tour manager throughout much of the 1980s, there was no direct evidence whatsoever of drug use. "One of us in the inner circle would have known about it. Prince didn't even pack his own toiletries, and we had regular access to his hotel suites. So surely we would have picked up remnants or telltale signs."

But drugs or no, there was a consensus among Prince's associates that his insular, cloistered existence—one that revolved almost exclusively around studios, nightclubs, concert halls, and movie theaters—had taken a toll on his creativity. For years, friends encouraged him to explore other countries (not as a performer, but as a visitor), meet people from outside his very limited orbit of Minneapolis musicians, and even to experience humble joys like a walk in the woods. He ignored every such suggestion. "He travels when he tours, but he doesn't do the type of traveling one needs to do to see the world more than five inches beyond your own face," lamented Badeaux.

To his band members, the growing emptiness at the core of Prince's songwriting was especially apparent. Forced into an existence that mirrored his, the New Power Generation members developed an acute sense of how limited Prince's horizons were. "Art is a reflection of life, and when you don't live anymore, what do you have?" mused keyboardist Barbarella. "Prince has created this world that he can't escape from, and it's consuming him."

But if both Warner Bros. and Prince's band members (along with growing numbers of fans) were disillusioned about his music and worried about his physical and emotional health, an even greater sense of despair set in among certain members of the media. During the 1980s, influential publications like *Rolling Stone* and the *Village Voice* had lionized Prince as a potential savior of rock 'n' roll—the only contemporary pop star who walked the same ground as earlier pioneers like John Lennon and David Bowie. That great promise had been squandered, many music scribes concluded. This was not a knee-jerk, temporary media backlash like that experienced when Prince released the quirky *Around The World In A Day* in 1985; writers seemed deeply saddened by what they saw as the decline of a once profoundly original artist. As written by Martin Keller of the *Chicago Sun-Times* in an insightful piece called "Prince: What Happened?":

> For more than a decade during the 1980s, Prince Rogers Nelson dominated popular music the way Elvis Presley shaped the '50s and John Lennon and Paul McCartney ruled in the '60s. The brave experimentation of songs like "Kiss" and "When Doves Cry," with their minimalistic rhythm tracks and cutting guitar solos, have been replaced by concessions to the rap marketplace and an aesthetic defined more by complacency than innovation. The edge that propelled his finest work as far back as *1999* in 1982 and as recently as *Graffiti Bridge* in 1990 seems duller with each recording in the '90s.

Whether he read such commentaries is unknown, but Prince seemed determined to redefine himself and to put the disappointments and frustrations of the last few years behind him. In public appearances, he kept emphasizing that "Prince" was dead. *The Gold Experience*—parts of which appeared on the Internet, placed there by fans who acquired the material on the bootleg market—contained segues between songs with spoken messages like "Prince esta muerte." Then, in a December 1994 appearance on the *Late Show with David Letterman*, he made the point even more explicit—after playing the unreleased "Dolphin" (a song about reincarnation) from *The Gold Experience*, he feigned his own death and was carried offstage.

But while the clear intent of Prince's various stunts was to foment outrage about Warners' treatment of him, the public response was bemusement, to the extent that anyone cared at all. His grievances, rather than being part of any larger movement for artists' rights, were transparently personal. In fact, the more meritorious parts of his campaign against Warners and the major label system—such as that artists received far too small a portion of their profits (generally less than fifteen percent)—were lost amidst his grandiose actions.

Come, released in August 1994, hammered the "Prince is dead" message home one more time. The black-and-white cover showed him outside the gates of what appears to be a cemetery (actually La Sagrada Familia cathedral in Barcelona, Spain). Below the word "Prince" are the dates "1958–1993," serving as a tombstone inscription.

Surely one of the few albums in pop history to have been intentionally fashioned as a mediocre project, *Come* was, unsurprisingly, a commercial failure. It sold 345,000 copies in the United States—the worst performance of his career to date—and reached only No. 15 on the Billboard Pop Chart. Neither Prince nor Warner Bros. did much to promote the record; it was, quite simply, contract filler.

Although Prince seemingly expected the public to understand that he had not truly sanctioned the release of *Come* and instead wanted it to have *The Gold Experience*, these distinctions were not nearly as widely appreciated as he thought. Instead, a great many fans simply found in the album another indication of his creative decline. "What concerned me was that he didn't understand what he was doing to his own career because of the feud with Warners," Badeaux observed. Added drummer Bland, "It was a collection of lackluster songs with dated production. I felt we were cheating the fans."

The media also failed to rally behind Prince's anti-Warners campaign and instead lambasted the new album. "*Come* is largely a toss-off that doesn't merit the excitement usually accorded Prince albums," observed the *Detroit Free Press*. Many of the reviews referenced Prince's misguided publicity stunts. "Ordinary artists just make duds; this guy specializes in public-relations catastrophes that confuse his loyal following and erode his stature as the major genre-busting innovator of the last decade," wrote *Rolling Stone*.

Seemingly oblivious to all of this, Prince continued to agitate for release of *The Gold Experience*. In his New Power Generation memorabilia store in Minneapolis, Prince had flyers circulated that asked patrons to petition Warner Bros. to "liberate" the record. Even as much of the public and most of his associates concluded that Prince's reputation was in free-fall, he remained fixated on what he considered an epic struggle between good and evil.

scape

Among the many ironies of Prince's crusade against Warner Bros., none
was greater than that his ceaseless and often vicious attacks were
mounted against executives who had created arguably the most artist-friendly label in
the entire music industry. Since teaming up at Warners in the mid-1970s, Mo Ostin
and Lenny Waronker had made creative considerations just as important as the financial bottom line. They followed a philosophy that was in many respects unusual for a
large record company. Interesting and challenging artists—not only Prince but the
likes of Van Halen, Maria Muldaur, Curtis Mayfield, and others—were given a chance
to develop over a series of albums, a practice that sometimes lost money in the short-
term. But Ostin and Waronker believed fervently that, over time, their nurturing
would pay dividends, and it usually did. Established artists like Neil Young and REM
chose Warners over other labels in large part because they were confident that their
creative freedom would be respected. And it was this very reputation that attracted
Prince to Warners in 1978.

The executives did not enjoy completely unfettered discretion—Warner Bros.
Records was just one part the Warner Music Group, which included the Elektra and
Atlantic labels. This in turn was part of Warner Communications, which included
Warner Bros. Pictures among other concerns. But through much of the seventies and
eighties, Ostin and Waronker's corporate overseers remained content with the profits
generated by the label and generally left them alone.

All of this changed with the 1989 merger of Warner Communications and Time,
Inc. This union marked the beginning of a disturbing trend, as over the subsequent ten
years numerous entertainment companies would be swallowed up by larger parents,
such as Disney's 1995 purchase of Capital Cities/ABC. Within these conglomerates,
conformity was encouraged and artistic adventurousness frowned upon. At Warner
Bros., Ostin and Waronker suddenly faced much greater pressure from the bureaucrats
proliferating above them.

At first, the autonomy of Warner Bros. Records was protected to some extent by Steve Ross, the charismatic chairman of Time-Warner and a stalwart supporter of Mo Ostin. But this ended with Ross' death in 1992 and the ascension of Gerald Levin to the top spot. Levin was the classic modern-era executive, a voraciously acquisitive figure who later became infamous for orchestrating the merger of Time-Warner and America Online, which decimated the market value of both companies. With Levin in charge, it became increasingly difficult for Ostin and Waronker to run Warner Bros. Records the way they wanted.

In summer 1994, one of the major players angling for influence within Time-Warner—Robert Morgado, the chairman of the Warner Music Group—altered the chain of command within the company. Ostin no longer reported directly to the chairman of Time-Warner (which had been the case during the Ross years), but now had to answer to Morgado. In practical terms, Ostin's authority was completely undermined. In August 1994, the chairman announced his resignation, representing the end of an era at the label.

Levin and Morgado anointed Waronker as the successor, but Ostin's longtime partner had no appetite for the ongoing palace intrigue at Time-Warner. Declining the powerful post, Waronker announced that he too was leaving, and in October 1994 Danny Goldberg—former manager of Nirvana—was appointed chairman of Warner Bros. Records.

Ostin and Waronker left behind a demoralized institution. Goldberg, while a well-liked figure in the music industry, lacked Ostin's gravitas and also seemed likely to himself become a victim of the instability at Time-Warner. He in fact lasted less than a year.

One person, though, felt hope amidst all of this turmoil: Prince. Despite the lengths Ostin and Waronker had gone to accommodate him, he viewed them as symbols of an industry that exploited artists—him in particular. While there was little basis for assuming that Goldberg would be easier to deal with, the shift in regimes offered the potential of a fresh start.

Goldberg began the relationship by offering Prince various olive branches. During a get-acquainted meeting, he agreed to release both *The Gold Experience* and *Exodus*, the New Power Generation's follow-up to *Gold Nigga*. And Goldberg believed he had extracted from Prince a commitment to stop bashing the label in public.

Their sit-down had not produced a true meeting of minds, however. Although Goldberg had not committed to any specific timetable for releasing the new albums, Prince assumed they would be rushed out almost immediately. When this failed to happen, he believed he had been misled. "There was a lot said in the initial meeting, and not much followed through," one Warner Bros. source said.

Prince resumed criticizing Warners in the media, and "slave" remained emblazoned on his face. In an article that appeared in *Esquire Gentleman*, he made reference to a new fifty-song album, called *Emancipation*, that he planned to release after his Warner Bros. contract expired. At the label, this was viewed as confirmation that he was recording strong material behind Warners' back while filling out his contract with mediocre releases. Troubled by this and viewing Prince's statements as a breach of his agreement to stop attacking the label, Warners officials cancelled the release of *Exodus*.

The war was back on.

* * *

Even as he was locked in combat with Warners, Prince's relationships with his own bandmates and other in-house personnel were also becoming fraught. In late 1994, he fell out with manager Gilbert Davison, arguably his closest confidant. They had clashed repeatedly over their joint ownership of the Miami Glam Slam club, and Davison decided he had had enough of trying to run Prince's increasingly disorganized business operations.

With Davison's departure, it became more difficult for Prince to ignore the precarious state of his finances. Running the Paisley Park complex produced a constant drain, and Prince's living expenses, which included salaries for cooks and clothiers, were astronomical. Something had to be done before he was driven into bankruptcy.

Duane Nelson, Prince's half brother, was put in charge of downsizing the Paisley Park staff. Firings occurred arbitrarily and without warning, and even key figures like soundstage director Mark White and chief financial officer Jenifer Carr were forced out. In many cases the cuts were ill-advised and only exacerbated the chaos at Paisley Park. After the purge was complete, left in charge were Duane Nelson and two of Prince's longtime assistants, Therese Stoulil and Juli Knapp-Winge. An operation that during the 1980s was run by some of the most creative professionals in the music industry now lay in the hands of a skeleton crew of administrative staffers.

One of the few high-ranking officials to keep his job—Levi Seacer, who in early 1994 relinquished his position as guitarist in the New Power Generation to become president of Prince's in-house record label—became extraordinarily demoralized as the wave of firings occurred. Seacer had little interest in running a label, particularly one so plagued with problems. An extremely proficient musician, between 1992 and 1994 he had emerged as a highly competent (if not especially imaginative) producer and arranger, and his reassignment to a managerial post left him (along with many others at Paisley Park) perplexed.

In November 1994, while Prince and the band were in Berlin playing the MTV European Music Awards, Seacer and his girlfriend Karen Lee (also Prince's publicist) cleaned out their desks and file cabinets at Paisley Park, leaving behind a letter of resignation but no forwarding address. His colleagues returned to find a deserted office suite. "It was like he went into the witness protection program," recalled drummer Michael Bland.

This left another hole in Prince's organization. Red ink continued to flow, and Prince made no meaningful effort to curtail his own spending. Even as key personnel lost their jobs in the name of cost-cutting, Prince continued to shoot expensive (and usually purposeless) videos at Paisley Park. And in an ongoing effort to establish himself as a business mogul, he maintained Glam Slam nightclubs in Los Angeles, Minneapolis, and Miami.

The biggest new strain on his coffers, though, was an elaborate stage set for a planned twenty-date European tour. This study in ridiculousness called "the Endorphinmachine" resembled conjoined male and female genitalia with a womb at the center. It was full of complex elements, including a conveyor belt that brought Prince onstage and a harness that swung Tommy Barbarella through the air as he played a keyboard solo. Making the set even more expensive was its cumbersome shape;

because it could not be packed into trucks efficiently, huge caravan of vehicles was required to move it from city to city.

Nor was the timing auspicious for a European tour. Prince had visited the continent six times since 1986, and was becoming just as overexposed there as in the United States. Predictably, ticket sales were slow, a situation that worsened as audiences learned that the concerts emphasized the unreleased *Gold Experience*. Without familiar songs to hold their attention, substantial numbers of fans left the shows early; some even asked for their money back.

Many customers were also dismayed by the poor sound quality. On recent tours Prince had been dissatisfied with his live sound staff, and on the Endorphinmachine tour he assumed the task himself by placing a mixing board in the backstage area in the set's "womb." The results were disastrous; because the onstage mix was different from that heard by the audience, Prince lacked any meaningful reference point, leading to serious imbalances in the sound.

After a series of disappointing shows in London indicated that the tour was not going to be successful, Prince made a belated concession to fiscal reality by ordering that a portion of the giant set be left behind. Starting with a March 10 show in Manchester, he and the band had to adjust to the stripped-down stage. Malfunctions started occurring, giving the show a flavor not unlike the film *Spinal Tap*. One evening, Barbarella missed his landing point on his dramatic mid-air trip across the stage and came crashing down on his keyboard, creating a cacophony in the middle of the song "Endorphinmachine." Another night, Prince forgot to turn on his guitar from the backstage mixing board before stepping on the conveyor belt that ferried him out to his microphone stand. He danced his way to the front of the stage as the band played a groove, only to discover this problem; he then had to flip the conveyor belt into reverse mode and boogey his way backwards. After fixing the glitch, he re-emerged from behind the curtain as his band members snickered.

Ticket sales for the shows remained weak, and Prince reluctantly ordered that additional pieces of the stage show be left behind in various cities to save money. By the time the tour reached Scotland, the grandiose set was down to almost nothing. "It was just a flat stage, no backdrop, no props at all," recalled Barbarella.

This tour, which Prince dubbed the Ultimate Live Experience, marked the effective end of his long romance with European audiences. During the mid- and late 1980s, he had built a passionate following in France, Britain, Germany, and other countries. Everything about Prince's approach—his sexual openness and androgyny, the incorporation of jazz textures into his music, his courageous development from one album to the next—seemed perfectly tailored to a European audience. But these same fans watched with dismay in the early 1990s as Prince abdicated his role as a musical pioneer and began following trends like gangsta rap. By the time the ill-fated Endorphinmachine set arrived on the continent, many of Prince's former loyalists had nearly run out of patience; these unsatisfying shows pushed many over the edge, leaving it unlikely that he would ever receive the adoration from European fans that he had enjoyed in the 1980s.

These shows also pointed toward the end of Prince's association with the New Power Generation, most of whom had begun to find him nearly impossible. Almost

uniformly cold and callous towards his colleagues, Prince often chided them for what
he perceived as sub par performances. "I developed a tremendous pool of negativity
within me that I needed to survive in that environment," one band member said.
"Fighting off that vacuous black hole took everything I had, and at the end of the day
I'd be so edgy and insensitive."

Former Revolution-era saxophonist Eric Leeds, whom Prince invited to Europe to
play several nightclub aftershows, found that Prince's personality had changed considerably over the years. He treated his band members thoughtlessly; after ordering Leeds
and the rest of the group to arrive at the nightclubs by midnight, he kept them waiting
until two or three in the morning. "He was out bar-hopping," Leeds remembered.
Often, by the time Prince's set began there were fewer than a hundred people left in
the audience.

Amidst all of the conflict in his world, Prince did have one source of emotional
sustenance: his relationship with Mayte Garcia, which finally passed from a platonic
courtship into a full-blown romance in early 1995. In appearance and personality,
Mayte very much fit the model of Prince's previous lovers, and in some ways seemed to
combine their qualities. Her skin tone and facial structure were not far removed from
Vanity or Apollonia; her low-key manner was very much like that of Anna Garcia. Her
compact bustiness suggested a Latina version of Carmen Electra. And the reflective,
almost mysterious air she exuded was reminiscent of Ingrid Chavez, Prince's spiritual
muse of the *Lovesexy–Graffiti Bridge* period.

For three years, since joining the band as a dancer on the *Diamonds And Pearls* tour
in 1992, Mayte had served an apprenticeship—part personal, part professional—with
Prince. They had not been especially close—their conversations were sporadic and
often short—but he fantasized about a much larger role for her in his life. On the 1993
Act I tour (Prince split the ♀ tour into three segments, entitled Act I, Act II, and Act
III) he created a stage show in which she played a sixteen-year-old princess whom
Prince (as the monarch of a fictional Middle Eastern country) tries to seduce. And long
before their relationship became sexual, associates were conscious of his strong attraction toward her. The very night he met Mayte on the 1990 Nude Tour, Rosie Gaines
predicted to Prince that he would one day marry the young woman.

It had been eight years since Prince had had a relationship that seemed likely to
lead toward marriage. That romance—with Susannah Melvoin, sister of bandmate
Wendy—had been the most passionate of his life. It was also the most challenging;
while Susannah's poise and sophistication stimulated him, they also threatened him.
Prince had been unwilling to accept her independence (or her demands that he be
monogamous), and the relationship ended painfully.

When they met, Susannah was nineteen and Prince twenty-six. In the future, the
age gap between Prince and his lovers steadily increased; he continued to select eight-
een- and nineteen-year-olds as his lovers, most of them far less urbane than Susannah.
Aside from his brief romance with Kim Basinger in 1990, he seemed unwilling to
explore relationships that he could not easily control.

Mayte Garcia was in many ways the logical conclusion of this trend. Almost uniformly described by Prince's associates with adjectives like "nice" and "sweet," Garcia

was hardly an especially articulate or imaginative young woman, even considering her youth at the time. Prince's attentions further discouraged her from forging her own identity, and he used her as a mouthpiece both for his music and his statements to the world. (During one interview, for example, he refused to answer questions directly but instead whispered his responses in Mayte's ear, which she then related to the questioner.)

In 1994 Prince started working on Mayte's planned first album, *Child Of The Sun*, but this was not an endeavor Mayte had any inherent passion for; rather, it was just another part of serving Prince. Even before joining Prince's band she had tried briefly to become a professional vocalist, but enjoyed little success with her cover versions of songs like Mister Mister's maudlin "Broken Wings." Not even Mayte herself had much faith that *Child Of The Sun* would make her a star; Prince was the sole true believer. "He basically made her do it," recalled Tommy Barbarella.

The album was created in secrecy. No one else remembers seeing Mayte record any vocals, indicating that Prince did not want her embarrassed by her frequent sour notes. The project seemed mainly an excuse to spend more time with her.

In summer 1995, the talented singer-songwriter Sandra St. Victor (formerly of the band the Family Stand), who had recently signed a deal with Warner Bros., was pleasantly surprised to hear from label officials that Prince wanted to meet her and possibly collaborate on some songs. Like many R&B musicians, she considered Prince a seminal figure and gladly agreed to sit down with him at Warner Bros. Records in Los Angeles.

St. Victor was waiting alone in a conference room when Prince was brought in by an aide, who immediately left. For atmosphere, she had dimmed the lights and placed New Age crystals on the table. Prince was shy and uncommunicative and appeared almost child-like as he sat down, sucking on a large lollipop he had brought. But he listened carefully as St. Victor played him some songs she had recently recorded, and he gradually opened up conversationally. He was especially complimentary about her lyrics and asked her to send him copies.

St. Victor, pleased by his enthusiasm, had her work delivered to him shortly after the meeting. Not long thereafter, she received in the mail a copy of a song he had built around some of her lyrics. While receiving the package was a thrill, after opening it and listening to it she was nonplussed—not only by the song, which seemed to her musically subpar—but also by the process that led to its creation. St. Victor had assumed that she and Prince would work together face-to-face in the studio, where an artistic dialogue could take place. In a rather difficult phone conversation, she explained that she had misunderstood the type of collaboration he wanted.

"I don't think either of us should have to work in a vacuum," she ventured.

"Well, I work best in a vacuum," Prince responded.

St. Victor was taken aback. "Well, what kind of vacuum are we talking about here—a Kenmore, or an Acme?" she asked, trying to determine the level of isolation and distance Prince required when he "collaborated" with other musicians.

"Acme," he responded without hesitation.

Feeling let down, St. Victor nonetheless agreed to keep sending him lyrics. But when they spoke, he was no longer as enthusiastic or friendly as he had been during their initial meeting; he seemed offended that she questioned his preferred way of working. St. Victor came to see that he had no intention of treating her as an equal partner, but simply wanted to make use of whatever interesting ideas she might have to offer. She realized that her frustration was probably quite similar to that experienced by other independent-minded female artists, such as Rosie Gaines, who had worked with Prince. While the notion of collaborating with him had at first seemed like the opportunity of a lifetime, it had, for the moment at least, ended disappointingly.

"When Prince shines that light on you, that energy, that respect, that admiration, it's easy to want to put your life in his hands," St. Victor reflected. "It's a very bright, warm, God-like light. But when he shuts it off, you've never known cold like that."

september 26, 1995: release of the gold experience

Finally, years after most of it had been recorded, Prince's next album was issued by Warner Bros. under ♀. The media and fans found the long-delayed project an overdue return to form. "With this LP, our former Prince turns in his most effortlessly eclectic set since 1987's *Sign O' The Times*," weighed in *Rolling Stone*. *Entertainment Weekly* called it "a buoyant, raucous effort, imbued with funk, passion, and playfulness."

With its bevy of strong and focused songs, *The Gold Experience* is indeed Prince's strongest work of the 1989–95 period that marked his artistic decline. Signs of genuine inventiveness—something largely missing from his music since *Lovesexy*—are found on cuts like "Pussy Control," which features a crazed synthesizer line and a humorous, quasi-rapped vocal by Prince. The song's lyrics, among his wittiest in years, address the power that a woman's sexuality gives her over men. But by far the album's most interesting cut is "Shy," a drumless piece that blends Grateful Dead–like folk-rock, James Brown–influenced funk, and even hints of electronica. A fascinating pastiche of styles, "Shy" finds Prince operating outside any constraints of commercialism or formula. Another powerful cut is "Gold," which for most of its five minutes bumps along simply as a melodious pop song but offers a surprising touch at the end—the abrupt introduction of a descending, multi-tracked vocal harmony that cuts across the song's chords rather than following them.

The album as a whole is somewhat less than the sum of its parts; unlike *Sign O' The Times* or *Lovesexy*, it lacks any unifying theme and at times feels muddled. But if it is an arbitrarily assembled collection of songs, *The Gold Experience* still reaches many more high points than Prince's previous efforts of the 1990s.

The album's release, though, proved something of an anti-climax. After so many delays, Prince had lost interest and now viewed *The Gold Experience* as just one more step towards the completion of his Warners contract. For hardcore fans who had long ago downloaded most of the material from the Internet or purchased it on the bootleg market, the album offered few surprises. And the general public, which in a different time might have embraced the album, continued to associate Prince more with name changes and other publicity stunts than with music. The record's commercial performance, while stronger than that of *Come*, was only modest; 530,000 units were sold in the in the United States, with the album reaching No. 6 on the Pop Chart and No. 2

on the R&B Chart. Thus, what might have been a comeback album for Prince in the end had little impact.

january 1996: tour of japan

A brief series of concerts that began in Tokyo marked the complete breakdown of relations between Prince and his bandmates. After an opening-night show that he perceived as slipshod, he gave the New Power Generation members the silent treatment, refusing to even communicate instructions before subsequent shows. "Prince acted in a manner that I had never seen him act before with this particular lineup ever," drummer Bland recalled. "He was really and truly angry with us."

The NPG members rallied together for emotional support as Prince continued to treat them caustically, even threatening to dock them hundreds of dollars in pay for any minor mistake during a show. Offstage contact between him and the band became minimal. Prior to this tour, Prince and his mates had always engaged in a joint prayer before going onstage. But before one of the Japanese shows, a bodyguard informed them that Prince wanted to pray alone. "That was particularly mean; I'm a Christian man, so I have to forgive, but I'll never forget that," Bland recalled. "From that night on, we never prayed with him again."

Later in the tour, Prince did an about-face and became friendly again, but the damage had been done. One evening while the NPG were eating at a Hard Rock Cafe restaurant, Prince arrived and as usual went with his bodyguards to a private room above the restaurant floor. When he sent down a messenger to invite his comrades up to eat with him, they sent word back that they weren't interested.

Back in Burbank, California, another regime change had occurred at Warner Bros.: Danny Goldberg was out and vice chairman Russ Thyret assumed the top job. Since the 1970s, Thyret had been a key member of the Ostin-Waronker team, and he shared his former mentors' commitment to preserving the creative freedom of artists on the label. Thyret had also been instrumental in getting Warners to sign Prince in 1978 and remained one of his biggest boosters at the label for many years.

Even as he ascended to the CEO position, though, Thyret remained at the mercy of the suits who now controlled Time-Warner. The rapid turnover of high-ranking executives continued. Robert Morgado, whose machinations had driven Ostin from the company, was himself ousted by Levin; Morgado's replacement, former HBO executive Michael Fuchs, fired a host of key executives below him in an effort to consolidate power, creating yet more instability; then Fuchs himself was axed in late 1995. Key artists on the Warner Bros. roster such as REM began to openly question whether the label was the right place to be, and a once-vibrant company was gradually turned into a shell of its former self. "To watch what happened to Warner Bros. after Mo and Lenny was heartrending," vice president Badeaux said. "It was rape and pillage, the parade of people who came through there."

With so much else to worry about, new chairman, Thyret, had little appetite for dealing with Prince's many complaints and demands, and he concluded that the label needed to end the relationship. While Warners' lawyers (including general counsel David Altschul) remained very much in the loop, a decision was also made that bringing suit against Prince would be counterproductive. Although certain of his actions—giving the label intentionally mediocre albums like *Come* and attempting to obliterate the powerful trademark of his own name, among others—may have been breaches of contract, Thyret and the attorneys advising him concluded the public relations fallout from such a lawsuit would be catastrophic. Just such a claim was brought in 1983 by entertainment mogul David Geffen against Neil Young, claiming that Young was giving the label "uncharacteristic" music; Geffen was ridiculed throughout the industry, forcing him to quickly settle. Warners did not want to create a sequel to that fiasco.

There were other compelling reasons for Warners to wind down its dealings with Prince. As a result of the name change and his other high-profile shenanigans, huge segments of the public viewed him more as an eccentric buffoon than the musical force of nature he had been in the 1980s. It seemed unlikely that his image would ever completely recover from the battering it had received in recent years.

In early 1996, negotiations began between Warner Bros. and Prince's new attorney, a shrewd and dashing young man named L. Londell McMillan. Quickly, an agreement was reached that Prince would immediately deliver two albums of material from the Vault to the label, which would then release him from his contract. For Prince, it was a joyous development: Finally, he would have the freedom to issue new albums whenever he wanted, and he would also own his future master tapes. The only concession McMillan was unable to wrest from Warners was ownership of the masters Prince had previously recorded for the company.

At a conclusive meeting with Warners, Prince delivered two new records, complete with cover art: *Chaos And Disorder* and *The Vault . . . Old Friends 4 Sale*. Each was very short and contained almost nothing in the way of interesting or strong material. Prince was slamming his door on the way out, offering no alternatives to these shoddy records. "It was presented as a 'take it or leave it, fuck you' situation," said one Warner Bros. source. With some reluctance, label executives struck the pact, and the long, nightmarish feud with Prince—or at least the most important chapter of it—was over.

One afternoon in early 1996 as Tommy Barbarella was working at Paisley Park with Prince, Mayte Garcia popped into the control room, as she often did. Always pleasant, today Mayte seemed especially full of smiles, and Prince also broke into a wide grin as soon as he saw her.

"Did you tell Tommy?" Prince asked her.

Barbarella looked over at Mayte. She walked toward him and held out her hand to reveal a huge engagement ring. He hugged her and kissed her briefly on the lips, but immediately pulled back for fear of offending Prince.

Notwithstanding Prince's propensity for making major life decisions on a whim, his associates detected something in his relationship with Mayte that perhaps justified this major step. "I'd seen him with a lot of women, but I'd never seen him kiss anyone, publicly show affection, or even do anything really nice for anyone but Mayte," observed Barbarella. For the moment, the steady parade of sexy women in and out of Paisley Park had ceased, and all of Prince's amorous attentions seemed focused on

Mayte. "He had that glimmer that someone has when they're really in love," commented Marylou Badeaux.

The wedding ceremony took place before a small group of family members and associates on Valentine's Day, 1996, at Park Avenue United Methodist in Minneapolis, where Prince had attended Bible-study classes. Invitees included Mattie Shaw and her husband, Hayward Baker; conspicuously absent was John Nelson, with whom Prince remained in a state of estrangement.

Mayte, when taking her wedding vows, did not utter Prince's name but rather pointed to a representation of the ♀ symbol that hung around her neck. A song that Prince composed especially for the occasion, "Friend, Lover, Sister, Mother/Wife," was played twice.

Several days later, Prince opened an official website called "The Dawn" where he posted the eight-page program from the wedding. Entitled "Coincidence or Fate?" it described the Prince-Mayte coupling in almost mythological terms, claiming that Prince's name change and his discovery of his "true soul mate" were both predestined.

But if the wedding program read more like a cultish pamphlet than a humble expression of love, Prince's associates did believe that he cared deeply for Mayte. At age thirty-eight, Prince seemed to want to begin a new chapter in his life—one marked not only by freedom from the constraints of the major label system, but also by a new approach to romance. Despite all that had happened during the nineties, it seemed possible that Prince might rediscover his muse and his direction in life. Perhaps instead of generating soap opera-like drama through his simultaneous courtship of numerous women, Prince would explore the meaning of commitment. Perhaps the bilious side of his personality that had dominated in recent years would be replaced by someone friendlier and more centered.

Despite the mediocrity of most of his music in the 1990s, few who watched his career closely believed that he was truly tapped out. *The Gold Experience* indicated that the creativity was still there somewhere; now perhaps it could again be unleashed.

CHAPTER SIXTEEN

Gone

A round the time Prince and Mayte were married in February 1996, she became pregnant. This brought out an even greater intensity in Prince's feelings toward his wife, and in the coming months he celebrated marriage, impending fatherhood, and freedom from Warner Bros. by recording a host of new songs that included some of his most focused work in years.

For most of the 1990s, Prince had found very little to write about. From *Graffiti Bridge* through *The Gold Experience*, his lyrics focused primarily on nebulous spiritual topics, along with a smattering of social issues that seemed to stir little real passion in him—racial relations ("Race" from *Come*), the Persian Gulf War ("Live 4 Love" from *Diamonds And Pearls*), and grassroots activism ("New Power Generation" from *Graffiti Bridge*) among them. Even his explorations of sex became strained and tired, as if he had little more to say on the subject. Songs like "We Can Funk" from *Graffiti Bridge*, "Come" and "Orgasm" from *Come*, "Sexy MF" from 🕊, and "Gett Off" from *Diamonds And Pearls* sounded like rehashings of his explicit material of the 1980s. Notwithstanding the stronger material on *The Gold Experience*, Prince had spent most of the past five years in a rut, churning out song after song that rarely added anything meaningful to his canon.

But in early 1996, he discovered a mission—expressing his commitment to Mayte and his joy over the impending arrival of their child. Over the spring and summer, he threw himself into these subjects with zeal as he developed what would become his first post–Warner Bros. album. Continuing in the vein of his wedding song, "Friend, Mother, Sister, Lover/Wife," Prince wrote love song after love song for Mayte, including the fusion-influenced "Savior," which climaxes with a torrent of passionate screams; the sultry R&B ballad "One Kiss At A Time"; and "The Holy River," where he claims to be finished with relationships based on empty carnality. He also composed songs about their unborn child, such as the piano ballad "Let's Have A Baby," a heartfelt, if simplistic evocation of family life; the mid-tempo rock song "My Computer," where he expresses confusion over how he will explain the world's violence and corruption to his child; and the funk number "Sex In The Summer," which relies upon a sample of the baby's heartbeat.

Prince had long been fascinated with children. In the early 1990s, when bandmate Levi Seacer won custody of his son (who was about seven at the time), Prince graciously set aside a playroom for him at Paisley Park. For some time Prince had been considering having children of his own, although, to a significant extent, the prospect intimidated him. On "Vicki Waiting" from 1989's *Batman* he poignantly questions whether it would be appropriate to make a "copy" of himself. It was only with the arrival of Mayte in his life that Prince began to feel more confident about handling the monumental responsibility of parenthood.

Prince's new music was also a conscious attempt to present a fresh vision of himself to his colleagues and the world. Dropping his sex-obsessed persona, he instead portrayed himself as a family man and a devoted husband. There were nonmusical changes in Prince's life at this time as well. In early 1996, he made a radical dietary shift, becoming a vegan and avoiding all animal products, including milk and eggs; soy milk and tofu became his primary sources of protein. He turned into something of an evangelist for the vegetarian lifestyle, attempting to convince associates that this was a healthier and more moral course.

Consistent with his newfound enlightenment, Prince made a genuine effort to treat band members and staffers at Paisley Park more humanely. But just as his purported spiritual transformation at the time of *Lovesexy* failed to live up to its billing, this latest epiphany fell short. His business affairs remained fraught with conflict, due in large part to the financial disarray at Paisley Park. Band members, employees, and outside vendors still had difficulty getting paid, and Prince showed no hesitation in using lawyers to fend them off. When former members of the NPG claimed that they had been cheated out of songwriting royalties for *Exodus*, Prince resolutely refused to pay up.

Because the last vestiges of stable administration at Paisley Park had disappeared with the exit of longtime staffers Therese Stoulil and Juli Knapp-Winge, it was unclear even where complaints should be directed. At one point, Eric Leeds, who had been promised a weekly wage for participating in rehearsals in 1995 and 1996, couldn't even find anyone to give his paperwork. In September 1996, with several payments well overdue, Eric was forced to approach his employer directly; during a stilted conversation, Prince denied that any money was owed. Relying on what sounded like a half-baked legalism, Prince claimed that if any agreement to pay Eric existed, it was made without his authority. Recalled Eric: "Unfortunately I can't put it in any other words — it was a complete lie. He said people who had worked for him had made the deal with me without his knowledge, which was completely untrue — he and I had had subsequent conversations about it."

Things had indeed deteriorated to the point where Prince was unable to pay his band members. In March, the current members of the NPG were abruptly told that the group was going on hiatus and that they were being removed from the payroll. Keyboardist Tommy Barbarella recalls getting the news in a phone call from a Paisley Park staffer just a day after an in-person meeting with Prince, during which he had said nothing about it.

For those that continued to collaborate with Prince in the recording studio, working with him became in essence a pro bono gig. When Rosie Gaines was invited to make a guest appearance on a new song called "Jam Of The Year," she received nothing for her contributions.

The various pressures in Prince's life—financial problems, impending fatherhood, the climax of his struggles with Warners—led to his meltdown on April 21 that put him briefly in the emergency room of Fairview Southdale Hospital. In the subsequent weeks and months, Prince took steps both to put his affairs back in order and—just as significantly—to relax. Spending time with Mayte in New York, Chicago, and Los Angeles, Prince found time to shoot a video for the song "Dinner With Dolores" but also took in an NBA Finals matchup between the Chicago Bulls and Seattle Supersonics, caught a couple of musicals on Broadway (*Rent* and *Bring In Da Noise, Bring In Da Funk*), and went nightclubbing.

Whether Prince continued to have chest pains is unknown, but there were no repeats of the April 21 incident as he took steps to take control of both his business situation and his emotions. In June, he re-formed the New Power Generation with two new members who had been recommended by Sheila E.—Kathleen (Kat) Dyson on guitar and Rhonda Smith on bass. Prince liked the sexy, cool image that the two women brought, and they were also extremely effective players. Another new recruit was Mike Scott, a guitarist and experienced studio musician. Kirk Johnson, who had been working in the studio with Prince for several years, took over the drummer's seat, and Morris Hayes continued on keyboards. The band members were reportedly paid, although it is unlikely that they were compensated as well as the NPG members who had been laid off in spring 1996. Rehearsals were fruitful as Prince began teaching the band his new material in preparation for a tour after the release of *Emancipation*.

Prince believed that many of his current problems, financial and otherwise, would disappear once he released a new album. The market, however, remained cluttered with material previously submitted to Warner Bros. *Chaos And Disorder*, the first of two complete albums he had recently delivered to the label, appeared in stores with practically no fanfare on July 8. The recording, like *Come*, was mere contract filler; everything from the sloppily constructed cover to the liner notes, which stated brusquely that the songs had been intended only for circulation among Prince's friends and associates, suggested a half-hearted effort. Much of the music (which was recorded primarily live in the studio with the original NPG prior to the group's disbanding) is rock-oriented, featuring heavy guitar and conventional structures. The melodies and chord progressions of songs like "I Like It There" and "I Rock, Therefore I Am" are pedestrian and underdeveloped. As with most Prince records, there are still a few interesting moments, such as the energetic, playfully rocking title cut and the caustic "Had U," based around only a distorted guitar and strings, whose bitter lyrics (which conclude with the line "fuck you") come across as a kiss-off to Warner Bros. But the ratio of filler to strong material is disturbingly high, marking arguably Prince's weakest album to date.

Little was done by either Prince or Warners to support the album; one of his very few promotional appearances was a performance of "Dinner With Dolores" on *The Today Show* in July. Not surprisingly, the album fared miserably on the charts, moving just 140,000 copies in the United States and fewer than 500,000 worldwide. Most casual Prince fans remained unaware the record even existed, and the slow sales also demonstrated that Prince's hardcore base was rapidly shrinking. Although a legion of fans still existed that would purchase virtually anything he released, the following that had numbered as many as two million in the late 1980s now stood at only about half a million, representing a decline of roughly seventy-five percent.

Reviewers blasted the album. "At its best, the record sounds like a collection of polished demos," observed a writer in *Rolling Stone*. "More often, though, it seems like the work of a Prince impersonator—someone who has closely studied the star's moves and mannerisms but has nothing new or substantial of his own to say." Jim Walsh in the *Saint Paul Pioneer Press* wrote that *"Chaos And Disorder* appears to be an uninspired collection of warmed-over jams, sketches, snatches and leftovers."

Prince did his best to ignore the record's poor performance and the hostile critical response. He was confident that fans and reviewers alike would be stunned by the breadth and creativity of his forthcoming first effort as an independent artist—a three-album set called, appropriately, *Emancipation*. As he wrapped up work on the project in late summer, attorney Londell McMillan, who remained a close advisor after helping broker the exit from Warner Bros., put out feelers to record companies. While Prince had no interest in signing a standard pact with a major record label, McMillan's plan was to have one of them handle the set's distribution. The lawyer laid down several non-negotiable demands to interested companies; among them was that Prince retain ownership of his master tapes and receive a significantly higher rate of return than the fifteen percent typically given to artists by the majors.

Despite Prince's years of attacks upon Warner Bros. and the record industry in general, there was no shortage of potential suitors. Although the executives who ran the world's major entertainment conglomerates viewed him as an erratic figure, they also saw him capable of uncorking a hit like *Diamonds And Pearls* practically at will. In September, McMillan began active negotiations for the release of *Emancipation* with Capital-EMI, a company run by Charles Koppelman, father of Michael Koppelman, Prince's engineer on *Diamonds And Pearls* and other projects. They quickly reached agreement in principle on a "pressing and distribution" deal, through which Prince assumed all of the costs of recording and promoting the album while the label simply manufactured and distributed the copies. In return for shouldering most of the responsibility, Prince retained his masters and also the majority of the profits.

The record was conceived as a masterwork that would silence anyone who viewed Prince as an artist in decline. At three discs of an hour each, *Emancipation* would be likely the longest new release in pop history—yet another milestone set by this stunningly prolific musician. Prince was pumped with excitement as he prepared to show the world what he could accomplish when he was truly free.

But even as preparations entered high gear for the release of *Emancipation*, another disturbing development occurred in Prince's personal life. At some point in early September 1996—the exact date is not known—he and Mayte were advised by physicians that her pregnancy was not proceeding as expected and that their baby was likely to have birth defects.

Prince seemed unwilling to recognize that anything was wrong. Discussions continued between McMillan and EMI, and he took no steps to halt or postpone them. On October 10, Prince and McMillan met with EMI executives in New York and played them the now-finished album. The label's representatives were delighted with the material, and contractual details were quickly finalized. *Emancipation* was slated for release in November.

Four days later, on October 16, Mayte gave birth at Abbott Northwestern Hospital in central Minneapolis. The baby, born with a rare skull disease called Pfeiffer's Syndrome, had an enlarged head, many related medical problems, and required a ventilator to breathe. From the beginning, the prognosis was grim.

A day later, EMI's Koppelman, who had no knowledge about what had transpired at the hospital, issued a press release announcing plans for the release of *Emancipation*. Again, Prince made no attempt to halt the promotional machinery gearing up behind the album.

The child endured a painful week of operations and other medical interventions to keep him alive. But despite the best efforts of physicians, including top specialists that Prince had flown in, it quickly became apparent that there was no hope. On October 23, the baby was taken off life support and died.

Justifiably concerned about unwanted attention from tabloids and other media outlets, Prince and Mayte took various steps to protect their privacy. They made no public statements, and Prince's representatives at Paisley Park remained resolutely mum. The baby's birth certificate omitted any mention of a father, although "Mayte Jannell Garcia-Nelson" was listed as the mother.

In the days and weeks following this tragedy, Prince threw himself into *Emancipation*-related promotional activities. On October 25, two days after the baby died, he played a concert in Hawaii. The next day, he returned to Paisley Park, where 150 music industry and media representatives were invited for an *Emancipation* listening party and press conference. A few days later, on October 30, he left for a promotional trip to Japan and did not return to Minneapolis until early November, when he shot a strange video for *Emancipation*'s "Betcha By Golly Wow!" in which Prince arrives at a hospital wearing medical garb to attend to a pregnant and smiling Mayte.

By this time, as Prince had feared, reporters were sniffing around the story of the baby's death. His refusal to provide any information whatsoever only generated more curiosity, and rumor-packed articles began appearing in tabloids. The mainstream media seemed more reluctant to pursue a story of such tragic and personal dimensions, but on November 4, when Prince and Mayte were interviewed by Oprah Winfrey for a segment to be broadcast later that month, the famous host delicately raised the subject. In response, Prince replied, "It's all good—never mind what you hear." Winfrey also asked questions about the references to the baby on "Sex In The Summer" and "Let's Have A Baby"; each time, Prince gave brief, agreeable responses that offered no hint of any problem.

While Prince and Mayte were certainly justified in not publicly discussing the tragedy, the lack of candor nonetheless created awkwardness, especially given the other activities occurring in his life. *Emancipation* was being billed as a celebration of marriage, birth, and family, topics that were sure to come up in interviews. By declining to postpone the album, and instead going forward with its November 19 release, less than a month after the baby's death, Prince helped create an unfortunate blurring of the private and the personal.

In addition to proceeding with the ill-timed release of *Emancipation,* Prince took steps that—while they may have simply been reasonable efforts to protect his privacy—came across to some as excessively manipulative. On November 4, the same day as the Oprah interview, a death certificate for the baby was filed with the Hennepin County Medical Examiner. It listed his name as "Boy Gregory" and the mother as "Mia Gregory." Just as on the birth certificate, no father was listed, but in other key aspects, the birth and death certificates did not match.

The woman who filed the death certificate, Erlene Mojica (called "Nanny" by both Prince and Mayte), had spent much of the pregnancy by Mayte's side. Her sister Arlene, a professional bodybuilder, was also an employee of Prince's organization and served as Mayte's bodyguard. Strongly invested in their care of Mayte and in her pregnancy, the women were left devastated by the death of the baby.

On December 23, the sisters were abruptly fired from their employment with Paisley Park Enterprises for undisclosed reasons. In early 1997, they were contacted by freelance journalist Tom Gasparoli, one of the reporters investigating the story. Unlike the tabloid writers who had been drawn to Minneapolis, Gasparoli was a solid journalist with years as a television reporter behind him. Initially reluctant to speak to him, the Mojicas soon opened up and seemed eager to tell their story. Many of their allegations—including that Prince may have ordered that the baby be taken off life support, and that he had forced Mayte to follow a vegetarian diet during her pregnancy—troubled Gasparoli, and suggested the possibility of a major story.

The sisters spilled out waves of emotion to him during a three-and-a-half hour interview. Gradually, Gasparoli's role shifted; he remained in part a journalist working on a potentially explosive story, but also found himself becoming an informal counselor and friend to the Mojicas, who were financially broke, emotionally devastated, and anxious to unburden themselves about the whole matter. As reported in several Minneapolis news outlets, Gasparoli encouraged the Mojicas to approach the authorities, which they did. He also set up a meeting between the sisters and two news outlets interested in the story—*Dateline NBC* and the *News Of The World,* a British tabloid. Although Gasparoli suggested that *Dateline* would be a more credible choice, the Mojicas went with *News Of The World,* which (unlike *Dateline*) was offering money.

Prince, meanwhile, continued to refuse to acknowledge that there had been any complications with Mayte's pregnancy. Undertaking more interviews than he had at any point during the 1990s, he deflected the questions and tried to keep the focus on *Emancipation.* In an interview with *USA Today,* Prince said, "There is a rumor out that my baby died. My skin is so thick now. I care much more about my child than about what anyone says or writes." As a result of these cryptic statements, some articles erroneously confirmed that the baby was in fact alive. "The artist formerly known as Prince has a new wife, new baby and a new attitude," read an article caption in *Ebony.*

But as a result of the Mojicas coming forward, more facts gradually emerged. On March 2, 1997, the *Minneapolis Star Tribune* reported that the Minneapolis police department and the Hennepin County Medical Examiner were investigating the death of the baby, prompted at least in part by claims made by the Mojicas. The nature of those allegations became clear on March 9, when the *News Of The World* published its account by reporter Stuart White under the unfortunate headline "Prince Pulled Plug on Baby." This luridly written story repeated claims previously made by the Mojicas to Gasparoli, such as that Mayte had been forced to sneak out to a local restaurant to get meat during her pregnancy and that Prince declined to have the baby undergo an operation that may have allowed him to breathe normally.

Ultimately, nothing the Mojicas told investigators (nor any of their assertions in the *News Of The World* story) provided specific evidence of any illegal actions by Prince. In June, the Hennepin Medical Examiner reported its finding that the baby died of natural causes. Authorities apparently concluded that Prince had made a difficult and painful, but also justified, decision. With the baby unable to breathe on his own, and facing an extremely difficult and compromised future, removing him from life support was a choice that—however questionable in the eyes of the Mojicas—was arguably compassionate. Legally, it was not a decision that authorities believed they could second-guess.

As for the claims that Prince had prevented Mayte from eating meat during pregnancy, these allegations—if they were indeed investigated and found truthful—could not have been linked to the problems suffered by the baby. Medical studies have found no connection between diet and Pfeiffer's Syndrome; the disorder is caused by a genetic mutation, and occurs largely as a fluke. Although the genes of the parents play a role, a couple that has a child with Pfeiffer's Syndrome is not necessarily at risk with respect to later children.

Concerned that the Mojicas might repeat their story to other media outlets, Prince did his best to muzzle them after the appearance of the *News Of The World* piece. His attorneys went before Carver County District Court in March to argue that the Mojicas had violated a confidentiality agreement signed as part of their employment with Paisley Park Enterprises. The court, showing immediate sympathy for this argument, closed the hearings to the public. The Mojicas argued, however, that they had never signed the purported agreements and that their signatures had been forged. Because the court proceedings continued under a veil of secrecy, it is not clear how the case was resolved. But given that the Mojicas have made no further disclosures, it is likely either that the court ruled that they were bound by a confidentiality agreement, or that the women simply agreed to keep quiet.

If the whole episode proved anything, it was that Prince's attempts to conceal information only fueled interest in the story. While he remained determined not to discuss the matter in any detail, Prince gradually edged toward public acknowledgment of the tragedy.

In an interview with Bryant Gumble at the end of 1996, Prince responded to questions about his baby's death by stating that "anything that happens, we accept."

"It sounds like there's been a problem, but you're of the belief that whatever has happened has happened for the best," Gumble countered.

"It's happened for a reason, yes," Prince said.

During a conversation with Spike Lee for *Interview* magazine in early February 1997, Prince responded to similar questions by making reference to a new piece of music. "I have written a song that says: 'If you ever lose someone dear to you, never say the words, "they're gone," and they'll come back,'" he said.

The song, called "Comeback," appeared on an album called *The Truth* a year later. A beautiful but sad number on which Prince sings accompanied by only an acoustic guitar, its words speak of a cool wind that Prince feels blow by him on the street one day, a wind that represents a departed spirit. "Comeback" is the sort of song Prince has rarely written—a piece that touches honestly on a traumatic experience.

At the same time, the lyrics reveal Prince's propensity for emotional denial. The message of "Comeback" is that pain and loss should not be accepted, but ignored. Rather than following the path of those who have poured their anguish into their art— for example, John Lennon's songs about the death of his mother, or Lou Reed's wrenching depictions of his own heroin addiction—Prince in essence refused to acknowledge, even to himself, that his baby was gone. He would not write about the subject again.

Even as speculation and innuendo swirled about his personal life, Prince did his best to focus on *Emancipation*, which he promoted more vigorously than any album of his career. In several interviews, he called it "the album I was born to make."

If *Emancipation* lacks the experimental flair and raw energy of albums like *1999*, *Parade*, or *Sign O' The Times*, it is nonetheless one of his most focused and consistent works. The three-album set demonstrates thematic coherence, focusing on his union with Mayte, his parting of ways with Warner Bros., and his spiritual development. Although it runs nearly three hours, *Emancipation* contains surprisingly little filler. Certainly Prince's most effective album since *Sign O' The Times*, it is a striking reminder of his talent.

There are myriad highlights. The opening "Jam Of The Year," while at first glance a rather standard piece of mid-tempo dance music, is elevated by various interesting touches—scat-like vocals from Rosie Gaines, a pristine funk guitar deep in the mix, and a descending piano figure that emerges at the end. "New World," based around a taut synth motif, is nearly as incendiary as anything on *Dirty Mind* or *Controversy*. "The Love We Make" is a soaring rock ballad with a stunning melody.

While the album's tone is for the most part upbeat and even celebratory, there are a few moments of darkness on tracks that obliquely address Prince's years of tension with Warner Bros. "Face Down," an odd and quirky number on which Prince half-raps and half-speaks, is charged with angst, but there is also an element of wit, and the song adds up to an archly amusing take on the record industry. "Slave," another strange piece in which a multi-tracked vocal hovers over a collage of drum-machine beats and samples, features impressionistic lyrics that reveal the isolation and pain Prince felt during his struggle with Warners.

The main deficiency of *Emancipation* is that, notwithstanding its consistently strong material, it fails to add anything genuinely new to Prince's sound. Instead, some of its songs are strongly derivative of contemporary R&B trends. "Emale" features an ambience remarkably similar to that created by producer Dr. Dre on Snoop Dogg's *Doggystyle*, and laid-back dance numbers like "Somebody's Somebody" aim for the glossy, radio-ready sound of groups like TLC and Boyz II Men. Given the lengths Prince had gone to free himself from Warner Bros., one would have expected a more challenging and experimental album than *Emancipation;* in the end, the most adventurous aspect of the album is its length.

Still, the media lauded the album as Prince's most satisfying effort in nearly a decade. "*Emancipation* is a whopping reminder that the former Prince is one of the most creative musical innovators of the late 20th Century—at least when he feels like it," weighed in the *Detroit Free Press.* "Not since *Diamonds And Pearls* has [Prince] made such a consistently successful album, and not since *Sign O' The Times* has he given his fecund, unknowable intelligence such free reign," asserted *Q* magazine.

Commercially, the album performed much more strongly than *Chaos And Disorder,* but its overall sales figures were short of Prince's expectations. Part of the problem was that EMI, shortly after the release of the album, began experiencing financial problems and then shut down altogether in spring 1997, hampering distribution. Moreover, Prince's selection of the weak "Betcha By Golly Wow!" (a cover of a song by the Philadelphia soul group the Stylistics) as the first single destroyed any momentum *Emancipation* might have gained on the radio. In the end, the album sold about 570,000 units in the United States. (It nonetheless received a double-platinum certification, indicating sales of two million, since one sale was counted as three by the Recording Industry Association of America.) All told, it was his best-selling new release since ♀, though it did not come close to re-establishing him as a major player on the pop charts.

While *Emancipation* was presented primarily as a one-man show, some of Prince's associates who contributed to the record raised the familiar grievance that he hadn't been entirely fair with songwriting credit. Sandra St. Victor was surprised to see on the album the song "Soul Sanctuary," for which she had written most of the lyrics during their brief collaboration in 1995. Not only was she not notified that the song would be released, but the album's liner notes indicate only that she cowrote just a single line of the song. Nor did she receive the publishing rights or royalties typically given to a cowriter. "He sent me a card, a picture, and a check," St. Victor said. "I told him, 'That's nice, but we didn't agree on anything.'"

But while St. Victor felt cheated out of her proper credit and remuneration, she ended up not pushing the matter. "I thought about doing something, but in the end I realized that he has much bigger lawyers than I do, and why should I waste the energy and time," she said. "There's more music to be made, so I've been doing that."

Another *Emancipation* cut that has been questioned is "Dreamin' About U," which Eric Leeds claims relies heavily on a saxophone melody he had created at a rehearsal. "That should have been credited to me as co-songwriter," Leeds said. These assertions thus joined a long line of declarations proffered by Prince associates who feel under-credited for their input into his music.

january 1997: emancipation *tours of the united states*

The first leg of Prince's promotion of his new record, called the Love4OneAnother Charity Tour, took in twenty-one cities, where at each stop some of the proceeds were donated to local charities. The concerts featured the revamped lineup of the New Power Generation. The shows were energetic and often powerful, if somewhat standard in their approach. Prince used timeworn stage routines (such as a segment where he coyly asked the women in the audience if their man "has an ass like mine"), leading to some complaints that he was failing to update his act. The set included various tunes from *Emancipation*, among them the opening number "Jam Of The Year" and "Get Yo Groove On," both of which became raw funk workouts in their live incarnations. Also performed were favorites like "Purple Rain," "Take Me With U," and "If I Was Your Girlfriend."

In July, the charitable component of the tour ended and a more conventional swing through larger arenas began. Called the Jam of the Year, the tour was unusual in its business aspects. Concerts were announced just two or three weeks in advance to discourage the scalping of tickets at prices higher than the face value, a practice that irked Prince. Despite the short notice, sales were strong. While few of the venues (which typically had capacities of 15,000 or more) sold out, in many markets Prince drew upwards of 10,000 people. Most of the promotional tasks were handled directly by Prince's organization, minimizing overhead. The stage show was stripped-down, featuring few props. In essence, Prince's approach to the tour mirrored the marketing of *Emancipation*; he handled most of the work and took in most of the profits, leaving a much smaller role for intermediaries such as concert promoters, ticket agencies, and record companies.

As the tour continued, most of the songs from *Emancipation* were gradually dropped from the set and replaced by older hits. For fans and critics who viewed the album as a creative rebirth, this was disappointing. Some were not surprised, though, that Prince was now distancing himself from an album that he now linked with a personal tragedy. "It is clearly an album he associated with Mayte and the child," noted one longtime observer. "I think it would be almost painful for him to perform many of those songs."

Prince remained true to his strategy of emotional denial. He poured himself into his concerts and the swirl of other activities on the road, which included frequent late-night and early-morning visits to nightclubs. The pace was more exhausting than exhilarating, but it served to distract Prince from his pain. Mayte was usually absent from the road, spending most of her time in Minneapolis.

Thus, the *Emancipation* period—one that began with the promise of a new approach to life and art—ended with things looking not so different after all. Prince was back on tour, essentially alone despite the coterie of band members and handlers that remained at his beck and call. He was playing the songs that had made him famous years earlier and living the same cloistered lifestyle. For associates who had hoped that the changes heralded by *Emancipation* would be lasting, it was not a pleasant sight. Observed one former band member, "I was kind of hoping that after the baby died it would be his crash and burn, and that he would be a phoenix and rise from the ashes, but that didn't happen."

CHAPTER SEVENTEEN

Larry

As the Jam of the Year tour made its way across America, a fateful stop took place on August 12, 1997, when Prince and the New Power Generation played the Nashville Arena in Tennessee. Following the concert, the band visited a nearby club called the Music City Mix Factory to play an aftershow. Those attending the event included former Sly & the Family Stone bassist Larry Graham, along with members of his group, Graham Central Station, who were in Nashville as part of a tour organized by the comedian Sinbad.

Born in Beaumont, Texas, on August 14, 1946, Graham, not unlike Prince, gravitated toward music at an early age and was playing piano by the time he was eight. As a teenager, he played organ in his mother's band, the Dell Graham Trio. Happenstance led him to the bass guitar, the instrument that would define his career. During a show, a malfunction in Graham's keyboard forced him to reach for whatever was nearby, which happened to be a bass; he discovered an instant knack for the instrument. A few gigs later the group's drummer quit, further altering Graham's musical trajectory. To cover for the lack of percussion, Graham began playing the bass in a fashion that involved whacking his thumb against the strings, generating a fierce, staccato sound. Graham thus became the acknowledged inventor of the style known as "slap bass," which emerged as an integral part of funk and modern jazz. One of the earliest recorded examples of this technique was Graham's intro to the Sly Stone classic "Thank You Falletinme Be Mice Elf Agin," which reached No. 1 on the Billboard Pop Singles Chart in 1970.

After leaving Stone's group in 1972, Graham enjoyed a fruitful solo career for much of the decade with Graham Central Station. In 1974, though, his music experienced a shift from free-flowing funk to more introspective and spiritual material as a result of Graham's conversion to the Jehovah's Witness faith. In the late 1970s and early 1980s he moved in the direction of balladry, which reinvigorated his commercial fortunes (the single "One In A Million You" reached No. 1 on the R&B Singles Chart in 1980) but made his sound less distinctive.

After several years of semi-retirement, he re-formed Graham Central Station in the 1990s and resumed touring. By 1997, when Graham encountered Prince in Nashville, he was no longer well-known among the public but remained a respected elder statesman of funk. Prince, who had covered both Sly Stone and Graham Central Station as far back as his teenage years, was delighted to meet this longtime musical hero and invited him to join in the aftershow performance. Prince, Graham, and members of both bands packed onto the club's tiny third-floor stage and jammed on "It Ain't No Fun To Me" (an Al Green number that appeared on Graham Central Station's 1974 debut album), "Thank You Falletinme Be Mice Elf Agin," and others.

The joyous onstage energy that resulted from this meeting prompted Prince to ask Graham and his band to join the Jam of the Year tour as the opening act. Graham agreed, and he and Prince soon developed a fast friendship that centered around their discussions of spiritual issues. Prince was curious about the Jehovah's Witness faith, as Graham recalled in liner notes for a 2001 Rhino Records retrospective. "He asked questions, [and] I started answering his questions from the Bible," Graham recounted. "Not in my own words; I was simply showing what the Bible said. The more I showed him, the more he wanted to know."

Prince seemed very receptive to Graham as a spiritual mentor. In the months that followed their meeting in Tennessee, the bassist emerged as the very center of Prince's personal life, for the most part replacing Mayte in this role. To a significant extent, there was also a melding of Graham's stage act with Prince's own, particularly at the more informal aftershows. During Graham Central Station's sets—which featured Graham's songs and also a liberal helping of Sly Stone numbers—Prince would often function as a member of the backing band, playing keyboards or guitar as Graham led the proceedings. Graham would then sit in on bass during Prince's sets.

From the perspective of fans, the sudden prominence of Graham was not an entirely salutary development, notwithstanding the bassist's talent and stature. Graham Central Station in its late-nineties incarnation was in some sense a cover or tribute band, relying heavily on classics written and initially sung by Sly Stone. It made little sense for an artist as important and original as Prince—however much he admired both Stone and Graham—to become part of this exercise in imitation. But Prince, badly needing spiritual support and a new focus in his life after the tragic developments of 1996, wanted Graham to play as large a role as possible, regardless of the artistic consequences.

In April 1998, a major transition became complete when Graham and his family moved to Chanhassen, settling into a modest home near Paisley Park Studios. Spirituality remained an essential part of the relationship between the two men. While Prince did not immediately proclaim himself a Jehovah's Witness, over the remainder of the tour signs of Graham's influence in this area increased. Tour staffers began handing out Jehovah's-oriented flyers before shows, and Prince even began altering lyrics of his songs to adhere to Jehovah's Witness doctrine. He changed the name of the classic "The Cross" from *Sign O' The Times* to "The Christ" in light of the Jehovah's teaching that Jesus Christ died not on a cross, but on a device of torture called a stauros. Prince also re-examined his use of profanity, something that the religion forbids. Eventually, the angry and curse-filled version of "Face Down" that had been a highlight of the Jam of the Year sets was dropped. And in an appearance at Madison Square Garden for an awards ceremony, Prince praised Graham for showing him "the truth" and made a confusing speech about the term "stauros" while the word was broadcast on a video screen behind him.

The incorporation of the Jehovah's Witness faith into his life represented Prince's latest spiritual epiphany. Beginning with 1988's *Lovesexy*, he had been on a relentless quest to connect with God on a deeper, more personal level, and he had undertaken a variety of public actions (including changing his name, purportedly for spiritual reasons) in furtherance of this goal. Each time, Prince presented himself as a transformed and newly enlightened person; this had happened again just as recently as his 1996 marriage to Mayte, which he claimed had awakened him to a higher morality. With the arrival of Graham in his life, he embarked on yet another new path, one that took him closer toward organized religion than anything since the Seventh Day Adventist services he had attended as a child. And interestingly, he had chosen a faith that had sprung from the Seventh Day Adventist faith and shared many of its doctrinal tenets.

It was all part of Prince's steady, inexorable journey from rebelliousness toward a more conventional and conservative world view.

If there was one area in which Prince could rightly still claim the mantle of a pioneer, it was in his approach to the business of music. Now free from the major label system, he was anxious to create a new paradigm that allowed for more rapid and direct delivery of songs to his fans. While *Emancipation* was distributed and promoted by a major label, he envisioned more idiosyncratic projects that would be handled exclusively through his own NPG Records. By doing so he could both maximize his own profits and diminish costs associated with promotion and distribution.

His first major effort in this respect was *Crystal Ball*, a five-album, mail-order set that Prince began marketing through the Internet in mid-1997. This project, which included mostly studio outtakes recorded years earlier, was Prince's means of reclaiming control of his unreleased music. For years, he was troubled by the wide availability of studio outtakes in the form of "bootlegs"—unauthorized collections of material created by black-market entrepreneurs. Although there were numerous songs in his Vault that fans had never heard, there were also hundreds of unreleased songs that ended up in circulation. This problem developed in large part because, during much of the eighties, Prince freely handed out cassettes of new songs to friends and acquaintances. By the mid-1990s he had tightened up this practice, but remained unhappy about the large number of bootlegs still available on the market.

Bootlegging of concerts and unreleased studio material was hardly uncommon in pop music, particularly among the cult-like fans of groups like the Grateful Dead, Bruce Springsteen, and Frank Zappa. The views of artists regarding this practice were mixed. To some, such as the Grateful Dead, bootlegging (particularly of live shows) was considered a part of being a serious fan. Zappa viewed the practice less charitably, believing that it cheated him out of revenues, and in 1991 he released on Rhino Records an enhanced box set of previously bootlegged material called *Beat The Boots*. Prince's views were in line with Zappa's, and *Crystal Ball* represented his own attempt to strike back at bootleggers.

From the start, though, the effort was plagued with problems. *Crystal Ball* was much more of a do-it-yourself effort than anything Prince—or probably any major pop artist—had attempted before. The album was advertised through his website and through word-of-mouth among the significant community of Prince die-hards on the Internet. Fans were encouraged to pre-order the set—at a sixty-dollar price tag—by calling Prince's "1-800-NEW-FUNK" phone number. His serious fans were excited about the prospect of this orgy of material, and anticipation built that *Crystal Ball* could be a masterpiece of unreleased gems.

By late 1997, about 84,000 people had pre-ordered the set. This level of demand, while small compared to that for a major label album, proved overwhelming for the limited infrastructure that Prince established at Paisley Park to process the orders. When album was released in January 1998, the delivery of *Crystal Ball* to fans was chaotic; some received it late, some got multiple copies, and still others had to badger Paisley Park incessantly before their orders were filled. Angry comments flew on Internet chat boards attacking Prince for his inability to run a business. To make matters worse, he reversed a previous decision not to sell the album through retail outlets; some hardcore fans were still waiting for their mail-order copies when *Crystal Ball* arrived in stores like Best Buy.

Artistically, *Crystal Ball* is a sprawling, poorly organized set that falls far short of the definitive statement fans had anticipated. Of the five discs in the set, the first three constitute Prince's reimagining of the aborted 1986 album *Crystal Ball* (parts of which had been reworked into *Sign O' The Times*). Starting with the lengthy title track, it continues through a hodgepodge of tunes recorded primarily in the mid-eighties and mid-nineties. While much of it is intriguing, there are few outstanding tracks. "Crystal Ball," which seemed adventurous in 1986, sounds meandering and unfocused after more than a decade on the shelf. "Ripopgodazippa," a pseudo-reggae exercise used in the 1995 film *Showgirls,* has an agreeable verse melody but lacks an effective chorus. "What's My Name?" is a mildly interesting curiosity awash in sound effects, while "Make Your Mama Happy," one of the stronger tunes, is an effective tribute to Sly Stone. As a whole, though, the album is oddly sequenced and sloppily constructed; even some of the segues between songs are awkward.

More successful is the fourth disc, a mostly acoustic effort with the portentous title *The Truth*. The record starts with two tense, dark pieces, "The Truth," and "Don't Play Me," both of which are effective and powerful. Another point of interest is "Circle Of Amour," the title and feel of which are reminiscent of Joni Mitchell's "The Circle Game" (from the 1970 album *Ladies Of The Canyon*). One of Prince's lines in the song even recycles the phrase "circle game."

The fifth disc of the collection—given only to those who had mail-ordered *Crystal Ball*—is an album of instrumental, classical-influenced music called *Kamasutra*. Prince's goal seems to have been to create a mixture of classical and ambient New Age music, but the results sound artificial and hollow, and most of *Kamasutra* is virtually unlistenable.

While some reviewers found in *Crystal Ball* yet more evidence of Prince's protean genius, most found it less than completely satisfying. "As usual, the music is funky and often fun—but most of it is for fanatics and completists only," noted the *Minneapolis*

Star Tribune. "There are good reasons most of this stuff wasn't released." Added *Entertainment Weekly:* "Ultimately, *Ball* is for aficionados, making crystal clear that [Prince] isn't a prepackaged pop star but an idiosyncratically brilliant fringe dweller who had a few big chart smashes."

The entire *Crystal Ball* endeavor—the botched marketing and delivery, along with the inconsistent nature of the album itself—further eroded Prince's core fan base. And among those who remained, there was an increasing sense of disgruntlement. On the large number of Internet sites devoted to discussion of Prince's career, the chatter became increasingly negative.

Prince, an Internet surfer who stayed in touch with former associates through emails, was aware of the complaints and viewed them with disdain. He was also troubled by the occasional critical article in *Uptown,* an internationally circulated fanzine devoted completely to the discussion of Prince's music. He believed that his fans should be unconditionally supportive and also felt that—as in the case of those who marketed bootlegs—*Uptown* and the websites were exploiting his image and making money off of him.

In late 1998, Prince and his in-house counsel, Traci Bransford, discussed the possibility of trying to shut down *Uptown* and various fan sites on the Internet through legal action. They enlisted the respected New York firm Thelan, Reid & Priest to draft lawsuits, which were then served on the fan groups in early 1999. His principal claims were that these entities violated so-called unfair competition laws by profiting off of his image and implying that they were sanctioned by Prince, and also that they violated his copyright in the ♀ symbol by reproducing it.

Of the many Internet sites sued, only a few had any connection to bootlegging, and it is unlikely that many profited from their activities. Most were shoestring operations developed by fans out of the sheer joy of discussing Prince's music. The same was largely true of *Uptown,* a magazine with a circulation of only about 2,000 worldwide. The claims that these organizations had violated his copyright were particularly preposterous; Prince had, after all, asked that he be identified only by the symbol and had even disseminated it to the media on computer discs. The unfair competition claims were nearly as thin—even though the sued organs wrote almost exclusively about Prince, none of them had claimed his official imprimatur.

Just the same, contesting these claims required legal representation that these organizations could not afford. One by one, the websites closed, generating a new level of outrage among fans who could scarcely believe that Prince was suing his most ardent fans. Only *Uptown,* which secured pro bono legal representation from the author of this book, was able to fight back. After pre-trial wrangling, a settlement was reached in which the magazine both agreed to stop calling Prince by the symbol and adopted a disclaimer announcing that it was not an official Prince publication. Finally, it stopped writing about any bootlegged albums, although it retained the right to discuss unreleased songs.

While *Uptown* continued publishing, the Prince Internet community was decimated by the lawsuits, leaving a bad taste in the mouths of many core supporters. After proclaiming himself a "slave" because of the restrictions placed on him by the record industry, he was now using his power and financial clout to deny fans the right to comment on his work. Once again, his own actions turned many aficionados into former fans of Prince.

For Mayte Garcia, life as Prince's wife turned out to be quite different from the picture of matrimonial bliss described on *Emancipation*. From the beginning of the Love4OneAnother Charity Tour through the end of the Jam of the Year swing, Prince was away from Minneapolis for much of a twelve-month period, playing more than 100 concerts and aftershows. Publicly, Prince continued to present Mayte as his exclusive love interest. On the first anniversary of their marriage (February 14, 1997), Prince threw a lavish party for her at Paisley Park. Still, given how infrequently they saw each other, it was hard for associates to escape the conclusion that the relationship had rapidly cooled.

In fact, Prince had already, by mid-1998, begun to develop eyes for another woman, a twenty-one-year-old Paisley Park employee named Manuela Testolini (known as "Mani") who came to the organization to work primarily for his Love4OneAnother charity. Testolini at first glance looked much like Mayte—caramel-skinned, beautiful, and only slightly less curvaceous. Yet her assured personality seems to have been important in attracting Prince. A highly religious young woman, Testolini spoke with Prince about God and spirituality at every opportunity, which further piqued his interest. He soon gave her a significant promotion by making her his personal assistant, and although the relationship did not immediately become romantic, it was clear where things were headed. "He and Mani got close, and the closer they got, the more he distanced himself from Mayte," said a knowledgeable source.

By mid-1998, Prince's public appearances with Mayte were mainly for public consumption, designed to prevent speculation that his marriage was ending. He still brought her along to some of his interviews and still seemed intent on presenting himself as the enlightened, monogamous family man of *Emancipation*. At times, though, he lowered the facade and began to prepare his fans for a change in his status. In July 1998, an announcement appeared on Prince's www.love4oneanother.com website stating that Prince had purchased a mansion for Mayte in Marbella, Spain. Shortly thereafter, Mayte relocated there and was visited infrequently by her husband. Then, in December, Prince held a press conference to make a strange announcement: He and Mayte were annulling their marriage, although they ostensibly remained a couple. He framed the decision in terms of his rejection of all "contracts," including marriage vows, and promised that the couple would renew their bond in a ceremony of their own choosing. This announcement, despite its confusing and ambiguous nature, amounted to more evidence that Mayte was gradually being cast adrift.

june 20, 1998: release of newpower soul

Prince's creative efforts during 1998 were directed toward three projects, none of which would be released under his name: a new album by the New Power Generation, and records by Larry Graham and Chaka Khan for his NPG Records label. The New Power Generation project, entitled *Newpower Soul*, was essentially a solo project;

Prince handled most of the vocals and instruments, even though members of the NPG are credited on the sleeve. Still, he did not go terribly far to conceal his pervasive involvement; the cover features a picture only of Prince.

Distributed worldwide by BMG Music, *Newpower Soul* suffered from promotion and delivery problems, again indicating that Prince's shoestring approach was a poor substitute for the machinery of a major label. The album performed about as poorly as *Chaos And Disorder*, reaching No. 22 on the Pop Chart and No. 9 on the R&B Chart and selling only about 100,000 copies. Nonetheless, he profited handsomely from the record's modest sales due to his higher percentage take. In interviews, Prince emphasized that he didn't need to sell millions of records to make huge sums of money; at times, his comments indicated an excessive obsession with financial issues.

Newpower Soul is among the most disappointing albums of Prince's career, finding him in an even worse creative funk than during the early 1990s. In contrast to the heartfelt *Emancipation*, the album is full of phony frivolity. Tracks like "Newpower Soul" and "Push It Up" strain to create the ambience of raucous, George Clinton–like party music, instead coming across as dull and lifeless. Lyrically, few of the songs address subjects other than sex or dancing, as titles like "Mad Sex," "Freaks On This Side," and "(Eye Like) Funky Music" indicate. The album's most interesting track, the subdued funk ballad "Wasted Kisses," is buried at the end of the disc as a "hidden" cut (and the listener is forced to scroll through more than thirty empty tracks to find it).

The media almost uniformly found the album an empty exercise. *"Newpower Soul* recycles the clunky hip-hop and stale jamming that have cluttered most of Prince's recent work," complained *Rolling Stone.* Added *New Musical Express:* "Most of *Newpower Soul* is bad George Clinton right down to the rubber-kneed basslines and appallingly shoddy cartoon sleeve."

Prince actively promoted the album, going so far as to call it "a landmark record for me" in an interview with the online magazine *Addicted To Noise.* With journalists, though, he continued to display the paranoid mindset that had prompted his lawsuits against his fans. During the *Addicted To Noise* session, the reporter was told that he could not use a tape recorder because Prince feared that his words might be purloined. "He's concerned about people using his image, likeness, and voice in ways that it was not originally intended [to be used]," Londell McMillan explained after the interview.

Even as *Newpower Soul* performed poorly, neither of the other two NPG Records releases during 1998—Larry Graham's *GCS 2000* and Chaka Khan's *Come 2 My House*—had much impact, either among critics or on the charts. Prince was heavily involved with both albums, which share the funk-lite sound of *Newpower Soul.* A more appealing presentation of the music on these three projects took place during Prince's concerts, where both Graham and Khan often showed up; seeing these three funk veterans play off of each other was rarely less than a treat.

Still, the continued lack of inspiration in Prince's songwriting was troubling to many of his former associates, who had hoped that his long-sought escape from Warner Bros. would open new vistas in his music. Instead, Prince's creativity reverted to the point found on lackluster albums like *Come* and *Chaos And Disorder.* From the perspective of former NPG keyboardist Tommy Barbarella, the continuing decline in Prince's work reflected an internal struggle between his desire to be a serious artist and his tendencies toward bacchanalian excess. "At the time I left the band, he was becoming a vegetarian, and we started to have deeper conversations about spiritual issues," Barbarella recalled. "But then he'd go upstairs and write a song called 'Good Pussy.' It got to the point where I was embarrassed being associated with some of the things he was doing."

However committed Prince had felt to Mayte and the principle of monogamy while recording *Emancipation*, his resolve on this issue began to waver rather quickly. New songs like "Good Pussy" and "A Good Dick And A Job" (both of which remain unreleased) and *Newpower Soul's* "Mad Sex" hinted that he had resumed seeing other women, something he gradually acknowledged. "Let's say I'm monogamous with God," he said in an interview with the British publication *Megastar*. And according to Barbarella, Prince also developed a fascination with seeing women have sexual relations with each other. The problem, however, was that none of this was inspiring him on an artistic level; the notion of Prince as a prophet of sexual freedom had long ago ceased to be interesting.

Ironically, even as his fan base shrunk and everyone from critics to former band members found his new music less vital, Prince's influence among young, up-and-coming musicians remained strong. His status began to resemble that of his longtime hero Joni Mitchell, an artist who by the late 1990s was perhaps more beloved by aspiring songwriters than the general public. As the end of the millennium neared, a variety of soul men and women began releasing albums that openly acknowledged a debt to Prince. The talented singer and instrumentalist D'Angelo debuted in 1995 with *Brown Sugar*, an album that drew immediate Prince comparisons. With song titles like "Shit, Damn, Motherfucker," D'Angelo emerged as an uncompromising and edgy figure not unlike the Prince of the early 1980s. The artist Maxwell, while more conventional in his approach than D'Angelo, also adopted an overall sound and image that owed much to Prince. A charismatic heartthrob, Maxwell took his cue from songs like "Do Me, Baby" and "Pink Cashmere" on his 1996 debut *Urban Hang Suite*.

And there was more—in 1996, Spike Lee's film *Girl 6*, the story of a phone sex operator, was packed with classic Prince songs. Cover versions of his songs, by artists ranging from the prominent to the obscure, were commonplace. In 1997, Mariah Carey covered "The Beautiful Ones" from *Purple Rain*, and Tom Jones continues performing live renditions of "Kiss." Young fans who might have been less familiar with his work found ample opportunities to discover his music.

With his legacy and influence secure, the question remained whether Prince would fall by the wayside or re-emerge as a force in contemporary pop music.

CHAPTER EIGHTEEN

omeBack

L. Londell McMillan, Esq., found himself in an unusual situation: He needed to boost the confidence of The Artist Formerly Known As Prince. For once, McMillan's most famous client was anything but cocksure; after a string of commercial disappointments, Prince seemed utterly uncertain of his next move. With this being the year his groundbreaking 1982 hit, "1999," had pointed toward, he faced undeniable pressure to raise his profile. Many felt the combination of the year and the song would be like a convergence of stars, presaging wonderful things for him. Lacking a plan to exploit this opportunity, Prince came to New York in April seeking McMillan's advice.

McMillan, only in his early thirties, could gaze at the platinum records on the walls of his tony 57th Street office and accurately describe himself as a player in the entertainment industry, with clients including Wesley Snipes, Def Jam Records, Ruff Ryders Entertainment, and Spike Lee. Since extricating Prince from his Warner Bros. contract in 1996, he had become one of his few trusted advisors. With his sophisticated understanding of the R&B market, McMillan knew what would put Prince back on the charts: funky grooves, catchy hooks, and an image that appealed to younger people—or at least didn't alienate them. Even at the age of forty-two, Prince could provide all of that, but there was another essential ingredient as well: promotion. Prince needed a massive, high-octane campaign to convince consumers he wasn't just an aging, eccentric legend who had changed his name to a symbol.

Since *Emancipation*, none of Prince's releases had made an impact in terms of record sales or critical attention. A significant part of the problem, McMillan believed, was that Prince's independent NPG Records label lacked the resources to generate a hit. His two 1998 albums, *Crystal Ball* and *Newpower Soul*, were undermined by disorganized promotion and distribution. Gaining independence from Warner Bros. and the major label system proved to be something of a mixed blessing for Prince, since he now lacked the means to adequately expose his work.

The limitations of Prince's independent business model again became apparent at the end of 1998, when he and Warner Bros. engaged in a tussle over the song "1999." Warners, which owned all of the Prince recordings made prior to his departure from the label in 1996, announced it would rerelease the song as a single to celebrate the new millennium. Prince was infuriated. He was free to perform his songs, but the physical representations of his pre-1996 music—the master tapes that he had unsuccessfully sought to wrest from the label—belonged to Warners, and he had no rights in the original recording of "1999."

Prince decided to strike back by remaking the song and releasing a competing version. Working frenetically at Paisley Park, he tossed off a creation that was actually a blend of the original "1999" and embellishments improvised on the spot by himself and several associates. (Old friend Rosie Gaines participated, but says she again was not paid.) Various alternate mixes were added and released with the main version as a maxi-single entitled *1999—The New Master*. This pastiche was hustled into stores by early February but sparked little reaction from fans or critics, reaching only No. 150 on the Pop Chart. Warners' release of the original "1999" fared better, climbing to No. 10 on the British pop chart. Once again, Warners' star-making machinery made NPG Records' efforts look anemic by comparison.

Believing a radical new strategy was needed to avert more commercial failures, McMillan presented Prince with an idea that would have been unthinkable a year ago: partnering with a major label, not just for distribution of an album, but for promotion as well. Of course, any deal would have to be strictly on Prince's terms. But McMillan confidently told Prince that he could broker a pact that guaranteed both creative control and ownership of the master tapes.

On its face, the notion of rejoining the major label system seemed ludicrous. Prince had spent the last three years blasting the record industry, claiming that it exploited artists of color, and he risked being called a hypocrite if he rejoined it. Throughout 1998 and early 1999, he continued to gripe publicly about Warners' continued ownership of his master tapes, calling the company a symbol of a corrupt and doomed system. "*Purple Rain?* I do not own that!" he snarled at live performances. "*Diamonds And Pearls?* I do not own that!" He claimed that independent labels such as NPG Records empowered artists and would soon render the major labels obsolete. On his website, Prince posted anti–major label polemics, including an "open letter to Madonna" asking for her help in reclaiming ownership of his master tapes. (She did not respond.)

Prince was worried about remaining relevant in the world of commercial pop. With some hesitation, he followed McMillan's advice and agreed to visit several companies, meeting briefly in April 1999 with executives at Arista, Sony, and elsewhere. But he had hardly made the psychological adjustments necessary for such a fundamental shift. He came away from the meetings disillusioned, complaining to friends that the label bosses kept urging him to emulate the sound of *Purple Rain* and other dated hits.

Unconvinced that a deal could be reached, Prince tacked the other direction with another salvo against Warner Bros. He announced in a *USA Today* interview that he planned to rerecord each of his seventeen Warner Bros. albums, which in theory would render the company's valuable Prince catalog obsolete. "Fleetwood Mac would be hard pressed to do something like this," Prince said, referring to the 1970s supergroup that split over personality conflicts, "but the only people I would have to argue with are the people in my head." Although *USA Today* credulously reported the statement, other media outlets expressed skepticism that Prince could pull off such a dubious and time-consuming project, or that the new versions would recapture the magic of his hits.

Prince returned to Minneapolis and his Paisley Park studio complex but took no steps to rerecord any old material. He performed a series of impromptu concerts at Paisley Park, events that began at two or three in the morning and were sometimes sparsely attended due to the absence of publicity. Bassist Larry Graham continued to play a major role in these and other shows throughout the year.

When not performing, Prince tinkered with new material in the studio, unsure when or if the songs would be released. For the remainder of the spring and summer, he divided his time between Minneapolis and Manhattan. The New York jaunts were primarily social in nature, with many evenings spent dancing at the trendy Club Life with MTV video jockey Ananda Lewis, an attractive young woman whose life had become a vortex of gossip and media flattery. By now, it was clear that Prince's relationship with Mayte was all but over—the ceremony that he had promised would renew their vows following the annulment never materialized. Prince also began dating Mani Testolini, who was sometimes mistaken for Mayte during public appearances.

Some of Prince's former associates, who had encouraged him to visit foreign countries and develop interests outside of music, remained perplexed at his choices of diversion. "He's over forty, and he's still hanging out at nightclubs, just hanging out," said one recent band member. "It has taken its toll, the lifestyle of recording studios and discos and nightclubs—when that's your whole world, you can't grow."

Prince stayed in touch with McMillan, who remained hopeful of linking his client with a major label and thought he saw an opening. Arista Records president Clive Davis, one of the executives who had spoken with Prince in April, came away from the meeting intrigued, despite Prince's obvious lack of enthusiasm. After four decades in the business, Davis still relished the challenge of working with artists that others found too difficult or eccentric; he had already scored in 1999 with Carlos Santana's *Supernatural,* an unlikely blockbuster that he saw as a paradigm for what could be accomplished with Prince.

By the late 1990s, Carlos Santana (born in 1947 in Autlan, Mexico) remained a household name among older rock fans but was viewed as well past his prime. His group, Santana (formed in 1966), spearheaded the "Latin rock" movement, which blended jazz, funk, and traditional Latin music elements into a celebratory but complex style. Santana's early records were commercial smashes and earned him immense respect as a guitarist, but as years went by his output was less consistent, and at age fifty-two he seemed an unlikely hit-maker, especially in the current climate. Pop music in 1999 incorporated a bewildering array of trends and countertrends, and most of the major stars were in their early twenties or younger. Rap and heavy metal combined noxiously in high testosterone groups like Limp Bizkit and Rage Against the Machine; country artist Shania Twain continued to sell records in numbers once unthinkable; introspective alt-rockers Nine Inch Nails and Radiohead were the new critics' darlings; and grinning teen puppets like Britney Spears and the Backstreet Boys stood atop the commercial heap.

Davis faced a good deal of skepticism over his signing of Santana, particularly from his corporate overseers at Bertelsmann, the German media conglomerate that owned Arista Records. There was talk in the record industry that Bertelsmann wanted to replace Davis with someone younger, which made the Santana deal especially risky. But the shrewd executive developed a plan that helped make *Supernatural* not only 1999's most successful album, but also one of the best-selling pop releases ever. He brokered collaborations between Santana and a host of contemporary hitmakers from various genres; these songs made up about half of the album, with the remainder devoted to more traditional Santana material for his core constituency. The collaborations were hugely successful, most notably "Smooth" (with Matchbox 20 front man Rob Thomas) and "Maria, Maria" (with former Fugees member Wyclef Jean), both of which shot to No. 1. The album won a host of Grammy Awards, including Album of the Year, and Santana tendered an emotional thank-you to Davis at the ceremony.

Supernatural had been a gamble, but bold plans were Davis' trademark and a major reason he had become one of the most influential music executives of his time. A bald, modestly overweight man with a ruddy complexion, Davis usually maintained an avuncular air but could quickly become fierce and intimidating when it suited his aims. Raised in a working class section of Brooklyn, Davis had no particular interest in music when he graduated Harvard Law School in 1956 and entered practice as a corporate lawyer. But after being laid off by his first employer, he ended up with a firm whose clients included CBS, owner of Columbia Records. This led to a job as an executive with Columbia, where he rose quickly and was installed as president in 1967. Despite having little knowledge of pop or rock music, he quickly gravitated toward such artists, shifting the focus of the formerly staid label away from classical music and jazz. Davis showed an ability to discover acts that combined chart potential with an aura of artistic respectability. His first signing as president was Janis Joplin, whom he saw perform at the 1967 Monterey Pop festival. "She was breathtaking and soulful and just the best white soul singer imaginable, but with a rock edge," said Davis. With the arrival of the 1970s, Davis' decisions began to shape the sound of the decade, as he scored a remarkable trifecta in 1972, signing Billy Joel, Aerosmith, and Bruce Springsteen. Davis had a spot-on ear for talent and was willing to put in the time in clubs and concert halls needed to separate out the Springsteens, Joels, and Joplins from a sea of hungry and driven, yet marginal performers.

Seeking to develop artists free of corporate interference, Davis founded Arista in 1975, naming the label after his high school honors society. His first signing was Barry Manilow, whose debut, "Mandy," shot to No. 1, a strong start that showed that Davis, rather than running a boutique for quirky artists, would focus on the bottom line. Davis knew that blockbuster successes like Barry Manilow brought in the dollars needed to develop more challenging artists. Over the years, Davis worked with sensitive souls like Carly Simon, Patti Smith, and Sarah McLachlan, as well as tough urban artists like Antonio "LA" Reid and Sean "Puffy" Combs, both of whom developed massively successful subsidiary labels at Arista.

If the eventual acquisition of Arista by Bertelsmann limited Davis' flexibility, it also made him a millionaire many times over. He remained an active dealmaker, and the triumph of *Supernatural* made him hungry for more. Although his meeting with

Londell McMillan in the summer of 1999 focused on other artists on the attorney's roster, Prince's came up early in the conversation. Davis was mystified by the artist's lack of direction. "He hasn't had the right record for a while," Davis said. McMillan seized the opportunity; Prince was not only busily preparing music for a new album, but was right in New York with a cassette full of great songs.

McMillan reported the encounter to Prince, emphasizing Davis' respect for his work and desire to help him mount a comeback. While knowing little about Davis' history, Prince was well aware of Carlos Santana's success at Arista, and he agreed to another meeting. He arrived at the Arista offices in a limousine, and Davis descended from his office to listen to several new tracks in the car. Most of the songs had a strong pop-rock orientation, in contrast to the R&B flavor of *Newpower Soul*. "This is exactly what you need," Davis said enthusiastically. "These songs will be hits." When Prince raised the sensitive topic of master tapes and his struggles with Warner Bros., Davis was reassuring. "Of course you can own your own music," he told Prince. "It's yours."

Prince came away impressed by Davis' directness and enthusiasm, and told McMillan to negotiate a deal with Arista. The lawyer secured a one-record pact that obligated Arista to promote and distribute the record, while giving Prince complete creative control and ownership of his master tapes. If Prince had any lingering doubts about the deal, they were allayed by the $11 million advance payment proposed by Davis, a remarkable figure considering that Prince's 1992 contract with Warner Bros. called for a $10 million per-record advance (though only if his previous album had sold five million copies worldwide, which never happened again after 1991's *Diamonds And Pearls*). The same factors that made the signing of Carlos Santana risky—fading commercial prospects, lack of trendiness, and, arguably, declining creativity—applied with equal force to Prince. But Davis, after the success of *Supernatural*, was feeling anything but cautious, prompting him to give Prince a generous, no-strings package.

Signing with Arista was only half the battle. Prince still had to finish the album and faced a tremendous public relations task: squaring the deal with years of anti–major label rhetoric. Prince had analogized the labels to slave owners while heaping praise on artists, such as Public Enemy and folk-rocker Ani DiFranco, who bucked the system by starting their own labels. He had tried to follow the same path with NPG Records, and the Arista deal seemed dangerously close to an admission that he had failed.

In media interviews, both Prince and McMillan downplayed Prince's commitment to Arista, characterizing the pact simply as a means of exploiting the label's resources. Prince took pains to note that the Arista deal was a different animal than his Warners contract and was only for one album. McMillan blandly described the pact as a "straightforward licensing and distribution deal," comparing Prince to an actor who prefers small art films but occasionally works on big budget productions.

Davis' reputation as a nurturer of artists helped blunt criticism of Prince, and the Arista chairman pitched in by praising him as "an artist, poet, and renaissance man." The signing was officially announced in August through a *USA Today* article where both Davis and McMillan were quoted extensively about the forthcoming album. "I loved it, and I didn't stint in my praise, because it came from my heart," Davis said. "The music says it all. You can talk about respect for accomplishment and a special place in history, but we're looking at the future. He's as contemporary and adventurous as ever. This is going to be a huge album. The hits are there in depth."

After inking the deal with Arista, Prince returned to the studio to record additional songs for the project. Taking a page from the *Supernatural* playbook, he recruited "special guests." First, he incorporated rap in recognition of its appeal to the youth market. Eve, a new artist from the ensemble Ruff Ryders, rapped on the R&B number "Hot Wit' U," and Chuck D. of Public Enemy, one of the pioneers of rap and now something of an elder statesman, appeared on "Undisputed," which sampled Public Enemy's seminal "Bring The Noise."

Prince next approached folk-rocker Ani DiFranco, an unabashed experimentalist with an intense, edgy vocal style who was nearly as prolific as himself, releasing a steady stream of intriguing, albeit inconsistent albums on her independent Righteous Babe label, also home to other artists of DiFranco's choosing. She had repeatedly declined lucrative offers from major labels, fearing encroachment on her artistic freedom, and Prince frequently lauded her business model and independent spirit. "She's taking $7 an album where some rapper [on a major label] is getting $1.50 and out of that he has to pay all his costs," he said in a 1999 interview with the British music magazine *Mojo*. In the same interview, he pointed persuasively to the group TLC, a trio of African-American women who suffered financial problems despite a string of hit records, as a prime example of the majors' exploitative behavior.

When DiFranco performed at Minneapolis' Midway Stadium in July, Prince approached her backstage to chat about his new project. Flattered by the attention, she agreed to come back to Paisley Park to jam and lay down some tracks. Prince found DiFranco remarkably unrestrained and easy to talk to, and it struck him that by refusing to accept the major labels' booty, she completely avoided the type of painful struggle he fought against Warner Bros. While they relaxed outside the studio control room, DiFranco curled up in front of her chair rather than sitting in it, an action Prince found disarmingly child-like.

Later in the evening, they were joined by DiFranco's touring saxophonist Maceo Parker, a longtime hero to Prince who represented a living history of funk music. Parker had spent years with James Brown, delivering memorable solos on "Cold Sweat," "Mother Popcorn," and other signature hits. Prior to such solos, both live and on record, Brown would bark out affectionate cues such as "Maceo—blow your horn!" With his sassy, exuberant style of playing sax, Parker did as much as anyone to make the instrument part of funk as well as jazz. After James Brown he had worked with George Clinton, the quirky funk artist whose sounds influenced a generation of musicians, including Prince. Parker had also released excellent solo albums, such as *Life On Planet Groove* (1992).

After Parker arrived at Paisley Park, the trio moved into the recording studio and got to work. DiFranco added an acoustic guitar part to Prince's just-completed piano ballad, "Eye Love U But Eye Don't Trust U Anymore," and Parker, appropriately enough, played saxophone on the James Brown homage "Prettyman." (Prince even called out Parker's solo in the same fashion James Brown had.) Weeks later, Prince returned DiFranco's favor by contributing backing vocals to DiFranco's song "Providence," which appeared on her 1999 album *To The Teeth*.

But when DiFranco and Parker left Paisley Park, some of the carefree spirit they brought seemed to disappear. As Prince continued work on the upcoming album, he strived to please each of the constituencies he had disappointed in recent years, giving the project a tone of calculation rather than artistic inspiration. Stung by hardcore fans who claimed that his music was no longer bold and experimental, Prince for the first time in years used his Linn LM-1 drum machine, which had been employed to great effect on "1999," "When Doves Cry," "Let's Go Crazy," and other 1980s hits. His retrieval of the device from storage was a direct attempt to connect the new album with his 1980s' innovations.

In another nostalgia-tinged move, he entitled the album *Rave Un2 The Joy Fantastic*. Prince had recorded a song of the same name a full decade earlier, but shelved it because of obvious similarities to his 1986 hit "Kiss"—minimalist instrumentation, falsetto vocals, and a dry snare-drum sound. But now he resurrected "Rave" as essentially an off-the-shelf item from the Vault, believing it, too, would appeal to fans of his 1980s music.

Then there was the contemporary R&B market to consider, which was dominated by slick, glossy artists like R. Kelly, TLC, Boyz II Men, and Destiny's Child. The sounds of such hitmakers were remarkably similar, relying on sparkling harmonies, catchy synthesizer riffs, and laid-back rhythmic patterns. McMillan, whose advice now extended even to creative matters, urged Prince to include material in this vein to enhance the album's appeal among R&B fans. Prince agreed and returned to the studio to record several songs that were in marked contrast to the rawer pop-rock material already committed to tape.

Among the new songs Prince recorded was the mid-tempo ballad "The Greatest Romance Ever Sold," which Clive Davis tabbed as the lead single. The Arista chairman continued his hyperbole, predicting to the press that "Greatest Romance" was going to be "number one all over the world." Prince, during his tenure with Warner Bros., often clashed with label executives over the selection of singles, but with *Rave* he was surprisingly willing to let Davis make such key decisions. A new Prince seemed to be emerging, one quite different from the angry and petulant figure who spent so many years lambasting Warner Bros.

Prince's openness extended to the media, and over the course of the campaign to promote *Rave Un2 The Joy Fantastic*, he gave more interviews than at any other time in his career, speaking with outlets ranging from the prominent (*People* magazine) to the highly specialized (*Guitar Player*) to the bizarrely obscure (a website called www.genegeter.com).

This campaign began with the crown jewel of the fourth estate, the *New York Times*. When reporter Anthony DeCurtis arrived at Paisley Park, he was greeted politely but coolly by Prince, who initially refused to preview any material from the new album, and the conversation got off to a tepid start. "I don't even know how many albums I've made now," Prince said when the reporter asked about his notoriously prolific nature.

"Is it fair to say that this upcoming album is something of a comeback effort for you?" DeCurtis asked.

"A comeback from what?" Prince shot back, emphasizing that he had released records independently only to avoid the meddling of major label executives. "I've had people [at labels] tell me, 'Everybody has to answer to somebody,'" Prince said. "I'd say, 'I answer to God, fool.'"

As the session neared the end, Prince loosened up and offered to give DeCurtis a taste of the new album. He sat down at a huge mixing board and blasted "The Greatest Romance Ever Sold." Prince gyrated to the music and danced over to DeCurtis to bellow explanatory comments, and while the journalist had trouble hearing what was said, something came through clearly: "Tell me that's not a hit!" Prince shouted. As DeCurtis recounted in his article:

> I turned to look at him. His chest was puffed out and he was smiling. His hips and shoulders were moving. But in his dark eyes beneath the bravado, there was a vulnerability he refused to acknowledge, as well as a hope that the answer would be what he needed to hear.

Prince's next public relations step was to generate an air of suspense through the announcement that an unnamed outsider would produce the album. While surprising for an artist who had self-produced each of his recordings, this idea seemed consistent with Prince's comradely dealings with Arista; perhaps, some observers speculated, he was ready to surrender a measure of control in the interests of a successful outcome. Internet sites percolated with chatter about the producer's identity. Only *Uptown*, the long-running Prince fan magazine that he had tried to shut down through legal action in 1998, remained skeptical, writing that "we have our doubts that he's going to be willing to actually take a back seat and let someone else make the production decisions."

Despite the efforts of Prince and Davis to generate buzz, the task facing Arista in promoting *Rave* was daunting. Notably, not everyone at Arista thought Prince had delivered a great album. Davis had not sought corroboration from others at Arista of his high regard for *Rave* and did not even play the album for colleagues at the label until the signing of Prince was a fait accompli. When other Arista executives finally heard it, they found it impossible to imagine what hits Davis thought he had heard.

While in most respects very favorable to Prince, the deal reached between Davis and McMillan did have an inherent flaw: Because the term was for one album only at Prince's insistence, Arista lacked incentive to methodically rebuild his career over a series of projects. The partnership would result in a quick score, or perhaps nothing. Mid-level executives and staffers in the trenches, who in any event did not see *Rave* as another *Supernatural*, simply had no reason to consider Prince a long-term investment, especially given his recent attacks on the major label system.

But Davis himself remained deeply involved in the promotion of *Rave* and treated it as a showcase release. In September, with the album completed and awaiting release, he hosted a "*Rave Un2 The Joy Fantastic* Listening Party" in a 500-capacity auditorium in the Equitable Building in Manhattan. Davis hand-picked the audience of journalists and music industry impresarios. Inauspiciously, the event was held during torrential rains brought on by Hurricane Floyd, a storm system that blew into the East Coast from the tropics. But a capacity crowd turned out nonetheless, and Davis, dressed rather more casually than usual in a light blazer and black turtleneck, still looked every bit the industry mogul as he spent over an hour alone onstage playing each track on the album, some more than once. He prefaced each song with an anecdote about its creation, indicating he had discussed the album extensively with Prince.

With the audience growing impatient, Prince finally appeared, wearing red pants and blouse, yellow boots, and a red scarf draped over his head like a monk's hood. Davis extended his arms from the podium, and the men shared a brief, awkward hug. Prince smiled wanly for the cameras and quickly disappeared. But Davis then raised a curtain to reveal Prince and his band, who launched into the 1986 song "I Could Never Take The Place Of Your Man." A fifty-minute set followed. But while the event demonstrated Arista's commitment to Prince, few of the invited reporters wrote about it. The media buzz that once surrounded Prince was notably absent.

Nor did the *Rave* campaign get much of a boost from the October 1999 release of "The Greatest Romance Ever Sold" to stores and radio. The single's layers of vocal harmonies and shiny lacquer of synthesizer gave it a superficial resemblance to much of the music in heavy radio rotation. Missing, though, was a powerful hook in either the verse or chorus, to say nothing of any interesting instrumental passages. A key innovation of Prince's pre-1990s production approach was to elevate subordinate elements of songs— vocal grunts, guitar embellishments, string orchestrations—to a central position in the mix. On "Greatest Romance," he turns this approach on its head by emphasizing the song's prosaic melody and forcing everything else to march in lockstep behind it.

More of the excitement was drained from *Rave*'s release when the "outside producer" was unmasked. *Rave*, like *Emancipation* and *The Gold Experience*, was released under his ♀ name. But Prince revealed in interviews in fall 1999 that the listed producer of *Rave* would be none other than "Prince." Prince/♀'s explanations to interviewers had an awkwardly schizophrenic quality. "In the studio, the producer has the last word," he said. "Prince was a really good editor, a good decision-maker. He was always stubborn about getting the sounds." In fact, the word "Prince" on the album was a transparent commercial device and an implicit admission that using a symbol as his name had hurt sales.

Arista released *Rave* on November 9, 1999, and Prince continued to throw himself into promotion of the project, planning a mini-tour of the United States and a video shoot for "The Greatest Romance Ever Sold." Davis' superiors at Bertelsmann had other ideas, though, and insisted that early promotion focus on European markets, a decision driven by the presence of the company's headquarters in Germany. Prince resisted, arguing to Davis that the U.S. market was crucial and that European appearances would delay the video shoot. But Davis had no real choice, and Prince reluctantly sat for interviews on television shows throughout Europe. These, and his visits to American programs such as *The Today Show*, were brief, stilted affairs that did little to stir enthusiasm for the album. Larry Graham was a distracting presence during many of the interviews, as Prince wasted valuable promotional time lauding his friend. "This is the best bass player I've ever had," Prince said when Graham joined him on the Swedish show *OP Reis*. "Larry is as important as anyone, anywhere, anytime."

Arista worked hard to push the album in Europe and in the United States, with mixed results. In London, the company blundered by giving away copies of the record as a promotion, which made it completely ineligible for the British pop charts. The initial absence of a video for "Greatest Romance" proved damaging as well, destroying the crucial marketing synergy between radio and television. The vital youth market showed little interest in the song, which reached only number 63 on the Pop Singles Chart and number 23 on the R&B Singles Chart. Both Prince and Davis believed "Greatest Romance" to be a powerful romantic ballad that would appeal to women and teenage girls. Instead, it began to free-fall down the charts.

Critical reaction to *Rave* was at best mixed. Some outlets, such as *USA Today*, called it Prince's strongest work in years. Other longtime Prince observers, such as Jim Walsh of the *Saint Paul Pioneer Press*, were less enthusiastic; he called it a "strong record," but "one that ultimately feels more workmanlike than inspired." The *Los Angeles Times'* Natalie Nichols also had her doubts, saying the album was "an echo of the innovator [Prince] once was." Steven Thomas Erlewine of the *All Music Guide* criticized its commercial concessions: "It's shocking to hear how perfunctory most of the performances are on *Rave*, yet it's stranger to hear Prince gunning for the pop charts."

Rave is not without its pleasures, but it lacks the conviction and thematic coherence of *Emancipation*, Prince's strongest album of the 1990s. Where *Emancipation* had devoted much of its three discs to celebrating Prince's marriage to Mayte, *Rave* finds him retreating to familiar lothario territory on tracks like "Baby Knows," an objectifying depiction of a female with a "butt that goes round" (written about Ananda Lewis), and "So Far, So Pleased," a fantasy of late-night seduction. A pair of more heartfelt songs, "Man O' War" and "Eye Love U But Eye Don't Trust You Anymore" seem to address Prince's breakup with Mayte, but do not probe deeply. The album's stronger outings include the minimalistic and abstract "Strange But True," the James Brown tribute "Prettyman," and the title cut.

Rave sold strongly at first as hardcore fans purchased copies. The general consumer, though, quickly lost track of the album amidst other holiday season releases, and sales tailed off along with radio play for "Greatest Romance." But Prince was not prepared to concede defeat after having invested so much hope and effort in the project. In mid-December, he videotaped a live performance at Paisley Park for broadcast on pay-per-view television on New Year's Eve. The atmosphere was festive, as guests like Lenny Kravitz and George Clinton stopped by to jam. Backstage, Prince percolated with ideas for jump-starting *Rave*, such as releasing a second single and linking with Carlos Santana for live performances. But like many aspects of the *Rave* campaign, the event was marked by missteps. Instructions for would-be attendees were posted on Prince's website, and fans traveled from throughout the country and the world seeking admission. But the instructions had been misleading as to the number of tickets actually available, and hundreds of fans were forced to line up for hours behind barricades in scathingly cold Minnesota temperatures, with only a handful ever gaining admission. Prince's friends and invited celebrities, by contrast, were immediately escorted in. After the show, fans flocked to Internet chat rooms to vent frustration.

The concert itself had a diffuse character, as Prince at times got lost in the whirl of special guest stars. The reunited Time played a perfunctory mini-set. Larry Graham took over a segment of the show with his usual Sly Stone covers. And with Lenny Kravitz's arrival onstage, Prince became a sideman on a plodding cover of the Guess

Who's "American Woman." The $19.99 pay-per-view broadcast received mixed reviews from fans and failed to reinvigorate *Rave*'s sales figures.

By the time the show was broadcast on December 31, Prince's mood had soured considerably, as he realized *Rave* was likely doomed to a quick exit from the charts. He felt he had done his part. Hadn't he delivered a collection of songs that Clive Davis promised would be hits? Believing the absence of radio airplay to be Arista's fault, he complained bitterly to McMillan and other close associates that the label had botched its marketing of the album. Abruptly, he discontinued his promotional efforts and made little further mention of *Rave* in interviews.

january 2000: paisley park studios

The Recording Industry Association of America quickly certified *Rave* as a gold album, indicating sales of 500,000 units. This was little cause for celebration, however, as the album was already, by the end of 1999, rapidly losing steam. For an artist who aspires to be a commercial force, anything less than a platinum record (one million copies sold) is considered a serious disappointment. If platinum is the minimum benchmark of stardom, then a gold record is just a knock on the door. Both Prince and Clive Davis knew it.

While the model for *Rave* was supposed to have been *Supernatural*, sales figures showed a canyon-like gulf between the two albums. By March 2000, *Supernatural* had climbed all the way to No. 1 on the Pop Chart and was certified as having sold nine million copies. By the same date, *Rave* had entirely dropped out of Billboard's Top 100. *Supernatural*'s hold on the charts spanned a sixteen-month period, whereas *Rave* peaked and faded over a period of about thirty days. But Davis believed that it was much too early to abandon the album. He had invested significant time and political capital in the project, as well as $11 million of Bertelsmann's money. Hoping to revive Prince's commitment, Davis flew to Minneapolis for a visit to Paisley Park. But he was met with a chilly reception, and Prince seemed more interested in assessing blame than moving forward. He expressed his frustration with Arista's promotional efforts and reminded the chairman of the hits he had promised. Davis, in turn, made it clear he had taken a personal risk to revive Prince's career. "I thought you'd be different from what I've read about you," Davis said. "Everyone warned me." Prince held firm: Arista had failed, and he wasn't investing any more time on promotion unless the company rushed out a second single. Davis, offended by such pressure tactics, made no assurances. The meeting went nowhere, and the two men parted sullenly.

Prince then made a series of public attacks on Davis. In early March, he posted on a message on his website that "Clive Davis and Arista Records allows [sic] *Rave Un2 The Joy Fantastic* to languish at the netheregions [sic] of the chart (ain't nobody really trippin')." A second message days later stated that Prince had postponed a limited edition of *Rave* with remixes and extended versions. Throwing Davis' optimistic predictions about the album back at him, Prince wrote that the delay "will give Mr. Davis time to make good on his promise to deliver a couple of real hit singles to 'the top of the charts.'"

Davis, despite his penchant for bombastic statements in the press, had no interest in a public spat with Prince. Instead of responding in kind, he quietly passed word down the ranks at Arista that the company was winding down the *Rave* effort. Months later, asked by a reporter why *Rave* fared so poorly compared to *Supernatural*, Davis was diplomatic. "Prince made a great record, but it didn't appeal to the thirteen- to nineteen-year-old age bracket, which means the demographics weren't sufficient to create a hit," he said. "It wasn't bad. I mean, it was a hit among a certain bracket. But it didn't go down with the youth."

Davis had bigger problems. Even after his massive win with *Supernatural*, Bertelsmann wanted new blood at Arista and decided to install Antonio "LA" Reid as president. The expensive failure of *Rave*, while not the only factor behind this move, did little to help Davis. He would not go quietly, however. Davis complained publicly that he was being forced out, and a chorus of prominent musicians quickly rose to his defense. Barry Manilow called "[this] blatant attempt to remove [Davis] offensive and alarming...there is no one in the entire music industry with the constant successful track record and future potential of Clive Davis." A representative for Carlos Santana said that "the only reason Carlos came to Arista was because of Clive...He can't believe this is happening."

Bertelsmann, troubled by the negative publicity, went forward with its succession plans but also provided lavish funding for a joint venture with Davis called J Records (named after Davis' middle initial). "This is not a start-up," said a mollified Davis. "We will be a major record label with our own marketing staff, our own promotion staff. It's unprecedented. And it's a very fulfilling dream."

Davis' new venture enjoyed a prosperous start. Hot artists like Wyclef Jean signed on, and J Records' first release, by the group O-Town, was a No. 1 hit. Davis' miscalculations regarding *Rave* seemed to have been a rare lapse in judgment, rather than an indication he had lost touch. "At 66, I am at the peak of my powers," he said following the announcement of the formation of his new label. Other than Prince, few were inclined to disagree.

chapter nineteen

Xenophobia

In January 2000, the rising R&B singer D'Angelo, who had grown up idolizing Prince, released *Voodoo*, an album that confirmed his position as a possible heir apparent to the leading figure in funk. *Voodoo* bore strong resemblance to *Dirty Mind* in its stripped-down production approach, and almost everything about D'Angelo's vocal delivery—falsetto harmonies, guttural growls, exuberant yelps—was reminiscent of Prince. Yet the recording also bore strong hallmarks of originality, particularly its swampy texture and song structures that favored hypnotic repetition over melody. D'Angelo's music, while not terribly commercial, was building him a rock-solid base of fans who were willing to patiently endure the long waits between releases. (His debut album *Brown Sugar* was released in 1995, and the follow-up to *Voodoo* is not expected until sometime in 2003 at the earliest.) To those who followed the careers of both men (including former Prince confidant Alan Leeds who became D'Angelo's tour manager), the young singer's career strategy was in many ways more appealing than that of his progenitor, who released torrents of undistinguished music and had most recently attempted to cater to the mainstream with *Rave Un2 The Joy Fantastic*.

In August 2000, D'Angelo and his band visited Minneapolis to play the Orpheum Theater. Prince invited him and Ahmir Questlove—the band's drummer as well as the leader of the respected group the Roots—to Paisley Park for a jam session the night before the show. For these two young musicians, this was something akin to a pilgrimage—a chance to socialize and play with one of R&B's most important and influential artists ever. Unfortunately, D'Angelo and Ahmir were treated with haughtiness, if not outright condescension from the moment Prince greeted them. He lectured them on how to succeed in music, rarely letting them get a word in, and he questioned the trajectory of their careers.

By the time Prince proposed moving into a rehearsal room to play, the excitement of the evening had cooled considerably. He picked up a guitar but made it impossible for anyone else to join in; he refused to play anything but new material his guests were completely unfamiliar with. D'Angelo noodled lamely on a set of keyboards as Prince instructed Ahmir how to play the beats correctly. Feeling excluded, D'Angelo mentioned he needed a breath of fresh air and stepped outside.

Later, when a pause presented itself, the two musicians excused themselves from the premises as quickly as possible. As a courtesy, they invited Prince to their concert but were told that his travel plans made this impossible. Saying goodbye and exiting Paisley Park, they felt a deep sense of relief. D'Angelo looked at Ahmir and said, "Why do I feel like I have to take a shower?"

Prince's dubious treatment of his guests was not atypical of his behavior during this time. Erstwhile colleagues with continuing ties to his organization received various reports of Prince's moodiness, irritability, and closed-mindedness. Ex-Revolution drummer Bobby Z. Rivkin, who visited Paisley in 2000, was forced to listen to Prince and Larry Graham engage in a homophobic rant, according to another former band member whom Rivkin told about the meeting. Prince explained to Rivkin that prior to any reunion of the Revolution (an idea discussed several times over the years), Wendy and Lisa would be required to publicly renounce their homosexuality. As Rivkin listened incredulously, Prince said he would insist that the women hold a press conference and "apologize" for their lifestyle.

From there, the discussion veered toward religion and race; Prince and Graham got on a bizarre jag about the word "Jew" meaning "black." Rivkin, who had been looking forward to this rare visit, exited Paisley Park in a state of disgust. Afterward, he told a former bandmate that he didn't care if he ever saw Prince again.

One knowledgeable source attributed Prince's erratic behavior in part to his alleged regular use of Percodan, a prescription painkiller that contains the addictive narcotic oxycodone. "He's been doing a lot of it, to the point where it's worrying people and has altered his personality," said this source. "His dark side is taking over more and more." According to another former associate, Prince was first exposed to this drug in the mid-1980s after he injured his leg during a tour. While having no first-hand evidence that Prince continued to use the drug after the injury healed, the source says that based on reports from others in the entourage, this may have indeed been the case. "It wouldn't surprise me if he acquired a taste for the high of prescription painkillers, and rumors did float within the immediate camp to that effect," the source said. "And the nature of Percodan—marathon days, dramatic mood swings—is in keeping with what were his unpredictable behavior and moods."

Whatever the causes—prescription medications, his continuing fury toward the record industry, his creative malaise, or some combination of these elements—Prince seemed profoundly ill-at-ease. Part of the problem, associates said, was that he couldn't accept the inevitable truth that his youth had slipped away along with his prominence in the pop world. "This is not a cat that's going to age gracefully," predicted one former band member.

The demise of *Rave Un2 The Joy Fantastic*, an album that Prince thought would reestablish him as a commercial force, contributed to angst. After his partnership with Arista Records deteriorated, the next step in Prince's career was wholly unclear. Should he seek another major label deal or resume the independent distribution model of *Newpower Soul?* In recent years, neither approach had worked particularly well.

Initially, Prince leaned toward making another stab at a comeback through a traditional major label release. Most of the material he wrote in 2000 was straightforward, unadventurous pop-funk in the vein of *Rave*. He assembled a new album called *High* that included "My Medallion," a funky-but-repetitive groove built around a single hook; "When Eye Lay My Hands On U," a slow, melodramatic number with dense harmonies and guitar work; and "High," a perky but insubstantial pop song.

In another effort to boost his public profile, in May 2000 he made an announcement that many had long expected: He was discarding the symbol name and returning to "Prince." The explanation for this shift was, not surprisingly, inconsistent with his rationale for having changed his name in the first place. At a New York press conference, he said that the ♀ name had been a means of escaping "undesirable relationships"—that is, his contract with Warner Bros. In 1993, though, he framed the name change not as a legal subterfuge but as a spiritual imperative. Which was true?

The announcement was widely publicized in news briefs, and millions of casual observers of pop culture learned that they no longer had to bother calling him "The Artist Formerly Known As Prince" or simply "the Artist." Still, it was hardly greeted as earth-shaking news. "I think the reason he did it was that he wasn't getting attention; people didn't care anymore," said a former Warner Bros. official. "And then he had this big press conference in New York, and, unfortunately for him, people still didn't care."

The lack of attention, coupled with *Rave*'s rapid exit from the charts, prompted Prince to radically shift his strategy. He decided that rather than trying to reclaim commercial success, he would cater to loyal fans and completely sidestep the machinery of major labels. He understood that his previous attempt at a fully independent distribution model, the problem-fraught *Crystal Ball*, had left many supporters and industry observers doubtful that such an endeavor was feasible. But he had a new plan. The Internet, Prince believed, would allow him to eliminate the logistical snafus that plagued *Crystal Ball* and provide music to fans in the simplest, most direct possible way: With a few clicks of a computer mouse (and the inputting of a credit card number) they could download songs. Even better, the lead time between his creation of music and its delivery to consumers would be reduced to practically zero.

Thus was born, in February 2001, the enterprise that Prince called the New Power Generation Music Club (or NPGMC). For an annual fee of $100, members were given access to new songs each month. The first postings on the website included numbers previously slated for *High* (an album that was never released), along with various pieces that hadn't been slated for any particular project, including "Silicon," an ominous, claustrophobic number that warns of the dangers of meat and dairy products.

The club received little attention from the general public and mainstream media. Obviously, only hardcore followers (and then only those with Internet access) could be expected to join and to spend the time necessary to download the songs that Prince posted on the site. This was especially true given the experience of *Crystal Ball*, which left even serious fans wary of doing business directly with Prince. Still, despite some dissatisfaction over the quality of the music, many who joined the club were pleased to have such quick access to new music. New songs were posted monthly, including rarities like a version of "Rebirth Of The Flesh" (a track from the aborted *Camille* album). Members received other perks as well, such as preferred seating at concerts.

Still, some music industry observers questioned the whole enterprise and wondered whether it wasn't just another sign of an imploding career. "If all he is doing is singing to the choir, he can't really expect to generate a younger or wider audience," Bob Merlis, former vice president of publicity at Warner Bros. Records, told the *Minneapolis Star Tribune* in a July 2002 article. "And if he doesn't keep the diehard fans happy, then he really might be in trouble."

But Prince paid no heed to warnings. While his organization released no public information about membership levels (an article in the *Minneapolis Star Tribune* quoted independent estimates of between 5,000 and 50,000, a range that seems reasonable in light of his recent sales figures), it is likely that the endeavor was quite lucrative for him, given the low overhead and high profit margins. In many respects, he seemed to be succeeding at using the Internet to establish a direct connection with consumers. Perhaps, as he had been arguing for years, major labels would soon become unnecessary.

As Prince began recording his next full album, *The Rainbow Children*, Jehovah's Witness doctrine emerged as a prominent element in his music. So too did tinges of anti-Semitism, along with dollops of patriarchal sexism. The song "Muse 2 The Pharaoh" demonstrates both tendencies, positing a gender hierarchy where men make the decisions and produce great art while women serve them. The song also makes an invidious comparison between the Holocaust and the enslavement of black Americans, arguing that extermination is preferable to a loss of freedom.

How did this former rebel, who during the 1980s had been pop's leading advocate of sexual freedom and cultural diversity, re-emerge in the 2000s as such a moralistic and narrow-minded figure? The answer in part is that Prince had never wholeheartedly embraced the role of revolutionary; this was simply one of many guises he adopted. The Prince of *Dirty Mind*, *Controversy*, and *1999* represented an important (and for a time dominant) part of his personality, but streaks of piousness and moral superiority were apparent even then. The trend in his work toward religious conservatism, which became more prevalent after his marriage to Mayte Garcia in 1996, was dramatically accelerated by Larry Graham's arrival on the scene in 1998. By the time *The Rainbow Children* was released in December 2001, Prince had committed, privately and publicly, to the Jehovah's Witness faith, and continued to extol Graham as his most trusted spiritual advisor. In an interview that appeared in *Gotham* magazine in 2001, he revealed that—at Graham's prompting—he was eliminating all profanity from his music.

At least on its surface, *The Rainbow Children* sounded radically different from anything Prince had released in recent years. Cool jazz textures and New Age inflections dominate tracks like "The Rainbow Children," "Mellow," and the "The Sensual Everafter." A pair of songs near the end of the disc, "Family Name" and "The Everlasting Now," represent a return to full-fledged funk and make much greater use of analog instruments (including sixties-esque keyboard and guitar sounds) than any of Prince's 1990s music. Structurally, songs like the title track, "Digital Garden," and "The Last December" are more adventurous than anything on *Rave* and incorporate unexpected twists. Composed and also performed almost entirely by Prince (with the exception of drumming by new recruit John Blackwell), the album showcases his musicianship and treats commercial considerations as secondary. In this sense, *The Rainbow*

Children demonstrates progress toward the creative liberation that many Prince fans expected after his departure from Warner Bros.

Still, there is less to the album than first meets the eye. Notwithstanding the intriguing song structures, the core musical ideas and melodies are often rather dull, and too much of the music sounds like pseudo-jazz. The circular riff that provides a foundation for "The Rainbow Children" is pedestrian, and "Muse 2 The Pharaoh," after a promising start, degenerates into a morose rap. "The Sensual Everafter" is one-step removed from lounge music, and the dance number "1+1+1 Is 3" recycles nearly all of its elements (right down to the bass line) from Prince's 1984 B-side "Erotic City." While the album's analog textures are appealing and much of the guitar and keyboard work quite skillful, *The Rainbow Children* illustrates the continued lack of inspiration in Prince's songwriting. Probably the most enjoyable track is "The Work, Part I," a fairly derivative James Brown homage that nonetheless is irresistibly funky and playful. Still, like every one of his albums since 1996's *Emancipation*, *The Rainbow Children* fails to deliver even a single song that belongs in the canon of Prince classics.

The album was received more warmly by critics than were recent efforts. Some found greater experimentation in *The Rainbow Children* than in perhaps any Prince record since *Sign O' The Times*. "Peerless production, experimental glee and brilliant musicianship add up to one of Prince's most challenging and fascinating works to date, whatever your take on the enigmatic valentines to God," wrote Edna Gunderson in *USA Today*. Still, probably an equal number found the record unsatisfying. "Bible-thumping sincerity doesn't suit Prince well; the album's light jazz-funk grooves sink under the weight of his sanctimony," opined *Entertainment Weekly*.

Prince's attempt to weave a spiritual narrative through the use of a distorted voice during segues was roundly criticized as annoying and distracting. Otherwise, the Jehovah's Witness content provoked little substantive discussion. The lyrics of "Muse 2 The Pharaoh" and "Family Name" (another song that hints at anti-Semitism through its dismissive invocation of Jewish or pseudo-Jewish names like "Rosenbloom," "Pearlman," and "Goldstruck") were too ambiguous to generate any real outcry, especially at a time in popular music when artists like the rapper Eminem were overt in their use of slurs against minority groups such as gays. Once pop's prime creator of controversy, Prince was now making music that was too obscure to offend.

Despite the fairly positive media response, *The Rainbow Children* sold poorly, topping out at about 130,000 copies. It failed to crack even the Billboard Top 100, the first time this had happened since his debut album. For the fourth time in recent years (the other instances being *Newpower Soul*, *Chaos And Disorder*, and *The Vault*), Prince released an album whose sales were at best comparable to a modestly successful alternative rock band. His profits again remained high due to his business model, but the sales figures indicated that Prince's hardcore fan base at best remained static.

december 31, 2001: hawaii

With much less fanfare than had marked his union with Mayte Garcia, Prince married for the second time, this time to Mani Testolini, in an intimate ceremony.

(Whether coincidentally or not, Prince chose as his wedding date the birthday of ex-girlfriend Anna Garcia.) Prince and his representatives provided no information, although media reports indicated that the proceedings adhered to Jehovah's Witness doctrine. A few months later, it was reported that Prince, through a company called Gamillah Holdings, Inc. (named after "Gamillah," a song released through the NPGMC), had purchased a home in Toronto, Testolini's hometown. The couple began spending more time in the city, where they were spotted at professional basketball games and elsewhere.

While Prince remained guarded about his new relationship (and refused to publicly confirm that he had married), there were indications from within his circle that he was very serious about Testolini. She was a visible presence at Paisley Park events, and fans found her accessible, friendly, and engaging. She also seemed to have a positive effect on Prince, as some of the sourness that characterized his mood in the aftermath of *Rave* lifted. And with the release of *The Rainbow Children*, he seemed to come to terms with being an independent artist with a cult following, as opposed to a major pop star. According to one former associate, he even began to shed some of the trappings of his former fame, firing his bodyguards as he commenced a tour in support of *The Rainbow Children*. "I don't need to pay a bunch of guys to follow me around anymore," Prince reportedly told tour coordinator Billy Sparks. "It looks kind of silly and it's expensive. If someone wants to kill me badly enough, those guys weren't gonna stop it anyhow."

Other aspects of the so-called One Night Alone tour, which visited American and Canadian cities in spring 2002, were encouraging as well. For years, former associates such as Alan and Eric Leeds had urged Prince to create a live show that emphasized musicianship over imagery and new material instead over timeworn hits. After years of resisting this advice, he now followed it almost to the letter, assembling a crack lineup of versatile players and giving them plenty of freedom to show off their chops. The set list consisted primarily of loose, funky versions of the *Rainbow Children* material along with some intriguing unreleased songs. Maceo Parker joined on saxophone for several dates as did Eric Leeds, with whom Prince's relations had soured in 1997 after a dispute over pay. (Eric, declining to reveal how the matter was resolved, said simply that his renewed association with Prince was profitable, both creatively and financially.) Alan Leeds, even before his brother was recruited, came away from the shows raving and wrote a review in the *Minneapolis Star Tribune* declaring that Prince's career was revived.

Backstage at the shows, Eric Leeds found a Prince who was more relaxed, friendly, and unconstrained than the tense and beleaguered figure of 1996–97. "Prince definitely seems comfortable with where he is in today's marketplace, and I sense that he's grateful to have such a loyal and musically knowledgeable fan base," Eric observed.

Prince found ways to reward his most zealous followers. During the tour, members of his New Power Generation Music Club were not only given preferred seating, but were allowed to attend sound checks before the shows, after which Prince often chatted affably with them. At one of these events, comedian Chris Rock was forced to sit in the balcony while members of the club gathered next to the stage. Prince cracked over the microphone that Rock would have gotten a better seat if he had joined the NPGMC.

And in June, Prince held his second annual "Celebration," a festival-like week of concerts and activities at Paisley Park. (The event was subtitled "Xenophobia"—also the reputed title of a new album in the works—indicating something about Prince's insularity.) Fans throughout the world were given a chance to tour the studio complex and see Prince perform multiple times, including a memorable solo acoustic show. More remarkably, he attended so-called discussion groups during which spiritual issues were debated by fans and moderators. While his views on religion seemed transparently dogmatic to some fans, most were pleased by his accessibility and friendliness. After years of actions that had alienated many loyal followers—including the botched *Crystal Ball* effort and his suits against *Uptown* and other fan-run organizations—Prince was seemingly trying to make amends.

Still, whether Prince's newfound security with his fans, spiritual life, commercial status, and musical trajectory will translate into true artistic growth remains to be seen. The relatively small group of people who belong to his Internet club are likely to continue to purchase virtually anything that he puts out, guaranteeing him at least a limited audience for his work. But while Prince has apparently (and laudably) given up aspirations to *Purple Rain*–like fame, one also hopes that he can reach beyond the limited cult that constitutes his current fandom. There are countless former supporters, music critics, and fellow musicians who believe Prince is capable of returning to the form that marked his finest hours. "What he had—I can't believe it's gone away, I just can't," said former Warner Bros. vice president Marylou Badeaux. "It's got to still be in there." But for now, most of the millions of serious, passionate, and intelligent followers who once viewed him as so many things—the heir to Sly Stone in his ability to blend funk and rock; a figure akin to David Bowie in his ability to reinvent himself and connect with underground subcultures; and a songwriter with the rare ability of a John Lennon to write pop music that matters—remain unconvinced that "Prince is back." At the same time, many of these former fans also remain hopeful that his dormant creativity will someday burst back to the surface.

It is unlikely, however, that Prince's current lifestyle will provide the stimulation he needs to rediscover the full measure of his creativity. Despite his new openness to informal interactions with fans, he in many respects remains a voluntary prisoner at Paisley Park, rarely exposing himself to new ways of seeing the world. His devotion to the Jehovah's Witness faith—which in some ways has liberated him from commercial pressures—does not necessarily indicate greater open-mindedness. "It certainly is a very important part of his life," observed Eric Leeds. "Whether it becomes a platform for investigating other ideas and cultures, or whether it reinforces his current 'comfort zone,' only time will tell."

There remains a strong streak of anger in Prince's music, much of it perhaps misdirected. A new song called "Avalanche," released over the Internet, declares that Abraham Lincoln was a racist and carries forth the theme of racial struggle raised during his battle with Warner Bros. While Prince's condemnations of society's white-dominated power structure are hardly indefensible, they do not seem part of a coherent world view. For the moment, his political and social views have an ad hoc flavor and remain a grab bag of moralistic preaching and generalized hostility.

It is likely Prince's rage stems from unresolved personal issues. His strategy of denial regarding emotional traumas—such as the death of his child and dissolution of his first marriage—has undoubtedly impacted his music and contributed to the void at the core of his work. As one former band member said, the vast majority of Prince's music over the past decade constitutes "a surface experience"—it very rarely finds the artist probing his own psyche. "I don't think Prince is entirely comfortable with himself," the musician continued. "I had hoped that after I was gone, he'd become more sincere, but that hasn't happened. It's time for him to go deeper."

Unless he can find a way to do this, future musical historians are likely to conclude both that Prince was among the most influential musicians of his time and that his impact was less significant than it could have been. Although Prince has created a vast catalog of music most likely larger than that of any other artist in the history of popular music, it is a canon more notable for its quantity than its quality.

His long-term impact remains obvious. In 2002, *The Boston Globe* noted that he has become one of the most covered artists of his time, with contemporary artists like Alicia Keys (who that year released a version of "How Come U Don't Call Me Anymore?" as a single) echoing aspects of his sound. D'Angelo—no matter how disappointing was his visit to Paisley Park—still turns to Prince's earlier music for inspiration. And even as interesting artists like D'Angelo, Macy Gray, and India.Arie show Prince's influence, the stripped-down funk sound that he perfected in the 1980s remains a significant strain of mainstream pop music, and can be heard in the danceable hit singles of Jennifer Lopez, Britney Spears, and numerous other chart toppers.

Yet, it has been many years—arguably since 1996's *Emancipation*—since Prince released a significant album, or even a truly brilliant song. Some of his experiments, such as the 1997 acoustic record *The Truth*, offer interesting moments, but in the end have made little genuine impact. Stylistically, Prince has become something of a dilettante over the last ten years—neither acoustic excursions like *The Truth*, nor forays into jazz (parts of *The Rainbow Children* and *The Vault . . . Old Friends 4 Sale*), nor the efforts at guitar rock (*Chaos And Disorder* and the Internet release "Habibi") demonstrate real mastery of these various genres. What does Prince stand for musically, beyond shallow eclecticism? Nothing he has released recently answers this question.

For the moment, despite some hopeful signs, Prince remains a true enigma—a brilliantly talented musician and composer who works as furiously as ever but remains unable to recapture the magic that characterized his best music. If Prince has indeed become a happier person over the past year or so—and there are signs that this is the case—perhaps it is simply because he has achieved the level of power required for him to be content. He answers to no one, except perhaps to the God he believes in so fervently. His relationship with his fans is direct and unmediated. Corporate chairmen like Mo Ostin and Clive Davis no longer have any license to interfere. His closest musical associate, Larry Graham, is someone who will never challenge Prince artistically. His universe is smaller than it has been in years, and it continues to shrink. But within that universe, his authority is absolute; Prince is in control.

DISCOGraPHY

A n entire book could be written documenting Prince's recorded output between 1977 and 2002. The following list attempts to be comprehensive without being duplicative. The primary intent is to document (1) each of Prince's released studio recordings (including side projects which he controlled or substantially participated in), and (2) each unreleased Prince studio song known to exist. Excluded from the list are remixes and alternate versions; for example, the songs "Gangster Glam" and "Violet The Organ Grinder" are not included because they are derivations of "Gett Off." The specific criteria for inclusion of unreleased material on the list are discussed below under "Unreleased Songs." This discography also includes songs written by Prince for other artists.

PRINCE ALBUM RELEASES
The entries below include the following information for all Prince albums released as of the date of publication of this book: title, release year, label and catalog number, the date and location of the recording, instruments played by Prince, other musicians/songwriters involved in each project, and the titles of the tracks on each album. The information regarding other musicians and songwriters is derived from the credits of the albums and also the reporting for this book. Any lead vocalists other than Prince are listed after the title of the track. In various cases, the credits on Prince's albums are incomplete or inaccurate, resulting in the need for additional reporting.

For You (1978)
Warner Bros. 3150

Recorded: Oct. 1977 to Feb. 1978 at the Record Plant, Sausalito, CA, and Sound Labs, L.A.
Prince: Producer, vocals, guitars, bass, drums, percussion, synths, and piano.
Other musicians/songwriters: Tommy Vicari, executive producer. David Rivkin, engineer.

Patrice Rushen, additional synths and synth programming on "Baby" and other songs. Charles Veal, strings on "Baby." Chris Moon, cowriter on "Soft And Wet" and "My Love Is Forever."
Tracks: For You / In Love / Soft And Wet / Crazy You / Just As Long As We're Together / Baby / My Love Is Forever / So Blue / I'm Yours

Prince (1979)
Warner Bros. 3366

Recorded: Apr. to June 1979 at Alpha Studio, L.A., and Hollywood Sound Recorders, L.A.
Prince: Producer, vocals, guitars, bass, drums, percussion, synths, and piano.
Other musicians/songwriters: André Cymone, backing vocals on "Why You Wanna Treat Me So Bad?"
Tracks: I Wanna Be Your Lover / Why You Wanna Treat Me So Bad? / Sexy Dancer / When We're Dancing Close And Slow / With You / Bambi / Still Waiting / I Feel For You / It's Gonna Be Lonely

Dirty Mind (1980)
Warner Bros. 3478

Recorded: May to June 1980 at Prince's home on Lake Minnetonka, Minneapolis; mixed in June at Hollywood Sound Recorders, L.A.
Prince: Producer, vocals, guitars, bass, drums, percussion, and synths. (There is no piano on *Dirty Mind* because the studio was too small to accommodate one.)
Other musicians/songwriters: Matt Fink, cowriter and synths on "Dirty Mind" and synth solo on "Head." Morris Day, cowriter on "Partyup." André Cymone, songwriting input on "Uptown."
Tracks: Dirty Mind / When You Were Mine / Do It All Night / Gotta Broken Heart Again / Uptown / Head / Sister / Partyup

Controversy (1981)
Warner Bros. 3601

Recorded: Summer 1981 at Prince's new home studio in the Lake Riley region of Minneapolis, Hollywood Sound Recorders, L.A., and Sunset Sound, L.A.
Prince: Producer, vocals, guitars, bass, drums, percussion, synths, and piano.
Other musicians/songwriters: André Cymone, songwriting contributions on "Do Me, Baby." Lisa Coleman, backing vocals on "Controversy" and "Ronnie, Talk To Russia." "Jack U Off" is a live band recording featuring Coleman (keyboards), Bobby Z. Rivkin (drums), and Matt Fink (keyboards).
Tracks: Controversy / Sexuality / Do Me, Baby / Private Joy / Ronnie, Talk To Russia / Let's Work / Annie Christian / Jack U Off

1999 (1982)
Warner Bros. 23720

Recorded: 1982 at Prince's Lake Riley home studio, Minneapolis, and Sunset Sound, L.A.
Prince: Producer, vocals, guitars, bass, drums, percussion, synths, and piano.
Other musicians/songwriters: Co-lead vocals on "1999" by Jill Jones, Lisa Coleman, and Dez Dickerson. Dickerson, guitar solo on "Little Red Corvette." Backing vocals/handclaps on various songs by Coleman, Jones, Wendy Melvoin, Vanity, Mark Brown, Peggy McCreary, Jamie Shoop, and Carol McGovney.
Tracks: 1999 / Little Red Corvette / Delirious / Let's Pretend We're Married / D.M.S.R. /

Automatic / Something In The Water (Does Not Compute) / Free / Lady Cab Driver / All The Critics Love U In New York / International Lover

Purple Rain (1984)
Warner Bros. 25110

Recorded: Aug. 1983 to Mar. 1984 at Prince's Lake Riley home studio, Minneapolis, First Avenue nightclub, Minneapolis, a rehearsal warehouse in St. Louis Park, MN, and Sunset Sound, L.A.
Prince: Producer, vocals, guitars, bass, drums, percussion, synths, and piano.
Other musicians/songwriters: The Revolution—Wendy Melvoin (guitar), Lisa Coleman (keyboards), Matt Fink (keyboards), Mark Brown (bass), and Bobby Z. Rivkin (drums)—appears on "I Would Die 4 U," "Baby, I'm A Star," "Purple Rain," and "Let's Go Crazy." Melvoin and Coleman, backing vocals on "Computer Blue." Apollonia, backing vocals on "Take Me With U." Strings on "Take Me With U," "Baby I'm A Star," and "Purple Rain" arranged by Coleman and Prince, conducted by Coleman and Melvoin, and performed by Novi Novog (violin and viola), David Coleman (cello), and Suzi Katayama (cello). Songwriting input by Fink, Coleman, Melvoin, and John L. Nelson on "Computer Blue."
Tracks: Let's Go Crazy / Take Me With U / The Beautiful Ones / Computer Blue / Darling Nikki / When Doves Cry / I Would Die 4 U / Baby I'm A Star / Purple Rain

Around The World In A Day (1985)
Warner Bros. 25286

Recorded: Jan. to Dec. 1984 at a rehearsal warehouse on Flying Cloud Drive, Minneapolis, Sunset Sound, L.A., and Capitol Studios, L.A., and mobile recording studios.
Prince: Producer, vocals, guitars, bass, drums, percussion, synths, and piano.
Other musicians/songwriters: The Revolution (see *Purple Rain*) appears on "America" and "The Ladder," and also receives songwriting credit on "America." David Coleman, cowriter of and plays oud, darbouka, and finger cymbals on "Around The World In A Day." John L. Nelson, songwriting input on "Around The World In A Day" and "The Ladder." Sheila E., drums on "Pop Life." Taja Sevelle and Susannah Melvoin, backing vocals on "The Ladder." Eddie Minnifield, saxophone on "The Ladder" and "Temptation." Brad Marsh, tambourine on "America." Strings on "Paisley Park," "Raspberry Beret," and "Pop Life" composed and conducted by Wendy Melvoin and Lisa Coleman and performed by Novi Novog (violin and viola), David Coleman (cello), and Suzi Katayama (cello).
Tracks: Around The World In A Day / Paisley Park / Condition Of The Heart / Raspberry Beret / Tambourine / America / Pop Life / The Ladder / Temptation

Parade: Music From Under The Cherry Moon (1986)
Warner Bros. 25395

Recorded: Between Apr. and Dec. 1985 at a rehearsal warehouse on Washington Avenue, Minneapolis, and Sunset Sound, L.A.
Prince: Producer, vocals, guitars, bass, drums, percussion, synths, and piano.
Other musicians/songwriters: Wendy Melvoin, lead vocal on "I Wonder U" and acoustic guitar on "Sometimes It Snows In April." Lisa Coleman, piano on "Sometimes It Snows." Melvoin and Coleman, songwriting input on "Sometimes It Snows" and "Mountains." Susannah Melvoin, backing vocals on various tracks. Sheila E., drums on "Life Can Be So Nice." Jonathan Melvoin, drums on "Do U Lie?" Marie France, French lines on "Girls & Boys." Clare Fischer, strings and orchestrations on most tracks. John L. Nelson, songwriting input on "Cherry Moon" and "Venus De Milo." Mazarati, backing vocals on "Kiss." David Z. Rivkin,

songwriting contributions, coproduction, and arrangement credit on "Kiss." "Mountains" features the expanded Revolution (see *Purple Rain*), which includes Miko Weaver (keyboards), Eric Leeds (saxophone), and Matt Blistan (trumpet).

Tracks: Christopher Tracy's Parade / New Position / I Wonder U / Under The Cherry Moon / Girls & Boys / Life Can Be So Nice / Venus De Milo / Mountains / Do U Lie? / Kiss / Anotherloverholenyohead / Sometimes It Snows In April

Sign O' The Times (1987)
Warner Bros. 25577

Recorded: Primarily between Mar. and Dec. 1986 at Sunset Sound, L.A., and Prince's new home studio in Chanhassen, Minneapolis; "It's Gonna Be A Beautiful Night" recorded live in concert on August 25, 1986 in Paris.

Prince: Producer, vocals, guitars, bass, drums, percussion, synths, and piano.

Other musicians/songwriters: "It's Gonna Be A Beautiful Night" features the expanded Revolution (see *Parade*) and Jerome Benton, Greg Brooks, and Wally Safford on backing vocals. Sheila E., raps on "It's Gonna Be A Beautiful Night" and percussion on "U Got The Look." Susannah Melvoin, cowriter on "Starfish And Coffee," backing vocals on "Beautiful Night," "Starfish And Coffee," and "Play In The Sunshine." Jill Jones, backing vocals on "Beautiful Night." Wendy Melvoin, guitar/backing vocals on "Slow Love," tambourine and congas on "Strange Relationship." Lisa Coleman, backing vocals on "Slow Love" and sitar and wooden flute on "Strange Relationship." Eric Leeds, saxophone on "Housequake," "Slow Love," "Hot Thing," and "Adore." Matt Blistan, trumpet on "Slow Love" and "Adore." Clare Fischer, strings on "Slow Love." Backing vocals on "Housequake" by Gilbert Davison, Todd Hermann, Coke Johnson, Brad Marsh, "The Penguin," and Mike Soltys. Carole Davis, cowriter on "Slow Love." Eric Leeds and Matt Fink, cowriters on "Beautiful Night."

Tracks: Sign O' The Times / Play In The Sunshine / Housequake / The Ballad Of Dorothy Parker / It / Starfish And Coffee / Slow Love / Hot Thing / Forever In My Life / U Got The Look (duet with Sheena Easton) / If I Was Your Girlfriend / Strange Relationship / I Could Never Take The Place Of Your Man / The Cross / It's Gonna Be A Beautiful Night / Adore

Lovesexy (1988)
Warner Bros. 25720

Recorded: Dec. 1987 to Jan. 1988 at Paisley Park Studios, Chanhassen, Minneapolis.

Prince: Producer, vocals, guitars, bass, drums, percussion, synths, and piano.

Other musicians/songwriters: "Eye No" is a full-band recording featuring Miko Weaver (guitar), Levi Seacer, Jr. (bass), Matt Fink (keyboards), Boni Boyer (keyboards), Eric Leeds (saxophone), Matt Blistan (trumpet), and Sheila E. (drums). Leeds and Blistan also appear on "Alphabet Street," "Anna Stesia," "Dance On," "Lovesexy," and "Positivity." Sheila E. and Boyer, backing vocals on various tracks. Ingrid Chavez, spoken intro to "Eye No."

Tracks: Eye No / Alphabet Street / Glam Slam / Anna Stesia / Dance On / Lovesexy / When 2 R In Love / I Wish U Heaven / Positivity

Batman: Motion Picture Soundtrack (1989)
Warner Bros. 25936

Recorded: Feb. to Mar. 1989 at Paisley Park Studios.

Prince: Producer, vocals, guitars, bass, drums, percussion, synths, and piano.

Other musicians/songwriters: Brief sampled snippets from various sources appear. Clare Fischer's strings that appear in "The Future" are from the previously unreleased track "Crystal Ball." The

Sounds of Blackness Choir is sampled in the same song. Sampled portions of the film are interspersed into various songs, most noticeably in "Batdance."

Tracks: The Future / Electric Chair / Arms Of Orion (duet with Sheena Easton) / Partyman / Vicki Waiting / Trust / Lemon Crush / Scandalous / Batdance

Graffiti Bridge (1990)
Warner Bros. 27493

Recorded: Dec. 1983 to Mar. 1990 at Paisley Park Studios, Sunset Sound, L.A., Washington Avenue Rehearsal Warehouse, Minneapolis, and other studios.

Prince: Producer, vocals, guitars, bass, drums, percussion, synths, and piano.

Other musicians/songwriters: Duets indicated next to song titles below. "Release It" and "Love Machine" cowritten by Prince, Levi Seacer, Jr., and Morris Day. George Clinton, cowriter on "We Can Funk." Day, cowriter on "Shake" and drums on "New Power Generation." Junior Vasquez, mixing and post-production on "Round And Round." Candy Dulfer, saxophone on "The Latest Fashion," "Love Machine," and "Release It." Backing vocals on various tracks by Rosie Gaines and the Steeles. T.C. Ellis, raps on "New Power Generation (Pt II.)." "Graffiti Bridge" features Seacer (bass), Boni Boyer (organ), Sheila E. (drums), and Clare Fischer (orchestra).

Tracks: Can't Stop This Feeling I Got / New Power Generation / Release It (vocals by Morris Day) / The Question Of U / Elephants & Flowers / Round And Round (vocals by Tevin Campbell) / We Can Funk (duet with George Clinton) / Joy In Repetition / Love Machine (duet between Elisa Fiorillo and Morris Day) / Tick, Tick, Bang / Shake! (vocals by Morris Day) / Thieves In The Temple / The Latest Fashion (duet with Morris Day) / Melody Cool (vocals by Mavis Staples) / Still Would Stand All Time / Graffiti Bridge / New Power Generation (Pt. II)

Diamonds And Pearls (1991)
Warner Bros. 25379

Recorded: Dec. 1989 to May 1991 at Paisley Park Studios, Olympic Studio, London, Warner Pioneer Studios, Tokyo, and Larrabee Studio, L.A.

Prince: Producer, vocals, guitars, bass, drums, percussion, synths, and piano.

Other musicians/songwriters: Various members of the New Power Generation—Levi Seacer, Jr. (guitar), Sonny Thompson (bass), Tommy Barbarella (keyboards), Rosie Gaines (keyboards), Michael Bland (drums), Tony Mosley (raps and background vocals), Kirk Johnson (percussion and backing vocals), and Damon Dickson (percussion and backing vocals)—appear on all tracks, save "Thunder." Eric Leeds, flute on "Gett Off." Clare Fischer, strings on "Push." "Willing And Able" cowritten by Seacer and Mosley. "Jughead" cowritten by Mosley and Johnson. "Live 4 Love" cowritten by Mosley. "Push" cowritten by Rosie Gaines.

Tracks: Thunder / Daddy Pop / Diamonds And Pearls / Cream / Strollin' / Willing And Able / Gett Off / Walk Don't Walk / Jughead / Money Don't Matter 2 Night / Push / Insatiable / Live 4 Love

⚤ (1992)
Warner Bros. 45037

Recorded: Primarily between May 1991 and July 1992 at Paisley Park Studios.

Prince: Producer, vocals, guitars, bass, drums, percussion, synths, and piano.

Other musicians/songwriters: Members of the New Power Generation—Levi Seacer, Jr. (guitar), Michael Bland (drums), Tony Mosley (raps), Tommy Barbarella (keyboards), and Sonny

Thompson (bass)—contribute to most songs on the album. DJ Graves, scratching. Mosley, cowriter on "My Name Is Prince," "The Flow," and "Sexy M.F." Seacer, cowriter on "Sexy M.F." The NPG Hornz—Michael B. Nelson, Kathy Jensen, Dave Jensen, Brian Gallagher, and Steve Strand—appear on various tracks. Eric Leeds, saxophone on "Blue Light." Michael Koppelman, bass on "Blue Light." Carmen Electra, raps on "The Continental." The Steeles, backing vocals on "3 Chains O' Gold."

Tracks: My Name Is Prince / Sexy M.F. / Love 2 The 9's / The Morning Papers / The Max / Blue Light / Eye Wanna Melt With U / Sweet Baby / The Continental / Damn U / Arrogance / The Flow / 7 / And God Created Woman / 3 Chains O' Gold / The Sacrifice Of Victor

The Hits/The B-Sides (1993)
Warner Bros. 45440

This compilation contains well-known Prince songs (in some cases edited versions), along with single B-sides (often edited), and four previously unreleased songs: "Pink Cashmere," "Pope," "Power Fantastic," and "Peach." The version of "4 The Tears In Your Eyes" differs from the version on the *We Are The World* album, being an acoustic take on the song.

Tracks: When Doves Cry / Pop Life / Soft And Wet / I Feel For You / Why You Wanna Treat Me So Bad? / When You Were Mine / Uptown / Let's Go Crazy / 1999 / I Could Never Take The Place Of Your Man / Nothing Compares 2 U / Adore / Pink Cashmere / Alphabet Street / Sign O' The Times / Thieves In The Temple / Diamonds And Pearls / 7 / Controversy / Dirty Mind / I Wanna Be Your Lover / Head / Do Me, Baby / Delirious / Little Red Corvette / I Would Die 4 U / Raspberry Beret / If I Was Your Girlfriend / Kiss / Peach / U Got The Look / Sexy M.F. / Gett Off / Cream / Pope / Purple Rain / Hello / 200 Balloons / Escape / Outta Stop (Messin' About) / Horny Toad / Feel U Up / Girl / I Love U In Me / Erotic City / Shockadelica / Irresistible Bitch / Scarlet Pussy / La La La, He He Hee / She's Always In My Hair / 17 Days / How Come U Don't Call Me Anymore? / Another Lonely Christmas / God / 4 The Tears In Your Eyes / Power Fantastic

Come (1994)
Warner Bros. 45700

Recorded: Primarily between Jan. and May 1993 at Paisley Park Studios.
Prince: Producer, vocals, guitars, bass, drums, percussion, synths, and piano.
Other musicians/songwriters: New Power Generation members Sonny Thompson (bass), Tommy Barbarella (keyboards), Morris Hayes (keyboards), and Michael Bland (drums) appear on "Dark," "Papa," and "Space." David Henry Hwang, lyric writer on "Solo." Backing vocals on various songs provided by Mayte, Kathleen Bradford, and Jearlyn Steele Battle. Eric Leeds, flute on "Letitgo." Ricky Peterson, keyboards on "Letitgo." The NPG Hornz (see ♀) appear on "Letitgo," "Come," "Race," and "Dark." Vanity, sampled moans on "Orgasm."
Tracks: Come / Space / Pheromone / Loose! / Papa / Race / Dark / Solo / Letitgo / Orgasm

The Beautiful Experience (1994)
NPG Records/Bellmark

This EP contains seven different versions of "The Most Beautiful Girl In The World."

The Black Album (1994)
Warner Bros. 45793

This much-bootlegged LP was finally given an official release by Warner Bros. in November 1994.

The tracks and mixes are the same as those on the release that was cancelled in late 1987.

Recorded: Between Sept. 1986 and Mar. 1987 at Sunset Sound, L.A., Washington Avenue Rehearsal Warehouse, Minneapolis, Prince's home studios, and other facilities; "When 2R In Love," recorded late 1987 at Paisley Park Studios.

Prince: Producer, vocals, guitars, bass, drums, percussion, synths, and piano.

Other musicians/songwriters: Sheila E., drums on "2 Nigs United 4 West Compton," sampled vocals on "Dead On It" (from "Holly Rock" on the soundtrack of the film *Crush Groove*), and backing vocals on "Cindy C." Boni Boyer, backing vocals on "Cindy C." Eric Leeds, saxophone, and Matt Blistan, trumpet, on "Le Grind," "Cindy C.," and "Rockhard In A Funky Place." Cat Glover, raps on "Cindy C." Susannah Melvoin, backing vocals on "Rockhard."

Tracks: Le Grind / Cindy C / Dead On It / When 2 R In Love / Bob George / Superfunkycalifragisexy / 2 Nigs United 4 West Compton / Rockhard In A Funky Place

The Gold Experience (1995)
Warner Bros. 45999

Recorded: Primarily between Sept. 1993 and Mar. 1994 at Paisley Park Studios.

Prince: Producer, vocals, guitars, bass, drums, percussion, synths, and piano.

Other musicians/songwriters: Most of the tracks feature instrumental input by the New Power Generation (see lineup on *Come*), including Mayte, backing vocals and spoken word portions. Ricky Peterson, keyboards, arrangement, and post-production input on "We March," "The Most Beautiful Girl In The World," "319," "I Hate U," and "Gold." Nona Gaye, cowriter on "We March." Gaye and Sonny Thompson share the lead vocal on "We March." Kirk Johnson, drum programming on "We March." James Behringer, additional guitar on "Beautiful Girl." The NPG Hornz (see ♀) appear on "319" and "Now." Michael B. Nelson, co-credit for horn arrangement on "Billy Jack Bitch." The NPG Operator (who delivers spoken segues between songs) is Rain Ivana.

Tracks: P Control / Endorphinmachine / Shhh / We March / The Most Beautiful Girl In The World / Dolphin / Now / 319 / Shy / Billy Jack Bitch / I Hate U / Gold

Chaos And Disorder (1996)
Warner Bros. 46317

Recorded: Between May 1993 and April 1996 at Paisley Park Studios.

Prince: Producer, vocals, guitars, bass, drums, percussion, synths, and piano.

Other musicians/songwriters: Most tracks feature instrumental input from the New Power Generation (see lineup on *Come*). Rosie Gaines, co-lead vocal on "I Rock, Therefore I Am" and backing vocals on various tracks. Steppa Ranks and Scrap D., raps on "I Rock, Therefore I Am." The NPG Hornz (see *Symbol*) appear on "Right The Wrong," "I Rock," "Into The Light," and "I Will."

Tracks: Chaos And Disorder / I Like It There / Dinner With Delores / The Same December / Right The Wrong / Zannalee / I Rock, Therefore I Am / Into The Light / I Will / Dig U Better Dead / Had U

Emancipation (1996)
EMI 54982

Recorded: Primarily in 1995 and 1996 at Paisley Park Studios.

Prince: Producer, vocals, guitars, bass, drums, percussion, synths, and piano.

Other musicians/songwriters: Kirk Johnson, associate producer; handled much of the drum programming, contributed to arrangements, and played additional synths on some numbers.

Rhonda Smith, bass on "Get Yo Groove On," "We Gets Up," "Eye Can't Make U Love Me," "Sex In The Summer," and "Dreamin' About U." Kat Dyson, guitar on "Sex In The Summer," "Emale," "Dreamin' About U," and "The Love We Make." Former New Power Generation members Tommy Barbarella (keyboards), Sonny Thompson (bass), and Michael Bland (drums) play on "Betcha by Golly Wow!" and "Saviour." Ricky Peterson, additional keyboards on "Sex In The Summer" and "Saviour." Mike Scott, guitar on "La, La, La, Means Eye Love U." Todd Burrell, additional keyboards on "Eye Can't Make U Love Me." Savion Glover, tap dancing on "Joint 2 Joint." Poet 99, sampled vocal on "Joint 2 Joint," "Right Back Here In My Arms," and "Face Down." Cesar Sogbe and Joe Galdo, additional programming on "The Human Body" and "Sleep Around." Scrap D., raps on "Mr. Happy" and "Da, Da, Da." Rosie Gaines, vocals on "Jam Of The Year." Kate Bush, backing vocals on "My Computer." The NPG Hornz (see *Symbol*) appear on "Sleep Around." Eric Leeds and Brian Lynch, horns on "We Gets Up." Backing vocals on various numbers also provided by Rhonda Smith, Kat Dyson, Montalbo Stewart, Kathleen Bradford, Rhonda Johnson, Chanté Moore, Mayte, Smooth G., Scrap D., and Michael Mac. Sandra St. Victor, lyrics for "Soul Sanctuary." Brenda Lee Eager and Hilliard Wilson, cowriters on "Somebody's Somebody." Michael B. Nelson, co-horn arranger on "Damned If Eye Do." Eric Leeds, songwriting input on "Dreamin' About U."

Cover songs: Bonnie Raitt's "I Can't Make You Love Me" (James Shamblin and Mike Read), The Stylistics' "Betcha By Golly Wow!" (Thom Bell and Linda Creed), The Delfonics' "La, La, La, Means I Love You" (Thom Bell and Bill Hart), Joan Osborne's "One Of Us" (Eric Bazilian).

Tracks: Jam Of The Year / Right Back Here In My Arms / Somebody's Somebody / Get Yo Groove On / Courtin' Time / Betcha By Golly Wow! / We Gets Up / White Mansion / Damned If Eye Do / Eye Can't Make U Love Me / Mr. Happy / In This Bed Eye Scream / Sex In The Summer / One Kiss At A Time / Soul Sanctuary / Emale / Curious Child / Dreamin' About U / Joint 2 Joint / The Holy River / Let's Have A Baby / Saviour / The Plan / Friend, Lover, Sister, Mother/Wife / Slave / New World / The Human Body / Face Down / La, La, La, Means Eye Love U / Style / Sleep Around / Da, Da, Da / My Computer / One Of Us / The Love We Make / Emancipation

Kamasutra (1997)

This instrumental, neo-classical album is attributed to the NPG Orchestra. It was sold through Prince's 1-800-NEW-FUNK line and also included as a bonus disc in the *Crystal Ball* package for those who ordered through 1-800-NEW-FUNK. It was recorded at Paisley Park Studios.

Tracks: The Plan / Kamasutra / At Last ... "The Lost Is Found" / The Ever Changing Light / Cutz / Serotonin / Promise/Broken / Barcelona / Kamasutra/Overture #8 / Coincidence Or Fate? / Kamasutra/Eternal Embrace

Crystal Ball (1998)

This release, which was first made available through 1-800-NEW-FUNK and later sold in stores, contains two separate albums: the three-disc set *Crystal Ball* and a single disc called *The Truth*, an album of primarily acoustic material.

CRYSTAL BALL

Recorded: Between Mar. 1983 and mid-1996 at various facilities.

Prince: Producer, vocals, guitars, bass, drums, percussion, synths, and piano.

Other musicians/songwriters: Clare Fischer, strings on "Crystal Ball" and "Goodbye." Morris Day, drums on "Cloreen Baconskin." Eric Leeds, saxophone on "Last Heart," "Crucial,"

"Sexual Suicide," and "Make Your Mama Happy." Kirk Johnson, programming and remixes on various tracks. Mike Scott, guitar on "18 & Over." Nona Gaye, vocals on "Lovesign." Brenda Lee Eager and Hilliard Johnson, cowriters on "Hide The Bone." New Power Generation (NPG) members Tommy Barbarella (keyboards), Sonny Thompson (bass), and Michael Bland (drums) appear on "Hide The Bone," "The Ride," "Interactive," "Calhoun Square" and "Strays Of The World" (the latter four songs also with Morris Hayes, keyboards). "Days Of Wild" recorded live in concert. The NPG Hornz (see *Symbol*) appear on "2morrow." NPG members Thompson and Bland and NPG Hornz member Kathy Jensen appear on "Ripopgodazippa." Susannah Melvoin, backing vocals on "Crystal Ball," "Dream Factory," and "Last Heart." Wendy Melvoin and Lisa Coleman, backing vocals on "Dream Factory." Boni Boyer, sampled vocal on "Acknowledge Me." Poet 99, sampled vocal on "Days Of Wild."

Tracks: Crystal Ball / Dream Factory / Acknowledge Me / Ripopgodazippa / Lovesign (Shock G's Silky Remix) / Hide The Bone / 2morrow / So Dark / Movie Star / Tell Me How U Wanna B Done / Interactive / Da Bang / Calhoun Square / What's My Name / Crucial / An Honest Man / Sexual Suicide / Cloreen Baconskin / Good Love / Strays Of The World / Days Of Wild / Last Heart / Poom Poom / She Gave Her Angels / 18 & Over / The Ride / Get Loose / P Control (remix) / Make Your Mama Happy / Goodbye

THE TRUTH

Recorded: Fall 1996 at Paisley Park Studios.
Prince: Producer, vocals, guitars, bass, drums, synths, and piano.
Other musicians/songwriters: Rhonda Smith, bass on "3rd Eye," "Animal Kingdom," and "One Of Your Tears," percussion on "Fascination," and cowriter on "Animal Kingdom" and "Man In A Uniform." Kat Dyson and Kirk Johnson, backing vocals on "Fascination." Mike Scott, guitar solo on "Fascination." Kirk Johnson, drum programming on "Circle Of Amour" and "One Of Your Tears."
Tracks: The Truth / Don't Play Me / Circle Of Amour / 3rd Eye / Dionne / Man In A Uniform / Animal Kingdom / The Other Side Of The Pillow / Fascination / One Of Your Tears / Comeback / Welcome 2 The Dawn

Newpower Soul (1998)
NPG Records/BMG 79872

Although it was billed as a release by the New Power Generation, this was in all essentials a Prince solo project and pictured only him on the front cover. It is thus included in this discography as a Prince release.

Recorded: May 1997 to Feb. 1998 at Paisley Park Studios.
Prince: Producer, vocals, guitars, bass, drums, percussion, synths, and piano.
Other musicians/songwriters: Kirk Johnson, drum machine and synth programming. The Hornheadz—Michael B. Nelson, Kathy Jensen, Dave Jensen, and Steve Strand—appear on various tracks. Additional horns on "When U Love Somebody" by Pierre Andre-Baptiste, Clark Gayton, and Wayne DuMain. DJ Brother Jules, scratching on "Mad Sex" and "Push It Up!" Chaka Khan, vocals on "Push It Up!" and "Come On." Kat Dyson, bottleneck acoustic guitar on "Come On." Doug E. Fresh, raps on "(Eye Like) Funky Music" and "Push It Up." Rhonda Smith, fretless bass on "The One."
Tracks: Newpower Soul / Mad Sex / Until U're In My Arms Again / When U Love Somebody / Shoo-Bed-Oooh / Push It Up! / Freaks On This Side / Come On / The One / (Eye Like) Funky Music / Wasted Kisses (hidden bonus track)

The War (1998)
NPG Records

Best termed either a long single or an EP, this album was released directly by Prince's NPG Records on cassette and five-inch compact disc. In many cases, it was mailed free of charge to fans who had previously ordered *Crystal Ball* through 1-800-NEW-FUNK. The release consists of the 26-minute song "The War," a live performance by Prince and the New Power Generation. Although it was attributed to the NPG, the song is listed here as a Prince release because he sings the lead vocal. The NPG lineup that appears is unknown, but Larry Graham plays bass.

The Vault . . . Old Friends 4 Sale (1999)
Warner Bros. 47522

Recorded: Between April 1985 at Feb. 1996 at Sunset Sound, L.A., Paisley Park Studios, Studio 301, Sydney, Australia, and other studios.

Prince: Producer, vocals, guitars, bass, drums, percussion, synths, and piano.

Other musicians/songwriters: Various lineups of the New Power Generation appear on most of the songs; personnel include Michael Bland (drums), Sonny Thompson (bass), Tommy Barbarella (keyboards), Morris Hayes (keyboards), Kirk Johnson (drums), Levi Seacer, Jr. (guitar), and Sheila E. (drums). Clare Fischer, strings on "Old Friends 4 Sale."

Tracks: The Rest Of My Life / It's About that Walk / She Spoke 2 Me / 5 Women / When The Lights Go Down / My Little Pill / There Is Lonely / Old Friends 4 Sale / Sarah / Extraordinary

Rave Un2 The Joy Fantastic (1999)
Arista 14624

Recorded: June 1998 to Sept. 1999 at Paisley Park Studios; title track recorded July 1988 at Olympic Studio, London.

Prince: Producer, vocals, guitars, bass, drums, percussion, synths, and piano.

Other musicians/songwriters: Kirk Johnson, computer programming on various songs, drums on "So Far, So Pleased," and percussion on "Man O' War." Michael Bland, drums on "Baby Knows." Mike Scott, guitar on "The Greatest Romance Ever Sold." Rhonda Smith, bass on "Tangerine" and "So Far, So Pleased." Chuck D., raps on "Undisputed." Eve, raps on "Hot Wit U." Gwen Stefani, co-lead vocal on "So Far, So Pleased." Sheryl Crow, backing vocals and harmonica on "Baby Knows." Ani DeFranco, acoustic guitar on "Eye Love You, But Eye Don't Trust U Anymore." Maceo Parker, saxophone on "Prettyman." The Hornheadz, featuring Michael B. Nelson, Dave Jensen, Kathy Jensen, Steve Strand, and Kenny Holman, appear on "Hot Wit U" and "Man O' War." Clare Fischer, orchestra on "The Sun, The Moon And Stars" and strings on segue before "Man O' War." Larry Graham, backing vocals on "Everyday Is A Winding Road." Backing vocals on various tracks by Kirk Johnson, Morris Hayes, Kip Blackshire, and Adele C.

Cover version: Sheryl Crow's "Everyday Is A Winding Road" (Crow, Jeff Trott, and Brian McLeod).

Tracks: Rave Un2 The Joy Fantastic / Undisputed / The Greatest Romance Ever Sold / Hot Wit U / Tangerine / So Far, So Pleased / The Sun, The Moon And Stars / Everyday Is A Winding Road / Man O' War / Baby Knows / Eye Love U, But Eye Don't Trust U Anymore / Silly Game / Strange But True / Wherever U Go, Whatever U Do / Prettyman

1999: The New Master (1999)
NPG Records 71999

This EP contains various new versions of "1999" consisting of material from the original version released in 1982 and new vocals and instrumentation recorded by Prince, Rosie Gaines (vocals), Larry Graham (bass and vocals), Doug E. Fresh (raps), and Rosario Dawson (spoken word).

Rave In2 The Joy Fantastic (2000)

This limited edition version of *Rave* contains some remixes and alternate versions of songs on the album; others are essentially the same as on the original album. It also contains one previously unreleased track, "Beautiful Strange."

The Very Best Of Prince (2001)
Warner Bros. 74272

This greatest hits compilation was released by Warner Bros. against Prince's wishes. It contains edited versions of previously released songs.

The Rainbow Children (2001)
NPG Records/Redline 700004

Recorded: At Paisley Park Studios.
Prince: Producer, vocals, guitars, bass, drums, synths, and piano.
Other musicians/songwriters: John Blackwell, drums on all tracks. Najee, soprano sax and flute on various tracks. Larry Graham, bass on "The Work Pt. 1" and "Last December." Backing vocals on various tracks by Millennia, Kip Blackshire, Mr. Hayes, and Femi Jiya.
Tracks: The Rainbow Children / Muse 2 The Pharaoh / Digital Garden / The Work Pt. 1 / Everywhere / The Sensual Everafter / Mellow / 1+1+1 Is 3 / Deconstruction / Wedding Feast / She Loves Me 4 Me / Family Name / The Everlasting Now / Last December

One Night Alone (2002)
NPG Records (released only to members of the New Power Generation Music Club)

Recorded: 2001 to 2002 at Paisley Park Studios.
Prince: Producer, vocals, piano, bass, guitars.
Other musicians/songwriters: John Blackwell, drums on "Here On Earth" and "A Case Of U."
Cover version: Joni Mitchell's "A Case Of You."
Tracks: One Night Alone / U're Gonna C Me / Here On Earth / A Case Of U / Have A Heart / Objects In The Mirror / Avalanche / Pearls B4 The Swine / Young and Beautiful / Arboretum

B-SIDES
The following songs, which are listed in chronological order of their release, were included as non-album B-sides to album cuts released as singles. Most of these songs were later released on *The Hits/The B-Sides*, albeit for the most part in edited versions.

Gotta Stop (Messin' About)
How Come U Don't Call Me Anymore?
Horny Toad
Irresistible Bitch

God
God (Love Theme from *Purple Rain*)
17 Days
Erotic City
Another Lonely Christmas
4 The Tears In Your Eyes
She's Always In My Hair
Hello
Girl
Love Or Money
Alexa De Paris
La, La, La, He, He, Hee
Feel U Up
Shockadelica
Scarlet Pussy
Escape (Free Yo Mind From This Rat Race)
Take This Beat (unofficial title for extended version of "I Wish U Heaven")
200 Balloons
Sex
I Love U In Me
The Lubricated Lady
Get Off (different song than "Gett Off")
Loveleft, Loveright
Call The Law
Rock 'N' Roll Is Alive (And It Lives In Minneapolis)
Tricky (the Time)
Grace (the Time)

NEW POWER GENERATION MUSIC CLUB AND OTHER INTERNET RELEASES

In February 2001, Prince began regularly releasing music over the Internet. By paying an annual fee of one hundred dollars, subscribers to Prince's New Power Generation Music Club (NPGMC) are given access to downloadable song files and also files containing programs called "NPG Ahdio [sic] Shows" that include a mixture of new and old material. Various live versions of previously released songs have also been released. Because the present discography is concerned primarily with studio material, the live tracks are not listed. What follows is all previously unreleased studio tracks that have been released through the NPGMC. The album *One Night Alone*, which was released only to members of the NPGMC, is described under "Prince Album Releases." Some tracks are attributed to other artists and Prince side projects as noted after the titles of those tracks.

Unfortunately, most of the material Prince has released through the New Power Generation Music Club is marginal. "Habibi" is an ill-conceived Jimi Hendrix tribute; "Supercute" is saccharine pop. Probably the most interesting release to date is "Judas Smile," a blistering piece of funk featuring a lengthy second section on which Prince adds some convincing bass playing.

The tracks are listed here roughly in the order of their release. The first four songs were released on Prince's website for free prior to creation of the NPGMC.

U're Still The One (cover of Shania Twain song)
Madrid 2 Chicago
One Song
Cybersingle
When Eye Lay My Hands On U
The Funky Design
Mad
Peace
Splash
High
My Medallion
Golden Parachute
The Daisy Chain
Silicon
Habibi
Northside (with NPG)
The Work, Part 1
Murph Drag (the Time)
Sex Me, Sex Me Not
Hit U In The Socket (Rosie Gaines)
Props 'N' Pounds
Supercute
Y Should Eye Do That When Eye Can Do This?
Murph Drag
Goldie's Parade (with NPG)
Hypno Paradise
Sadomasochistic Groove
Van Gogh
I Like To Play
Asswoop (Madhouse)
2 Whom It May Concern
Judas Smile
Rebirth Of The Flesh (1988 rehearsal version)
Pearls Before The Swine
Underneath The Cream
Vavoom
Jukebox

PRINCE SONGS ON SOUNDTRACKS OR COMPILATIONS

The songs below are from film soundtracks and other compilations for which Prince was asked to contribute one or more songs. The list below does not cover soundtracks Prince recorded for his own films, such as *Purple Rain* and *Under The Cherry Moon*. Those albums and *Batman: Motion Picture Soundtrack*, for which Prince wrote and recorded all the music, are described under "Prince Album Releases."

4 The Tears In Your Eyes (*We Are The World* compilation, 1985)

Good Love (*Bright Lights, Big City* soundtrack, 1988)

Love Sign (duet with Nona Gaye; *1-800-NEW FUNK* compilation issued by Prince's NPG Records in 1994; also contains songs by Prince protégés and side projects)

Super Hero (New Power Generation featuring the Steeles; *Blankman: Music From The Motion Picture*, 1994)

Don't Talk To Strangers/She Spoke 2 Me/Girl 6 (*Girl 6: Music From The Motion Picture*, 1996—This film by Spike Lee used a wide variety of older Prince songs in addition to this smattering of unreleased material. "She Spoke 2 Me" was released again in 1999 in a longer version on *The Vault . . . Old Friends 4 Sale.*)

2045: Radical Man (*Bamboozled: Original Motion Picture Soundtrack*, 2000)

SINGLE-ONLY RELEASES

In the early part of the new millennium, Prince began occasionally releasing singles as a way of placing new music before his hardcore fans. None of the releases discussed below were extensively distributed, and radio play was modest at best.

U Make My Sun Shine/When Will We B Paid? (2001; A-side is a duet with Angie Stone, B-side is a cover of a Randall Stewart composition)

The Daisy Chain/Gamillah (NPG Records, 2001)

Supercute/Underneath The Cream (NPG Records, 2001)

Peace (NPG Records, 2001)

SIDE PROJECTS

The projects discussed below are termed "side projects" because (a) they involve lead vocalists other than Prince, and (b) were released under the names of other artists or groups. In actuality, Prince's involvement in all of these projects was pervasive. In addition to functioning as the (usually uncredited) producer on most of the albums below, he also wrote nearly all of the songs and played most of the instruments. Regarding The Family's eponymous first album, for example, saxophonist Eric Leeds (who performs extensively on that album) says, "I consider it as much a Prince album as anything else he's done."

The Time

THE TIME (1981)
Warner Bros.

Recorded: Apr. 1981 at Prince's Lake Riley home studio.

Musicians/songwriters: Morris Day, lead vocals on "Cool." Prince and Dez Dickerson, cowriters on "Cool." Dickerson, primary writer on "After Hi School." Lisa Coleman, songwriting input on "The Stick" and backing vocals on various tracks. Matt Fink, synth solos on "Get It Up" and "The Stick." All other songwriting, instruments, and vocals by Prince.

Tracks: Get It Up / Girl / After Hi School / Cool / Oh, Baby / The Stick

WHAT TIME IS IT? (1982)
Warner Bros. 23701

Recorded: 1982 at Prince's Lake Riley home studio and Sunset Sound, L.A.

Musicians/songwriters: Morris Day, lead vocals. Dez Dickerson, cowriter of "Wild And Loose." All other songwriting, instruments, and vocals by Prince.

Tracks: Wild And Loose / 777-9311 / OnedayI'mgonnabesomebody / The Walk / Gigolos Get Lonely Too / I Don't Wanna Leave You

ICE CREAM CASTLE (1984)
Warner Bros. 25109

Recorded: Between Mar. 1983 and Jan. 1984 at Sunset Sound, L.A., First Avenue, Minneapolis, and other studios.

Tracks: Ice Cream Castles / My Drawers / Chili Sauce / Jungle Love / If The Kid Can't Make You Come / The Bird

PANDEMONIUM (1990)
Paisley Park/Warner Bros.

Only songs written by Prince are included below.

Tracks: Jerk Out / Donald Trump (Black Version) / Chocolate / Data Bank / My Summertime Thang

Vanity 6

VANITY 6 (1982)
Warner Bros.

Recorded: 1981 in Prince's Lake Riley home studio and Sunset Sound, L.A.

Musicians/songwriters: Lead vocals by Vanity, Brenda Bennett, and Susan Moonsie. Terry Lewis, cowriter on "If A Girl Answers." Jesse Johnson, cowriter on "Bite The Beat." Dez Dickerson, writer, guitar, and production on "He's So Dull," drums on "3x2=6." All other songwriting, instruments, and vocals by Prince.

Tracks: Nasty Girl / Wet Dream / Drive Me Wild / He's So Dull / If A Girl Answers (Don't Hang Up) / Make-Up / Bite The Beat / 3x2=6

Apollonia 6

APOLLONIA 6 (1984)
Warner Bros.

Recorded: 1983 and 1984 in Prince's Like Riley home studio, Sunset Sound, L.A., and Flying Cloud rehearsal warehouse, Minneapolis.

Musicians/songwriters: Apollonia, lead vocals. Lisa Coleman, cowriter on "A Million Miles," keyboards on "A Million Miles," and backing vocals on "Some Kind Of Lover." Brenda Bennett, cowriter on "Some Kind Of Lover." Jill Jones, backing vocals on "Ooo She She Wa Wa." Susannah Melvoin and Mark Brown, backing vocals on "Mr. Christian." Sheila E., drums and percussion on "A Million Miles." Wendy Melvoin, guitar on "A Million Miles." All other songwriting, instruments, and vocals by Prince.

Tracks: Happy Birthday, Mr. Christian / Sex Shooter / Blue Limousine / A Million Miles (I Love You) / Ooo She She Wa Wa / Some Kind Of Lover / In A Spanish Villa

The Family

THE FAMILY (1985)
Warner Bros.

Recorded: June to Oct. 1984 at Flying Cloud Drive rehearsal warehouse, Minneapolis.

Musicians/songwriters: Paul Peterson, lead vocals. Eric Leeds, saxophone on various songs. Clare Fischer, strings on various songs. Bobby Z. Rivkin, songwriter on "River Run Dry." Wendy Melvoin, rhythm guitar on "Yes."

Tracks: High Fashion / Mutiny / The Screams Of Passion / Yes / River Run Dry / Nothing Compares 2 U / Susannah's Pajamas / Desire

Madhouse

8 (1987)
Warner Bros.

Recorded: Late Sept. to early Oct. 1986 in Prince's Chanhassen home studio; mixed in October at Sunset Sound, L.A.

Musicians/songwriters: Eric Leeds, saxophone and flute. All other songwriting and instruments by Prince.

Tracks: One / Two / Three / Four / Five / Six / Seven / Eight

16 (1987)
Warner Bros.

Recorded: Late July and early Aug. 1987 at Paisley Park Studios; "Nine" recorded in Prince's Chanhassen home studio March 1987.

Musicians/songwriters: Eric Leeds, saxophone and flute. Matt Fink, synth solo on "Sixteen." "Ten," "Eleven," and "Fifteen" are live recordings featuring Prince (keyboards), Leeds (saxophone), Levi Seacer, Jr. (bass), and Sheila E. (drums). Excerpts from the film *The Godfather* are used as segues between various tracks. All other songwriting and instruments by Prince.

Tracks: Nine / Ten / Eleven / Twelve / Thirteen / Fourteen / Fifteen / Sixteen

Sheila E.

THE GLAMOROUS LIFE (1984)
Warner Bros. 25107

Recorded: Dec. 1983 to Apr. 1984 at Sunset Sound, L.A.

Musicians/songwriters: Sheila E., vocals, percussion, and cowriter on "Noon Rendezvous." Jesse Johnson, songwriting input on "The Belle Of St. Mark." Jill Jones, additional vocals on "The Belle Of St. Mark" and "Oliver's House." David Coleman, cello on "Oliver's House" and "The Glamorous Life." Novi Novog, violin on "Next Time Wipe The Lipstick Off Your Collar." Nick DeCaro, accordion on "Lipstick." Larry Williams, saxophone on "The Glamorous Life." All other songwriting, instruments, and vocals by Prince.

Tracks: The Belle Of St. Mark / Shortberry Strawcake / Noon Rendezvous / Oliver's House / Next Time Wipe The Lipstick Off Your Collar / The Glamorous Life

ROMANCE 1600 (1985)
Warner Bros. 25317

Recorded: Dec. 1984 to Feb. 1985 during *Purple Rain* tour at Master Sound in Cleveland, Cheshire in Atlanta, and Sunset Sound, L.A.

Musicians/songwriters: Sheila E., lead vocals, percussion, and writer on "Merci For The Speed Of A Mad Clown In Summer." Sheila and her band perform "Merci." Eddie Minniefield, saxophone on various tracks. All other songwriting, instruments, and vocals by Prince.

Tracks: Sister Fate / Dear Michelangelo / A Love Bizarre / Toy Box / Yellow / Romance 1600 / Merci For The Speed Of A Mad Clown In Summer (no Prince involvement) / Bedtime Story

SHEILA E. (1987)
Warner Bros.

Only the songs written by Prince are listed below.

Tracks: One Day (I'm Gonna Make You Mine) / Love on A Blue Train / Koo Koo / Boy's Club / Pride And The Passion

Jill Jones

JILL JONES (1987)
Warner Bros.

Recorded: Between July 1982 and Oct. 1986 at Prince's home studios and Sunset Sound, L.A.; "All Day, All Night" recorded live at First Avenue, Minneapolis, with the Revolution in June 1984.

Musicians/songwriters: Jill Jones, lead vocals, coproduction on various songs. David Coleman, coproduction on various songs. Clare Fischer, orchestral arrangements on various songs. "For Love" features saxophone by Eric Leeds, drums by Jellybean Johnson, and bass by Paul Peterson. Leeds, saxophone on "Violet Blue." Matt Blistan, trumpet on "Violet Blue." "With You" (cover of song from *Prince*) recorded by lineup of New York session musicians. All other songwriting, instruments, and vocals by Prince.

Tracks: Mia Bocca / G-Spot / Violet Blue / With You / All Day, All Night / For Love / My Man / Baby, You're A Trip

Ingrid Chavez

MAY 19, 1992 (1991)
Paisley Park/Warner Bros.

Prince had compositional involvement in the songs mentioned below, with the exception of "Candle Dance," on which he had no compositional involvement but plays a guitar solo. The remaining songs on the album are not listed.

Tracks: Heaven Must Be Near / Candle Dance / Elephant Box / Slappy Dappy / Jadestone / Whispering Dandelions

Martika

MARTIKA'S KITCHEN (1991)

Prince wrote or cowrote several of the tracks on this album; songs in which he had no role are not listed.

Tracks: Martika's Kitchen / Spirit / Love. . . Thy Will Be Done / Don't Say U Love Me

Mavis Staples

TIME WAITS FOR NO ONE (1989)
Paisley Park/Warner Bros.

Prince performed most of the instruments and composed all of the songs save for two numbers that are omitted from the list.

Tracks: Interesting / Come Home / Jaguar / Train / I Guess I'm Crazy / Time Waits For No One

THE VOICE (1993)
Paisley Park/Warner Bros.

Prince had compositional involvement on all of the songs listed below. The remaining three tracks are omitted.

Tracks: The Voice / House In Order / Blood Is Thicker Than Time / You Will Be Moved / The Undertaker / Melody Cool / A Man Called Jesus / Positivity

Eric Leeds

TIMES SQUARED (1991)

While this album is probably more appropriately termed an Eric Leeds solo project than a Prince side project, it is listed here in light of Prince's compositional involvement with most of the songs on the record. (He had no involvement with "Lines" and "Kenya.") The album was produced by Eric Leeds.

Tracks: Lines / Andorra / Night Owl / Overnight, Every Night / Cape Horn / Little Rock / Easy Does It / The Dopamine Rush / Kenya / Times Squared / Once Upon A Time

Carmen Electra

CARMEN ELECTRA (1992)
Paisley Park/Warner Bros.

Tracks: Go Go Dancer / Good Judy Girlfriend / Go On (Witcha Bad Self) / Step To The Mic / S.T. / Fantasia Erotica / Everybody Get On Up / Fun / Just A Little Lovin' / All That / This Is My House

Elisa Fiorillo

I AM (1990)
Paisley Park/Warner Bros.

Prince had compositional involvement on all of the songs listed below. The remaining three tracks are omitted.

Tracks: I Am / On The Way Up / Playgirl / Love's No Fun / Ooh, This I Need

Mayte

CHILD OF THE SUN (1995)
NPG Records

Tracks: Children Of The Sun / In Your Gracious Name / If I Love U 2Night / The Rhythm Of Your Heart / Ain't No Place Like U / House Of Brick (cover of the Commodores' "Brick House") / Love's No Fun / Baby Don't Care / However Much U Want / Mo' Better / If I Love U 2Night (Spanish Version) / The Most Beautiful Boy In The World

New Power Generation

Prince's backing band from 1991 to 1995 was called the New Power Generation or NPG. Three albums were released under this moniker: *Gold Nigga, Exodus,* and *Newpower Soul.* The actual input of the band members varies considerably on each record, as discussed in more detail below. *Newpower Soul* is discussed under "Prince Album Releases" for several reasons. First, the NPG lineup that existed from 1991 to 1995 had completely disbanded by the time the album was released. Second, *Newpower Soul* was not only composed and performed mostly by Prince, but features only him on the cover and was promoted as a Prince release. Thus, notwithstanding the use of the NPG name, the album is considered by most to be an official Prince release.

GOLD NIGGA (1993)
NPG Records

Musicians/songwriters: This album features rapper Tony Mosley as the primary lead vocalist. Levi Seacer, Jr., guitar. Michael Bland, drums. Sonny Thompson, bass. Kirk Johnson, percussion and programming. Tommy Barbarella, keyboards. Morris Hayes, keyboards. Damon Dickson, backing vocals. The NPG Hornz (see *Symbol*) appear on most songs. Prince was involved heavily in the songwriting and plays various instruments.

Tracks: Goldnigga Part 1 / Guess Who's Knockin' / Oilcan / Deuce And A Quarter / Black M.F. In The House / Goldnigga Part 2 / Goldie's Parade / 2gether / Call The Law / Johnny / Goldnigga Part 3

EXODUS (1995)
NPG Records

Musicians/songwriters: This album features Sonny Thompson as the primary lead vocalist. Thompson also plays bass. Michael Bland, drums and vocals. Tommy Barbarella, keyboards and vocals. Morris Hayes, keyboards and vocals. Mayte, backing vocals. David Bauder, electric violin on "Hallucination Rain." All songs written by Prince, save "Get Wild," which was cowritten by Thompson.

Tracks: Get Wild / Newpower Soul / Count The Days / The Good Life / Cherry, Cherry / The Return Of The Bump Squad / Big Fun / New Power Day / Hallucination Rain / The Exodus Has Begun

UNRELEASED SONGS

A large universe of unreleased Prince songs circulates among collectors. A great many other songs have been said to exist by band members, engineers, associates, or Prince himself. The following criteria have been used to assemble the list below. First, only songs that are believed to have been substantially completed are included. Thus, recorded jam sessions and embryonic ideas are not listed. Secondly, songs whose existence have not been satisfactorily documented are not included. Of course, this requires some judgment calls. In cases where a particular song has been described in detail by a credible source or sources, the song is included on the list. By contrast, where songs have been alluded to by Prince or his associates, but where little or no information is available beyond the song's title (and in some cases the date and place of its recording), such songs are not included on the list. Thus, the song "Wally," which has been described in detail by several sources, is included, whereas the song "3 Nigs Watchin' A Kung Fu Movie" is excluded, even though it has been mentioned by Prince. Similarly, the song "Boy U Bad," while it has been discussed by a former Prince associate, is excluded because the information available is not sufficiently detailed to provide a "picture" of the song.

Not included on the list below are alternate versions of unreleased songs that have only minor differences with their official counterparts. For example, a slightly longer version of the track "Right Back Here In My Arms" (from 1996's *Emancipation*) exists, but is not mentioned below because there is little difference between the released and unreleased version. However, in cases where an unreleased version is radically different and/or features different personnel, the alternate version is listed below. An example is the track "We Can Funk," which was originally recorded in 1983 with the Revolution. "We Can Funk" was officially released on *Graffiti Bridge* (1990), by which time the song had changed substantially and featured backing vocals by George Clinton.

With respect to songs that have been played live and have turned up on bootlegs or on the Internet, only original Prince compositions—as opposed to cover songs—are included on the list.

The songs have been separated into categories that proceed chronologically. In some cases the category relates to a specific abandoned project such as the *I'll Do Anything* film project, which was aborted after director James L. Brooks decided not to make the movie a musical. In other cases, the categories are more arbitrary and have been created by the author as a means of organizing the songs.

Early Demos (1976–77)

"Machine" is not known to still exist but has been described by Prince and his early associates.

Darling Marie	Make It Through The Storm
Don't You Wanna Ride	Neurotic Lover Baby's Bedroom
Hello My Love	Nightingale
I Like What You're Doing	Rock Me, Lover
I Spend My Time Loving You	Since We've Been Together
Leaving For New York	We Can Work It Out
Machine	Wouldn't You Love To Love Me?

Post–*For You* Outtakes (1978–79)

"Donna" is a likeable but sappy love song with layers of falsetto vocals.

Baby, Baby, Baby
Donna
Down A Long Lonely Road
I Am You
Just Another Sucker (recorded with Pepé Willie)

Rebels Sessions (1979)

As discussed in Chapter 3, Prince formed a side project called the Rebels to explore a more rock-oriented sound after the release of *Prince*. Only the songs with Prince's songwriting input are listed below.

Hard To Get
If I Love You Tonight
Turn Me On
You

Dirty Mind/Controversy/The Time Outtakes (1980–81)

"Tick, Tick, Bang" is a different version of the song that appears on *Graffiti Bridge*.

Broken

Jealous Girl

Lisa

The Second Coming

She's Just a Baby

Strange Way Of Saying I Love U

There's Something I Like About Being Your Fool

Tick, Tick, Bang

1999/What Time Is It?/Vanity 6 Outtakes (1981–82)

Not all of these songs are outtakes from *1999*, but most of them share that album's cold, mechanical flavor and rely on the Linn LM-1 drum machine. The most well-known of the group is "Moonbeam Levels," an assured rock ballad. "Extra Loveable" and "Purple Music" are fairly monotonous funk numbers. "Something In The Water" is noticeably different than the version on *1999*, relying more on piano than synthesizer. "Irresistible Bitch" and "Feel U Up," which were cut in sequence almost as a single song, feature different instrumentation and vocal approaches than their released versions. "Girl O' My Dreams" is a different version than the one on T.C. Ellis' *True Confessions*.

Boom, Boom, Can't U Feel The Beat Of My Heart

Can't Stop This Feeling I Got

Extra Loveable

Feel U Up

Girl O' My Dreams

If It'll Make U Happy

Irresistible Bitch

Lust U Always

Moonbeam Levels

Moral Majority

No Call U

Purple Music

Something In The Water (Does Not Compute)

Turn It Up

U're All I Want

Purple Rain Period Outtakes (1983–84)

Several versions of "Computer Blue" exist that are significantly longer than the *Purple Rain* version and contain additional instrumental sections and spoken-word sections. Alternate versions of several other *Purple Rain* tracks exist, but they are not radically different and are not listed above. "A Million Miles" is a different version of the Apollonia 6 song with Prince on lead vocals. "Chocolate" also contains Prince's vocal (rather than Morris Day's) and has some different instrumentation than the version released on the Time's *Pandemonium*. Finally, "G-Spot" is different from and far superior to the Jill Jones version. "Vibrator" and "Wet Dream's Cousin" are Vanity 6 outtakes; "Vibrator" is amusing and features a vocal cameo by Prince as a dirty old man.

Computer Blue

Electric Intercourse

G-Spot

Love And Sex

Possessed

Traffic Jam

Vibrator

Wednesday

Wet Dream's Cousin

Post–Purple Rain Outtakes (1984–85)

"Feline" and "Miss Understood" are outtakes from *The Family*. "Our Destiny" and "Roadhouse

Garden," taken from a live concert with the Revolution at First Avenue in Minneapolis, are powerful rock numbers that show the influence of Wendy Melvoin and Lisa Coleman.

Feline
Miss Understood
Our Destiny
Roadhouse Garden

Parade/Dream Factory Outtakes (1985–86)

Parade, arguably the most collaborative released album of Prince's career, was followed by *The Dream Factory*, another project that featured prominent contributions from Wendy Melvoin and Lisa Coleman. The album was shelved when they left the band. Many of the songs below are discussed in more detail in Chapters 8, 9, and 10. This group of songs includes many of the most notable outtakes of Prince's career. "Data Bank" is substantially radically different from and superior to the version released on the Time's *Pandemonium*. The two versions of "Kiss" show the evolution of the song that is discussed in Chapter 7. "Love Or Money" is a raw version of the song that appears as the B-side to Prince's "Kiss" single; it contains several additional guitar parts and Prince's vocal part is much more fragmentary, and is sung in his standard low register (as opposed to the "Camille" vocal that appears on the released version). "Eternity" is a raw demo of the song later recorded by both Sheena Easton and Chaka Khan.

A Couple Of Miles
Adonis And Batsheeba
All My Dreams
A Place In Heaven
A Place In Heaven (vocals by Lisa Coleman)
Baby Go-Go
The Ball
Big Tall Wall
Can I Play With U?
Can't Stop This Feeling I Got
Coco Boys
Come Elektra Tuesday
Cosmic Day
Data Bank
Emotional Pump
Empty Room
Eternity
Everybody Wants What They Don't Got
Evolisdog
Euphoria Highway
Get On Up
Girl O' My Dreams
Go

God Is Everywhere
Heaven
In A Large Room With No Light
It Ain't Over Until The Fat Lady Sings
It's A Wonderful Day
Junk Music
Killin' At The Soda Shop
Kiss (acoustic demo)
Kiss (Mazarati version)
Little Girl Wendy's Parade
Love Or Money
Old Friends 4 Sale
Others Here With Us
Rebirth Of The Flesh (studio version)
Soul Psychodelicide
Teacher, Teacher
Train
U Gotta Shake Something
Visions
Wally
We Can Funk
Witness For The Prosecution
Wonderful Ass

The "Flesh" Sessions (1986)

These inspired instrumental jams featured Prince (primarily on drums), Wendy Melvoin, Lisa Coleman, Jonathan Melvoin, Eric Leeds, Sheila E., and Levi Seacer, Jr. A portion of "Junk Music" appeared as background music in *Under The Cherry Moon*.

Groove In C Minor

Groove In G Flat Minor
Junk Music
Slow Groove In G Major
Y'all Want Some More?

Lovesexy/Batman/Graffiti Bridge Outtakes (1987–90)

Various of the songs listed here were recorded for side projects and feature vocals by the likes of Morris Day, Jill Jones, and Margie Cox. The numerical titles were for a projected third Madhouse album. "People Without" is a dramatic number played in August 1988 at an aftershow in Rotterdam. "What Did I Do?" is also a live-only number from a 1987 Paris aftershow.

American In Paris	My Pony
Bed Of Roses	Nine Lives
Brand New Boy	No Changes
Come Back To Me	Number One
Corporate World	People Without
Curious Blue	R U There?
Dance With The Devil	Ruthie Washington Jet Blues
Flesh And Blood	Seven Corners
Fuchsia Light	Soul Company
Funky	Soul Psychodelicide
Girl Power	Stimulation
Girls Will Be Girls	Undercover Lover
God Is Alive	The Voice Inside
Good Body Every Evening	Warden In The Prison Of Love
Good Man	We Can Hang
The Grand Progression	We Got The Power
I Believe I Love U	What Did I Do?
If I Had A Harem	Your Love Is So Hard
Latino Barbie Doll	17 (Penetration)
The Line	18 (R U Legal Yet?)
Me Touch Myself	19 (Jailbait)
Move Me	20 (A Girl And Her Puppy)

Diamonds And Pearls/Carmen Electra Sessions (1991–1992)

Some of these are outtakes from *Carmen Electra* and other side projects. "Letter 4 Miles" is an instrumental tribute to Miles Davis.

A Positive Place	Hit U In The Socket
Boom Box	Hold Me
Carmen On Top	I Wonder
Crystal City Cry	The Juice
The Flow	Letter 4 Miles
Glam Slam '91	My Tree
Go Carmen Go	Oobey Doop
Heaven Is Keeping Score	Play
Hey, Louie Louie	Player
Hey, U	Power From Above

Powerline	Stroke
Schoolyard	Uh-Huh!
Something Funky (This House Comes)	Work That Fat

I'll Do Anything Sessions (1992)

"Empty Room" (written about Susannah Melvoin and originally recorded circa 1987) is considered one of Prince's most outstanding outtakes.

Be My Mirror
Empty Room
I Can't Love U Anymore
I'll Do Anything
Make Believe
Poor Little Bastard
Wow

Miscellaneous Sessions (1992)

"51 Hours" is an overwrought techno-funk number sung by sidekicks Diamond and Pearl.

The Ryde Divine
We Can Hang
51 Hours
1,000 Hugs And Kisses

Miscellaneous Sessions (1993–94)

"Days Of Wild" was originally slated for *The Gold Experience*. "Snow Man" is a notable outtake featuring Nona Gaye on vocals. "Good Pussy" is not in circulation but has been described (and ridiculed) by several former New Power Generation members.

Days Of Wild (studio version)
Good Pussy
It Takes 3
On Your Own
Parlor Games
Rootie Kazootie
Slave 2 The System
Snow Man

The Undertaker Sessions (1995)

These live performances were recorded for the limited edition film *The Undertaker*. The performances featured Prince, Sonny Thompson, and Michael Bland. The video is considered "unreleased" because it has never been released in the United States.

Bambi
Dolphin (different version from the one on *The Gold Experience*)
Honky Tonk Woman (Rolling Stones cover)
Poor Goo
The Ride
The Undertaker

Emancipation Outtakes (1995–96)

"Livin' 2 Die" and "Stone" are collaborations with Sandra St. Victor.
> Eye Am The DJ
> Feel Good
> Livin' 2 Die
> Slave 2 The System
> Stone
> 2020

Rave Un2 The Joy Fantastic Outtakes (1999)

> This Is Your Life

Although this list is sparser for the most recent years of Prince's career, this should not be taken as evidence that his pace of recording has slowed. There are two primary reasons for the dearth of unreleased material in the second half of the 1990s. First, Prince has taken greater precautions to prevent the circulation of unreleased material. Second, much of his non-album material of the last few years has been released through his New Power Generation Music Club.

SONGS WRITTEN BY PRINCE FOR OTHER ARTISTS

The following list contains songs that Prince wrote specifically for the use of other artists. It does not include the very large universe of Prince-written songs that other artists have chosen to cover. (For example, omitted are both Sinead O'Connor's version of "Nothing Compares 2 U" and Tom Jones' version of "Kiss.") With respect to many of the songs discussed below, Prince also played some or all of the instruments on the songs.

> I Don't Wanna Stop (Ren Woods, *Azz Iz*, 1982)
> Stand Back (Stevie Nicks, *The Wild Heart*, 1983; cowritten by Nicks)
> Sugar Walls (Sheena Easton, *A Private Heaven*, 1984)
> The Dance Electric (André Cymone, *AC*, 1985)
> You're My Love (Kenny Rogers, *They Don't Make Them Like They Used To*, 1986)
> 100 M.P.H. (Mazarati, *Mazarati*, 1986)
> Manic Monday (the Bangles, *Different Light*, 1986)
> Eternity (Sheena Easton, *No Sound But A Heart*, 1987)
> Telepathy (Debbie Allen, *Telepathy*, 1987)
> Baby Go-Go (Nona Hendrix, *Female Trouble*, 1987)
> Wouldn't You Love To Love Me?/If I Could Get Your Attention (Taja Sevelle, *Taja Sevelle*, 1988)
> Eternity/Sticky Wicked (Chaka Khan, *CK*, 1988)
> Cool Love/101 (Sheena Easton, *The Lover In Me*, 1988)
> Neon Telephone (the Three O'Clock, *Vermillion*, 1988)
> So Strong (Dale Bozzio, *Riot In English*, 1988)
> Shall We Dance (Brownmark, *Good Feeling*, 1989)
> Love Song (Madonna, *Like A Prayer*, 1989; cowritten by Madonna)
> Mind Bells/Bliss (Kahoru Kohiruimaki, *Time The Motion*, 1989)
> Yo Mister/Love 89 (Patti LaBelle, *Be Yourself*, 1989; Love 89 cowritten by Easton)
> If I Love U 2 Night (Mica Paris, *Contribution*, 1990)

The Sex Of It (Kid Creole and the Coconuts, *Private Waters In The Great Divide,* 1990)

And How/Skip 2 My U My Darlin' (Jevetta Steele, *Here It Is,* France version, 1991; Prince is cowriter with others on both songs).

Why Should I Love You? (Kate Bush, *The Red Shoes,* 1991; cowritten by Bush)

I Hear Your Voice (Patti Labelle, *Burnin',* 1991; cowritten by Labelle)

Girl O' My Dreams (T.C. Ellis, *True Confessions,* 1991)

Hold Me, Open Book (Jevetta Steele, *Here It Is,* U.S. version, 1991)

U (Paula Abdul, *Spellbound,* 1991)

Allegiance (Howard Hewitt, *Allegiance,* 1992)

Five Women (Joe Cocker, *Night Calls,* 1992)

With This Tear (Celine Dion, *Celine Dion,* 1992)

Qualified (Lois Lane, *Precious,* 1992)

The Big Pump (George Clinton, *Hey Man . . . Smell My Finger,* 1993; cowritten by Clinton)

The Halls Of Desire/Uncle Sam/Paris 1798430 (Tevin Campbell, *I'm Ready,* 1993)

Super Hero (Earth, Wind & Fire, *Millennium,* 1993)

Well Done (the Steeles, *Heaven Help Us All,* 1993)

Sunday Afternoon (Candy Dulfer, *Sax-A-Go-Go,* 1993)

Aguadilla (Eric Leeds, *Things Left Unsaid,* 1993; cowritten by Leeds)

Born 2 B.R.E.E.D./In A Word Or 2 (Monie Love, *In A World or 2,* 1993; cowritten by Love)

Get Blue/Dance Unto The Rhythm (Louie Louie, *Let's Get Started,* 1993; cowritten by Louie Louie)

The Tender Heart/I Want U: Purple Version (Rosie Gaines, *Closer Than Close,* 1995)

Pain (Chaka Khan, *Living Single: Music From And Inspired by The Hit TV Show,* 1997)

Van Gogh (Van Gogh, *Van Gogh,* 1998)

index

Italicized page numbers refer to photographs.

♀ (album), 183–184, 186–187, 189, 190, 204, 210, 218
♀ (name), 191–192, 193, 196, 206, 209, 224, 236, 242

A&M Records, 18, 19, 74, 78
ABC/Dunhill, 18, 19
Abdul, Paula, 31, 85
Academy Awards, 90, *143*
Act I, 204
Act II, *137*, 204
Act III, 204
Ad Company, 17
Addicted to Noise, 226
"Adore," 111, 116
Advision Studios, 94
Aerosmith, 32, 184–185, 188, 231
Ali, Muhammed, 196
"Allegiance," 183
All Music Guide, 237
"All My Dreams," 108
Ally, Kirstie, 187
"Alphabet Street," 126–127, 165
Alpha Studio, 28–29
Altschul, David, 208
America, 12
"America," 82, 170
American Artists, 17
American Bandstand, 30
American Music Awards, 78
"American Woman," 238
Anderson, André, 9, 10, 11, 12, 13, 14, 15, 17, 23, 25, 44. *See also* Cymone, André
Anderson, Bernadette, 9, 10, 11, 12
Anna Fantastic, 149, 158. *See also* Garcia, Anna
"Anna Stesia," 127, 152
"Anna Waiting," 157
"Annie Christian," 42
"Anotherloverholeinyohead," 104, 106
Apollonia, 25, 63–64, 106, 153, 204
Apollonia 6, 64, 65
Arista, 229, 230–233, 235–237, 238–239, 241
"The Arms Of Orion," 157
Around The World In A Day, 17, 77, 79, 80–83, 85, 86, 90, 91, 103, 109, 110, 116, 117, 122, 170, 198
"Around The World In A Day," 74–75, 77
Arsenio Hall, 176
ASCAP, 50
ASI Studio, 14
Atlantic, 200
"Automatic," 52, 53
"Avalanche," 246

"Baby, I'm A Star," 62, 76, 154, 156, 158, 170, 174
"Baby Knows," 237
Backstreet Boys, 230
Badeaux, Marylou, 35, 40, 59, 65, 70–71, 80, 114, 116, 118, 120, 123, *130*, 152, 159, 171, 176, 186, 189, 192, 195, 196, 198, 199, 207, 209, 246
Baker, Hayward, 8, 209
Baker, James, 70
Baker, Susan, 70
Balhaus, Michael, 91
"The Ball," 124
"The Ballad of Dorothy Parker," 101, 110, 111, 112, 117
"Bambi," 194
Bangles, 64, 180
Barbarella, Tommy, 170, 176, 177, 190, 192, 198, 202, 203, 205, 208, 211, 226–227
Barber, Lisa, 104, 105
Barnard, Michael, 126
Basinger, Kim, 157, 158–160, 162, 192, 204
"Batdance," 157
Batman, 156–158, 165, 211
"The Battle of Funk," 30
Batts, Don, 33, 40, 51
Beach Regency Hotel, 92
Beals, Jennifer, 160
Beatles, 26, 33, 58, 72, 74, 76, 77, 80, 81, 82, 85, 102, 104, 108, 116, 117, 129
"The Beautiful Ones," 66, 67, 227
Beck, Jeff, 32
Bee Gees, 24
Belize, 195
Bellmark Records, 195
"Be My Mirror," 184
Bennett, Brenda, 49, 64
Bennett, Roy, 35, 36, 37, 47, 48, 49, 50, 53, 55, 56, 65, 68, 70, 71, 101, 150, 151, 194, 197
Benton, Jerome, 48, 91, 93, 95, 99, 117–118
Berkoff, Steven, 92
Bertelsmann, 231, 236, 238, 239
Best Buy, 223
"Betcha By Golly Wow!," 214, 218
Beyer, Troy, 101, 177
"Big Tall Wall," 101
Billboard, 24, 46, 68, 80, 89, 116, 152, 157, 182, 193, 195, 199
"The Bird," 68
The Black Album, 121–124, 125, 126, 128, 150, 152, 155, 160, 165, 190
"Black MF In The House," 183
Blackwell, John, 243

Bland, Michael, *141*, 166, 169–170, 175, 178, 181, 183, 190, 193–194, 197, 199, 202, 207
Blaney, Joe, 124
Blinn, William, 61, 63, 67
Blistan, Matt, 86, 95, 106, 117, 118, 121, 152, 166
Blondie, 36
Bloom, Howard, 11, 32, 34, 35, 37, 66, 69–70, *70*, 94
"Blue Light," 187
BMG Music, 226
"Bob George," 121–122
Bono, 103
Borm, Rob, 194
Boston, 32
Boston Globe, 67, 247
Bowie, David, 52, 165, 198, 246
Boyer, Boni, 117, 118, 124, 153, 166
Boyz II Men, 29, 190, 217, 234
Bozzio, Dale, 181
Branch, Michelle, 155
Brandt, Gary, 29
Bransford, Traci, 224
Bream, Jon, 67, 187
"Bring The Noise," 233
Brooks, Albert, 184
Brooks, Greg, 95, 99, 117–118
Brooks, James, 184
Brown, James, 8, 12, 13, 29, 40, 55, 57, 72, 89, 95, 118, 125, 140, 153, 206, 233, 244
Brown, Mark, 10, 39, 40, 43, 45, 46–47, 71, 72, 75, 87, 88, 89, 90, 97, 99, 105–106, 107, 108, 166
Browne, David, 176
Buena Vista Music Group, 35
Burton, Tim, 156, 157, 158
Bush, George H.W., 171
Bush, Kate, 111, 114, 171–172

Cameron, James, 66
Camille, 111, 117
"Camille," 111, 114, 117, 121, 192
Campbell, Tevin, 160
Candlebox, 155
"Can I Play With U?," 99, 100
"Can't Stop This Feeling I Got," 161
Capital Cities/ABC, 200
Capital-EMI, 213
Capri Theatre, 27–28, 131
Carey, Mariah, 165, 189, 227
Carlos & Charlie's, 78
Carmen Electra, 188, 190
Carmichael, James Anthony, 20
"Carousel," 98
Carr, Ian, 129

Carr, Jenifer, 202
Cars, 32
Carwell, Sue Ann, 25, 26, 31
Casey, Terry, 89
Cavallo, Bob, 28, 35, 36–37, 49, 52, 53, 56, 57, 58, 59, 60, 61, 63, 65, 155, 156, 162, 186
Cavallo & Ruffalo, 28
Cavallo, Ruffalo & Fargnoli, 35, 49, 59, 156, 186
CBS, 231
CBS Records, 18, 19, 21
"Celebrate," 246
Centennial Theatre (Sheridan, Wyoming), 104–105
Central High Pioneer, 14
Champagne, 13–15, 17, 44
Chaos And Disorder, 208, 212–213, 218, 226, 244, 247
Chapman, Gayle, 25–26, 29, 34
Charles, Ray, 78
Chavez, Ingrid, 122–123, 124, 127, *144*, 160, 169, 182, 183, 204
Chaya Brasserie, 159
Chic, 20, 32, 164
Chicago Sun-Times, 198
Child Of The Sun, 205
"The Christ," 221
Christian, Terry, 88
Christian, Tony, 89
"Christopher Tracy's Parade," 86
Chuck D., 167, 233
Ciccone, Madonna Louise. *See* Madonna
The Cinderella Theory, 181
"Circle Of Amour," 223
Clapton, Eric, 32, 84
Clark, Dick, 30
Clash, 32, 36, 52, 111
Clinton, George, 38, 57, 68, 140, 160, 181, 226, 233, 237
Club Life, 230
CNN, 171
Cobain, Kurt, 189
Cocker, Joe, 183
"Coincidence or Fate?," 209
"Cold Sweat," 153
Coleman, David, 74–75, 81
Coleman, Lisa, 34–35, 36, 46–47, 52, 54, 56, 61, 62, 69, 71, 72, 73–74, 75, 77, 81–82, 83, 87–88, 92, 94, 95, 96, 98–99, 101, 102, 103, 104, 105, 106, 107–108, 109, 110, 111, 112, 114, 115, 116, 117, 119, 121, 125, 127, 129, *142*, 166, 169, 170, 241
Collins, Tyler, 195
Coltrane, John, 99, 128, 129
Columbia Records, 99, 231
Combs, Sean "Puffy," 231
Come, 9, 195–196, 199, 206, 210, 212, 226
"Come," 210
"Comeback," 217
Come 2 My House, 226
Commodores, 20
Concrete Jungle, 195
"Condition Of The Heart," 77
Considine, J.D., 187

Controversy, 39, 40–43, 46–47, 49, 51, 53, 59, 85, 217, 243
"Controversy," 40, 42, 168, 196
Cookhouse, 14
Costello, Elvis, 129
Cox, Margie, 181
"Crazy You," 23
"Cream," 171, 176, 177
"The Cross," 116, 221
Crystal Ball, 112, 113–114, 116, 120, 124, 161, 190, 222–224, 228, 242, 246
"Crystal Ball," 101, 108, 112, 223
Culture Club, 72
A Current Affair, 6
Cymone, André, 10, 25, 26, 29, 31, 34, 38–39, 40, 44, 88, *131*, *138*. *See also* Anderson, André

"Daddy Pop," 176
Damian, Michael, 184
"Dance On," 127
"Dance With The Devil," 157
D'Angelo, 38, 227, 240–241, 247
D'Arby, Terence Trent, 84 85
"Darling Nikki," 70
Dateline NBC, 215
Daugherty, LaVonne, 13–14, 44
Davis, Carole, 113, 170
Davis, Clive, 230, 231–233, 234, 235–236, 237, 238–239, 247
Davis, Miles, 6, 9, 74, 84, 85, 86, 98, 99–100, 110, 118, 121, 129, 165, 175, 176
Davison, Gilbert, 92, 98, 123, 178, 186, 191, 194, 202
"The Dawn," 209
Day, Morris, 13, 15, 38, 44–45, 46, 48, 49, 55, 61, 62, 63, 65, 67, 68, 93, *138*, 153, 160, 162
"Days Of Wild," 196
"Dead On It," 165
DeCurtis, Anthony, 234–235
Def Jam Records, 228
Delfonics, 195
"Delirious," 53
Dell Graham Trio, 220
Del's Tire Mart, 25–26
Denver, John, 12
Destiny's Child, 50, 234
Detroit Free Press, 104, 218
Devo, 32, 40, 53
"Diamond," *136*, 175
Diamonds And Pearls, *136*, 142, 171, 172–179, 183, 184, 185, 187, 189, 190, 197, 204, 210, 213, 218, 229, 232
Dickerson, Becky, 71
Dickerson, Dez, 26, 28, 29, 30, 31, 34, 37, 38, 40, 43, 46, 47, 50, 52, 53–54, 56, 61, 69, 70, 71, *131*, *140*, 166
Dickson, Damon, 178
Diddley, Bo, 89
DiFranco, Ani, 232, 233–234
"Digital Garden," 243
DiLeo, Frank, 176
Dinkins, David, 175

"Dinner With Dolores," 212
Dion, Celine, 183
Dirty Mind, 35–40, 41, 42, 45, 46, 55, 69, 87, 113, 129, 166–167, 217, 240, 243
"Dirty Mind," 33, 34, 36
Disney, 35, 200
"D.M.S.R.," 52
"Dolphin," 194, 198
"Do Me, Baby," 38–39, 41, 227
"Don't Play With Me," 223
Dorsey, Thomas A., 124
Dr. Dre, 163, 167, 168, 217
The Dream Factory, 98–99, 100–101, 102–103, 105, 108, 110, 111
"Dreamin' About U," 218
Dreams, 61, 63
Dreamworks Records, 188
Dr. Fink, 62, 167. *See also* Fink, Matt
Duran Duran, 93
Dylan, Bob, 5, 78, 104, 165
Dyson, Kathleen (Kat), 212

Eagles, 32
Earth, Wind & Fire, 19, 21, 32
Easton, Sheena, 68, 117, 157, 180
Ebony, 168
8, 100
Electra, Carmen, 25, 158, 169, 170, 173, 177, 183, 184, 188, 190, 193, 204
"Electric Chair," 157
Elektra, 200
"Elephant Box," 182
"Elephants and Flowers," 161
Elfman, Danny, 156
Ellington, Duke, 6, 68, 74, 85, 99, 118, 121, 129
Ellis, T.C., 166
Elm, Tommy. *See* Barbarella, Tommy
el-Qaddafi, Muammar, 112
"Emale," 217
Emancipation, 201, 212, 213, 214–215, 217–219, 222, 225, 227, 228, 236, 237, 244, 247
Emerson, Keith, 26
EMI, 213, 214, 218
Eminem, 244
Endorphinmachine, 202–203
Entertainment Weekly, 162, 176, 206, 224
Equitable Building, 235–236
Erlewine, Steven Thomas, 237
"Erotic City," 68, 244
Escape Club, 184
Escovedo, Pete, 66
Escovedo, Sheila. *See* Sheila E.
Esquire Gentleman, 201
Eurythmics, 72
Eve, 233
"The Everlasting Now," 243
Exodus, 201
Exposé, 184
"(Eye Like) Funky Music," 226
"Eye Love U But Eye Don't Trust U Anymore," 233, 237
"Eye No," 124, 127

Fabulous Flames, 95
"Face Down," 217, 221–222
Family, 13, 70, 85–86, 91, 93–94, 95,
    96, 109, 180, 192
The Family, 93–94, 112
"Family Name," 243, 244
Family Stand, 205
"Fantasia Erotica," 158
Fantastic, Anna. *See* Garcia, Anna
Fargnoli, Steve, 28, 35, 37, 39–40, 43,
    49, 52, 53, 55, 56, 59, 60, 61, 63,
    65, 68, 75, 79, 90–91, 106, 113,
    114, 125, 126, 150–151, 153, 155,
    156, 186
"Feline," 70
Fenn, Sherilyn, 102
Fink, Matt, 26, 29, 33, 34, 36, 38,
    46–47, 48, 49, 54, 58–59, 61, 62, 64,
    71, 72, 73, 75, 78, 87, 95, 102, 107,
    108, 117, 123, 152, 166–167, 170
Fiorillo, Elisa, 25, 173
First Avenue, 48, 62, 65, 135
Fischer, Brett, 112, 114
Fischer, Clare, 79, 85–86, 93, 112, 114
Fitzgerald, F. Scott, 5
"Five Women," 183
Fleetwood Mac, 12, 32, 229–230
Flesh, 100
"The Flow," 171
Flyte Tyme, 13, 180–181
Foley, James, 63
Fontano, Steve, 20, 22
Foreigner, 32
"Forever In My Life," 111, 112, 118
"4 The Tears In Your Eyes," 79
For You, 23–24, 25, 26, 27, 29, 31, 32,
    88
"For You," 22
"Freaks On This Side," 226
Fuchs, Michael, 207
Fugees, 231
Furious Five, 164
"The Future," 157

Gabriel, Peter, 111, 114
Gaines, Rosie, *142*, 166, 167, 168, 169,
    170, 171, 172–173, 176, 177,
    178–179, 181, 183, 184, 195, 204,
    206, 212, 217, 229
Game Boyz, 166, 167, 177, 178
"Gamillah," 245
Gamillah Holdings, Inc., 245
Gang of Four, 32
Garcia, Anna, 106, 149–150, 157, 158,
    160, 168, 179, 184, 192, 204, 245
Garcia, Mayte, 1, *137*, *139*, 168, 177,
    179, 183, 184, 187, 192, 193,
    204–205, 208–209, 212, 213, 214,
    215, 217, 219, 221, 222, 225, 227,
    230, 237, 243, 244
Gasparoli, Tom, 215, 216
Gaye, Marvin, 127, 180, 193
Gaye, Nona, 193
GCS 2000, 226
Geffen, David, 208
Geldoff, Bob, 78
Gershwin, George, 68

"Gett Off," 173, 176, 194, 210
"Get Yo Groove On," 219
Gibson, Lawrence, 79
"A Girl And Her Puppy," 175
Girl 6, 227
"Girls & Boys," 95, 103, 165, 193
The Glamorous Life, 67–68
"The Glamorous Life," 68
Glam Slam, 193, 202
Glam Slam Ulysses, 193, 195
Glieberman, Owen, 162
Glover, Cat, 117, 126, *144*, 152
"Go Go Dancer," 188
Gold, Jeff, 172, 174–175, 187
"Gold," 196, 206
Goldberg, Danny, 201, 207
The Gold Experience, 196, 198, 199,
    201, 203, 206–207, 209, 210, 236
Gold Nigga, 183, 184, 190–191, 192,
    201
"Goldnigga," 183
"A Good Dick And A Job," 227
"Good Love," 114
"Good Pussy," 227
Gordy, Berry, 180
Gore, Tipper, 70, 128, 163
Graffiti Bridge, 134, *144*, 153–156,
    158–162, 163, 164, 165, 166, 167,
    172, 173, 182, 185, 198, 204, 210
Graham, Bill, 43
Graham, Dell, 220
Graham, Larry, 13, *145*, 220–222, 225,
    226, 230, 236, 241, 243, 247
Graham Central Station, 13, 220–221
Grand Central, 12, 13
Grand Funk Railroad, 11
Grandmaster Flash, 163–164
Grateful Dead, 206, 222
Gray, Macy, 38, 247
"The Greatest Romance Ever Sold,"
    234, 235, 236, 237
Green, Al, 26, 74, 111, 127, 221
Guess Who, 237–238
Guitar Player, 234
Gumble, Bryant, 216
Gunderson, Edna, 244
Guns N' Roses, 128, 159

"Habibi," 247
Hackford, Taylor, 45
"Had U," 212
Hall, Arsenio, 176
Hall & Oates, 58
Hamilton, Jim, 9–10
Hammer, Jan, 26
Hammer, MC, 164
Hard Rock Cafe, 207
Harrington, Richard, 162
Harris, Jimmy "Jam." *See* Jam, Jimmy
Harrison, George, 111
Hasselmann, Bea, 10
Hayes, Isaac, 116
Hayes, Morris, 212
HBO, 207
"Head," 33, 34, 38, 46, 54, 70, 163, 167
"Heaven Must Near," 182
"Hello," 79, 80

Henders, Doug, 77
Hendrix, Jimi, 29, 32, 67, 72, 76, 170
Hendryx, Nona, 37
Hennepin, Louis, 5
Hewitt, Howard, 183
Hey Man . . . Smell My Finger, 181
High, 242
"High," 242
"High Fashion," 93
High Spirits, 17
Hilburn, Robert, 57
Hill, Dave, 38
Hiltbrand, David, 128
"Hippy Blood," 182
The Hit and Run Tour, 102
The Hits/The B-Sides, 192–193
Holden, Stephen, 29, 42
Holiday, Billie, 6
Hollywood Sound Recorders, 29, 40, 51
"The Holy River," 210
Homer, 193
Hookers, 49
"Hot Thing," 110, 116
"Hot Wit' U," 233
"Housequake," 116, 117, 193
"How Come U Don't Call Me
    Anymore?," 53, 247
Humphrey, Hubert H., 5
Huntsberry, Chick, 47, 48, 53, 55, 57,
    70, 78, 79, 87, 90
Husney, Brit, 22
Husney, Owen, 17–19, 21–22, 23, 24,
    25, 26–27, 28, 30, 34, 39, 45, 149

"I Am," 159
Ice Cream Castle, 67–68
Ice Cube, 163, 168
Ice-T, 164, 167
"I Could Never Take The Place Of
    Your Man," 110, 116, 236
"I Feel For You," 29, 68
"If I Was Your Girlfriend," 110, 112,
    117, 219
"I Like It There," 212
"I Like What You're Doing," 17
I'll Do Anything, 184
"I'm Yours," 23, 24, 32
"In A Large Room With No Light," 99
India.Arie, 247
"In Love," 24
Internet, 198, 224–225, 225, 242, 246
Interview, 216–217
"I Rock, Therefore I Am," 212
"Irresistible Bitch," 193
"It Ain't No Fun To Me," 221
"It's A Wonderful Day," 99, 102
"It's Gonna Be A Beautiful Night,"
    118, 165
"It's Gonna Be Lonely," 29
"I Wanna Be Your Lover," 28, 29, 32,
    40
"I Wanna Melt With U," 187
"I Wish U Heaven," 124
"I Wonder U," 86, 88

Jackson, Janet, 50, 85, 180–181, 185,
    188, 189–190

Jackson, Jesse, 175, 196
Jackson, Michael, 5, 7, 29, 32, 56, 58, 66, 72, 78, 82, 151, 176, 185
Jackson, Terry, 12
"Jack U Off," 41, 42, 43
"Jailbait," 175
Jam, Jimmy, 13, 45, 46, 48, 55, 62, 85, 180–181
James, Rick, 30, 164
"Jam Of The Year," 212, 217, 219
Jam of the Year, *137*, 219, 220, 221–222, 225
Jean, Wyclef, 231, 239
"Jerk Out," 88
Jet, 63
Jiya, Femi, 157
Joel, Billy, 187, 231
Joe Louis Arena, 68–69
Johnson, Becky, 91
Johnson, Cheryl, 191
Johnson, Coke, 89
Johnson, Jellybean, 12, 13, 45, 62
Johnson, Jesse, 45, 46, 48, 49, 50, 62, 68
Johnson, Kirk, 212
Jones, Jill, 41, 55, 66, 78, 80, 92, 101, 113, 181
Jones, Perry, 28
Jones, Quincy, 56, 78
Jones, Tom, 227
Joplin, Janis, 231
"Joy In Repetition," 114, 161
J Records, 239
"Jungle Love," 68
"Just Another Sucker," 14
"Just As Long As We're Together," 19, 21

Kael, Pauline, 65
Kamasutra, 223
Karlatos, Olga, 64–65
Karlen, Neil, 81
Keller, Martin, 198
Kelly, R., 234
Keys, Alicia, 247
Khan, Chaka, 29, 68, *145*, 225, 226
King, Larry, 9
King, Rodney, 164
Kiss, 31
"Kiss," 39, 89–90, 103, 105, 177, 180, 187, 192, 198, 227, 234
Knack, 36
Knapp-Winge, Juli, 202, 211
Kool & the Gang, 29
Koppelman, Charles, 213, 214
Koppelman, Michael, 167, 168, 169, 171–172, 182, 213
Kotero, Patricia. See Apollonia
Kraftwerk, 40
Krattinger, Karen, 68, 97–98, 101, 112–113, 115, 119, 123, 154, 156
Kravitz, Lenny, 237–238
KUXL, 12

LaBelle, Patti, 160, 181
"The Ladder," 77, 82, 170

"Lady Cab Driver," 9, 52
Lambert, Mary, 91, 92
"The Last December," 243
Late Show with David Letterman, 198
Lauper, Cindy, 78
"Leaving For New York," 16
Led Zeppelin, 26, 31, 32, 74
Lee, Brenda, 89
Lee, Karen, 202
Lee, Spike, 72, 216–217, 227, 228
Leeds, Alan, 35, 36, 41, 46, 49, 55, 56, 57, 59, 60, 62, 63, 65,68, 69, 72, 73, 74, 76, 86, 90–91, 92, 93, 98, 99, 100, 106, 107–108, 111, 112, 113, 114, 117, 118, 121, 125–127, 128, *140*, 151, 152, 154, 156, 164, 168, 169, 170, 173, 175, 181, 188, 191, 197, 240, 245
Leeds, Eric, 72, 74, 76, 77, 86, 87, 93, 95, 96, 98, 99, 100, 103, 106, 108, 111, 117, 118, 121, 124–125, 129, 152, 166, 169, 170, 191, 204, 211, 218, 245, 246
Leeds, Gwen, 92, 98
Leeds, Tristan, 98
"Le Grind," 121
"Lemon Crush," 157
Lennon, John, 33, 37, 42, 52, 198, 217, 246
"Let's Go Crazy," 62, 68–69, 81, 164, 177, 234
"Let's Have A Baby," 210, 214
"Let's Pretend We're Married," 52, 163
"Letter 4 Miles," 175
Letterman, David, 198
Levin, Gerald, 201, 207
Levinson, Gary, 17, 18–19
Lewis, Ananda, 230, 237
Lewis, Terry, 13, 45, 46, 48, 50, 55, 62, 85, 180–181
"Life Can Be So Nice," 86
Limited Warranty, 150
Limp Bizkit, 230
Lincoln, Abraham, 246
"The Line," 124
"Lisa," 34–35
Little Anthony and the Imperials, 14
Little Feat, 28
"Little Red Corvette," 52, 53, 56, 58, 84
Little Richard, 8, 74
"Live 4 Love," 171, 210
Loder, Kurt, 67
London Times, 157
"Loose!," 195
Lopez, Jennifer, 247
Los Angeles Coliseum, 42–43
Los Angeles Herald-Examiner, 52
Los Angeles Times, 57, 156, 237
Louisiana Superdome, 79
Love4OneAnother Charity Tour, 218–219, 225
Lovell, Glen, 105
Lovesexy, 124–125, 127–129, *135*, 150–153, 155, 156, 157, 160, 162, 164, 165, 166, 172, 173, 177, 190, 193, 204, 206, 211
"Love Song," 154

"Love 2 The 9's," 183
"The Love We Make," 217

"Machine," 14
Madhouse, 100, 175
Madison Square Garden, 222
Madonna, 5, 50, 72, 82, 103, 113, 151, 153–155, 158, 160, 162, 185, 229
"Mad Sex," 226, 227
Magnoli, Albert, 63, 64, 155, 156, 159, 162
"Make Believe," 184
"Make It Through The Storm," 25
"Make Your Mama Happy," 223
Mamas and the Papas, 53
Mamet, David, 154
Manderville, Shauntel, 14
"Manic Monday," 64, 180
Manilow, Barry, 231, 239
"Man O' War," 237
Marcil, Vanessa, 193
Matchbox 20, 231
Matthews, Denise. See Vanity
Maverick Records, 155, 185
"The Max," 187
Maxwell, 227
May 19, 1992, 182
Mayfield, Curtis, 200
Mazarati, 88–89
McCartney, Paul, 12, 24
McCreary, Peggy, 51, 89
McLachlan, Sarah, 231
McMillan, L. Londell, 208, 213, 214, 226, 228, 229, 230, 232, 234, 235
Mechanics, 184
Medina, Benny, 174, 175
Megastar, 227
"Mellow," 243
Melody Maker, 29, 116
Meltzer, Gordon, 175
Melvoin, Jonathan, 74, 75, 81–82
Melvoin, Susannah, 66, 73–74, 75, 85, 87–88, 91–92, 93, 95, 97–98, 101–102, 105, 112–113, 114–115, 119, 122, 127, 154, 169, 170, 179, 204
Melvoin, Wendy, 54, 56, 61, 62, 65–66, 69, 71, 72, 73–74, 75, 76, 77, 81, 83, 87–88, 92, 94, 95, 96, 98, 99, 101, 102, 103, 104, 105, 106, 107–108, 109, 110, 111, 112, 114, 115, 116, 117, 119, 121, 125, 127, 129, *142*, 166, 169, 170, 204, 241
Merlis, Bob, 243
Met Center (Minneapolis), 54
Miami Herald, 67
Michael, George, 84, 85
Mico, Ted, 116
Midnight Special, 30
Midway Stadium, 233
Miles, 99
Miller, Jim, 80
Milli Vanilli, 184
Mingus, Charles, 74
Minneapolis Star Tribune, 10, 187, 191, 215–216, 223–224, 243, 245
Missing Persons, 181

Mister Mister, 205
Mitchell, Joni, 13, 29, 67–68, 77, 111,
    121, 223, 227
Mockler, Bob, 29
Moir, Monte, 45, 48, 62, 85
Mojica, Arlene, 215–216
Mojica, Erlene, 215–216
Mondino, Jean Baptiste, 125
"Money Don't Matter 2Night," 171, 177
Monk, Thelonious, 6
Monroe, Marilyn, 79, 81
Monterey Pop Festival, 231
Moon, Chris, 14–15, 17, 18, 23, 44
Moon, Tom, 176
Moonsie, Susan, 41, 49, 50, 56, 64, 65,
    179
Moonsound, 14–17, 18, 44
Morgado, Robert, 201, 207
"The Morning Papers," 183, 187
Moroder, Giorgio, 20
Morrisette, Alanis, 155
Mosley, Tony, 167–168, 169, 170, 171,
    173, 176–177, 178, 183, 187, 190
"The Most Beautiful Girl In The
    World," 195, 196
"Mother, Sister, Lover/Wife," 210
Motley Crue, 63
Motown Records, 180
Moultrie, Fred, 156
Mountain Ears Studio, 31
"Mountains," 94, 101, 104
"Movie Star," 100
MTV, 56, 81, 91, 104, 176, 230
MTV European Music Awards, 202
MTV Video Music Awards, 176
Muldaur, Maria, 200
Mulligan, Jim, 194
"Muse 2 The Pharoah," 243, 244
Music City Mix Factory, 220, 221
"My Computer," 210–211
"My Little Pill," 184
"My Medallion," 242
"My Name Is Prince," 186, 187

Nashville Arena, 220
"Nasty Girl," 50
National Enquirer, 79, 81
Nelson, Alfred, 6, 8
Nelson, Duane, 9, 150, 194, 202
Nelson, John L., 4, 5–7, 8–9, 10, 45,
    77, 81, 97, 150, 209
Nelson, John, Jr., 5
Nelson, Lorna, 5
Nelson, Olivia, 9
Nelson, Prince Rogers. *See* Prince
Nelson, Sharon, 5, 16
Nelson, Tyka, 6, 9
Nelson, Vivienne, 5
New Edition, 29
New Musical Express, 38, 226
"New Position," 86, 104
New Power Generation (NPG), 1, 141,
    166–168, 169–171, 173–174, 176,
    177–179, 183–184, 187, 190,
    193–194, 197, 198, 201, 202–203,
    207, 211–212, 218, 220, 225–226
"New Power Generation," 166, 167, 210

New Power Generation Music Club
    (NPGMC), 242–243, 245
Newpower Soul, 225–226, 227, 228,
    232, 244
"Newpower Soul," 226
News of the World, 215, 216
Newsweek, 80
Newton, Wayne, 69
Newton-John, Olivia, 24, 58
"New World," 217
New Yorker, 65
New York Times, 82, 105, 234–235
Nichols, Natalie, 237
Nicholson, Jack, 156, 158
Nicks, Stevie, 106
Nietzsche, Friedrich, 169
1999, 52–56, 59, 69, 84, 85, 86, 88, 111,
    113, 117, 161, 164, 188, 217, 243
"1999," 52, 53, 56, 82, 156, 192, 228,
    229, 234
1999—The New Master, 229
Nine Inch Nails, 230
94 East, 14
Nolte, Nick, 184
"Nothing Compares 2 U," 93, 192
Nova Park Hotel, 90
NPG Records, 225, 226, 228, 229, 232
Nude Tour, *136,* 166, 171, 204
NWA, 128, 164, 168

O'Connor, Sinead, 93, 113, 192
"Old Friends 4 Sale," 79
O'Neal, Alexander, 13, 45, 181
"100 MPH," 88
"One Kiss At A Time," 210
One Night Alone, 245
"1+1+1 Is 3," 244
On Top, 188
OP Reis, 236
"Orgasm," 210
Orlando, Tony, 12
Orpheum Theater (Minneapolis), 240
Orwall, Bruce, 194
Ostin, Mo, 19, 20–21, 29, 32, 35–36,
    52, 59–60, 65, 113, 114, 123, 172,
    185, 189, 190, 191, 192, 196,
    200–201, 207, 247
O-Town, 239
"Our Destiny," 87

Pacino, Al, 63
Page, Jimmy, 32
"Paisley Park," 76, 77, 82
Paisley Park Enterprises, 186, 191,
    194–195, 195, 214, 216
Paisley Park Records, 88, 93, 140, 169,
    180–181, 182, 185, 188, 190, 191,
    195, 223
Paisley Park Studios, 1, 5, 97, 98, 108,
    118, 122–124, 141, 148, 149–150,
    151–152, 154, 157, 158, 160, 167,
    175, 183, 190, 193–194, 202,
    208–209, 211–212, 214, 221, 225,
    229, 230, 233–235, 237–238,
    240–241, 246, 247
Palmer, Del, 172

Palmer, Robert (critic), 82
Palmer, Robert (musician), 116
"Papa," 9, 195
Parade, 86–87, 88–90, 94, 95, 96, 98,
    99, 101, 102, 103–104, 105–107,
    109, 110, 117, 118, 128, 157, 165,
    170, 193
Parales, John, 157
Parents' Music Resource Center
    (PMRC), 70, 128
Parker, Dorothy, 101, 110, 111, 112,
    117
Parker, Maceo, 233–234, 245
Parliament/Funkadelic, 32
"Partyman," 157
"Partyup," 38, 44
Paster, Robbie, 17
Patrick, Tara Leigh. *See* Electra,
    Carmen
Paul McCartney & Wings, 12
"Peach," 192, 194
"Pearl," *136,* 175
"Penetration," 175
People, 64, 128, 234
Performing Songwriter, 45
Perry, Joe, 185
Peterson, Paul, 70, 85, 93, 94, 109
Phair, Liz, 129
Philadelphia Inquirer, 176
Phillips, Lee, 156
Phillips, Randy, 159, 160, 161, 166,
    178, 186
Picasso, Pablo, 161–162
"Pink Cashmere," 149, 192, 227
Pink Floyd, 32
"A Place In Heaven," 98, 105, 108
Plant, Robert, 84
"Play In The Sunshine," 111
Police, 32, 103
"Pope," 192
"Pop Life," 76, 79, 80, 82
"Positivity," 127
Power, Robin, 181
"Power Fantastic," 98, 102, 192
Preminger, Otto, 169
Presley, Elvis, 198
Preston, Billy, 21
Pretenders, 129
"Prettyman," 233, 237
Prince, 3, *130–137, 139, 143–145, 147*
    awards to, 78, 90, 143
    birth of, 5, 6
    death of child of, 214–217, 219
    and drugs, 123, 197, 241
    health of, 2, 30, 212
    marriages of, 1, 137, 209, 210–211,
        222, 225, 237, 243, 244–245
    name change of, 145, 191–192, 196,
        209, 236
    relationships of, 1, 28, 34–35, 41, 49,
        50, 55–56, 61, 62–63, 64, 65–66,
        73–74, 85, 87–88, 91–92, 95, 97–98,
        101–102, 105, 112–113, 114–115,
        119, 122, 143, 144, 149–150, 152,
        154, 158–160, 168–169, 170, 177,
        179, 193, 204–205, 208–209, 227,
        230
Prince, 29, 31, 32, 34, 36, 131, 132

Prince Rogers Trio, 6
"Private Joy," 40–41, 42
"Providence," 233
Pryor, Richard, 34, 183
Public Enemy, 164, 232, 233
Purple Rain, 5, 8, 9, 52, 62, 63, 64–72,
    73, 75, 76–78, 79, 80, 81, 82, 83,
    84, 85, 86, 87, 90, 91, 93, 104, 106,
    108, 109, 111, 113, 121, 122, 128,
    132, *133*, *143*, *145*, 152, 153, 155,
    157, 159, 161, 165, 166, 170, 173,
    185, 227, 229, 246
"Purple Rain," 59, 62, 67, 76, 78, 170,
    177, 196, 219
"Push It Up," 226
"Pussy Control," 206

Q, 116, 197, 218
Queen, 183
Questlove, Ahmir, 240, 241

"Race," 210
Radiohead, 230
Rage Against the Machine, 230
The Rainbow Children, 243–244, 245,
    247
"The Rainbow Children," 243, 244
"Raspberry Beret," 80, 81–82, 93
Rave Un2 The Joy Fantastic, 149, 173,
    234–239, 240, 241–242, 245
"Rave Un2 The Joy Fantastic," 149,
    234
Ready for the World, 84, 85
Reagan, Ronald, 42, 82, 116
Rebels, 31, 32, 38
"Rebirth Of The Flesh," 117, 242
Recording Industry Association of
    America, 218, 238
Record Plant, 22–23, 194
The Red Shoes, 172
Reed, Lou, 52, 128, 217
Reid, Antonio "LA," 231, 239
"Release It," 161
REM, 174, 185, 188, 200, 207
Reprise Records, 20
"The Rest Of My Life," 184
Revolution, 55, 61–62, 65, 69, 75–76,
    87, 88, 90, 95–96, 98–99, 102–103,
    105–108, 109, 111, 121, 123, 166,
    170, 192, 204, 241
Rhino Records, 221, 222
Richie, Lionel, 58, 78
"The Ride," 194
Righteous Babe, 233
Riley, Melvin, Jr., 84
"Ripopgodazippa," 223
Ritz, 37
Riverfront Stadium (Cincinnati),
    48–49
Rivkin, Bobby Z., 16, 17, 25, 26, 27,
    28, 34, 36, 39, 41, 44, 45, 46, 69,
    71, 75, 87, 95, 99, 105, 106, 107,
    108, 241
Rivkin, David Z., 14, 16, 17, 18, 22,
    23, 29, 30, 39, 62, 85, 88–90, 93,
    94, 159, 181

"Roadhouse Garden," 87
Robbins, Kenneth, 193
Robinson, Smokey, 26, 32, 180
Rock, Chris, 245
"Rock In Rio," 170
Rogers, Nile, 20, 37
Rogers, Susan, 6, 11, 45, 50, 61, 62, 64,
    66, 70, 77, 79, 82, 86, 87, 89, 94,
    95, 98, 100, 101, 102, 109–111,
    112, 115, 119, 120, 121, 123, 148,
    150, 165
Rolling Stone, 8, 29, 37–38, 42, 52, 67,
    68, 81, 88, 104, 127, 157, 161–162,
    191, 198, 206, 213, 226
Rolling Stones, 32, 42, 43, 74, 104,
    108, 116, 129, 185
"Ronnie, Talk To Russia," 42, 82
Ross, Diana, 78
Ross, Steve, 201
Roth, David Lee, 64
Roxy, 51
RSO, 18, 19
Ruff Ryders, 228, 233
Rufus, 85
Rundgren, Todd, 29
Run-DMC, 163–164, 165
Rupert's, 122

Safford, Wally, 79, 95, 99, 115,
    117–118
Saint Paul Civic Center, 77
Saint Paul Pioneer Press, 176, 194, 213,
    237
St. Victor, Sandra, 205–206, 218
San Jose Mercury News, 105
Santana, 11, 12, 66
Santana, Carlos, 21, 230–231, 232, 237
"Savior," 210
"Scandalous," 158
"Schoolyard," 172–173
Schooly D, 164
Scorcese, Martin, 91
Scott, Mike, 212
Scott-Thomas, Kristin, 91, 92, 94, *143*
"The Screams Of Passion," 93
Seacer, Levi, Jr., 39, 100, 117, 125,
    141, 166, 169–170,
    170, 173, 183, 202, 211
Seger, Bob, 58–59
"The Sensual Everafter," 243, 244
Sevelle, Taja, 25
"7," 186–187, 187
"777-9311," *54*
"17 Days," 64
"Sex In The Summer," 211, 214
Sex Pistols, 32
"Sexuality," 40, 42
"Sexy Dancer," 29
"Sexy MF," 183, 187, 210
Shaw, Mattie, 4, 6–7, 8, 209
Sheila E., 66, 67, 68, 69, 74, 76, 82, 86,
    87, 92, 94, 95, 99, 100, 101, 106,
    107, 113, 117, 118, 121, 124, 125,
    126, *144*, 152, 154, 166, 170, 212
"She's Always In My Hair," 80, 193
"She's So Dull," 50
Shoop, Jamie, 28, 49

Showgirls, 223
Shrine Auditorium, 78
"Shy," 196, 206
Sigerson, Davitt, 53, 104
Sign O' The Times, 52, 108, 110–111,
    116–119, 121, 122, 125, 127, 128,
    129, *144*, 151, 152, 157, 161, 164,
    165, 166, 176, 192, 193, 206, 217,
    218, 221, 223, 244
"Sign O' The Times," 116
"Silicon," 242
Silver Bullet Band, 58
Simon, Carly, 231
Simple Minds, 159
Sinclair, David, 157
"Sister," 33, 163
"6," 100
Sixx, Nikki, 63
"Slave," 217
Sly & the Family Stone, 12–13, 13, 25,
    26, 52, 178, 220
Smashing Pumpkins, 75
Smith, Charles, 6–7, 9, 10, 11, 12, 13,
    23, 25, 28, 34, 38, 44, 48
Smith, Patti, 129, 231
Smith, Rhonda, 212
Snipes, Wesley, 228
Snoop Doggy Dogg, 163, 168, 217
"Snow Man," 193
"So Blue," 22
"So Far, So Pleased," 237
"Soft And Wet," 16, 17, 22, 23, 24, 33
"Somebody's Somebody," 217
"Sometimes It Snows In April," 101,
    107
Sony, 185, 229
SOS, 68
"Soul Sanctuary," 218
Sound 80, 18, 21, 22, *130*
Sound Labs Studios, 23
"Space," 195
Sparks, Billy, 245
Spears, Britney, 230, 247
Spellbound, 31
Spice, 168–169
Springfield, Rick, 58
Springsteen, Bruce, 67, 72, 78, 82, 103,
    222, 231
Stamp, Terrence, 92
Staples, Mavis, 160, 178, 181
Starr, Jamie, 46, 50, 57, 63
Steeles, 39
Steely Dan, 32
Stefanelli, Simonetta, 63
"Step To The Mic," 188
Stern, Howard, 191–192
Stewart, Rod, 25, 159
Stiefel, Arnold, 159, 160, 161, 166,
    178, 186
Stiefel & Phillips, 159, 161, 178, 186
Stiffleman, Gary, 185, 186
"Still Waiting," 29
Sting, 103
Stone, Sly, 12–13, 38, 42, 53, 67, 72,
    116, 164, 170, 220, 221, 223, 237,
    246
The Stooges, 128
Stoulil, Therese, 202, 211

Strange, Steve, 39–40
"Strange But True," 237
"Strange Relationship," 108
Strayhorn, Billy, 118
Streisand, Barbra, 105
Stylistics, 218
Sugarhill Gang, 164
"Sugar Walls," 68, 180
Summer, Donna, 20
Sunset Sound, 40–41, 51, 65, 74,
    86–87, 88–89, 100, 102, 109,
    110–111, 114, 120, 148
"Superfunkycalifragisexy," 122
Supremes, 180
"Sweet Baby," 187
Sweet Potato, 42

"Take Me With U," 64, 219
"Tambourine," 82
"Teacher, Teacher," 99, 102
Teena Marie, 36, 41
Television, 32, 129
Temptations, 12, 29, 116
Testolini, Manuela, 225, 230, 244–245
Thelan, Reid & Priest, 224
"There Is Lonely," 184
"Thieves In The Temple," 161, 168
"39th Street Party," 14
Thomas, Rob, 231
Thompson, Sonny, 13, 166, 169–170,
    193–194
"3 Chains O' Gold," 183
301 Studios, 184
Three O'Clock, 181
Thyret, Russ, 18, 19, 26, 36, 207–208
Tiffany, 184
Time, 12, 13, 45–49, 53, 54–55, 57, 61,
    62, 63, 67–68, 85, 93, 94, *138*, 153,
    161, 180
The Time, 46, 48, 50
Time, Inc., 200
Time Waits For No One, 181
Time-Warner, 185, 201, 207
TLC, 50, 217, 233, 234
The Today Show, *145*, 212, 236
Tony Orlando & Dawn, 12
To The Teeth, 233
Tower Records, 152–153
"Train," 108
Tramps, 53
Travolta, John, 24
T Rex, 177
Troutman, Roger, 46, 68
"Trust," 157
The Truth, 223
"The Truth," 223, 247
Tucker, Ken, 37–38
Turner, Steve, 127
Turner, Tina, 78
Turturro, John, 72
Twain, Shania, 230
"2 Nigs United 4 West Compton," 121
Tyler, Steven, 185

"U," 31
"U Got The Look," 117

Ultimate Live Experience, 203
The Undertaker, 193–194
Under The Cherry Moon, 90–93, 94–96,
    101, 102, 104–105, 109, 121, 128,
    143, 155, 162
"Under The Cherry Moon," 86
"Undisputed," 233
Upsher, Kim, 28, 179
"Uptown," 36, 38, 43
Uptown, 224, 235
USA for Africa, 78
USA Today, 91, 162, 215, 229–230,
    232–233, 237
U2, 103

Valli, Frankie, 24
Van Halen, 64, 200
Vanity, 25, 49–50, 55–56, 61, 62–64,
    106, 204
Vanity 6, 49, 50, 53, 55, 57, 62, 63, 64,
    94, 180
Vanity 6, 50, 55
The Vault . . . Old Friends 4 Sale, 79,
    184, 208, 244, 247
Vega, Susanne, 174
Vicari, Tommy, 21–24, 30
"Vicki Waiting," 157, 211
Village Recorders Studios, 19
Village Voice, 42, 198
Virgin Records, 185
"Visions," 98–99, 105, 108
The Voice, 181

Waldorf Salad, 74
Wall, John, 29
"Wally," 115–116
Walsh, Jim, 213, 237
Warhol, Andy, 37
Warner Bros. Pictures, 59, 65, 91, 94,
    104, 118, 155, 157, 159, 161, 200
Warner Bros. Records, 1, 18, 19, 20–24,
    25, 26, 27–28, 29, 30, 32, 33,
    35–36, 37, 40, 44, 46, 52, 65, 77,
    78, 80, 90, 99, 104, 113–114, 117,
    118, 119, 120, 121–122, 123, 125,
    127, 130, 131, 153, 172, 173,
    174–175, 176, 179, 180, 181, 182,
    184–188, 189–193, 194, 195–197,
    198–199, 200–201, 202, 205, 206,
    207–208, 210, 212, 213, 217, 226,
    228, 229–230, 233, 234, 242, 243,
    244, 246
Warner Communications, 66–67, 158,
    200
Warner Music Group, 200, 201
Waronker, Lenny, 19, 20–21, 21, 22,
    29, 32, 35–36, 113, 114, 172, 189,
    190, 191, 192, 196, 200–201, 207
Washington Post, 162
"Wasted Kisses," 226
We Are The World, 79, 80
"We Are The World," 78, 79, 80, 91,
    114
Weather Report, 74
Weaver, Miko, 95, 99, 117, *141*, 161,
    197

Weber, Frederick, 153
"We Can Work It Out," 19
"Well Done," 39
Wembley Stadium, 171
Westlake Audio, 98
Wham!, 72, 84
"What's My Name?," 223
What Time Is It?, 54
"When Doves Cry," 64, 65, 66–67, 78,
    84, 180, 187, 192, 198, 234
"When Eye Lay My Hands On U," 242
"When 2 R In Love," 121
"When We're Dancing Close and
    Slow," 29
"When You Were Mine," 33, 38
White, Barry, 51, 121
White, Mark, 202
White, Maurice, 21
White, Stuart, 216
White, Verdine, 19, 21
"Why Should I Love You?," 171–172
"Why You Wanna Treat Me So Bad?,"
    28, 32
William Morris Agency, 27
Williams, Clarence, III, 64–65
Willie, Pepé, 11, 14, 24, 25, 26, 27,
    38–39
"Willing And Able," 177
Willis, Jill, 185, 194
Winfrey, Oprah, 5, 7, 8, 9, 214, 215
"With This Tear," 183
"Witness For The Prosecution," 102,
    108
Wonder, Stevie, 12, 13, 16, 24, 30, 32,
    78, 177, 180
"Wonderful Ass," 50
"The Work, Part I," 244
"Wouldn't You Love To Love Me," 25
www.genegeter.com, 234
www.love4oneanother.com, 225

"Xenophobia," 246

Yokohama Stadium, 107
"You," 31
Young, Neil, 200, 208

Zahradka, Gary, 194
Zahradka, Suzy, 194
Zapp, 46, 68
Zappa, Frank, 222
Zwicky, Chuck, 197
ZZ Top, 185